MOVIE FREAK

MOVIE FREAK

MY LIFE WATCHING MOVIES

OWEN GLEIBERMAN

BOOKS

NEW YORK • BOSTON

Certain names and identifying characteristics have been changed.

Hachette Books
Hachette Book Group
1290 Avenue of the Americas
New York, NY 10104
hachettebookgroup.com
twitter.com/hachettebooks

First Edition: February 2016

Hachette Books is a division of Hachette Book Group, Inc.
The Hachette Books name and logo are trademarks of Hachette Book Group, Inc.

The publisher is not responsible for websites (or their content) that are not owned by the publisher.

The Hachette Speakers Bureau provides a wide range of authors for speaking events. To find out more, go to www.hachettespeakersbureau.com or call (866) 376-6591.

Print book interior design by Jouve.

Library of Congress Cataloging-in-Publication Data
Names: Gleiberman, Owen, author.
Title: Movie freak : my life watching movies / Owen Gleiberman.
Description: New York : Hachette Books, 2016. | Includes index.
Identifiers: LCCN 2015039430| ISBN 9780316382960 (hardback) | ISBN 9781478960829 (audio download) | ISBN 9781478910909 (audio cd) | ISBN 9780316382946 (ebook)
Subjects: LCSH: Gleiberman, Owen. | Film critics—United States—Biography. | BISAC: BIOGRAPHY & AUTOBIOGRAPHY / Entertainment & Performing Arts.
Classification: LCC PN1998.3.G585 A3 2016 | DDC 791.43092—dc23 LC record available at http://lccn.loc.gov/2015039430

Printed in the United States of the America

RRD-C

10 9 8 7 6 5 4 3 2 1

For my mother

And for Sharon, Lily, and Sadie,
who save me every day

"So you think you're a Romeo,
playing a part in a picture show."
—*Supertramp,*
"Take the Long Way Home"

PREFACE

So how do you get to be a film critic?

In my life, that's the question I've been asked more than any other. I get asked it at parties, on playgrounds, in apartment hallways, in offices, on airplanes, on movie lines. There are a handful of other questions that run a close second. Questions like: *How many movies do you see a week? Do you take notes? Do film studios ever try to influence your opinion? Have you ever had your words twisted in a movie ad? What's your all-time favorite movie?* (The answers are: about five or six; yes, I always take notes; the studios wouldn't dare; once in a blue moon; and *Nashville.*) The questions generally get asked with a knowing smile, a slight winking tone of *come-on-let-me-in-on-it...*

In the popular imagination, the job of professional film critic is, more or less, the greatest job in the world. It's one that everybody thinks they would want to do; it's one that everybody thinks, deep down, they *could* do. You watch movies—lots of them, all day long! You write down your opinions of them! You get to see your words quoted in ads, your name up in lights! You become sort of famous! What's not to like?

There's an avid curiosity, and always has been, about what critics do. Just beneath that, though, the real curiosity is about who we *are.* When people pepper me with all those questions, what they're really saying is: What gives you the *right* to be a critic? What makes you so special that *you*—as opposed to, say, *they*—get to spend your entire life watching movies, deciding which of them is good or bad, and why?

It's actually a great question. And it deserves a great answer.

Let's get one thing out of the way fast. If you have any notion that this profession is, on some essential level, ridiculous, that it's simply fun beyond all shame, and that those of us who do it are basically slackers dignified by their salaries...well, to quote Martin Sheen in *Apocalypse Now*, you are *absolutely goddamn right*. The role of professional movie critic is, more or less, the cushiest job that Western Civilization ever coughed up. Maybe that's one reason why criticism is now dwindling; as Western Civilization declines, so go the people who were fortunate enough to make a living not creating art or entertainment, but *evaluating* it.

I admit it: I've been one lucky sucker.

That said, there's a dimension to being a critic that tends to get left out of people's "I wish I had a job as lazy as yours" formulations. And that dimension, in a word, is obsession. It's the thing that I've tried to capture in this book. I wanted to write about what you might call the secret history of being a movie fanatic, and what that really involves. For the truth about movie buffs, and film critics especially, is that there's a kind of religious mania that drives us, and you either have it or you don't. Before anything else, the primal act in our lives is going to the movies *by ourselves*, sitting there alone, with a nearly monastic sense of mission, "connecting" with images of life and reality on the big screen—even as, in doing so, we may be copping out on the very reality those images represent. I've been fortunate, all right, but not *just* because I stumbled into a preposterously enjoyable job. The real stroke of luck is that I was able to elevate the nerd madness of my solitary movie passion into an identity, an existence, a personality-defining role.

The world, of course, now overflows with mad-geek obsessives of every stripe (comic-book fans, sportsaholics, Sudoku addicts). But what's unique about movies as an art form is how totally and vividly and spectacularly they create a *you-are-there* facsimile of life as it really looks, a fully realized alternate earth that the critic inhabits and lives inside. In writing this book, my intent was to channel the deep eccentricity of that pursuit, to get in touch with the elemental *weirdness* of rabid film fanaticism. In my case, the weirdness isn't exactly compartmentalized; I'm kind of an obsessive guy in all ways. But then, that's part of what drew me to movies, which feed off obsession as though it were high-octane gasoline.

We now live in an age of pop-culture fixation, in which our country has evolved into the United States of Entertainment, with a great many other places right behind it. For all the (justified) chatter about the renaissance era of television, movies, in their power and grandeur and reach, their mythological scope, their ability to cast a larger-than-life spell in the dark, remain our stubbornly thriving and preeminent popular art form. The critic, in a sense, is the ultimate fan, but he's also the bridge between movies and the people who voraciously devour them. I've tried to set down an honest account of my experience, but I'm the first to admit that it may all seem a bit…insular. The true confessions of a film critic? Of a person who watches movies too much? That sounds like a book that should be entitled *White People Problems 3.0*. Yet take a look around: We've become a veritable society of watchers. I hope that my story will speak to the movie freak who lives inside so many of us.

MOVIE
FREAK

CHAPTER 1

I LOST IT AT THE DRIVE-IN

The oversize letter 'U' loomed up large at the entrance to the University Drive-In Theater. Filled with dozens of tiny hot-pink lightbulbs, the letter dazzled and glowed, like it was made of lit-up bubblegum. And that felt right, since what this candified gateway heralded was a carnival of excess. It promised delights of a totally indulgent nature.

Ah, the drive-in movie theater! It's up there with the bowling alley, the $2 piss-water-beer dive bar, and the Friday night high-school football game as a tawdry specimen of Americana, a destination of low-kitsch nostalgic charm. The drive-in offers—or at least it once did—a moviegoing experience that is wholesomely amusing in a slightly scuzzy way. One thinks of tailgate parties and hot-summer make-out sessions, of monster movies and kung fu movies and Burt Reynolds idiot car-chase movies. But in 1967, when I was 8 years old, and 1968, when I was 9, the drive-in, for me, became a place of debased enchantment, a seductive theater of cruelty in which the curtain was drawn back on things I never, ever should have seen.

During those two years, mostly in the summer, my father, showing the combination of antsy compulsive desire and near-total indifference to his family's needs that would mark so much of his existence, developed a highly charged curiosity about the newly taboo-busting movies for adults that had begun to dot the American motion-picture landscape. My dad hadn't been a movie fan for quite some time. His most dedicated era of moviegoing was his youth, in the '30s and '40s, when you could still buy a ticket to a Saturday double feature for 15 cents. (He'd been mourning the rise in ticket prices ever since; one of the forms his pathological cheapness took was not ever fully accepting the concept of inflation.) He had once taken me to see a Hitchcock film (it was *Sabotage*, which in my 7-year-old way I enjoyed), and he came out of it muttering that Hitchcock—Hitchcock!—was a fraud, that his movies were "parrot shit." Normally, for my dad, the prospect of hauling his family off to a movie would have been as far from his mind as taking them on an expedition to Saturn. Yet for all my father's outward, plaid-jacket conservatism, the world of late-'60s sex and violence struck a chord in him. It was only years later, when I learned of his serial adultery and saw that he'd been a Jewish Don Draper in horn-rims, that I realized how much his inner appetites connected with the times.

Piling my mother, myself, and my two little brothers, 3-year-old Erik and 2-year-old Stefan, into the family Buick, he fed his appetites and literally took us along for the ride. During those two years, I saw twisted, sordid visions that haunted my head at far too tender an age. It was as if I was losing my cinematic virginity at a very skanky whorehouse. Movie buffs will tell you a story about how the first time their eyes popped open in wonder at the cinema, it was when they saw *The Wizard of Oz* or *Citizen Kane* or *2001: A Space Odyssey* or *The Godfather* or *Jaws*. For me, it was all about seeing the devil rape Rosemary before I was old enough to know what the devil or rape was. And the thing is, I drank up every depraved, inappropriate minute of it, even if it *was* the moviegoing equivalent of borderline child abuse.

There's something inescapably cozy about a drive-in movie theater. Jerry Seinfeld used to tell a very Jerry monologue joke about why he likes to drive so much because you're inside and outside at the same time. At the drive-in, you weren't just inside and outside: You were part of an entire audience from which you remained separate—a hermetically sealed moviegoing horde. I suspect that if my family had been there to see *The Jungle Book* or *Doctor Doolittle*, the experience would have been very warm and toasty in that leftover-1950s way. Instead, for me, there was a disturbingly sinister excitement to it. To get to the drive-in, you had to leave the woodsy hills and boulevards of our hometown of Ann Arbor, Michigan, and go out to a flat, drab no man's land, to badly lit roads with names like South Industrial. By the time we arrived at the University, or the Ypsi-Ann (so named for being halfway between Ann Arbor and the more downscale Ypsilanti), we had, at least to my eyes, abandoned civilization entirely.

We'd usually get there during what photographers call the magic hour, when the sun is saturating everything in its darkish-orange verge-of-twilight glow. Hanging the bulky curved gray speaker, which seemed to be made of graphite, onto the driver's-side window, we'd wait for the sound to start crackling through that oversize walkie-talkie. That would happen around dusk, a moment that always feels a little godless when it's just you and the shrub brush and the darkening outdoors. But then...there would be light! Just when it looked as if the wide, chalky billboard of a movie screen might fade right into the dusk, the projector would rattle to life, and we'd be subjected to that ancient drive-in ritual: the concession-stand trailer. The one with the booming-voiced announcer, who also seemed like he was from the '50s, selling popcorn euphoria, accompanied by images of movie junk food that were so old and grainy and worn that the hot dogs were green. That ancient snack-haven commercial was, in its slightly exotic way, innocuous, but what mesmerized me, every time, was the "Our Feature Presentation" trailer, with its psychedelic swirling rainbow and the modly syncopated clickety-clack horns from Keith Mansfield's "Funky Fanfare"—the clip that Quentin Tarantino has featured before several of his films, starting with *Kill Bill, Vol. 1*. That 18-second "dater" probably didn't make its debut until 1968, but in my memory, it plays at the start of every outdoor movie I ever saw, like a passageway into the forbidden night. Before Quentin had the video store, I had the drive-in. It was my open-air, dirt-and-gravel-floor grindhouse.

As the first film was about to start (for these were always double features), my mother, in her role as well-meaning if ineffectual protector, would turn around from the passenger seat and say to me, in what became a meaningless ritual, "Now, there may be a moment when I'm going to tell you to cover your eyes." I would dutifully nod, knowing that such a moment would never arrive. (It was presumed that my brothers would simply fall asleep, which they generally did within half an hour.) I would then pin my gaze, from the back seat, over the front seat and into the screen. Watching something like *You Only Live Twice* or *Hurry Sundown* or *The Dirty Dozen*, I was so possessed I felt like I would literally sit through the entire movie without blinking.

The first one I can remember seeing was *Penelope*, a leftover 1966 comedy starring Natalie Wood as a kooky kleptomaniac. What I recall best is Wood, who commits several thieveries in disguise, changing her look and costume so often (at one point she pencils on a facial mole) that her erotic identity seemed as tantalizingly ambiguous to me as Kim Novak's would decades later when I first saw her in *Vertigo*. There was also a "wacky" sexual-assault scene in which Jonathan Winters, as a mad anthropology professor, chases Wood, stripped to her underwear, around his office. I had no idea what the movie was actually about, but it seemed to be about something deeply kinky that was happening between the lines.

The debauchery was right there on the surface, however, in *The Penthouse*, a shockingly nasty little 1967 number from Britain. It took place almost entirely in a chilly-chic London apartment, where a couple who are having an affair wake up to start their day, and then the buzzer rings, and it's two men who have come to read the meter. Except that's not why they're there at all. Once inside the flat, they turn out to be hell-raising hooligans who spend the entire film tormenting and terrorizing the couple. They use ribbons, for some reason, to tie the man to a chair, then bully and ridicule him, then hold a switchblade up to his neck ("It's so thin you don't feel a thing when it goes in!"), then pour out great big cups of whiskey for the woman to drink, and she turns into a slurry, messy-haired harlot who sleeps with each of them, though it doesn't look like ever she had much of a choice.

It's as if someone had taken the "Singin' in the Rain" torture-and-rape scene from *A Clockwork Orange*, extended it out to feature length, and showed it to a wide-eyed 8-year-old. I have special memories of the moment when the cuckolded hero, strapped to his chair, shouts "*Nooooo! Nooooo!*" as his girlfriend stumbles around the apartment in a sloppy naked drunken daze, a din of cacophonous jazz flooding the soundtrack with insanity. And also the moment when one of the two intruders, having had his way with the heroine, says to the other one, with supremely lewd and lip-smacking understatement, "You know, Barbara is a *lovely* girl!" And I remember how the thugs, using their switchblade to carve off greasy slices of salami to snack on, maintain a tone of brutal, leering mockery, the threat of violence coming off them like steam heat.

Years later, I watched *The Penthouse* again, and I saw that it was a cleverly debased little art-exploitation movie, as if the young Roman Polanski had collaborated with a sub-rate Harold Pinter. The British actors all do their best to out–Richard Burton each other, even as they're licking their chops at the Swinging London model-turned-actress Suzy Kendall, who goes from innocent to pouty to poutier. In its grimy claustrophobic way, the film anticipates the hothouse sadism of Sam Peckinpah's *Straw Dogs*, as well as the power-play gimmickry of Michael Haneke's *Funny Games*. But what struck me most when I saw *The Penthouse* again is that the film's subtext—that this naughty adulterous couple somehow *deserves* the torment they're being put through—is what I would viscerally connect to as a child. I hardly understood the conversational intricacies of the movie, like the big allegorical speech about tiny alligators escaping into the London sewer. But what I did experience—the winks of lewdness, the outrageously *unexplained* bullying—was really the whole point. A hideous vengeance was being taken on guilty sinners. The film was a nightmare, and I couldn't get the evil of it out of my head. From that moment, I think I was hooked, with a preternatural lack of choice about it, on the sick thrill of the dark side.

I should emphasize that I had just completed the third grade. I also had a reasonably wholesome set of interests. I enjoyed schoolwork (I wouldn't grow utterly bored with it until I was 12), and I craved the Banquet turkey pot pies that my mother stuck in the oven for lunch. During family highway drives, I devoted myself to spotting the 1966 Mustang, especially a tomato-red one, which seemed the coolest automobile imaginable. (Who knew that it would still seem that way 50 years later?) At recess, I was an eager soccer player, despite the fact that I was a stumbling-limbs sort of athlete. I was also exceedingly proud of how I looked in my Cub Scout uniform, taking extra care to knot the kerchief so that the blue and yellow stripes lined up just so.

Without knowing it, though, I was already on my way to becoming a creature of...fixations. My first crush, in its third-grade way, was quite an obsession, to the point that I was so consumed by Julie Williams, with her thick flip of blonde hair, her heart-shaped angel face, and her comforting air of gravitas, that I thought about Julie for what seemed to be all day long, every single day, for the entire school year. At the YMCA, my father enrolled me in a chess class, and I was terrible at the game, never gaining the ability—or maybe it was just the patience—to think more than a move ahead. But the real action at the Y started after class. I would spend all Saturday afternoon in the dank lobby, shooting pool with kids from assorted sides of the tracks, and there, thanks to the jukebox, I discovered, for the first time, that there were glorious pop songs far beyond what I knew from *The Beatles* cartoon. I'd plop in the stray dimes I collected to play the same songs over and over again, like "The Letter" by the Box Tops, which I found so infectious that I could scarcely account for its hold on me, or "The Rain, The Park, & Other Things," a Cowsills tune that struck me as the most romantic thing I'd ever heard (*"I love the flower girl,/Was she reality, or just a dream to me?"*), or the song that possessed me more than any other: "Jimmy Mack," by Martha and the Vandellas. It was my first encounter with the Motown sound, that three-dimensional jangle of joy framed by the bounding bass and the shimmering tambourine. That song filled me with so much rapture that each time, as I listened to the lyrics (*"Jimmy Mack! Jimmy! Oh, Jimmy Mack, when are you coming back?"*), an inner-city anthem for all the women who'd been abandoned by scurrilous men, all I could think was: Why would anyone with a name as happy as Jimmy Mack want to run away?

I'd also begun to attach myself to books in the way that I later would to movies. I consumed the Laura Ingalls Wilder series over and over again, experiencing *Little House in the Big Woods* and its seven sequels as obsessional slices of rustic heaven: a period-piece dream of family life to counter my own neurotically close-knit but affectionless clan. In the Wilder books, the character of Pa—bearded, benevolent, protective— was the ultimate antidote to my distant, self-obsessed father. And as I entered the fourth grade, my personal bible became *Harriet the Spy*. Louise Fitzhugh's 1964 children's novel spoke to me almost more deeply than any book has since. It's the tale of an androgynous 11-year-old New York City girl in a hooded sweatshirt and big round spectacles who writes down, in her diary, her secret thoughts about everyone she encounters: her classmates, the adults she "spies" on, even her best buddy, a boy named Sport. It's a book that has often been celebrated by writers (like Jonathan Franzen), but to me, Harriet isn't merely a budding writer. She is one hundred percent a born *critic*: an analyst-observer of life, someone who drinks in and judges the drama of everything she sees. When her diary is discovered, and the other kids read what she's been saying about them, she is vilified and ostracized, cast out of grade-school society like a leper. Yet to me, the beauty of the book was that even though Harriet spends the rest of the story in turmoil, recoiling from what she's done... what, in the end, has she really done? She wrote down *her* thoughts, in secret, in *her* diary. The message, if there is one, seems to be: Keep your private reactions to yourself. But Harriet was already doing that. The real, and tantalizing, and scary message of *Harriet the Spy*—the message I took away from it—is that your thoughts and observations, if you really see what's going on in front you, might just be dangerous. And that's what makes them exciting.

Maybe that's why the movies I saw at the drive-in didn't feel like a violation to me. Their effect was to turn me into a child voyeur, like Harriet; they made me feel like I was peering behind a veil, seeing privileged secrets. And there was a shuddery fascination to that experience that linked it to the reverence I already had for the books and music I loved. By the summer of 1968, the movies my parents were going to see at the drive-in had, if anything, grown even more twisted and explicit. To my 9-year-old eyes, *Rosemary's Baby* was the ultimate terrifying bad dream. I quivered in its wake, like a mollusk without a shell. Everything in the movie seemed to worm its way into my soul—not just the demonic rape scene but Mia Farrow's hideously odd Auschwitz-by-Sassoon haircut and the behind-the-walls chanting of the devil cult. To me, Rosemary's warbled plaint during what I sort of realized was "sex," whatever that actually was (she cried, "This is no dream, this is really happening!"), seemed to express the spirit of the movie. It *all* seemed like it was really happening. Days after I saw it, I began to have a recurring nightmare, which lasted for close to a week, and it was all about the Ruth Gordon character, who in her noodgy banality reminded me of the aging women I met in my grandfather's Jewish co-op in the Bronx. In my dream, she was coming for me.

When the end credits rolled on a movie like *Rosemary's Baby*, my parents would say almost nothing about it, and I would say nothing at all. We would drive home, my eyes heavy with slumber, and the thought that was usually most prominent for me was how impressed I was that anyone could be awake at that hour, let alone awake enough to drive. The mood in the car was drained and dissipated, a kind of post-climax. And then, a few weeks later, the ritual of lowering-dusk excitement and chamber-of-horrors disturbance would begin again. In a funny way, I felt united with my parents in watching those movies. I knew that my father had chosen them, and that they said *something* about him (maybe more than he knew). And the fear and blood and alienation and dread that coursed through those films became, in effect, a mirror of the hidden alienation in my family.

If *Rosemary's Baby* creeped me out beyond words, the drive-in movie that may have had the greatest effect on me, because it's the one that I felt most connected to, was *The Boston Strangler*. It was a true-life, close-to-the-bone police procedural made in the shadow of *In Cold Blood* and the 1966 Richard Speck murders, with mod split-screen photography and an orgy of kinks that would never have been allowed in a Hollywood movie even one year before. Tony Curtis, an actor I had never heard of, donned the black wool cap and split personality of the working-class Boston serial killer Albert DeSalvo, and he did it with a private anguish that somehow spoke to me. The moment that was most vivid—it will always define my experience at the drive-in—is the one in which Curtis' DeSalvo, with his underhanded skill at talking his way into single ladies' apartments, has entered the home of a potential victim (played by Sally Kellerman). He is tying her wrists and ankles to the bedposts—a violent scene that very much plays as a sexual-bondage scene. I confess that I did find it a little erotic (much more so than the scaly devil having his way with Rosemary). Which made me a little queasy. But then Curtis looks up from his homicidal "work" and catches an accidental glimpse of his face in the mirror. And it stops him; he realizes what he's doing, what he *is*, and for a few seconds, he can't go on. The film, at that moment, wants the audience to look at his torment with a glimmer of empathy. But in my case the identification became total, because the fact that I was a 9-year-old boy sitting in a car with my parents, gazing up at an outdoor movie screen, watching someone do something so inexplicable and evil, and then seeing him catch a guilty glimpse of himself in the mirror, made me feel, at that moment, that we were *both* watchers. I felt, like the Boston Strangler, kind of bad about what I was doing. But part of the feeling was that, just like him, I knew I didn't want to stop.

CHAPTER 2

THE BIRTH OF A HEAD CASE

I consumed as much junk television growing up as any kid, and most of it—the dancing-on-the-edge-of-kitsch adventures of *Batman*, the sketch-comedy confetti of *Rowan & Martin's Laugh-In*, the theater-of-the-absurd sitcom crapola of *The Beverly Hillbillies*, *Gilligan's Island*, *Green Acres*, *Bewitched*, *I Dream of Jeannie*, *The Addams Family*, *Hogan's Heroes*, and so on—was so aware of its own cheese value that it was as if Susan Sontag's "Notes on Camp" had somehow, preposterously, become the new handbook/Bible of network TV executives. Way before I experienced any of those shows, however, I was possessed by a drama called *Branded*—or, rather, by the opening-credits sequence, which I watched week after week, spellbound by its ability to strike pity and terror in my six-year-old heart.

In stark black-and-white, we see military snare drums, then a fort, then U.S. Cavalry soldiers marching in rigid formation. Except that there's nothing noble about the ritual they're about to enact. A single soldier stands, mute and expressionless (he's played by that surly block of wood known as Chuck Connors). His commanding officer approaches, and the soldier begins to get...stripped. (There's no other word for it.) The officer tears off Connors' hat and tosses it to the ground. Then he tears off the epaulette on his right shoulder, then the epaulette on his left shoulder, then rips away his top shirt button, then the second button, then goes lower still, the camera closing in on Connors' face until he looks like a piece of rough trade; it's as if *Gunsmoke* had been directed by Pier Paolo Pasolini. Our hero is being cashiered, drummed out of the Army on a bogus cowardice charge. But to my young eyes, he was being violated in the most primitive and unspeakable way. No wonder I could never watch the rest of the show, in which Connors' disgraced hero roams the frontier in a cowboy hat, doing valiant deeds. It was all dry as dust next to those S&M credits, and I think it instilled in me a lifelong fear of being bored at Westerns.

Maybe the reason the credits of *Branded* struck such a mighty chord in me is that they seemed to echo the experience I had in October 1964. I wasn't a defrocked soldier—I was a kid in kindergarten, going to a cozy little public school in Ann Arbor. The school was called Eberwhite, named for the man who founded it: His name was Eber White. (Eber? I'm sorry, that's weird.) Somehow, the stubborn Puritan eccentricity of that name—why didn't they just call it, you know, White Elementary School?—only added to the flavor of my first days at an institution where everything seemed quietly, inexpressibly exotic. I was fascinated by a budding sociopath named Paul, who never smiled beneath his leftover Princeton buzzcut, and who, whenever we were asked to sit cross-legged in front of the piano, insisted on stage-whispering the word "Poop!" into the ear of whoever happened to be sitting next to him. It was his conspiratorial tone that got to me, as if he were sharing some deeply held private belief.

I was fascinated as well by the bizarre ritual of nap time, in which we would all lay down, for 20 minutes, on our personal woven multi-color mats, at which point I would pass the time by meditating on a question that feels, in hindsight, like it must have been my very first skeptical, anti-social, WTF-is-this-anyway? deep *critical* thought. *Why*, I kept wondering to myself, *do I have to lay my head down on this mat and keep looking at nothing, when I'm not tired at all?* (The answer, of course, was that someone needed a rest. The teacher did.) At Eberwhite, even recess seemed exotic. All of kindergarten was really just play, but then came the moment when we were let out...to really play. And so we screamed with delight as we scurried out the door. I took to running and yelling with such enthusiasm that I got chastised for running some poor kid over. I swear, I had no idea. Had I really trampled someone? Maybe having fun came with a price.

The fun ended suddenly, when two ladies arrived at the classroom door, and I was summoned forth, in front of the whole class, and led out into the hallway, with its off-white cinderblocks and omnipresent linoleum echo. I was a little scared, because the singling out made me feel like I had done something terribly and unforgivably wrong. Kindergarten was the most equal place imaginable, the pint-size version of democracy in action. We were all just recess jungle-gym players and nap-time mat-layers, who had to listen when Paul whispered "Poop!" in our ear. Then the day ended, and we went home for lunch. And that was all there was to it. Life was good! But now I was being sucked away, removed from that happy garden of kiddie-time leisure. And the fact that it was *just* me could only mean that I was special in some disturbing way. I was being cast out. I would now be separated from the horde. Right then and there, I was branded.

The two ladies marched me down to another classroom, and as I entered, things looked familiar but different. There were about the same number of kids, and they seemed fairly ordinary, but they were sitting at desks, and there was a lot of very official-looking stuff—numbers, writing—plastered on the walls. I was asked to sit at a desk in the back, next to a bulletin board that featured a great big pumpkin made of circles of orange construction paper, and that pumpkin, a preview of Halloween, made me feel good for a moment. I looked up at it and thought, "I guess this place will be all right. But where am I?"

I was in the first grade, having been placed there after six weeks of kindergarten. It was not a decision instigated by the officials of Eberwhite Elementary School. It was, rather, a move they went along with after being pushed into it by my mother, who was desperate for me to "get ahead," already overripe with eagerness to launch her campaign to turn *me*—as a representative of *her*—into the Smartest Kid In The Universe. It was her way of stacking the deck in my favor. Years later, when I saw *Almost Famous*, I nearly fell out of my chair when it was revealed that the 15-year-old hero is so much shrimpier than the other kids in his class because he has, in fact, been skipped ahead not one grade but two (including kindergarten). I'd never before seen a movie character who thought just like my mother until Frances McDormand's Elaine informs her son, with a hellbent twinkle of superiority, "You skipped kindergarten…because I taught it to you when you were four!" Then she adds, "Who needs a crowd? Who put such a high premium on being typical? You're unique! You're two years ahead of everybody!"

Talk about a step forward that's also a step back. I think that my mother, just like McDormand's Elaine, believed that she was saving me from the fate of being typical. Well, mission accomplished. You might say that I adjusted well. Once I got over my *Branded* moment, I settled into the first grade without much fear or fanfare. I was a quick-minded kid, and the schoolwork came easy. I was assigned to a reading group, and it didn't take long for me to catch up with the other dogged perusers of *Dick and Jane.* My mother, huddled with me on the couch, taught me the fundamentals of reading in two nights, using the book *Go, Dog. Go!* My adjustment to the first grade was not traumatic. My mother must have thought that everything was going according to plan.

Yet in a funny way, the ease of the transition camouflaged the number it did on my psyche. You must understand that this was not the era in which children start to read on their iPads in preschool, and by the time they reach kindergarten they're on to Proust and the Pythagorean theorem, all because their parents are desperate to get them onto the step ladder (next stop: Ivy League!) that will hoist them into the One Percent. When I came along, the difference between kindergarten and every other grade—it's the reason they didn't *call* it a grade—is that, with nothing academic in sight, all kindergarten *was*, in the end, was about being with other kids. It wasn't about "learning." It was about learning to be a social being. And so skipping a kid like me out of kindergarten after six weeks was a rather boneheaded thing to do. It said, in effect: *That social stuff is just fluff. It doesn't matter.*

I socialized in first grade without visible drama, but now there was a purpose, a mindful activity, to everything happening. The sheer irresponsible joy of kid-to-kid connection got waylaid. That may be why I could never totally grasp what was going on at summer camp, or in the soap opera of high school, or in the world of office politics; that may be why my personality is flavored with a pinch of Asperger obtuseness. What skipping kindergarten did was to abstract me from other kids, turning me into someone who stood almost reflexively *outside* a situation, someone who could only now "play well with others" via the brain. It locked me into a state of voyeuristic passivity, turning me into a person who doesn't so much stand up and do things as sit around and watch things, waiting for someone else to do them. (Trust me: You wouldn't want *me* to be the only other person at a dinner table if the Heimlich Maneuver was called for.)

From a young age, a pattern was established: *I watched things. I listened to things. I thought about things.* And that was enough. There's a photograph of me with my grandfather sitting in front of the tilted metal schematic globe sculpture at the 1964 World's Fair, and I'm looking into the camera with what was already a typical gaze for me: a little downbeat, a scrutinizing look in my eye, verging on a scowl, as if my 5-year-old self were pondering something terribly important. In gym class at Eberwhite, the gym teacher was a burly ex-Marine named Mr. Barrett who liked to treat us as if we were in basic training, and since I was smaller than the other kids, and uncoordinated enough to stand out (how in the world was I supposed to climb…a *rope*? or use my white-noodle arms to do a pull-up?), I was the butt of many a joke, the principal one being that Mr. Barrett insisted on calling me "*Glieg*-erman," as if my name was just too ethnic and irritating to ever get right. It shored up that even though I didn't hate sports, gym was never going to be my scene. Too much… *activity*.

So why did my mother, Lillian, push so hard for my six-week graduation from hanging out and having fun? It had to do with her own blend of brainy ambition and insecurity. Born in the Bronx in 1934, she was raised to be a nice Jewish girl, a role she struggled to live up to because she was too smart for it. She was pensive and kind, morose and easily crumpled—a wallflower of severity—and she was also beautiful, though she never totally knew it. She wore her hair in one of those pouffy cake-frosting 'dos made popular by Marilyn and Janet Leigh and Doris Day, yet by the early '60s, her choice of a short haircut had begun to morph from something stylish and pert into an almost unconscious way of martyring her femininity. The world could have been her oyster, but her life conspired to make her feel like a girl who didn't deserve pearls.

What happened was this: My mother's parents came over from a village in Poland, and whatever virtues of hardworking noble immigrant *blah blah blah* they brought with them (my grandfather, a tool-and-dye maker, launched a successful shop in Harlem), they created a domestic environment in which love was rarely, if ever, expressed; it was treated as a foreign emotion. One reason that I've never given much of a damn about my Jewish roots, apart from the fact that I never had a Jewish upbringing (my family always celebrated Christmas, albeit the *Charlie Brown*–meets–Santa Claus version), is that while I know that I was lucky to be born in 1959, years after the Holocaust, when I look back on my own clan (all the members of my grandfather's family were killed by Hitler), I see unspeakable tragedy, but I also see a family of people who were capable of using the forces of social oppression to explain away their own inability to love. While I honor the meaning of the cruelties of history (when you've seen as many Holocaust documentaries as I have, it's hard not to), I have no patience—none!—for allowing those cruelties to be treated as an excuse for shoddy personal behavior. When my mother was 4 and a half, she contracted pneumonia and was placed in the hospital for 17 days. There was a no-visitation policy on the children's ward, but her parents could have insisted on seeing her—and they never did. She thought that she had been abandoned. The event traumatized her, instilling her with an anxiety and rage that, by her own account, she never totally got over.

Growing up, she was a cautious but precocious girl who invested her ego in getting all A's (that's how she would be loved!), and then, when she was only 15, came the event that would mess up so much of the rest of her life: meeting my father. They had a romance right out of *Dirty Dancing*, hooking up at a Catskills resort in the summer of 1949. This was pre–rock & roll; instead, they shared a passion for classical music, which they instilled in me. (I nearly became a classical violinist.) Lillian was the jailbait ingenue, and my father, Eli, was the 18-year-old hunky busboy, a Brooklyn-born bodybuilder and sun worshipper, strikingly handsome, but with thick Clark Kent horn-rims, which gave him the look of a studly beach bully who was also an intellectual geek. In spirit, he was both those things. He told my mother that he wanted to marry her a month after they met, and in those days, they shared a lot. They had a communion, an attraction, an affection. Yet the desperate, self-fulfilling folly of their bond is that neither one of them loved the other in the way that each of them longed to be loved. They arranged, in effect, their own deeply flawed marriage of convenience, and it became a nest of codependent misery.

My father was blessed with a great deal—looks, talent, the gift of gab, and the ladies loved him—but he nursed twin demons of megalo-mania and self-doubt that made my mother's insecurities look heartwarm-ing. He planned to become a doctor, but got lousy grades in his science classes, then flirted with becoming an English teacher, then wound up going to medical school after all—in Lausanne, Switzerland, because it was easier to get in there for Americans whose pre-med resumes didn't cut it. It was like buying non-FDA-approved drugs in Brazil. (The paradox was: It was easier to get in...but you had to study medicine in French.) That's why I was born in Switzerland and spent the first year of my life there. I have no memory of the place, but given my general lifelong state of fingernail-chewing anxiety, it probably made my central nervous sys-tem a *little* calmer than it might have been otherwise. Switzerland in the late 1950s had to be one of the most placid places of the 20th century.

My parents got engaged, and appeared, at first, to be headed for the out-of-the-Jewish-tenement version of a storybook marriage. But there was one hitch: My dad had already begun to have liaisons with other women, and in plain view of my mother. He went to Lausanne early, fell in love (his words) with a schizophrenic girl who lived in the house he was staying at, and told Lillian about it. More than crushed, she was destroyed. Yet did she throw the bum out? No. (The fact that I now exist is the only thing keeping me from writing the words *big mistake*.) And he didn't cancel the wedding either, despite a telegram he sent that threatened to. The truth is that the two were deeply tied to each other. My mother had found her anchor, terribly flawed as he was, and she wasn't about to give up the diamond ring on her finger. She was scared she would never get another one.

She viewed me, her first son, as her prize surrogate, a symbol for the success and acceptance in the world that she craved. Yet she was also des-perate for a soulmate, someone to make up for the scoundrel my father turned out to be. From a very young age, I was her companion, and she explained the world to me, ardently and earnestly, with almost no consid-eration for the fact that she was talking to a child. She told me about the James Bond novels she was reading, about the soap operas she was watch-ing, about what a fast-food restaurant was. And she built plastic monster models with me, all the classics—the Wolfman, Dracula, the Hunch-back of Notre Dame, the Frankenstein monster—which became, in effect, my kiddie-store introduction to horror movies. She even watched a horror film with me on TV once: *The Mystery of the Wax Museum*, which spooked me deeply at age five, because I associated the images of beautiful waxy dead women with…my mom. (Was I glimpsing some lost-soul part of her?) There was almost no hugging in my house, and the words "I love you" were never spoken. My parents, too, did their bit to incinerate love. Yet there was a sweet vibrance to my mother's personality, expressed in her willingness to share the kinds of activities with me that my father should have been doing. It was expressed, as well, in this dangling conversation the two of us had, this never-ending *talk*, that was her skewed form of affection.

More than anything, my mother talked to me about the classical composers she adored. When I got to second grade, she took me to the stately, cream-colored performance hall of the University of Michigan's Hill Auditorium to hear the Tchaikovsky Violin Concerto. About 15 minutes in, when the shockingly beautiful downbeat of the piece's grand theme was first struck, it was, to me, such a blinding nuclear bomb of incandescence that I was like Alex in *A Clockwork Orange* having an aural climax to the great Ludwig Van. I'm not exaggerating when I say that from that moment on, I was a deeply religious person. It was simple, really: No world that contained this majesty, this sound, this *pleasure* could be said to be godless. I felt—I knew—that this sound was all a person would ever need to be happy. It was all *I* needed.

Tchaikovsky loomed large for me. Later in the second grade, I was listening to the family phonograph, which I'd learned how to operate, and the record on the turntable was *Swan Lake*. The famous theme music, which I'd never before heard, possessed me. So I picked up the tone-arm and played it again. And again. And again. It was sublime, satisfying my inner swoony Alex, yet now, somehow, I craved more. I was like a teenage boy staring at a gorgeous girl: The music was so beautiful that it was no longer completely satisfying just to hear it. I needed to be…inside it. How could I do that?

I went over to our piano, which my mother played (with a touching amateur choppiness), and picked out the melody. It was easy enough to do. But that wasn't enough. What made the music beautiful, I realized, wasn't just the melody, it was the chords. I would have to play those too! So I began to try out combinations of notes, and before long I had figured out the chords to *Swan Lake*. If I positioned my fingers just so, I could play the theme with my right hand and the chords with my left. And suddenly, right there, *that* was enough. I was no longer just hearing the music; I was inside it. A decade later, when I was a senior in high school, I wrote my first movie review: of Ken Russell's *Tommy*. But really, this was my first review. For me, becoming a critic was never primarily about judging a movie, it was about trying to crawl inside the experience, to merge with it. It was an act of consummation.

From that moment, I could play anything by ear on the piano that I wanted, and I did. Mostly, that meant pop music. A few weeks later, I was getting a ride home from another neighborhood mom, and a song came on the radio: "What the World Needs Now Is Love," sung by Jackie DeShannon. I was dumbstruck; I had never heard a melody so tender and sad, so liltingly bittersweet. The lyrics seemed directed right at me: What the world of my family needed was love, sweet love, but this song was saying that the whole *world* needed love, that there was just too little of it. I thought: If that's so, then everyone else needs love just as much as I do. At that moment, "What the World Needs Now" made *me* feel loved. I felt redeemed; I suddenly knew that I was just like everyone else. There wasn't much difference to speak of between the feeling that "What the World Needs Now" provoked in me and the feeling that the theme from *Swan Lake* provoked in me, and to this day, I think a great deal of pop music *is* classical music—it's just a lot shorter. To my surprise, the mother who was driving me, Mrs. Slater, began to sing along (*"We don't need another mountain..."*), and I thought: Wow, my mom would *never* do that. And somehow that seemed to symbolize everything about my mother that was contained, forlorn, withheld. Before long, I was playing "What the World Needs Now" on the piano. I think figuring out how to play things was my way of serenading her.

It's not like my father was going to do it. He loomed over us, but really, he had already checked out—of the marriage, and his family, too. He was a worldly and ruthlessly intelligent man, but also a hardass and an Olympic-level cheapskate: To him, money was more real than anything it could ever buy. He was like Howard Stern's father ("Shut up! Sit down!") crossed with a high-culture version of the Great Santini. My dad, like my mother, had a reverence for the classical music he listened to, especially if it was from the baroque era, and his appreciation was genuine, but the music also symbolized something for him. In his eyes, it gave him highbrow cred—and, just maybe, an honorary WASP membership card. On Sunday mornings, he would blare Bach organ music at top volume from the local classical radio station. I would be looking at the comics, or eating bacon and eggs, but in the background it sounded like the Phantom of the Opera had taken over the stereo. In essence, it was my father's way of going to church.

I have a strikingly gentle early memory of him taking me to his office when he was a medical resident. He let me peer through his microscope, then he played a game with me using a typewriter, saying that I would "hit the jackpot" each time the return bell rang (was this his eerie premonition that I'd become a writer?). In that moment, he was soft, soothing, fatherly—the way he almost never was after that. By the time I was in grade school, with two younger brothers (born in 1963 and 1964), I began to see him not so much as my enemy as someone who, for mysterious reasons, now viewed *me* as the enemy. And it all began when I was watching Saturday morning TV.

I became a fanatic for the Beatles not long after everyone else in the galaxy, though in a slightly different way: In 1965, when I was six, I was a devoted watcher of *The Beatles* cartoon series, which had been cooked up, and fast, to cash in on the group's success. It was a chintzy little show, with what looked like cutout replicas of John, Paul, George, and Ringo scurrying around spewing kiddie-sitcom Cockney one-liners. But it was my first link to the moptops. On Saturday mornings, I would sit there, hypnotized, watching the silly animated Beatles as they went through their adventures and, on each episode, cavorted to two early Beatles songs. I was entranced by "Misery," so bouncy in its heartbreak, and "I'll Follow the Sun," which haunted me with how I couldn't decide if it was a happy song or a sad song. It was like sunlight gleaming through the rain.

Each week, however, I would try to hide the fact that I was watching *The Beatles* cartoon, in an "Oh, is *this* on?" sort of way, from my father, who would tromp into the living the room and say, in a voice of testy disappointment, "Owen, what are you watching this garbage for?" He hated pop music, looked down on the very idea of it. There was a teenage girl who lived on the top floor of our apartment building, and she kept a transistor radio glued to her ear. My father would talk about how she was "crazy," and he meant it, as if he thought she was the only teenage girl in America with a habit like this. That's how out-of-touch his anger made him. But since I *wasn't* a teenager, fighting a cliché rock & roll battle with my father didn't make me defiant; it filled me with guilt. I knew that I dug the Beatles, and my father's rancorous attitude could hardly take that away. But his hatred toward something I revered so much discombobulated me.

When I was in the third grade, we moved to a storybook-looking but overly small two-story house, red with white pillars, with a backyard just across the fence from a dense woods. That miniature forest, with its cedar-chip path, led directly to the playground of Eberwhite, and I often wandered through it, drinking in the viny oddities of nature, usually meandering, at the end of my walk, over to the playground, with its slightly bent goalposts, because I liked looking at it when it was empty. But one Saturday morning, as I emerged from the woods onto the Eberwhite grounds, I saw a sight that left me in shock: From the parking lot streamed all these boys...who I knew...from my third-grade class. And all of them were there with their fathers. I had stumbled, as if by karmic accident, onto the very first day of tee-ball, the training-wheel version of Little League in which kids stand at home plate and knock a hardball off a standing tee. I wasn't a big sports kid, yet I was crushed. As far as I was concerned, the words "feeling left out" might have been invented for this occasion. Yet I stood there, humiliated, and watched the entire practice.

Standing on the sidelines of that practice, I blamed my father. He wasn't a nice, baseball-playing man like all these other dads. He was a gruff customer who gave me a hard time for watching *The Beatles* cartoon. No wonder I didn't know about tee-ball practice! Then again, it was really me—not my father—who had failed to register that tee-ball was starting in the first place. Why hadn't I known about it? I couldn't wrap my head around the answer to that question. Because really: How could you know about something you didn't know about? What I sensed, but couldn't quite voice to myself, is that if I had been more connected to the other boys in my class, I would have known.

But connection was something I was starting to have a problem with.

Or maybe just something I'd begun to have a profoundly ambivalent relationship to. And the first time I ever realized that was going to the movies.

I was about to see *The Sound of Music* for the second time: the first time that I'd ever gone back to see a movie twice. I had seen it the first time with my grandparents in New York City. It's literally the only film I can ever remember them seeing, and I was curious as to why they cherished it so much. Only years later did I figure out that it must have been the feel-good factor *plus* the family-entertainment-whips-the-Nazis inspiration-alism, which spoke to their Jewish old-country selves. But *The Sound of Music* had enveloped me, too. It's the first movie I ever saw that wasn't kids' stuff, and the songs were so entrancing that once we got home, I wore out the soundtrack and learned to play all of it on the piano. I was possessed by Julie Andrews, this soprano angel in the body of an innocently mis-behaved tomboy nun–turned–den mother.

I can't swear that my mother dropped me off at the theater and left me to see *The Sound of Music* all by myself, but that's how I recall it. What I know is that I stood there, alone, in the cavernous lobby of the Michigan Theater, alive with anticipation at the sights and sounds that I would soon be seeing. I still think *The Sound of Music* is a great film— impossibly square, to be sure, but a musical that tingles with a whole-some incandescence; it's not so much "sugary" as a stylized projection of pure goodness. Standing in that lobby, which was filled with children (it must have been a weekend matinee), I could hardly wait to drink in Andrews' benevolent glow, the splendor of the Alps, the heartstring tug of "My Favorite Things" and the lordly grandeur of "Climb Every Mountain." But gazing around at the other kids who were waiting to go in, I realized, at that moment, that I had a deep desire not to share the movie with any of them. I wanted to be the only one watching it. I was filled with a strange new sensation, a borderline jealousy of everyone else in the theater, as if none of them even had the right to be there. It's a feel-ing that I never had, at least consciously, again. Yet for a few seconds, I knew that watching *The Sound of Music* wouldn't be enough. I wanted to possess it, to fuse with it, to live inside it. I wanted it to be mine.

CHAPTER 3

THE COUNTERCULTURE KID

The smell was pungent, a little sweet, with an unsettling hint of crops on fire. I'd never encountered it before, but as the smoke wafted out over the audience, I knew what it was, because what else could it be? David, my new friend from seventh grade, who had brought me to the movie, leaned over and, with a knowing whisper, as if he was doing something other than pointing out the obvious, said, "*Marijuana!*" I just nodded.

The smell disturbed me, because it meant that we had truly snuck into the land of adults, who did things that you weren't supposed to do. *Marijuana was against the law.* I was still innocent enough to feel that meant something fundamental. And when I looked up at the screen, I can't say that I was comforted: There were multiple colliding images of hazy green farm landscapes, but what set the mood, syncing up with the rush of anxiety I got from flirting with those burnt-corn vapors, was the music on the soundtrack, with its ominous churn of guitars, and a voice ringing out as though it were singing about the end of the world: "It's been a *long...time...*comin',/It's going to be a *long...*time gone."

We were in a movie theater, of sorts. Actually, it was Angell Hall, a drab, sloping, not-very-large lecture hall at the University of Michigan that served as the prime space for one of several undergraduate film societies. The place was dingy even by Midwestern college standards, but that made it seem a little clandestine, like a speakeasy. The film we were watching was *Woodstock*, and in those opening minutes, I passed through a looking glass: With all of these long-haired college students lighting up their joints and hash pipes, it's as if the world of the movie had come off the screen and enveloped me. Moments later, the mood lightened: The sound of Crosby, Stills & Nash singing "Long Time Gone" gave way to "Going Up the Country," and those same farm images, now dotted with swaying hippies, took on a beatific glow. To this day, I've never liked "Going Up the Country" when it comes on the radio—it's often been pointed out that Canned Heat's lead singer sounds just like Kermit the Frog—but inside the fertile panoramas of *Woodstock*, he sounded like the Pied Piper tripping down a yellow brick road of debauched enchantment. He beckoned. The whole movie beckoned.

It was in the first week of seventh grade that I fixated, Harriet the Spy–like, on David, sitting in the back of English class. He was the only kid in Slauson Junior High with long hair, and he wore glasses that had gold wire frames (which were then not nerdy but exotic) and a necklace of tiny plastic beads. The thing that caught my eye, though, was that his prominent nose was buried in a thick, squat book with strange lettering and a drawing on the cover that looked like a woodland hallucination. Each day I would observe him as he paid absolutely no attention to the teacher, absorbed instead, for the entire class hour, in that book. What was it? From several seats away, I stared at the odd lettering and saw that it said *The Lord of the Rings*. After class one day, I went up to him and said, "What's that book you're reading?" He said, "*The Fellowship of the Ring*. It's about Hobbits." Hobbits?

I went downtown with David on a crisp fall Saturday, and it was on that outing that I began my puppy-love affair with the counterculture. I had no idea, of course, that I was falling for something that was already in its death throes. Middle Earth, Ann Arbor's one and only head shop, was a bent-ceilinged hovel, but the posters in the black-light room gave off a crazy chartreuse glow, and the whole place was suffused with a mystical spicy foreign scent so thick that you could just about bathe in it, and you could purchase that scent and take it home with you in thin brown sticks that came in packages bedecked with floating Asian figures with six arms. David then took me to the Bead Bag, a store that sold nothing but mounds and mounds of intricately designed and painted beads. We took our trays and picked out the beads we wanted, which you strung onto an elastic band to create—as I learned—not a necklace but a *choker*, which was okay for guys to wear, and which I began sporting that very day. At the waterbed store, we rolled around on top of what was apparently the gooshy future of sleep. It was all a big circus... with a cause.

What I couldn't get over is that the people in the stores, who looked like the groovy version of 19th-century American settlers, were so nice! It would not be radically unfair to describe 1969 to 1972 as the period in which a major swath of American youth pretended to drop out of the middle class so that they could all go to work in shops selling ornate psychedelic candles. To me at the time, this seemed a perfectly valid revolutionary notion. I wanted to feel like I belonged to their happy hippie universe, which was *so* not the depressing crush of junior high or the humdrum affection-free zone of my family. These people wanted to overthrow "the authority," and that, it struck me, was a very good idea. Together, we would all replace The Authority with nice people who sold candles!

My righteous romance with the counterculture, at the ages of 11 and 12, was certainly the naive, rosy-cheeked version of it. Yet in a funny way, the pre-teen years may have been the ideal developmental moment to be immersed in the love-in politics of the late '60s. My connection to the counterculture was absolutely Oedipal: *Get rid of the bad father.* Yet that was probably true of more than a few of the youth-culture revolutionaries who actually took up the cause. Born in 1959, I'm technically a boomer, but really, I was too young to experience the flowering of the '60s. Instead, I was plopped down right on the cusp between the boomers and Gen X. This left me a little rootless, but it gave me an aesthetic-perceptual advantage: I connected deeply to boomer passions, but only as a child...and so I could see, perhaps more than others, just how much inner child there always was guiding the boomer vision.

My own father certainly despised my new fixations. He ridiculed my choker ("Owen, *why* are you wearing that thing?"), and he instructed me not to go to Mark's, a hippie coffeehouse where he warned, in his most stern physicianly tones, that I might end up catching hepatitis. I think he literally believed that the people in the kitchen were all junkies, and I was just young enough that his paranoia got to me. When David, on one of our downtown jaunts, took me to Mark's, I sat there watching him consume his bean-sprout sandwich while I ended up faking a stomach ache and eating nothing.

I began to live in pinball arcades, not just because I got hooked on pinball and air hockey, but because there was something so seductively sleazy about those dank parlors of fun, with their dirty rugs, bad lighting, rows and rows of magical-mechanical playtime machines, and surly teenage clientele who all looked like they were either drug dealers or drug buyers. The pleasure of pinball was innocent enough, and I would often take my kid brother Erik along with me (growing furious any time he got a higher score than I did), yet in some indescribable way pinball seemed...*bad*. Sinful. Maybe that's because decades before videogames became a kind of digital freebase for kids, the culture recognized that too much indolence *was*, in fact, unhealthy. (Now it's all just good clean first-person-shooter fun.) I discovered that the greatest song to be playing on a pinball arcade's sound system was Led Zeppelin's "Black Dog." Few things could make me feel happier than going on a run of Target Pool or Fireball to those annihilating riffs topped with Robert Plant's orgasms.

I had less good luck reading *The Lord of the Rings*. I tried to get through it—twice—but each time I got stuck, like a truck driving through four-foot-deep mud, in the middle of *The Two Towers*, the second volume of the trilogy, which was, if humanly possible, even worse than the first. How could anyone read this gibberish, this turgid nonsense? Who cared about orcs and trolls and the intricate geography of all these places that sounded like they were named by a Turkish chemistry teacher? I had learned, by then, that *The Lord of the Rings* was a countercultural touchstone, that the good, pastoral, giant-pipe-smoking Hobbits were kind of like hippies (the same way that the Caterpillar in *Alice in Wonderland* was sort of getting high), and I desperately wanted to be in on the cachet of it all, but I decided that J.R.R. Tolkien was a writer of encyclopedias masquerading as a novelist.

The book that became *my* counterculture touchstone was the published transcript of the Chicago Seven trial. The line-by-line court proceedings had been whittled down to a 290-page Bantam paperback called *The Tales of Hoffman*, and in seventh grade, I carried it everywhere, reading it over and over, seeing the endless trial for what it was—not so much a criminal-conspiracy case as a reality-based war-of-the-generations stage play. I worshipped Abbie Hoffman and Jerry Rubin and Tom Hayden and Rennie Davis, drawing pictures of their faces in my spiral notebook the same way that I once drew pictures of the Beatles. I turned the Chicago Seven into pop icons. And that's because I loved listening to them stand up in open court, telling off...the man. The evil Judge Julius

Hoffman! A punitive scold just like my father. For someone who hated being part of any group larger than my grade-school class, I was cultivating a strong desire to become part of *the people*. In the end, though, what I revered about the Chicago Seven is that they stood up and told the truth. That was the aspect of the counterculture I romanticized.

My parents' drive-in-movie habits had faded to once or twice per summer, which is how I got to see *M*A*S*H*. (Donald Sutherland struck me as cooler than any rock star, though the football game at the end seemed to go on forever.) To sate my curiosity about the raciness of films made for adults, I now had to rely mostly on my subscription to *Mad* magazine, whose monthly issues I devoured, especially the movie satires. They were caustically funny, in their everything's-a-scam-and-everyone's-an-idiot way, but the true genius of *Mad* was that Mort Drucker's caricatures were so detailed, so insane in their exactitude (in the satire entitled *Botch Casually and the Somedunce Kid*, you could make out every hair in the stubble on Robert Redford's chin), that they were like a comic-book study of the grimy charisma of New Hollywood stardom. Reading those satires really was the next best thing to seeing the movies. (Sometimes, when I finally did see the movie, it verged on disappointing; I wished it was closer to the satire.)

I was addicted to monster movies and consumed them mostly on our family's 16-inch black-and-white television set with the random piece of tinfoil wrapped around the semi-broken antenna. Our local horror host came out of Detroit and called himself Sir Graves Ghastly, and he was an oddly vain broken-down actor in a Dracula suit and a teddible Transylvania accent. I enjoyed his antics, but mostly as a prelude to movies that, no matter how awful or cheesy or fake, left me with a taste of awe. Movies like *The Day of the Triffids* (about an attack of giant vegetables!) or *The Manster*, in which a man grows a savagely gnashing second head. (The best shot was that of an eye appearing where his nipple should be: the noggin just starting to grow!) Then there was the one film I saw on *Sir Graves* that actually, to my surprise, scared the holy living shit out of me: *Black Sunday*, a low-budget Italian ghost orgy of shadows and fog built around the nightmare image of a woman shut up in a casket that pierced her face with a spike. When the casket opened, I literally leapt off the couch in fright.

I first glimpsed the recklessness of the counterculture at the rock concerts I began to go to in 1971. A lot of them took place in Hill Auditorium, the stately performance hall where I'd heard the Tchaikovsky Violin Concerto (and saw God) just a few years before. There was something fantastically oxymoronic about seeing the stage of this elegant classical venue taken over by a group like Commander Cody and His Lost Planet Airmen, local country-rock badasses who turned "Hot Rod Lincoln" into a blast of anarchy. The smell of lit-up weed was now an old friend, but the audience intimidated me, because it wasn't just hippies, it was bikers: beer-guzzling dudes with stringy beards who looked like they wanted to beat someone up. Once, we went to see a furious bluesman named Luther Allison (who looked like a rapacious young Morgan Freeman), scrunching ourselves right up next to the stage, and I stared at his facial contortions as he shot out increasingly high-pitched guitar licks that seemed to pierce the universe. It all made me wonder: Was the '60s vibe I was grooving on truly about freedom and love? Or was it about how the pursuit of those things inevitably turned threatening?

The answer, I began to think, was the latter, especially after I saw my first R-rated movie at a traditional theater. David's father, summoned by a frantic last-minute phone call, came down to the Michigan Theater—the same place where I'd had my jealous breakdown over *The Sound of Music*—to buy tickets so that the two of us could get in to see *Easy Rider*, which was playing for a week on its third run. And suddenly, I had the novel sensation of watching an adult movie about people I felt I kind of knew. Billy and Captain America were us! The hippie rebels! During the opening credits, I took note of the fact that one of *Easy Rider's* two stars, Dennis Hopper, had "directed" the movie. I'd never thought about what it meant to "direct" a movie (though it was kind of obvious what it meant: to put the whole damn thing together), and throughout *Easy Rider*, I was amazed that Billy, who seemed so slovenly and drugged out, with his lackadaisical "*Man-n-n-ns!*," was actually the guy behind the camera. The film was sort of slow, and I only half got some of it, but then, at the end, came the first moment I had ever experienced in a movie that...well, what can I say? That blew my mind.

It was right after the two get shot to death by a trigger-happy, hippie-hatin' redneck. That was pretty intense, and the violence of it all was made memorable by the image of the smoking ruins of one of the two crashed-and-burned choppers viewed from way up in the sky... *the very same shot*, I realized, that had already been glimpsed in the hallucinatory acid-trip sequence set in New Orleans. In other words: The biker had foreseen his own death. *Fucking wow!!!!!!* The whole rest of the night, that haunted me. I could not get it out of my head.

If *Easy Rider* had a message, it was that the counterculture was running on empty. But that was something I had to discover in my own intensely personal and stupid yet necessary way. By the eighth grade, I was growing my hair long, which visibly disturbed both my parents. I was a straitlaced, pre-hormone-crazed 12-year-old hippie radical who believed in power to the people... but didn't like belonging to groups. I was more than a little confused. And all of the confusion came to the surface, and exploded, in Miss Walker's history class.

It was supposed to be American history, but Miss Walker, whose very first year of teaching this was, simply started at the beginning of the textbook, which commenced, in brain-glazing detail, with the *discovery* of America. Though I had liked learning about the explorers in grade school, this was the bone-dry factual version (a great deal of attention paid to words like *textiles*), and it became obvious that Miss Walker's notion of teaching was plodding through the textbook one page at a time. Near the end of the first semester, we still hadn't gotten to the Revolutionary War. I was bored down to my fingernails (literally), but more than that, I was now old and aware enough to figure out that the teacher didn't know what she was doing. And I was going to make her pay for it.

Looking to entertain myself, and to flex my new "rebel" muscles, I became not just the class clown but the class jackhole delinquent. I mouthed off at every opportunity, mocking the material and the teacher, not with any noteworthy wit, but with a great deal of conviction that disrupting the basic flow of the class was a deeply righteous thing to do. Every discussion of something that happened in history ("They made a deal to exchange crops for land rights...") was greeted by one of my knowingly doltish rejoinders ("Why would they want to do that?"). I turned eighth-grade history into my own personal Chicago Seven trial. What made this not simply an adolescent rite of passage, but a rather ugly one, is that Miss Walker was black, and she hailed from the inner city, and I could tell that she was teaching—literally—by the book, holding on to it like a life raft, and I was the smug little Jewish kid lording it over her lack of sophistication and experience. This was, make no mistake, a racist form of acting out, and the fact that I somehow convinced myself that I was "liberating" the classroom only made it worse. Miss Walker herself didn't know what to make of me. In exasperated tones, she would dress me down, as if this was a bad sitcom and I was her Vinnie Barbarino, and I was regularly banished to the assistant principal's office, which never had much effect on me. How could it? I had my cause! I was fighting the people's fight! Fighting the boredom! Fighting the authority! But really, I think I was just fighting to be heard.

• • • • • •

In Pioneer High School, where I became something of an artist at skipping class, my favorite activity was nearly Zen in its simplicity: I loved wandering around the school. Aimless. Without pretense or purpose. Long hair flopping in my face. Shirt untucked (my lazy, can't-be-bothered anticipation of the grunge look). Thinking and dreaming. I probably had more than a touch of ADD, which wasn't routinely diagnosed back then. And I say: Thank God it wasn't. Whatever I lost in terms of the information I failed to soak up in classrooms, I gained in not having my entire personality stamped with the lockstep calming/energizing spirit of Ritalin. I may have been an overly restless slacker, but at least I was me.

Walking through the empty halls while class was in session was a spiritual balm. It gave me a respite from the lack of privacy I had at home, where my father couldn't be bothered to fix the jammed-half-open sliding door that separated my bedroom from the kitchen. It also saved me from something I couldn't put into words, though it was probably related to the sensation characterized by Jean-Paul Sartre in the lovely line "Hell is other people." It's not that I didn't *like* other people. (I did have friends.) It's that I felt so much more serene when I had the luxury of not being in their company. My soul unclenched when I was all by myself. And the extraordinary thing—though I took it completely for granted—is that in Ann Arbor in the mid-'70s, you could actually get away with strolling through the halls of high school, day after day, without ever being bothered by a pesky administrator. The rules were *that* lackadaisical.

I was the beneficiary, or maybe the victim, of a new wave of "progressive" spirit that had rolled in from the counterculture, though without any real shift in educational policy. The forward-thinking cachet was all about the new code of discipline—i.e., you now had to look pretty hard to find one. There was a smoking lounge in Pioneer, an entire two-story room in which students could retreat to have a cigarette, and this was considered not demented but enlightened: a way of respecting student smokers by giving them a place to go. Though I didn't smoke myself, I would wander by the lounge and stare at what looked like all the impossibly grownup students who were seated there, enveloped in swirling clouds of toxic haze (there was so much smoke that it looked like there must have been a forest fire in the next room). In a high school graced with a smoking lounge, all a kid like me had to do to get away with being out of class was to look, however vaguely, like I was on my way to something.

I mastered that look, though the truth is that I was on my way to nowhere. The experience of imagining myself the Abbie Hoffman of eighth grade history had proved a disaster. My antics didn't inspire any revolutions, but they did get me hooked on not doing schoolwork, a form of indolence I decided was cool. I was a smart kid but way too easily bored, and paying attention in class was something I convinced myself was for squares.

Despite my compulsive class-cutting, I avoided the kids at Pioneer who skipped school and headed for the woods across the road to partake in ritual afternoon sips of Boone's Farm Apple Wine. And I didn't hang out with the gloomy-eyed, long-greasy-haired stoners who stood for hours at a time in the side-door foyers—though I did, in the midst of winter, adopt their delinquent uniform, which was to wear your big, dirty-green Michigan parka with the fur-lined hood *all day long*, never once taking it off, not in class and not in the hallways. The parka was cred, a scruffy sign that you didn't *want* to be in school. I wore the parka with a morose sort of pride, but apart from that, I avoided the clique of these junior substance abusers.

For an entire year, it seemed, the movie that everyone was talking about was *American Graffiti*. I didn't see it, though I did go to a few *American Graffiti*–inspired greaser nostalgia parties, mystified—or maybe just irritated—that the ubiquitous theme song of high school had become "Rock Around the Clock." The nostalgia was puzzling to me, because it was all about looking back at something that no one actually remembered.

The reason I was seemingly the only kid in my class who never saw *American Graffiti* is that in my rather solitary search for an identity, a *role*, I had become something of a snob-ignoramus about popular movies. I assumed that they were crap and would hold no interest for me. Sure, some of the films that possessed me, like *Rosemary's Baby* or *Easy Rider*, had been hits, but I took that fact to be nearly incidental to what I responded to in them. Movies that I regarded as obvious mass entertainment I could not have cared less about. Which is why, in addition to *American Graffiti*, the films that came out during my high school years that it never once occurred to me to go see included *The Exorcist*, *The Sting*, and *Jaws*.

I was more into watching *The Ghoul*, a syndicated jester of a late-night horror-movie host who was a knock-off of Ghoulardi, the character that Paul Thomas Anderson's father, Ernie Anderson, invented in Cleveland in the early 1960s. But what Ron Sweed did with the character had a more nutzoid, anything-goes '70s vibe—he was like a beatnik Howard Stern crossed with an amphetamine junkie trashing his basement on public-access TV. I thrilled to his antics, even as I'd begun to develop a rather odd relationship to the cruddy horror and sci-fi movies he was showing. Watching something like *The Strange World of Planet X* or *Beast with a Million Eyes* or *Target Earth*, I wasn't nearly as enthralled as I had been seeing those kinds of movies on *Sir Graves Ghastly*, but now I would fantasize that I was literally inside the films, standing there on those weirdly placid low-budget '50s movie sets, and I found the sensation comforting. I wanted to go live there.

· · · · · ·

The smoke flowed through my lungs, and it made me dizzy and a bit high, but that was all, because it wasn't weed—it was a cigar. I was standing with half a dozen other guys from the eleventh grade, all of us sucking on Tiparollos as we stood across the street from the Campus Theater, where we were getting ready to go into the first Friday night show of *Flesh Gordon*. It was the fall of 1974, and I'd been asked to go along by a kid named Peter, who sat with me in the back of English class, where we liked to spend the hour playing cards (that sterling Pioneer disciplinary code at work again!). Peter came from a conservative Middle Eastern family—sort of the Arab equivalent of my stuffy Jewish clan. He was a visibly uptight guy himself, but he compensated for it in a number of ways. He wrote hilarious short stories, he was a furious rock drummer, and he was obsessed with seeking out the most vulgarly strange and debauched movies he could find. (Decades later, he became a monk living behind the bars of a Greek Orthodox monastery; I guess the spirit of his parents won out.) I wound up tagging along with him and his partners in outré-movie crime to see *Flesh Gordon*, a movie that promised outer-space parody and horniness, though not necessarily in that order.

This was going to be a boys' night out, and though that was not really my thing, since I could never find the right what-the-hell tone of cocky flippancy, I was grateful to be there. The movie turned out to be a cardboard soft-core sci-fi spoof that was fun...at stray moments. A lot of shrill camp acting and horrible '70s jokes that knew they were horrible (which didn't make them any less horrible). But an attack of monsters called Penisauruses, complete with giant veins, was rather well done (it reminded me of the creatures in *Mysterious Island*, a 1961 Jules Verne–meets–Ray Harryhausen special I had seen several times on TV). And then there was the moment when Flesh, the frosted-blond space-warrior hero, gets together with some sort of sultry deposed space queen in her private shuttle shaped like a teapot, and as I watched her straddle him, her buttocks writhing, it made quite an impression on me. I carried that exploitation-film image around in my head for months.

I was still eager to see any film that fed my teenage hunger for the forbidden. I'd never lost the desire for that shock, that lurid *frisson*. Yet the shock value was getting harder to find. Nothing could truly match the spellbound awe I experienced as an 8-year-old at the drive-in peering behind a cinematic door marked "Do Not Enter." And now, my craving for the outrageous had fused with sex. Fortunately, I no longer had to depend on the satires of *Mad*. I could go to the campus film societies!

They would let anyone in, without carding you. So I kept tabs on the upcoming film schedules, and I made momentous plans to see a couple of major-event movies on the calendar. The key to the plans being: I would go to them all by myself. Hell is other people accompanying you to movies that feed your restless appetite for sin.

The first film I developed an obsession with seeing was *Last Tango in Paris*, and for obvious reasons. It was already the scandal of the '70s, and I knew all about it: It was a movie that consisted, in its entirety, of two people having sex in an apartment! That sounded right up my alley. The day of its showing arrived, and early on a Sunday evening, I headed downtown to the University's Modern Languages Building, which contained yet another lecture-hall-turned-makeshift-film-society-venue (though this one wasn't so much drab as sprawling and sterile). *Last Tango* had come out the year before, and given the slower release patterns of movies back then, that made it feel like it was still a fairly new film. So I was surprised when I got to the MLB and saw that two dozen people, at most, had shown up to see it. The scandal seemed to be evaporating before the movie even started.

Then it began, with Marlon Brando looking up into the air and screaming (I guess he didn't know yet that he was going to be having sex for two hours in an apartment). There was a really unpleasant scene featuring a woman who had slashed herself to death in a bathtub (why was that scene even there? And when was the sex going to start?). And then, at last, Brando got to the apartment, and there was the girl, and yes, she was gorgeous (her baby-doll poutiness reminded me of Linda Ronstadt), and the two of them had sex, though they didn't take their clothes off. That was okay; we still had most of the movie to go. But then the two started talking, and talking some more, and even when the sex scenes arrived, they weren't *sexy*, like the one in *Flesh Gordon*. The already famous "Get the butter!" scene was just…a long monologue. (Yes, a monologue delivered during an act of anal penetration, but you could hardly see what was happening.) What a letdown! *Last Tango in Paris* turned out to be a really talky, somber, hard-to-fathom movie for adults.

Years later, *Last Tango* would become one of my favorite films, as I came to see that it's really a scalding and mournful raw-nerve passion play about a mid-life crisis. I was hardly ready for it at 15. Yet if my adolescent libido was disappointed, I was also semi-captivated. The film's decadent languor, its tragic-romantic saxophone score, its whole late-afternoon melting look and mood stayed with me. No, its art kinkiness wasn't sexy—not really. But what was it?

I had a better experience with the next juicy movie I chose, which was the *other* scandal of the '70s, *A Clockwork Orange*. In this case, I had already read the book (in ninth-grade English class—probably the one assigned novel I read that semester), mastering the jaunty dystopian slang of words like "droog" and "horrorshow" and, my personal favorite, "yarbles" (which meant "balls"). As it happens, nothing that transpired on screen was quite as fraught as the conversation I had with my mother when I made the mistake of telling her that I was going to see *A Clockwork Orange*. "Oh, *Owen*," she said, her features crestfallen. "Why would you want to see that?" I couldn't begin to answer her. And I felt terrible, laced with guilt, as if I'd been caught with my hand in the evil-dream-factory cookie jar. All I could do was mumble something like, "I just want to see it..." In a funny way, that was the truth.

This time, the venue was packed. It was 15-year-old me and 800 college kids, and they were stoked. The "Singin' in the Rain" scene was too brutal to be erotic, but it fed my hunger, because it *was* shocking (though the main thing I took note of through my mesmerized gaze was that Alex, the ringleader rapist-hoodlum, was doing all of this sick stuff, yet somehow I still really liked him). The scene in which Alex picks up a couple of teenyboppers and has his way with them was disappointing, just like *Last Tango*: Yes, the scene was kind of witty, but since it was in super-fast motion, you couldn't really see anything. Oh, how I wished I could watch that scene at regular speed! Since I'd read the book, I felt that the ultra-nasty films they showed Alex to program him against violence weren't ultra-nasty enough. (In hindsight, this was my first demonstration of what became a core principle for me as a critic: If you're reviewing a movie based on a book, if at all possible do *not* to read the book—at least, not until after you've seen the film. Otherwise, all you'll be doing is comparing the two.) The ending, with Alex being fed like an infant by one of the men who had programmed him (who now grinned with friendly glee), left me completely baffled. Yet as I walked out of *A Clockwork Orange* and sauntered home, my head was spinning with the sounds and images I had seen. It was like some plastic satanic futuristic-but-not-futuristic dream. The movie was something of a washout on my teenage peter-meter, but even so, I watched it in a trance.

I started to talk to a kid at school named Greg about *A Clockwork Orange*, and he told me about a movie coming up at one of the campus film societies that *he* was planning to see. (So I wasn't the only one!) The movie had a strange name: It was called *Satyricon*. It was about sex and madness and ancient Rome. It was made by someone named Fellini. And somehow, the way that Greg spoke about it, he made it seem like not just a movie but a holy event. Greg and I skipped school one day, going down to Ann Arbor's tiny Centicore bookstore to see Andy Warhol, who was there promoting his volume of tape-recorded ramblings, *The Philosophy of Andy Warhol (From A to B and Back Again)*. When we got to the store, at 11:00 a.m., no one else was there, but there was Warhol, standing inside all by himself holding a flower, looking lost and forlorn. I didn't know much about him, but his art was so famous that Greg and I got the bright idea—probably repeating something that zillions of people had done—to go to a nearby grocery store and purchase cans of Campbell's tomato soup, which we gave to Warhol to autograph. He did it without saying a word.

Greg couldn't stop talking about *Satyricon*, and catching his fever, I started to talk about it too. I knew even less about Fellini than I did about Warhol, but his name had an aura about it, and I felt like I was preparing myself to see something at once forbidden and elevated. I imagined it as an *artistic* drive-in movie. And then, finally, the big night arrived. Greg and I went to Angell Hall, heading for that same sloping classroom-theater where I'd seen *Woodstock* in seventh grade. It was a full house. The film started, and I saw wildly stylized Roman-antiquity sets, and scene after scene of foppish, rather hideous-looking lecherous men lording it over boys and girls, and all that seemed, in its way, rather promising, but after a while I began to notice that I wasn't really follow-ing what was going on, and that I was growing a little restless, and then the restlessness turned to outright disinterest, and then I noticed that I was literally fighting to keep my eyes open. By the end, *Satyricon* had come to seem like the longest movie I had ever seen. I couldn't wait for it to be over.

It was awful! (Greg, though, really liked it.) Yet a funny thing happened on the way to the boring Roman orgiastic head-scratcher. By the time we finally saw *Satyricon*, I was mind-bogglingly disappointed in what the movie turned out to be. Yet my hopes for it, built up over a month of chatter, had taken on such a life of their own that I was still immersed in the movie I *longed* for it to be. I told my mother about it, and I think she was greatly relieved to hear that I'd gone to a movie by Fellini in the wake of seeing *A Clockwork Orange*. A few weeks later, she gave me a book as a present, which was quite uncharacteristic of her outside of birthdays and Christmas. The book was called *The Cinema as Art*. It was a smallish paperback full of fairly dense prose, and I can't say that I could get through much of it. But in the middle, there were several sections of stills, all tarnished-silver black-and-white, from films that the book talked about, none of which I had ever seen or heard of, and each of those photographs hit me as if I was a child staring at the magical cover illustration on a book of fairy tales. An ominously huge fireplace from *Citizen Kane*. A looming close-up of a deeply shadowed, impossibly glowering man in long whiskers from *Ivan the Terrible*. A bald man with bat ears grasping his heart and literally fading away before the sunrise in *Nosferatu*. Two dead donkeys lying inside two grand pianos in *Un Chien Andalou*. Again and again, I would take the book and page through those photographs. I had to see the films those images came from! They seemed like pure windows into the forbidden, though with an added element, a shimmer of mystery.

Greg didn't talk about movies, he talked about "film," and I realized that that's what those stills were about. Film! The word, so simple yet suggestive, made my heart beat with curiosity. So one Saturday night, I went with a couple of my more art-conscious acquaintances over to Greg's house, and instead of watching *The Ghoul*, I sat around with all of them and watched, on PBS, an Ingmar Bergman film called *Wild Strawberries*. It was a lot more somber and slow-moving than *Satyricon*—just watching it seemed like some gravely hushed ritual—but this time, I could follow the story, and I got caught up in the plight of this old man who felt like nobody ever really loved him. It was a little static, but it was touching. It was like *It's a Wonderful Life* (which I'd seen on TV) remade in an oddly severe way. Over the next year, we would periodically go over to Greg's house to watch a Bergman film (they always played on PBS), and the act of sitting there in the dark with my friends seemed, to me, very adult and kind of cool. I hadn't become a film buff yet; this was more like the early chrysalis stage of my buff-dom. I was getting hooked on the notion that each new movie, good or bad, was a package of surprise, a revelation waiting to happen.

In the fall of my senior year, I went to see *Tommy*, the 1975 movie of the Who's rock opera. I knew the music well and was captivated by a few scenes (like the Marilyn Monroe church), but I didn't really know what to make of it. For reasons I still can't remotely remember—maybe it was that I was stoked by my new hobby of moviegoing, or maybe it was just a whim—I decided to write a review of *Tommy* for our high school newspaper, *The Optimist*. It was my very first movie review, and it was written in a stodgy, joyless tone that was all bluster and no insight:

"At first it seemed to me that there must be some obvious significance to the plot: however I decided after about 12 seconds of thought that it was totally meaningless and that it had probably been thought up by someone at about 1:30 A.M. following a bad episode of The Tonight Show." I also noted that "many of the sequences are very effective visually, and they contribute to a total imagery that is sometimes quite admirable." But there is one line in my badly written, broad-brush review that hints at something: "There is no actual dialogue," I noted, "only singing. However there is music going constantly. This gives the film the peculiar effect of not having any genuine emotional ups and downs." In my stumbling way, I was trying to deal with Tommy's moment-to-moment effect on me.

I had one more piece of true shock cinema in store. It was another highly planned event with Peter and his band of naughty-movie droogs. There was a film they had seen several times, and they were going back again, because they couldn't get enough of it. "You won't believe it!" Peter told me. It was called *Pink Flamingos*, and every time the subject came up, Peter, who did a great impersonation of Curly from the Three Stooges, would erupt into Curly-ish whoops and spin around on the floor. He wasn't hiding anything about the film, either: By the time the night arrived to see *Pink Flamingos*, I already knew that it was the movie in which you got to see someone eat dogshit. Who on earth wouldn't want to see that?

We arrived at the campus film venue, this time a vertically tiered science-lecture hall, and as soon as the film started, with an endless grainy shot of a trailer home and this weirdly cruddy-sounding early rock & roll guitar, the whole underground aura of it seemed beyond forbidden; it felt like we were going to watch a snuff film. I should have been thrilled, but instead I was actively nervous. And when the main character came on (she was called Divine, and she was *played* by somebody named Divine...how strange), she was amazingly hideous, a clown monster with a snarling grin, and then she got really, *really* angry, at which point it began to seem like she was insane. Then a couple of characters came on with blue and red hair (which seemed as jarring, back then, as if they'd each had seven fingers), and they, if possible, got even more ragingly mad than Divine did.

As I watched *Pink Flamingos*, it never occurred to me that Divine was actually a man. I thought I was seeing the single most aggressive woman I had ever beheld. And though everyone in the audience, including Peter and his pals (who I guess I was now part of), giggled hysterically, and I could certainly tell that the film was supposed to be funny, I found it so disturbing that my chuckles were forced. At the end, when the villains were tried and killed, I was not at all sure that the actors *hadn't* been executed. I may not have known what a drag queen was, but I did know what a documentary was, and this movie, despite its awkward storyline about a competition to be "the filthiest person alive," seemed to be about real (sick) people. The dogshit scene was the ultimate proof of that. As the narrator said, "What you are about to see is real!" Watching that scene made me a little ill, yet it did deliver on the forbidden-awe factor. The scene was, in the truest and deepest meaning of the term, *awesome*, and like the rest of the movie, it scared the bejesus out of me. Coming out of *Pink Flamingos*, I felt my entire worldview shift. It had never even occurred to me that I shared a planet with people like this, but now I knew that I did. My craziest drive-in-movie dreams had been fulfilled, and trumped. I now realized that even I couldn't go any further.

And then, without my wanting or expecting it, the moment came when the light streamed in. It was in the winter of 1975, when I was 16 years old, and my mother, who had never done this before, asked me if I'd like to go to see a movie with her. It sounded like a nice thing to do, so I said: Sure, why not? The two of us went down to Angell Hall, and she explained that this was a movie about the making of a movie, and that the film's director also played the director in the movie (which made me think, for a moment, of Divine playing Divine). His name, she said, was François Truffaut.

The movie started, and sure enough, it showed a movie being shot, with people walking out of a fake subway, and then a scene unfolded with two men and a gun, but what seized me, after they shouted "Cut," was the music that flooded the soundtrack: It was a startling brass chorale, with trumpets that sounded like something by George Frideric Handel, only it was succulent and contemporary in a way that I couldn't quite explain. Hearing those notes, I surged with happiness. The music came on again and again, and it made me happy each time, but before long, I began to feel how the pleasure of the music was also expressing something: the nearly unspeakable joy that the people on screen were taking in making the movie. And I could certainly see why: What amazing fun it looked like! It was like a melodramatic magic show, a series of intricate acts of make-believe that, each time, made you believe. The off-camera goings-on struck me as very grownup (adulterous affairs, a man in love with another man, two of the film workers casually taking off their clothes and sneaking into the woods to have sex), but I could follow them all, and I felt sophisticated doing so. And what I started to notice was that there was all this life flowing around the making of the movie, and there was also the glorious fakery involved in actually making the movie, but the magical part was the way that the life flowed into the fakery, flooding it until it all became...real. And somehow, seeing this, I felt more than captivated. I felt tickled, dazed, enchanted.

Sitting in Angell Hall that night, watching François Truffaut's *Day for Night*, I turned my head to the side and looked around me, taking in the darkness. I turned to look at my mother, and then I turned back to stare at the big, crowded rectangle of light at the front of the room. I saw the people on screen and felt their passion, and I knew, all of a sudden, that it was my passion too. These people weren't just movie characters— they were my people. And right then and there, I realized that I didn't need anything else. Because *this* was it. This is what I had been wandering around and searching for. This was everything.

I was home.

CHAPTER 4

THE BIRTH OF A MOVIE FREAK

It was your basic, everyday dorm-room prison cell: a cinderblock cubicle, with green-and-gray walls and just enough space for a pair of desks and shelving units. A lot of students would tape a schedule from one of the campus film societies onto the wall, along with their Blue Öyster Cult and "Hang in there, Baby!" kitty-cat posters. For me, though, during my freshman year at the University of Michigan, the film schedules weren't just about another random activity you could do at night. They were sacred scrolls, the focal point of my existence. And this, of course, had to be reflected in how I displayed them. So I took the posters for the four film groups—the Ann Arbor Film Co-op, Cinema Guild, Cinema I, and Mediatrics—and arranged them, like an art collage, until they covered the entire inside of my polished plywood dorm-room door. (My roommate didn't mind; he was a tea-sipping William Buckley fanatic who cared about nothing but reading the classics.) I was even compulsive about cutting out a tiny circular hole in one of the posters that would fit, ever so snugly, around the door's half-inch-diameter wide-angle peephole. This, you see, was more than a door—it was my Wall Of Life, The Representation Of Who I Now Was. The movie schedules were being displayed, but mostly to myself. Part of the beauty of becoming a film buff is that it meant I didn't need anyone else.

I'd spent the summer engaged in my favorite pastime—doing nothing much at all—while catching a handful of movies on campus. I had yet to figure out, in the fading vapors of my adolescent snobbery, that commercial movies were something a movie buff might actually be interested in. I was still making the "film" vs. "movie" distinction that I would soon figure out was preposterous: a meaningless dichotomy. To bolster my loyalty to the "film" end of things, I made regular trips to Borders Books—not the chain store, but what was, back then, the one and only Borders in the world, a long, high-shelved, reverently silent paperback-smelling independent sanctuary launched in Ann Arbor by two U of M grads in 1971, years before it grew up into a brightly lit cultural McShopping Mall. I haunted the film section, browsing and drinking in the pictures in books like *Film as a Subversive Art* and *The Film Director as Superstar*, and taking in, for the first time, the parameters of movie history, a subject that I now realized, with a tingle of time-machine sentience, was actually quite short. If you dated it, for convenience, back to *The Birth of a Nation*, in 1915 (I was aware that there were rumblings of cinema before then, but in the grand scheme of things, not that much to speak of), you could say that the entire history of motion pictures, in 1976, was just...60 years old. Compared to, say, English literature, movies were a 3-day-old infant. That fact thrilled me. It made me feel that I could ingest it all, that I could make the movies mine and that, in doing so, I would also belong to them.

I was goosed along by my early experiences in freshman classrooms. I hadn't abandoned my school-is-for-the-birds attitude of smug academic neglect, and I figured, on some level of projected idiocy, that the kids around me would now be enlightened enough to share that attitude: that all of us would be too clued in to care about the stuffy irrelevant drudgery that "they" were shoveling at us. Did I ever have a wake-up call coming! I'd gotten into the University of Michigan with my mediocre high-school grades only because it was a state school, and the campus, which was woven throughout the downtown area, was so familiar that it was like my buddy. What I was clueless about is that the U of M was, in fact, an elite institution that kids across the country competed to get into, and though a number of my comrades from Pioneer had gotten in, most of my classmates weren't Midwestern slackers like me. They were prep-school go-getters, often wealthy, looking to bite into the future. It's not just that they did the assigned reading—they actually *liked* talking about things like the plays of Aristophanes and the rise of the Byzantine Empire. There was no way I could keep up (though I did enough homework to hold my grades above water), because the bottom line was that I had no desire to.

From the start, I was drawn to realms outside of academia. Early in the semester, I wandered on a whim into the offices of *The Michigan Daily*, the U of M college newspaper, where I asked to see the arts-page editor. She was a chipper, snappy sort named Lois, and after being introduced, I asked her if I could start writing some reviews of classical music. This turned out to be one of the worst ideas I'd ever had, and a mercifully short-lived one, though it led me to the place where I would spend most of my undergraduate career: the college newspaper office. Aside from my one random, badly written review of *Tommy*, I had never demonstrated the slightest interest in writing anything, and I didn't necessarily feel the impulse now. I think this came closer to being my desperate attempt to keep one hand in the classical-music world.

Lois assigned me to review a concert by the University Philharmonic, and not long after my snooty, choppy review appeared in the paper (giving me a little jolt of adrenaline that made me recall Harriet the Spy getting her first article published), I bumped into an acquaintance from high school, a proto-computer wizard named Jon, who had always been notable to me for having the most raging volcano field of acne I had ever seen. He told me that he'd read my review. A bit flattered at the recognition, I asked him what he thought. "I hated it," he said with a sage grin. "I thought it was . . . pompous." I wanted to sink into the earth, because I realized, on the spot, that he was right. The built-in problem with reviewing a classical music concert is that the event itself has already faded into the ether, and if you write something like "the clarinet solo in the third movement was dutiful but lacked zest" . . . well, who gave a fuck if it did? You sounded like a parody of the critic as nitpicking cad. But I was on the beat and continued, for a couple of months, to churn out this dross. It says something about how much my status as a film buff was purely about *watching* movies, rather than any desire to write about them, that it never even occurred to me to try my hand at writing another movie review. I'm not sure, to be honest, that I had ever even read one. The form meant nothing to me.

Despite having volunteered for the *Daily*, I had a genuine ambivalence about putting myself *out* there, especially when it came to sex. To say that I was behind in that area would be phrasing it kindly. At 17, I was a virgin (and, as it turned out, three years away from losing my virginity). That fact, however, wasn't all that shameful to me. The truth—and this *did* shame me—was that I had never so much as kissed a girl, and had never even been on a date. (I boycotted my senior prom in a fit of leftover-'60s, *I wouldn't be caught dead in that parade of phonies!* pique.) And I wouldn't do either of those things for two more years. I did have opportunities, like the girl from Grosse Pointe who rubbed my arm outside my dorm room and suggested that we "go inside." Why didn't I? The thought of transforming desire into flesh (even mere lip flesh) filled me with a dread I could hardly account for. I was like a trembly Irish Catholic wallflower from 1862, terrified of what I desired. Sex was what I craved and what I somehow, mysteriously, couldn't imagine myself doing.

But movies, which I was entering into the earliest days of my love affair with, would now be *my* domain, my realm of passion and mastery. Proudly, I propped up my new film books on the dorm-room shelf: a volume of the writings of Sergei Eisenstein, which I pored over to learn about his intricate yet, to my mind, borderline loopy theories of montage (it was obvious to me that the "collision" of two images didn't work in the way that he described it), or Carlos Clarens' *An Illustrated History of the Horror Film*, an elegant treatise that colored in my love of the Famous Monsters of Filmland era, now allowing me to experience it as an organic slice of cinema history. And make no mistake: Lousy dorm meals aside (it's not that they tasted bad; it's that everything from the meat to the vegetables seemed to be made of the exact same Waxy Food Product), cinema history was now the banquet on which I feasted every night.

Looking at the schedules that covered my door, where I'd circled each film I planned to go to, I saw the entire history of movies laid out, night by night, double feature by double feature, in an arresting high-meets-low, art-meets-bubblegum sprawl, each pair of films organized by director or actor or genre or simply according to the programmer's whim: *Dog Day Afternoon* paired with *Scarecrow*, *Night of the Living Dead* paired with *Carnival of Souls*, *The Searchers* paired with *Fort Apache*, *Blow-Up* paired with *The Passenger*, *Harold and Maude* paired with *King of Hearts*, *The Music Lovers* paired with *Women in Love*, *Written on the Wind* paired with *Imitation of Life*, *Z* paired with *The Parallax View*, *Aguirre, Wrath of God* paired with *Even Dwarfs Started Small*, *Bonnie and*

Clyde paired with *Gun Crazy*, *The French Connection* paired with *French Connection II*, *Knife in the Water* paired with *Cul-de-Sac*, *Beyond the Valley of the Dolls* paired with *The Day of the Locust*...

What's nearly impossible to communicate, in the era of DVDs and VOD and streaming and Netflix and Turner Classic Movies and a thousand other ways to watch whatever you desire, is the shiver of anticipation it gave one to stare at such a roster of films when it was literally *the only way that you could see them.* Some of the more popular double features showed up regularly, every couple of semesters, but if you missed that chance to catch *Medium Cool* or *Solaris* or *A Woman of Paris* or *Bring Me the Head of Alfredo Garcia*, you felt like you might not have the opportunity for years. And maybe you wouldn't. After all, no one knew that the videocassette revolution was coming; it would have sounded like science fiction. In the early '80s, after I got my first VCR, I loved renting videos as much as anyone, in no small part for the kid-in-the-candy-store feeling that a video store gave you. Yet if I had to say whether something was lost—as well as gained—in the early age of videocassettes, I'd venture to say that yes, maybe it was. Any given film became a little less rare and, perhaps, a little less magical.

It's hard to think of a year more tailor-made for treating the experience of college as a ginormous revival house than 1976. The New Hollywood, which had been named but not yet made iconic, had more or less just ended. I personally think that a key spear in its side was *Rocky* (which opened December of my freshman year), with its *On the Waterfront*-redone-by-Capra sentimentality and its tearful happy ending that revived, after a decade of downer scuzziness, the whole feel-good ideology of happy endings. In many ways, *Rocky* was the dawn of Reaganism. But when I started college, a lot of the great films of the '70s were still on their way to becoming fabled. This was the moment a lot of them were being discovered.

And the sensation—the hope—of discovery was the religion that sustained me, night after night. There's a creative side to having a touch of ADD, one that feeds into the life of a movie buff: You can consume an entire work in 90 minutes to two hours, and then, just like that, you're on to the next one. It's the perfect aesthetic surrogate for sex, because the two have so much in common: No matter how any individual movie works out, the *promise* of ecstasy is always there. When I would show up at Angell Hall, the forbidden movie palace of my youth, only now to see something like *Gilda* (in which I found Rita Hayworth to be not just madly sexy but a tragic romantic presence), or *Sweet Movie* (a deadly serious allegory of political oppression that was nevertheless extreme enough in its bodily fluids to rival *Pink Flamingos*), or *Jules and Jim* (my first Truffaut film after *Day for Night*—and, to me, a staggeringly turgid and precious movie), or go to the ramshackle Architecture Auditorium to take in *Ivan the Terrible, Parts I* and *II* (three and a half hours that moved like a glacier yet still somehow made good on the eerie shadow-puppet grandeur promised by that still from *The Cinema as Art*), I would feel that I was about to witness a nearly sacramental ritual.

A word on *Jules and Jim*: It was my first experience of seeing a classic film I thought was second-rate, and the lesson I took from that particular evening was simple and eternal, and rooted in the (relatively) brief history of movies: If you found an acclaimed film to be disappointing, or uninteresting, or downright bad, then so what? *That's what you thought of it.* I held the history of cinema in reverence, but it wasn't a reverence that could trump my own experience of two hours spent in a movie theater. There were other venerated films I didn't care for—*Nights of Cabiria, She Wore a Yellow Ribbon, The Magnificent Ambersons*, almost anything by Godard— and though I always thought about what I'd seen afterwards, I never gave the fact that I didn't *enjoy* a movie a second thought. I was insecure about a lot of things, but I trusted my pleasure centers. It seemed obvious to me that they weren't correct or incorrect. They were simply mine.

They were certainly operating on overdrive when I got to see my first Woody Allen film: *Love and Death*, a perfect introduction, since it contained bite-size parodies of Bergman. I quickly saw that Allen was a clown-genius of neurotic lunacy, especially after I took in the perennial campus double bill of *Bananas* and *Everything You Always Wanted to Know About Sex But Were Afraid to Ask*. Yet what hit me as much as the comedy is how wildly I identified with Allen the long-frizzy-haired, horn-rimmed yammering-intellectual horndog. More than just a hilarious loser, he was Supergeek, the anxious, decidedly strange-looking man who, in movie after movie, could actually get the girl. When you were as sexually backward as I was, Woody Allen was a culture hero. He was the movie star who gave you hope.

The films at Angell Hall would often be introduced by an Ann Arbor Film Co-op stalwart named Rip, who appeared too old to be an actual student, but whose long hair and bandana and autodidactic intros qualified him as a roving herald of movie mania. To introduce something like Ken Russell's creepy-crawly possessed-nuns psychodrama *The Devils*, he would stand up on stage and bellow, "A lot of people have said they think the violence in this film is gratuitous. Well, we don't think it's gratuitous. We think this is a bold work of art!" All that was missing was a "right on!" Just like that, the freedom-fighter politics of the '60s had turned into the daring-movie aesthetics of the '70s.

The communal feeling inside almost any movie theater is primal, mysterious, animalistic, and healing. In college, I reveled in that sensation, though I wasn't necessarily seeking it out. For one of the touchstones of being a film buff was the essential act of liking, and choosing, to go to the movies by yourself. We've all seen lonely guys at movie theaters: the schlub slumped in his seat, his jaw resting lazily on his hand. For a lot of people, going to see a movie by yourself, at least on a regular basis, would seem to be a desperate, sad-sack activity. And maybe it is. But I've spent a major portion of my life going to the movies alone, and from the outset, doing so was an element of the mystique I was creating about the pop-culture form I'd already fashioned into my mistress. Going alone transformed moviegoing from a pastime into a nearly sacramental ritual. It's what made it a holy romance.

For the true movie buff, being at the movies, even if you're with other people, means that you *are* alone. The essential experience has almost nothing to do with the quality of what you're seeing. It begins with the sheer existential bliss of leaving yourself behind to merge with whatever's taking place on screen, and with taking a simultaneous deep dive into the reactions of your own mind. With all of that going on, who needs another person? Even a makeshift college movie theater could become a velvet womb, its comfort promising the chance to be reborn. For me, that womb was a hiding place, a stimulation chamber that soaked up my ADD, and a trance-inducing meditation space in which I watched grownup movies that exerted the power of childhood fables. It's where my restless nature could melt into whatever I was watching.

Going up to the ticket desk, I would plop down my $1.50 and wander inside, choosing a seat that provided a good vantage point, and before the movie started I would be intensely aware of the audience: the stray clusters of friends, the people on dates, the occasional other lonely guy who, I presumed (with a touch of competitive wariness), was also one of the movie-buff anointed. I wondered, at moments, what it might be like to actually *go* on a date, but the thought was always short-circuited, because whatever movie I was seeing, in effect, *was* my date. It was the entity I was going to be having a dialogue with. I was a little like the Joaquin Phoenix character in *Her*, conducting a deeply satisfying relationship with something that may not have been human, but that was okay, because it looked and felt human to me.

I think that point is crucial when applied to the gritty, mirror-image-of-reality movies of the 1970s. My new life as a film buff hooked on the glories of solitude wasn't all that different from that of the bookworm who spends his time sitting in a room immersed in the journey of a 600-page novel. But where books can come alive on the page, movies, as the film buff experiences them, don't have to "come" alive. They *are* alive. You're staring at real people—a version of reality that comes to seem more real *than* reality. The result isn't just a wholesome love of art (though a lot of film buffs pretend it is). It's a sweet sickness, a metaphysical addiction, a way of entering into a cocoon that you're convinced, in some part of your being, is more perfect and transcendent than life.

It's not like I *never* went with a friend. I met my first fellow movie buff on my dorm-room floor, a glad-handing fellow named Andy from upscale Chicago who could hardly have been more different from me. He slept with a lot of girls, won so many honors for his poetry that he counted on the awards for income, and considered himself the world's foremost authority on Stanley Kubrick. Andy took me to my first showing of *2001: A Space Odyssey*, mostly so he could show that he knew the film's every line and music cue by heart, and my conversations with him were exhilarating, because they demonstrated something I'd never fully encountered with my Ann Arbor friends: that a pivotal part of the pleasure of movies is *talking* about them. He also blasted through the last shards of my anti-commercial-movie bias, since Andy, whose father worked in advertising (he'd invented the Pop-Tarts mascot Milton the Toaster), guzzled commercial movies like soda. For the first time, I began to venture out to first-run theaters to see things like *The Seven Percent Solution* or *Car Wash*, and that set the stage for what would be the most influential month of my life, from late November to early December of my freshman year. It was the moment that would mark my transformation from eager, polite, budding Film Buff to full-on cinema-syringe Movie Freak.

It all started Thanksgiving weekend. I was back at my parents' house for the holiday, all of six minutes away from campus (that's how cozy and small Ann Arbor was), and on Friday, the day after Thanksgiving, I decided to take in a matinee. There was something playing called *Carrie* that looked like an offbeat horror film, and that roused my curiosity, so I drove over to Briarwood, our local shopping mall, which housed a primitive '70s multiplex, and I went in to see it. I had never heard of the film's director, Brian De Palma, or the writer, Stephen King, on whose novel it was based. But as *Carrie* started, with a slow-motion scene in a steamed-up girls' locker room, I thought, "Yes, this is my kind of movie," and when Sissy Spacek's Carrie had her period right there in the shower, blood dripping through her hands beneath her horrified gaze, only to find herself attacked by the cinema's original onslaught of mean girls, I was so disturbed, and simultaneously so giddy that the opening of a movie could provide such a desperate jolt of emotion, that it was as if I had already entered some hyper-charged version of movie heaven.

Carrie never let up. The tormented battles between Carrie and her Christian psycho mother seemed to have come out of some witches'-brew version of *The Glass Menagerie*, and the wallflower-goes-to-the-prom plot seemed to tap every masochistic feeling of being out of the loop of mainstream life that I had ever had. Granted, I'd done my share of cultivating an outsider stance, but that didn't mean it wasn't alienating, and *Carrie* was a sullen young geek's catharsis. When the prom sequence began with a single glorious shot, the camera edging from the air toward the disco ball and the surging crowd of dolled-and-tuxedoed dancers, I remember thinking that no moment I'd ever seen in a movie had made me *this* excited, this delirious. The hideously cruel trick played on Carrie, and the bloodbath of her response, was a mini Hitchcock opera of mad vengeance that turned sadism into moviegoing bliss. And when the final shocker arrived, with Carrie's hand popping out of the gravesite, I literally *stood up* in terror, as if I was trying to scramble away from the screen and over the back of my seat. I felt a shudder of fear pass through my body like a ghost.

Coming out of *Carrie*, I was so ecstatic that I didn't know what to do, so I got in the car and drove and drove and thought about the movie, then drove some more, and thought about it some more, then came home and talked to my mother about it, then went out, looking for friends to tell about it. I was manic, like someone who'd just done six lines of cocaine and was suddenly possessed by the knowledge that *Carrie* wasn't just a movie, *it was the secret of life.* I thought about the film for days, and talked about it for days. I decided that it was the one film I'd ever seen that was almost literally a dream. I couldn't get its itchy, ticklish power out of my system.

A week or so later, I was sitting in the living room of a friend's family, waiting for her to come downstairs, and to kill time, I picked up a copy of *The New Yorker* magazine, which I never looked at (even though my parents subscribed to it). I saw on the contents page that there was an article about "the current cinema," so I turned to it. And I started reading. It was a review of *Carrie*, and from the opening words ("*Carrie* is a terrifyingly lyrical thriller"), it seemed to express everything I thought about the film yet, somehow, didn't know that I had thought. Reading the review, I felt like I was reliving the movie, and a few of the lines really jumped out at me. One was when the writer said that "Sissy Spacek uses her freckled pallor and whitish eyelashes to suggest a squashed, froggy girl who could go in any direction; at times, she seems unborn—a fetus." *Whitish eyelashes!* (Yes, I could just *see* them...) Another was when she said, "Who but De Palma would think of using old-movie trash, and even soft-core pornos, to provide 'heart' for a thriller?" I thought: *Yes!* The film *did* have a trashy/soft-core/drive-in-movie dimension, but what an amazing, and ironic, and right-on idea that *that* side of it provided the film's heartfelt core. Finally, the writer said, "*Carrie* looks like a piece of candy." I didn't even know why that was such a perfect description, yet it was. The movie glittered like candy, all right, and it *was* candy. The review was signed by someone named Pauline Kael. I thought: This person's writing is like candy. I must eat more.

Over the next couple of weeks, I read Pauline Kael's reviews, in *The New Yorker* and, mostly, in her latest collection, *Reeling*, which I went down to Borders to buy. It was a big, dense, packed book with a boldly colorful jacket—and every review in it crackled with the same hypnotic rhythms and startling perceptions, the same rush of ideas and images and sensations and judgments. Kael's descriptions of just about everything carried a snap of objectivity: Whatever she wrote about, she seemed to be describing it just as it was, and there was something narcotic about the effect of that. She seemed to have a 20-20 reading on what the material world looked and felt like. She also seemed to understand everything about how the culture of movies worked—the way it was a layer cake of passion and pretension. Even if you loved movies, seeing through the sham of what certain films were up to was, for her (and, by implication, for you), part of the fun of being a moviegoer. It wasn't just about watching a movie; it was about glimpsing the hidden layers of the cake. There was also something about Kael's writing that took me a while to realize: She wrote about every character in a movie—even a flat, mediocre movie—as if that character wasn't a "character" at all but, in fact, a real live human being, standing right in front of you. Which is kind of what a movie character is. In her descriptions ("Charlie, you can see in his tense ferret's face, feels he was born to be punished," "Michael [Corleone]'s attempt to be the man his father was has aged him, and he can't conceal the ugliness of the calculations that his father's ceremonial manner masked"), Kael was a mercilessly incisive therapist laying bare the personalities she observed. And this made a thrilling kind of sense, since movies, good and bad, featured actors who brought every quirk and furrow of their personalities to the screen, sometimes unintentionally. Kael wasn't just writing movie reviews. She was inventing a new kind of reality-based criticism for the ultimate "reality" art form. And the astuteness of her live-wire movie therapy was uncanny.

As crazy as it sounds, I began to imagine, quite literally, that Pauline Kael was my mother—an idealized, heightened version of her. I had no idea at the time that the two had much in common. They were hyperarticulate Jewish women, both a little over five feet tall, both possessed by the power of art, and born 15 years apart (Kael in 1919, Lillian in 1934). But my mother, for all her perceptions of the world, was tangled up in her insecurities. Kael was like a supreme, pearly-voiced Lillian 2.0 who soared on worldly wings. For all the caustic sting of her wit, there was something nearly angelic about the earnest, sentence-by-sentence directness of her attempt to express the truth of what she saw. The catharsis of it was the permission it gave you to believe in—and express—*your* truth. Her reactions to the world were so analytic yet sensual, so fully felt and satisfied, that the woman who came across on the page seemed to exist in a state of grace. I wasn't just thrilled and fascinated by the slangy poetic turn of Kael's mind. I was moved and transported by it. I felt as if I knew her.

Within weeks, she'd become "Pauline," my companion, and all I wanted to do was see more movies, read Kael's reviews of them, and think about those movies—perceive them—in the way that she did: to cut to the X-ray core of what was going on in each one of them. She showed me that that core existed, and that it was the truth of what any movie was, and that you could find it, with her help, or on your own. It didn't even matter when I disagreed with her; I would read what she wrote about a movie that I loved and she didn't (like, say, *Midnight Cowboy*), and her words would have the same magical effect on me. I would chime with the bulk of her perceptions and ideas even when I *didn't* agree with the assessment they led her to. She seemed right even when she was wrong. It was as if Pauline Kael made *your* brain into a movie review, and *she* was turning the pages and reading it, and *you* were having thoughts you never had, which were her thoughts, but they became yours.

And then came the moment that changed...everything. The movie that revolutionized my life. It was in the middle of December, just as everyone was cramming for finals. I, too, tried to squeeze in a ramped-up study schedule, but that didn't mean I stopped going to the movies every night, and one that I'd been intensely curious about from the moment I read the description of it on the schedule was *Nashville*, a country-and-Western ensemble epic directed by Robert Altman, the maker of *M*A*S*H*. I saw it at Angell Hall, and during the shadowy opening credits, the first thing I noticed was the sheer size of the image, a rectangle that seemed staggeringly thin and wide, like a razor blade. (It was called

Panavision.) Then the movie began, with Henry Gibson, who I remembered from *Laugh-In*, as a country star seated in a darkened recording studio singing, "We must be doing something right to last 200 years." I could tell that the chucklehead patriotism was supposed to be funny (a handful of people in the audience giggled at it), and it *was* funny, but it was also weirdly emotional in a way that I couldn't account for. The song was a joke, but it had a power. And then, when the scene ended, the people in the movie started talking all at once, as if they were being filmed without knowing it, and that feeling didn't stop, even as individual characters started to emerge. Each of the film's 24 characters seemed to be the star of his or her own movie, yet miraculously, the stories weren't just linked—they dipped in and out of each other, flowing together as one, so that almost any scene appeared to be unfolding in three dimensions at once. The intensity of love you could feel for a character in a movie got multiplied almost exponentially.

Nashville was a drama and a documentary, a soap opera and a musical, a formally radical tale of random wandering nobodies, and a mind-boggling image of America. It was a *vision*. It was the most radically enthralling movie that I had ever seen. (It still is.) Yet I think what so possessed me about it, and what made my response to it extraordinarily personal, is that Altman, in letting 24 characters mingle and wander freely, bumping into each other only to disconnect, caught something that had happened to this country by the middle of the '70s that was already beginning to haunt me: He captured how Americans, after the breakdown of the '50s and then the breakdown of the counter-culture, were now *apart* from one another, even as we continued to gather together. In the scene where Ronee Blakley's willowy, reverent, screw-loose Barbara Jean sings "Dues," I sat in my seat just about trembling, because she seemed to be singing not only about a broken marriage but about the connection that she—and everyone else—had lost. In America, we were now united by entertainment, by the sea of media we swam in, and we socialized and interacted boisterously, yet in some nearly indefinable way we had stopped talking *to* each other. *Nashville* captured and defined that. It channeled the new, splintered reality by incorporating it right into the freewheeling DNA of its messy, liberated narrative sprawl. The movie was made two decades before the rise of the Internet, yet in many ways it throbs with the niche-happy, together-yet-separate, babbling-ourselves-to-death spirit of digital culture. It was, and still is, the movie of our time.

When it ended, I wandered in a daze out of Angell Hall, and I couldn't speak. The movie had gone to my head like peyote. I thought about it all night. I thought about it the next day. I thought about it the next week. I thought about it, for seriously extended portions of each and every day, for the next four or five months. The film lived inside me, and I lived inside it. *Nashville* was so bold and vast an experience that, to me, it added up to an alternate reality that one *could* live inside. But what could I do with that feeling?

Fate had an answer for me. Altman, by the time he made *Nashville*, had become a very hip filmmaker, especially on campuses. A group of U of M students had organized a Robert Altman festival, and it was set to run throughout my second semester, from January through April. The dozen or so features that Altman had made would all be shown (I hadn't seen any of them, except for *Nashville* and *M*A*S*H*), and the festival would also feature a series of speakers, including Elliot Gould, the *Village Voice* critic Andrew Sarris, *Nashville* screenwriter Joan Tewkesbury, and Altman himself. It was the ideal primer for a born-again Altmaniac like me—but more than that, I realized that it was a perfect event for me to cover for *The Michigan Daily*. I volunteered to do so, and that (*Tommy* review aside) was the first writing that I ever did about movies. The pieces themselves, half of which were previews, were just perfunctory college journalism (I interviewed Tewkesbury and reported on Gould's space-cadet humor; I never did get to meet Altman). But they cemented the connection for me between movies and writing. I also attended the party for Andrew Sarris, who I had never read, but I did know a little about him, like the fact that he was supposedly rivals with Pauline. I buttonholed him at the party and spent about 10 minutes peppering him with questions about Kael, which he clearly grew annoyed at but was a good sport about, finally dismissing me with a curt, "She and I don't get along."

Altman's films, as I watched them during the festival, were a revelation, especially the gauzy transcendent Western-mural-come-to-life *McCabe & Mrs. Miller* and *Brewster McCloud*, which I sat through three nights in a row; it was a fairy tale of doomed freedom, starring Bud Cort as a boy who wanted to fly, that hooked the adolescent rebel-prankster in me. I noticed that I disagreed with Pauline about *Brewster McCloud* (she hated it), and about *Thieves Like Us* (she thought it was like a Faulkner novel; I thought it just sat there). But Kael's writing on Altman, especially her reviews of *Nashville* and *McCabe*, did much to show me what an intoxicating form film criticism could be. Her reviews were tethered to the movies, yet they took on a full-scale aesthetic life of their own. What I cherished about Kael's writing is the way that she caught the flash of reality right on the page, like lightning in a bottle. My thought was simple, and it was also huge: *I want to do that too.*

In March, I spent spring break in New York City with my friend Lise, my first trip there as an adult, and I filled the week with a litany of rite-of-passage coming-of-age pleasures. I ate my first Szechuan meal (then très exotic), I had my first mixed drink (a rum-and-Coke), and I saw Charles Mingus play the Village Vanguard and got to watch him, true to legend, chew out a member of his band onstage. We had a very cool celebrity sighting: At an Upper East Side matinee of *Fellini's Casanova*, one of the rare movies that Pauline had admitted in print to walking out of, there were a dozen scattered people in the audience, and one of them, I nudged Lise to notice, was Kurt Vonnegut. He left after 45 minutes.

For me, New York was the city of Woody Allen, and I made a point of seeking him out, going to eat at Elaine's on the off-chance that we might spot him having dinner (the amazing thing was: He was there! having dinner!), and going to see him play ragtime clarinet at Michael's Pub. In that case, we knew he'd be there, because he famously performed at Michael's every Monday night, so the challenge I set for myself was: Could I find a way to meet Woody? During the set break, I steeled myself and wandered up to the stage, and there he was, in his flannel shirt, looking small and lithe and not even mildly intimidating, so I went up to him and said that I was a fan and asked if I could talk to him for a bit. He said, "Sure," sitting down on one of the stools.

He was very serious, cracking a slight smile only once (ironically, it was when I mentioned the Bergman parodies in *Love & Death*), and he could hardly have been nicer to a pushy, nervous 18-year-old college kid. I threw him a few questions about his movies, making a point of letting him know how inspired I found *What's Up Tiger Lily?*, his hilarious dubbed version of a Tokyo-à-go-go Japanese spy movie. "That was a lot of fun to do," he said, sounding sincere yet still deeply serious about such a nutty movie. I asked if he kept up on current films, and he said very much, and when I told him how much I loved *Nashville*, he said, "Yes, I quite admired it too," though he added, "It's not really my kind of picture." Finally, I asked him when his next movie was coming out. "I've got one opening in a month," he said. "It's called *Annie Hall.*" A month later, when I saw *Annie Hall* on opening night in Ann Arbor, it cemented what had already come to feel like my synergistic triangular relationship with New York City, the nerd valor of Woody Allen, and the romance of romance. I couldn't get enough of *Annie Hall*, because of how totally it fed that triad.

Just after the semester ended, I went to Briarwood to see another new movie on opening day, and it never occurred to me to see this one more than once, even though I found it an enveloping experience. It was called *Star Wars*. The early showing I'd gone to was packed, but I had been to packed opening shows before, so that didn't seem like a very big deal. There were times the movie came off like true science fiction, especially when the hypnotically nasty, voice-of-doom character of Darth Vader was on screen. The climactic dogfight was breathlessly exciting, and I saw that there was something seductively new in the awesome precision and light-speed of the effects. The film began slowly yet revved itself, ending up as pure movement. For all the technology, the story, by its finale, roused me to tears. When I came out, I thought: Terrific movie! And that was about all I thought.

Until I saw the line.

It was 3:30 in the afternoon, and the line for the next show of *Star Wars* extended back from the ticket counter and right into the sparkly, fake-marble-floor shopping mall, bending around the corner. I glanced to the side and noticed that the T-shirt store across the corridor was selling *Star Wars* T-shirts. Hmmmm, I thought, that's awfully fast. Curious, I wandered back, following the line for the movie, and I took a right turn and saw that the line...just kept going. At that point, I still had no idea—no one did—what *Stars Wars* would turn out to be. To me, the film was space-age candy corn done with new-fangled zing, which was nifty—but not, to my mind, any sort of revolution. But the size of that line was a bit major, a bit daunting. It pointed to the future, perhaps, more than the movie itself.

One of the reasons that people have always gone to see hit movies is that other people are seeing them. If you went to see *Jaws* or *The Exorcist*, then you were joining the *Jaws* or *Exorcist* club. That day, standing in Briarwood, I caught a glimpse of a new kind of club that people were now going to join when they saw *Star Wars*. It was a new kind of club because it was bigger than big. The name of the club was... *every single person in the galaxy*. The club would come to be measured by the size of the box office, a number that would now cue you to which movies everyone in the galaxy was seeing. And once that happened, did you want to see the movie to see the movie? Or did you want to see it to be in the club? The two experiences would become impossibly gummed up together. *Star Wars* was the ultimate popcorn smash; it was also a little like seeing the rise of Walt Disney's Triumph of the Will. It would be a while, however, before I realized that the galaxy we were talking about was the new American entertainment state, the new planet earth. And it would also be a while before I realized that a movie like *Nashville*, supreme work of art though it was, would now be playing in a galaxy far, far away.

CHAPTER 5

MY OWN PRIVATE ANIMAL HOUSE

There comes a moment in the life of every young man when he transitions from thinking about sex to going out and actually having it. We tend to imagine that moment as something that simply happens to you when you're ready. Yet losing one's cherry, more often than not, is far from an accident. Sex happens because you've sought it out, because you've made a conscious commitment to move from what we might call the masturbatory lifestyle to a more engaged, proactive, do-or-die mode. Ultimately, I would go through that experience. But back when I was still in the early stages of viewing life through a scrim of cinematic images, my first go-for-broke, *the-time-is-now!* action regarding sex wasn't, in fact, about hooking up with anyone. It was when I made the decision to graduate to porn.

I owe it all to Jackie Bissett in a wet T-shirt.

It was the summer of 1977, and I'd landed a cruddy job as a porter at a roadside Holiday Inn on the outskirts of Ann Arbor. Every day, from 3:00 to 11:00 p.m., I donned a blue jumpsuit to take out giant garbage bags and wheel around baskets of hot steamed laundry, after which I could relax and sink into the real nitty-gritty of the job: eating oversize gobs of chocolate-brownie ice cream out of the hotel restaurant's kitchen freezer, and delivering room-service orders, which wasn't that much of a bother since I always got tipped, and because I found the process to be a bit of an adventure due to the voyeuristic peeks into other people's lives that it afforded you. There's something tingly and a tad predatory about working behind the scenes of a dingy anonymous two-story motel. You feel like Holden Caulfield spying on the real America, and there's a sneaky liberation to that.

Maybe that's why, on the job one night, I finally worked up the courage—in the dumbest, most embarrassingly inept way possible—to "ask someone out." Delivering dinner in white Styrofoam compartments to a family that was on the road, I noticed that the daughter, who appeared to be about my age, was adorable, and I thought she smiled at me, so after hearing one of the parents use her name (it was Beth), around 15 minutes later I called the room and asked to speak to her. A sweet voice came on the phone, and I explained that I was the guy who had just delivered room service, and wanted to know if she'd like to "get together." Those are the exact unfortunate words I used, and writing them now makes me want to crawl into a dark pit. "Get *together?*" she said with a slight giggle. "Sorry, we're busy."

"Okay, I didn't mean to bother you," I said. "I just thought I'd ask." And I hung up, bringing to a brisk conclusion the lamest moment of my life so far. But I guess another way to look at it is: It was a start. The truth is that sex didn't seem real to me; it was a fairy-tale kingdom of flesh that I could only dream one day of joining. One night, a businessman I delivered a glass of Scotch to asked me if I knew of "a good place to go," and when I asked, in all innocence, "For what?," he grinned like one of Dean Stockwell's goons in *Blue Velvet* and said, nearly whispering the word, "*Pussy.*" I thought he was disgusting, even though he was really just talking about the very thing I wanted. I gave him the name of a college nightclub I never went to, since I hated the noise and the crowds, and he grinned again and closed the door.

For me, sex seemed to be taking place on the other side of a great divide. So in that recessively longing, look-but-don't-touch spirit, I figured that I would take in a new Hollywood movie that seemed all but designed for vicarious pleasure: *The Deep*, starring Nick Nolte and Jacqueline Bissett. The entire film was being sold as a big-budget wink of an exploitation punchline, because even though it was a scuba-diving drug thriller based on a Peter Benchley novel, and therefore an official second cousin to *Jaws*, its real hook was the heavily advertised underwater sequences in which Bissett swam around in a billowy white T-shirt. The true concept of the film was: *A wet T-shirt can't get any wetter than this!* On one of my nights off, I went to an early evening show, and Bissett, under the sea, did indeed look alluring in a *Playboy* Sex in Cinema sort of way, but within 45 minutes I thought I would drown in tedium. *The Deep* turned out to be one of the worst movies I'd ever seen. And such a disappointment in terms of erotic daydream fodder! I sat there bored, and horny, and lonely, and frustrated, and then—there it was!—a glowing blue lightbulb went off over my head. For the first time, it dawned on me: *I am now 18 years old.* (I had been for three months.) I am a legal adult. I can buy a ticket to a porn film, with no muss and no fuss. It was something that I'd never thought about doing, yet clearly had thought about in some hidden compartment of my brain.

Within moments, I had gotten up and walked out of the movie—the first time I ever did that, an act that took on a glimmer of significance, since it was as if I was making a statement to the film geek in myself: "Attention, film geek! Sex trumps movies!" (It sure does. Especially when a movie is as awful as *The Deep*.) I got into the car and turned on the ignition, knowing just where I was headed: to the only porn theater in the area, which was in Ypsilanti, Ann Arbor's sleazy low-budget sister city, home of Eastern Michigan University and the serial killer John Norman Collins. The advertisements for a theater called the Erotic Art Museum, listing X-rated titles, appeared in *The Ann Arbor News* nearly every day. I remember noticing them early on in high school, when *Deep Throat*—advertised with a generic drawing of a nurse who was more Florence Nightingale than Linda Lovelace—played there for an entire year. I didn't know the streets of Ypsi, but no matter: I would drive around and find the Erotic Art Museum. I was on a mission. Forget my years of teenage *Penthouse* fantasies, forget *The Deep* and *Last Tango* and *Flesh Gordon*, forget everything I had ever seen. I was now, at last, going to experience the fuck-film version of nirvana.

I had been to Ypsilanti just once in my life. It was for one of my family's twice-a-year dinners out to a restaurant, when we'd gone to a place called the Spaghetti Factory, where there must have been some bottomless-pasta-bowl bargain night taking place, since otherwise my father would never have bothered schlepping us out there. Ypsi was six miles away, and a few minutes after I reached the town and began to drive around randomly, I spotted the Erotic Art Museum, a glowing white cake wedge of an early-'60s movie marquee that lit up an otherwise dark and dusky block. I felt a shiver of nervous excitement. This was going to be…a consummation. I parked the car a strategic couple of blocks away, and as I strolled over to the theater, I realized that I was terrified of being seen, of being found out. This felt like the sleaziest thing to do I could have imagined. I desperately wanted to go, and by now it hardly felt like a choice; I was driven, compelled. I felt like Raskolnikov entering the anticipatory, heat-seeking stage of my triumphant crime!

I opened the door of the theater and went inside, and there was a ticket counter, where I paid what felt like the insane sum of $10 (at the time, a movie ticket on triple steroids), and then, for some reason, you had to push through a turnstile, which seemed like something that would be required if you were going to see a movie in prison. Even in the lobby, the place reeked of disinfectant (and you knew why, but you didn't want to think about why). Then I opened the door—the forbidden door!—to the theater, and there, up on the screen, was a woman with strawberry blonde hair in mid-straddle, and I stood in the back, my eyes adjusting to the darkness, and within 10 seconds of watching her swivel-hipped gyrations and listening to her sulky, nearly angry words of pleasure ("Oh, yeah…*fuck* me like that"), I knew, in some deep chamber of my heart, that I was hooked. This is what I had been searching for.

As my eyes adjusted to the darkness, I saw that there were maybe 25 rows of seats, and about 15 people in the audience, all of them men, most of them "older," each one sitting a number of seats away from the others, each locked in his own private lecherous viewing sphere. I took my own strategically distant-from-everyone-else seat. The movie that was already on (I didn't know what it was called) ended in a few minutes, but what I'd seen already had the desired effect, and the previews of coming attractions just skyrocketed the horny factor because of the orgiastic way they piled on the climaxes; the arousal I felt was already nearly too much to bear. I started to wonder if I might come without touching myself—something I had never done, but the salty lust was building up in my system, like steam that felt like it was about to pop a valve.

Another movie started, this one with the promising title of *She's No Angel*. It would mark the first time that I registered the distinctive, come-hither look and personality of a porn star—in this case, the young Sharon Mitchell, whose sneering clown mouth, slightly sad-eyed gaze, and caustic tomboy demeanor made me think that she was some sort of

Jewish American Princess (which she wasn't at all). For 60 minutes, she gave herself to one guy after another, or maybe it was more accurate to say that she *took* them, since I had never conceived of a woman this nakedly aggressive in her desire. I watched it all in a hormonal delirium, barely paying enough attention to the plot to have even a conscious thought of how awkward and fake it was. My simple reaction was: What's happening up on screen is heaven. Or, more accurately, heaven would be getting to be a guy up on that screen.

Later, after I'd driven back to Ann Arbor and returned to the bare-bones room that I'd rented for the summer, the act of relieving myself of all that erotic buildup was a shuddery deliverance that flirted with being an anti-climax. My orgasm, intense as it was, was all too familiar. Yet seeing what sex actually *looked* like had been a revelation, a rapturous new drug. I'd been blind, and now I saw. I was haunted by the mad-dog carnal enthusiasm with which Sharon Mitchell—I didn't know her name yet, I just thought of her as "that incredibly sexy JAP"—engaged in the act of giving head. Sex on screen looked "natural," but it also looked sinful as hell. The whole evening had been a deep dive into sin. But that, it turns out, is what I craved. I had just enough of the counterculture in me that the old boomer trope "If it feels good, do it" now made itself felt with an empowering abandon. There was no doubt: Sex made me feel really good when it looked *this* bad. That's why porn, right off, was something to believe in, even if my attraction to it was drenched in shame.

Every few weeks, I went back. Over the summer, into my sophomore year, and for the rest of my time at the U of M, the Erotic Art Museum became my secret dirty-deeds home away from home, the godless scummy house of worship that I attended to fuel the religion of my desire. My shame, to be clear, did not derive (or not simply) from some neo-Victorian, neo-altar boy cosmic guilt about sex. Sure, I did have some of that. But I also felt, quite literally, alone in my pursuit. Today, porn has become an officially universal, bordering-on-non-taboo activity. Men look at it, women look at it, teenagers look at it, kids whose brains it is probably actively damaging look at it. That's all because the Internet has fashioned porn into a more seductive big business than ever: It's capitalism with a hard cock. But when I would go on my grungy voyages out to the Art Museum, I felt like the only student at the entire University of Michigan—undergrad population: roughly 35,000—who was going to see porn films. And the evidence bore that out. In four years, I never saw anyone there who so much as resembled a college student (though I did once see Mr. Fleischer, one of the teachers from my old elementary school; we nearly bumped into each other at the turnstile, and exchanged a meaningful silent glance). This was the only porn venue in the area, so I think I was justified in feeling: *I'm a warped slave to my libido.* I was odd boy out.

And yet: I was also a movie geek. And the fact that these grainy, badly made fuck films *were* movies—real movies, with scripts and sets and stories and actors playing roles—was far from incidental to their appeal. In the 21st century, where porn exists as a bite-size utilitarian commodity, you're three clicks away from watching anything you want, and when you do, that five-minute-and-37-second clip is what it is, and even when it pushes your boundaries, you're in control of the boundaries, free, at any moment, to order up more of the same. The porn movies of the '70s were different. They had a mischievous dazed ebb and flow, and what's often misunderstood about them is that everything in the films that people now mock—the beyond-terrible acting, the full-bush hairiness, the whole Scotch-tape inadequacy of '70s porn as "drama"— worked in their favor as erotic mythology. Every scene, whether it took place in a rec room or a trucker's bar or a dentist's office, began with the cartoon premise that the two people in it totally wanted to have sex but were constrained by their societal "roles." They had to pretend (for about a minute and a half) to be proper civilized beings. The unspeakable acting, which tended to take the form of exaggerated camp snipery (the Andy Warhol school of amateur overstatement), became, in its very badness, an expression of the thin veneer that society was: people *pretending* to be this or that, when all they really wanted to do was fuck. In the '70s, the cardboard laughability of porn said that sex is the only reality. These delirious fleshpot features showcased a raw fever that made civilization itself seem a sham, a joke, a mere cover-up of desire.

That theme was actually at the center of some of the old movies that were starting to seduce me. For nearly a year, I'd been giving myself a crash course in vintage Hollywood cinema, not all of which I liked. I responded to the back-and-forth flirtatious scuffle of screwball comedy,

I found Westerns to be stodgy and dull (it would be decades before I was savvy enough to appreciate them), and I adored anything by Hitchcock. But like a lot of people born too late to have grown up with Old Hollywood, I found that I related in an intensely personal way to one genre way above all others, and that was film noir. These tales of crime and dread and desire struck me as sexy and ageless in a way that other classic Hollywood films did not; they seemed way, way ahead of their time. One can go on about their dramatic chiaroscuro lighting, their whole drenched-in-darkness mood of elegant pulp passion. Yet what remains strikingly contemporary about film noir—and what both men and women relate to, albeit in different ways—is the luminously tawdry, boldly empowered figure of the femme fatale. At my first showing of *Double Indemnity*, once I got past the shock of seeing Fred MacMurray, the genial dad from *My Three Sons*, as a sleazy sap who called women "baby," I began to fixate on just what it was that made Barbara Stanwyck, as the snarling manipulator in an ankle bracelet, so alluring. It was her mean sultriness, and what that hinted at: the promise of a sexuality that was decidedly not nice. All the film noir vamps and vixens (Lana, Rita, Barbara) had it: the promise of something nasty in the bedroom. That's what made them worth killing and dying for. Here, then, was what had emerged as the quintessential screen goddess of the 20th century: the woman who was defiantly *not* an angel. Yet it was all done with implication. The metaphorical poetry of film noir was that the audience completed the film, using their imaginations to fill in the details of the sublime nastiness that Lana and Rita and Barbara suggested.

In porn, the actresses were like the film noir fallen-angel tramps with their clothes off. Suddenly, nothing was left to implication. Yet the fantasy being delivered to the audience was the same one that drove so many noirs: the vision of a kind of sexuality that found transcendence in the muck. Seeing actual sex on screen was intoxicating, but the true hook of porn, for me, was the feverish fury of the way the women *were*. That's why they were porn stars. The fact that the films were threadbare enough to be documentaries of their own making was the proof that what you were seeing was "real." Then again, what you were seeing was also a depiction of hellbent feminine sexuality in which a woman's desire got fused with the go-for-broke aspect of the male libido. The fantasy, in an odd way, was that the women on screen existed so entirely apart from the procreative aspect of sex that they were as free to fuck as any belt-notching stud. And they were. But that truth also contained the glimmer of a lie—a myth of insatiability. That myth projected how women could now be, but not necessarily how most of them *wanted* to be. The women in porn were eager vessels of flesh, and that became, for a long time, the irresistible destructive muse of my romantic-erotic life.

My porn binges were like crack highs. Each time I traveled to the Art Museum, I felt the same rush that I felt going in the first time, the same giddiness of anticipation at what new libidinous frenzy I was going to be seeing, the same feeling that the curtain, at long last, was going to be drawn back (just as it was at the drive-in), and that I was going to witness...the naked truth. The truth of pleasure. Every few weeks the porn oasis lay waiting for me, and I was fine with being so compartmentalized about it. The anticipation sustained me.

Returning to earth from planet porn, I found my other home away from home in the tattered, high-ceilinged offices of *The Michigan Daily*. They occupied the second floor of the Student Publications Building, which was designed in the Gothic gingerbread style of Yale architecture, though inside there were few frills or pretensions to this hive of undergraduate journalists. Everywhere you looked, there were dozens of randomly discarded miniature green-glass Coke bottles, which came out of an ancient machine that charged five cents a bottle. That was the main perk of working for the *Daily*. The place was also littered, at what seemed like post-tornado levels, with grayish-brown sheets of recycled-pulp copy paper (this was before recycling was chic—at the *Daily* it was just cheap): first drafts of stories, second drafts of stories, abandoned leads, all scattered over typewriters and desks and onto the floor in what looked like the aftermath of a dirty-tan confetti parade. It was a place I found completely comforting in its litter-strewn, Coke-stained, who-cares-about-cleaning-up way. (Actually, the janitors cared. The student journalists would then start fresh the next afternoon, working up to the midnight mess.)

Early in my sophomore year, I got corralled into working for the *Daily* in what turned out to be a fairly standard recruitment ritual. Lois, the arts editor who had first agreed to print my classical music reviews, called me over to her desk and explained that she was leaving the paper, at which point she informed me that the next arts editor was going to be... me. I sputtered in protest, and explained what seemed all too obvious: There was no way I could do the job, I had no experience, I knew nothing about editing, and what's more, I didn't even think I wanted the job. She waved off my protestations. "It's easy," she said. "You'll pick it up in no time."

I didn't want the job, but I didn't *not* want it either. I would never have volunteered, but now that someone was dumping the arts editorship in my lap, I began to think: Well, hmmm, why not? Journalism, by the mid-'70s, had acquired a new degree of cultural cachet on the heels of the mythic scoops of Watergate and the Pentagon Papers, but it still hadn't entirely shaken off its roots as a profession that wasn't quite respectable—a job for curmudgeons and borderline social misfits. I was an arts dude, not an aspiring reporter, but I already related to that pesky-outsider aspect of working at a newspaper, and I felt at home at the *Daily* because of the fellow rumpled cranks I was starting to meet there.

There were several film reviewers at the *Daily*, and one of them became a key figure to me, even though—or maybe because—he was certainly not a perfect ten on the sanity scale. Christopher wasn't a college student; at the time, he was a 32-year-old dishwasher with what I thought was a touch of schizophrenia (yes, it's possible to have just a touch), bald, with twinkly eyes and a red beard that made him look like a slightly demented young Santa Claus, and he was someone who lived, each day, inside the cave of his movie obsession. He was allowed to write for the *Daily* because... well, no one quite knew why. He'd simply found a perch there that everyone honored. At moments, usually when no one else was in sight, he would go into 40-ounce-beer-fueled rages, leaving the corner area around the arts desk trashed, but most of the time he was very personable, and he had audacious intuitions about movies that he expressed, in his reviews, with a slightly unhinged effrontery that taught me: *This is how to do it.* Chris showed me that movie criticism had a pedal-to-the-metal aspect, that it was about letting your most out-there insights take wing. I didn't yet have the skills to do that, but talking to him became, for me, like consulting some scraggly Ann Arbor cinephile Buddha.

On the rare occasions that I tried my hand at writing a movie review, I was strikingly bad at it. I hardly felt confident enough to weigh in on the schlock of the week (*The Island of Dr. Moreau, Twilight's Last Gleaming, Oh, God!*), because I feared I didn't know enough about the actors' or directors' careers. But what really stymied my writing was how much I had to fake having any experience of *life*. I scarcely knew what it meant to hold a job, file a tax return, have a relationship, kiss a girl. I longed— oh, how I longed!—to write with the audacious knowingness of Pauline Kael. But really, how knowing could you be when you didn't know anything? In my kitschy attempts to come off as "authoritative," I wound up channeling the hanging-judge voice of my father, twisting my sentences into knots of gloom to analyze whatever I was writing about. "This particular attempt at realistic drama functions effectively as a chronicle of inner-city prison ills," I wrote in a review of *Short Eyes*. "But its contrived set-ups and intentionally earthy style contribute to a confusion of intent, as well as a message that rings as falsely as the commercial films from which it superficially appears to deviate." I would say that's a review that rates four out of four sticks-up-the-butt.

In a way, I was too much of a *fan* to be a critic yet. Working at the *Daily* gave me a foothold in the tsunami of students that was U of M, but going to movies without a thought to writing about them was still my prime activity. Often, I would smoke a joint beforehand, taking advantage of the fact that in Ann Arbor, with its famous five-dollar pot law, you could toke up while just walking down the street, any street. Digging into the nickel bag I kept in a drawer, I would do that on the way to certain films, usually the ones that *weren't* head films. It was my way to hear their subtext, to discover what they were truly, madly, deeply about. (I developed a fine appreciation for the psychological subtleties of *Pillow Talk* only because I saw it stoned.)

Apart from *Nashville* and *Carrie*, no movie dominated my world with the obsessive delirium of Martin Scorsese's *Mean Streets*. At first, I vastly preferred *Taxi Driver*, because the voluptuous voyeurism with which Scorsese reveled in the scuzz underground of New York City— boy, could I relate to Travis Bickle's lonely-guy porn fixation!—made it seem like the most badass movie ever made. The first time I saw *Mean Streets*, on a double bill with *Taxi Driver*, it seemed drab by comparison.

But on a second viewing. I experienced *Mean Streets* for what it was: not just the first film to show you what guttersnipe mobsters were really like, but the most mesmerizing livewire rock & roll street opera ever made. It was the ultimate movie-as-existential-album-of-your-life, and Robert De Niro's Johnny Boy spoke to the former teen radical in me in a way that transcended all reason. The film presented him as an irredeemable fuckup—a volatile, bomb-tossing flake who systematically messes everything up for the hero, Harvey Keitel's earnest Charlie, a character I had much more in common with. Yet when De Niro was on screen, he made Johnny Boy into such an electric figure precisely *because* there was no defense of his destructive antics. *He simply did not care.* Watching Johnny Boy tapped the same reckless liberation I felt listening to my favorite Sex Pistols song, "No Feelings" ("No feeeel-*ings*...for anybody else!"). At the end of the movie, when he's getting ready to jump in a car that will lead him to a rendezvous with a hitman's bullet, De Niro, the picture of sociopathic nonchalance, does an amazing little hand shuffle to Smokey Robinson and the Miracles' "Mickey's Monkey" that made me feel, more than any moment I had ever seen in a movie: *I want to be that guy.* Even though—no, *because*—he's a totally selfish crazy loser dog.

I was still, at heart, an old-school romantic pushover, and that's why I also got hooked on the slick glories of *Saturday Night Fever*. I had a profoundly personal connection to it. The year before it was released, my youngest brother, Stefan, who had always been a little troubled in a high-strung way, was diagnosed with Tourette syndrome. Now that he was bedeviled by a thicket of tics, which seemed to be fighting for control of his very being (he stuck out his tongue, he raised his middle finger to strangers), he was trapped in a special dungeon of teenage hell. He withstood it courageously, and one of the things that got him through was that he was the original fanboy of my family. He saw pop characters as avatars, living directly through them. The first one that he attached himself to was Fonzie, then came Gene Simmons from Kiss, and then John Travolta's Tony Manero, a swarthy, strutting Fred Astaire–as–street stud who Stefan dropped into at least two conversations a day for the next five years. He was seismically obsessed. Tony, the cocky cutthroat dancing on air, was who he wanted to be.

I went with Stefan, four or five times, to see *Saturday Night Fever*, and each time I could feel the film's percolating dance-floor bliss, and the simultaneous swagger and desperation of Travolta's performance, floating into the diorama of Stefan's aspirational fantasy. He got himself a long leather jacket and pointy shoes and swept back his thick black hair just like Travolta's. In Stefan's mind, he became Tony, and I was father Frank, Tony's sweater-nerd fallen-priest brother standing on the sidelines of the disco, and their ranting father ("*One* pork chop!") was our dad. After a while, I started to experience the movie that way too. In outline, *Saturday Night Fever* had an early-blockbuster-era gaucheness (it seemed to be cashing in on about three trends at once), but that's part of what I loved about it. It was an example of Hollywood alchemy, a film that transformed its faintly tinny high-concept premise into emotional gold, and in doing so it revealed to me how soulful a flagrantly commercial movie could be.

Though I was still shy about doing movie reviews, I decided on a whim to try and write a feature about Michael O'Donoghue, the visionary of shock comedy who had taken the clubbing-baby-seals outrageousness that he'd originally pioneered at *The National Lampoon* and transformed it into the bedrock aesthetic of *Saturday Night Live*. I thought of O'Donoghue as a black-comedy sage, but more than that, he seemed like a showbiz outlaw, and I was fascinated by his mystique. He agreed to be interviewed, and I traveled to New York on my own dime to do it. The hours I spent hanging out with O'Donoghue thrilled me, because I idolized his blasé sense of danger, and beneath his flip hostility he turned out to be a personable guy who liked to go to places like the New York Racquet Club. When I went back to visit him, he complimented my article, saying that it didn't read like something out of a college newspaper (he was being kind), and he got me tickets to see *Saturday Night Live*. Journalism was starting to look like a kick.

I was tuned into the scandalous purity of a figure like O'Donoghue, but *National Lampoon's Animal House* had come out during the summer, and as it gathered force as a hit on campus, to me it was merely funny in a disposable, lightweight way. I wanted it to have more hardcore *Lampoon* in it. What I scarcely recognized is that *Animal House* was a transformative movie: the one that would take frat houses and kick them up into something much, much bigger—would make them over from a slightly shady subculture into the newly universal Spring Break/party-till-you-puke way of life for American college students. In the fall of '78, toga parties invaded the campus, and while I never attended one, I did make it to one frat bash, and it was like visiting a low circle of hell. I was so unable to sustain even 10 seconds of conversation with anyone I met, male or female, that I might as well have been speaking Urdu. I knew I didn't belong there, yet as I looked around at what felt like an orgy with clothes on (I didn't stay long enough for any of them to come off), I realized, in the back of my mind, that I was really a world-class hypocrite, because I yearned to sleep with the same girls that the frat guys did, the ones I obsessed over in porn films, but I didn't have a clue as to how to get them. I was living—trapped—in my own private animal house.

Yet something had shaken loose in me. After suffering through an English class hour devoted to the couplets of Alexander Pope, I walked down the stairs and out the door with a fellow classmate named Sue, not even thinking about what we were talking about, and as I looked over at her, with her short clipped hair, tight body, too-many-potato-chips complexion, and general aura of polite repression, I realized that she was a nice Catholic girl, and that I, for all the bad-boy movies I devoured, was a nice Jewish boy, and a little voice went off in my head that said: "This is someone you should ask out. What are you waiting for? *Just do it, idiot!*" And just like that I did, crossing the line ("Would you like to go out sometime?"), and just like that she said yes ("Sure, how about this weekend?"), and I thought, "Wow, good answer. That wasn't so difficult..."

I didn't take her to a movie, because that seemed like it would be too unimaginative. Instead, I decided to go for "class": I would take her to a play. A university production of Tom Stoppard's *Travesties*, which sounded like it would be amusing, since it was about three catchy historical figures (James Joyce, Vladimir Lenin, and Tristan Tzara) mixing it up, but the play turned out to be all numbing verbiage (as, to this day, I think all of Tom Stoppard is), and it was interminable, and I felt vaguely embarrassed at having asked her ("*I hope she doesn't think I* like *this shit*"). But afterwards, we went to the Cottage Inn, a U of M pizza-and-beer hangout, and at her suggestion we drank Irish coffees, about three of them apiece, which was enough to get me swoony and agitated at the same time, which I probably would have been anyway, especially once she led me back to her apartment.

I knew something was about to happen, and I was terrified. As in: I had to pretend to use her bathroom to literally try and calm my nerves, my brain, my heart, my vaguely shaking limbs. I returned to the living room and sat down next to Sue on the couch, and we talked for a few awkward minutes, and I knew this was the moment of truth, and what I did next was not, in the scheme of things, in any way remarkable, gently curling my hand behind the nape of her neck, drawing her mouth to mine—I was doing what everyone else I knew had done long before me. But as our lips touched, and our tongues slipped into each other's mouths, I thought that this was the most delicious feeling in the world, and the fact that I had waited so long, until I was nearly 20, to actually do this was a kind of madness, and I had no idea why it had taken so long, but the delay did have a good side, because oh, the endless desert I had endured... and coming out of it now was like guzzling cold clear water after a 20-year thirst. Sue and I never did sleep together; in fact, we never had another date. (She kept turning me down.) But something had clicked, because we kissed for more than two hours, and when we were done, I walked out into the 4:00 a.m. air and felt like I had taken my first steps into the land of the living.

CHAPTER 6

"I HOPE TO GOD IT'S NOT KRAMER VS. KRAMER!"

The sun-roasted, bone-dry weather of Wichita, Kansas, at the height of the summer—no breeze, the thermometer pushing 100—seemed to complete something about the locale itself, much as the hanging-in-the-air heat of the Deep South does. On the main commercial drag, with its limestone glint, everything appeared to be standing still; the city was as listless and barren as a moon colony. What was a Midwestern brainiac film geek doing in Wichita? It was 1979, and I'd arrived for what was once a hallowed ritual of aspiring journalists: the college newspaper internship. I'd applied for it in much the same way that I did so many things—because it's what I was "supposed" to do—and after getting turned down by other, better papers (no surprise, since I didn't have any real reporting clips), I found myself at *The Wichita Eagle-Beacon*, a cookie-cutter daily in the Knight-Ridder chain. There, I wrote dumb stories about topics that no one, including me, could have cared less about, like people who take 50-mile commutes to work, exotic gardens, and the office politics of a local Native-American art museum.

At the *Eagle-Beacon*, I struck up a camaraderie with the paper's film critic, a man named Bob in tight permed curls who smoked punctiliously thin brown cigarettes and seemed as out of place at the paper as Richard Simmons at a Knights of Columbus meeting. I liked talking movies with Bob, and he seemed to relish my company—at least, until he went on vacation for two weeks and I filled in for him. During that time, *The Muppet Movie* opened, and though I had nothing against the

Muppets, having grown up with their rascally felt-faced cuddliness, I found the movie to be overly cute and endless (something I've thought about every Muppet movie since), and that's what I wrote in my one-star *Eagle-Beacon* review. When Bob returned from vacation, he was so outraged that someone actually had the arrogance to *pan* the Muppets that he wrote and published a second review of the movie, this one a four-star rave, just to set the record straight.

That summer, in between getting the primal heebie-jeebies from *Alien* and taking in all the multiplex movies of the week, from the is-it-cool-or-just-inept flying-killer-silver-ball horror cheapie *Phantasm* to *Escape from Alcatraz*, I went to see Woody Allen's *Manhattan* once a week, every week, on Friday afternoon, for the entire three months that I was in Wichita (movies stayed in theaters a lot longer then), paying a kind of ritual weekly visit to Woody and Mariel Hemingway and Michael Murphy and Diane Keaton and George Gershwin. What surprised me, even at the time, about my complete emotional fusion with the movie was how much deeper it was than the connection I'd had to *Annie Hall*. Two years before, *Annie Hall* had seemed like everything— the comedy that proved that Woody Allen, the post-macho, less-than-handsome, smart-mouth-dweeb role model to dweebs like myself, could get the girl, and that therefore you could too. *That* was a catharsis. Yet the more I watched *Annie Hall*, the more I noticed that there was an odd quirk at its center: The reason that Alvy Singer, in that one scene, could scarcely bring himself to utter the word "love" ("I lurve you!") is that it never truly, totally felt like he *did* love Annie Hall. He *liked* her a lot; maybe he even adored her. And yes, he was a "neurotic" narcissist. But then, lots of people live up to that description and are still able to fall in love. Woody Allen, by contrast, came off as a solo vessel looking for an audience. There was something about his tweedy, whiny, contempo-vaudeville persona that was like a forcefield against romantic tenderness.

In *Manhattan*, he dithered around with Diane Keaton once more, and got dumped again, and seemed even more upset by it, yet the upshot of the movie was that Woody's Isaac Davis truly did belong with Mariel Hemingway's 17-year-old Tracy. It was the sweetly enticing, strawberry-ice-cream vulnerability of a child-woman that melted *him*—a scandalous pairing, to be sure, but a far more convincing one, and one that Woody, as an artist, was startlingly up-front about. (Who would have guessed that he was portraying his future? And who, including Woody, could get away with such a frank self-portrayal today?) In the end, the *real* romance of *Manhattan* was the triangle that embraced Woody and the audience and Manhattan itself. I kept going back to the movie to imagine myself as every one of the characters in those to-die-for settings—getting tipsy-philosophical at the end of a late meal at Elaine's, or standing around at a gala at the Museum of Modern Art (a scene that always gave me a tingle of knowingness because of my friendly connection with Michael O'Donoghue, who had an amusingly stilted cameo in it), or moving from Isaac's glorious duplex to that smaller flat with the brown water and the sound of a man sawing a trumpet in half coming through the wall. It was in those settings where the entanglements of love met the glory of talk met the never-ending flux of New York City. With its luminous black-and-white vistas, its wised-up view of life as a cabaret of conversation, *Manhattan* became a kind of shelter for me, not just a movie but a place to go. For 90 minutes each week, I escaped the sauna of Wichita and lived on Woody's bittersweet verbal-cosmopolitan island, wishing that I could take up residence there.

At *Eagle-Beacon* parties, I learned, for the first time, how much I liked to drink. There's a photograph of me in an *Eagle-Beacon* newsletter lying passed out on a picnic table (the sorry result of grain-alcohol punch), but my supreme moment of clarity regarding drinking occurred one evening in the bathroom during a Saturday-night work kegger, when I was buzzed to the gills, letting a bunch of beer pass through my system, and my one and only thought was simple, direct, and beautiful: What in the world could be the downside of *this*?

During the last two weeks, I also succeeded in losing my virginity to a fiery, curly-haired photo intern named Liz whom I'd become platonic friends with over the summer. In theory, the experience was something out of a bad indie romcom, like *The Way, Way Back* set in flyover country: Nerd obsessed with going to the movies is too shy to make a move, but finally does, stumbling into a late-summer liaison. But here's how it played out: The kissing by the fountain was great, the finger-fucking in the dark outside was sublime...but then, back in my dingy fluorescent room at the Wheat Shocker apartments, with the lights halfway on, I had this tender naked girl in front of me, and I was caught up short, right there in bed, by the realization that all the porn films I'd been consuming over the last two years had done a number on my psyche. They had mind-fucked me. I'm not sure what I expected from sex, but it was probably along the lines of more voluptuous dirty talk and orgiastic positioning, less breathy affectionate kisses and trembly writhing. And less *sensation*. The skin-on-skin sensuality of it all felt like an intrusion, and what I realized after the fact, with a rush of anxiety that made me suspect I'd been forever spoiled, was that sex had been constructed in my head, by porn, as a *visual* experience. The way that a mouth actually felt on my penis seemed to have nothing to do with what a blowjob, to me, really was: a heady turn-on for the eyes. I would spend more than a few years trying to take those two versions of sex—the visual and the sensual—and merge them, to transform my erotic life into the movie of my dreams.

The other thing I did that summer was to write a letter to Pauline Kael, just as she was going on hiatus from *The New Yorker* to try her hand as a consulting Hollywood producer/kibitzer/guru. No one, including Kael, knew when she was coming back (or even if she would), so I figured that this might be my last real chance to send her a fan letter. I told her how much I would miss her writing, and to let her know that I wasn't *just* a fan but a kindred spirit, I informed her that I wrote movie reviews, too—for my college paper.

If I say that I sent that letter with no careerist intentions, that it never once occurred to me that Kael would ever reply, it may sound like the lamest of hindsight rationalizations. We live, after all, in an era when preschool is the new prep school, when kids start seriously networking by the age of 8. But, in fact, I wrote that letter because I idolized Kael and wanted to let her know that I did. When she sent a note back, and it arrived, in a small cream envelope decorated with *The New Yorker*'s Irvin font, with a black fountain-pen scribble on the back, I knew, instantly, what it was, yet I couldn't believe it. Kael was a rock star, and you don't expect a rock star to answer your fan gush.

"*Dear Owen Gleiberman*," the note began in Pauline's breathless penmanship (I was struck by how she used my entire name, as if not to project any folksy false intimacy).

Thanks for your generous words. If you have written anything you'd like me to read, send it on.

> Best,
> Pauline Kael

At that point, a careerist volt shot through my body. The tone of the note was neutral, and it was just two brief sentences, but Pauline Kael was asking to see my work; she was asking me aboard. I had no idea that she had a network of devoted followers whom she praised and cultivated— the feeling in my gut was that she was interested in *me*—but I wasted no time in gathering a few college clips together, including a review I'd done of Robert Altman's *A Wedding*, a rambling unpublished essay on *Carrie*, an article on rock & roll in the movies, and several others, and sending them along to her. Since it was getting to be late in the summer, I included the return address of the seven-bedroom house in Ann Arbor that I'd been sharing with friends and would soon be returning to.

Sure enough, a few weeks after I got back to Ann Arbor, another bite-size *New Yorker* envelope arrived. This time the note began *"Dear O.G."* and said:

> *Yes I got your pieces and I particularly liked the Altman piece and parts of the Rock & Roll on Reels. Why don't you keep sending me the reviews you're proudest of? I'll try to say something helpful—if I can.*

> Best,
> Pauline Kael

I was pleased that she praised me (in what even I could read was a fairly generic way), but the thrill didn't come close to matching the arrival of that first note. In an odd way, I already felt like I knew her. So I sent off a fresh batch of pieces, including reviews of *Manhattan* and *Richard Pryor Live in Concert* that I'd written, from Wichita, for the *Daily*. And I waited. And waited. And waited. And no more *New Yorker* notes arrived. A disappointment, to be sure, but Pauline was still a rock star, and I didn't really expect anything more from her.

I knew that I lived for movies, that I was consumed by sex (even though I'd only just started to have it), but apart from those two burning addictions, I was a voyeur without a role, and I still nurtured an ambivalence about the popular aspect of pop culture. One day, I stood on Maynard Street, across from Ann Arbor's one and only hip clothing store, which was called Renaissance, and I got into a tangled war of identity with myself over a pair of sunglasses. As the decade of scruffiness declined, a new era of fashion was starting to come into focus, and I got bitten by the chic novelty of it in the form of a gogglish pair of tinted spectacles. The person who inspired me to want to wear them was Chris Stein, the leader of Blondie who was also Debbie Harry's boyfriend. (In 1979, if you were a guy in college, that was like being married to Marilyn Monroe.) Blondie had made my favorite album of the new wave—*Parallel Lines*, a divine piece of jingle-jangle punk that rarely left my turntable—and at the age of 20, I was periodically told that I resembled Stein: We had the same thick square eyebrows, the same trying-a-little-too-hard short-Jewish-guy insolence. Stein wore those sunglasses, and I wanted to wear them, too. And now, I had seen them in the display case of Renaissance. I would buy them! I would be affectlessly handsome in them just like Chris Stein! I would be cool!

I went into the store, tried on the glasses, gazed into the big round mirror sitting at eye level…and saw, gazing back at me, the image of a college student wearing Chris Stein's sunglasses and, as a result, looking like an utterly obvious and embarrassing poseur-fool, a walking zombie of the consumer culture. I could not handle that image. So I took off the glasses and left. But I couldn't walk far, because as soon as I got out the door, I stopped in my tracks and thought: "Damn! I really wanted to buy those fucking glasses!" I decided that I was actually scared of attempting to look cool, that it was a kind of fear of success that I needed to conquer. So I went back into the store, put on the glasses, gazed into the mirror, and began the whole cycle again. It went on—back and forth, in and out of the store—for close to an hour, as if I was the Hamlet of aspiring Eurotrash. In the end, I couldn't buy the glasses. Something inside me wouldn't let me.

A few weeks later, I was standing in the kitchen, popping our group house's nightly communal feast of Tater Tots into the oven, when the phone rang. One of my housemates burst in and said, "Owen, Pauline

Kael is calling for you!" I said "What?" as I stumbled into the next room and picked up the receiver and said hello. I'm not exaggerating when I say that it was like hearing the voice of God at the other end. "Hi, it's Pauline Kael! I figured I'd give you a call because I thought I'd never write you." (I took her meaning; I was lazy too.) Her voice was thick with insinuation, and girlishly saucy in its singsong clarity. She asked me if I had any plans, and I said (because what else could I say?), "I want to be a film critic." Actually, I usually told people that I was "pre-law," because it sounded like something respectable to say, and I figured that law school was probably something that I could do. When I told Pauline that I wanted to do what she did, I guess I expected a rousing endorsement of the idea. Instead she said, "But movies are so shitty now!" It was my first taste of the Kael vocabulary, and it was a shock. "Well," I said, struggling to find a way to answer that, "I still think there's a lot of good ones." She talked about how hard it was to be a critic—to earn a living, that is—and since I'd never thought much, or in fact at all, about any of that stuff, I rolled with her warnings, barely taking them in. (Why was *Pauline Kael* complaining about *that*?) I just thought—I knew!—that I wanted to meet her. And so I asked if I could, telling her that I was planning a trip to New York over the Christmas vacation. She said that she would be in the city, starting near the end of the month, and that we should have dinner. I don't recall how the conversation ended. I was too excited, and nervous, at the prospect of meeting God.

••••••

It was New Year's Day, 1980, around 6:00 p.m. when I entered the Royalton Hotel, where Pauline stayed whenever she was in New York. The hotel was right across the street from the Algonquin, with its mythological cocktail bar, and one block up from *The New Yorker*. So the Royalton, if only by association (and the fact that Kael was staying there), seemed venerable in a literary way. I was anxious as I knocked on the door, because I'd never met a true idol before, let alone someone who struck me as the most brilliant and admirable woman in the universe. Pauline opened the door and gave me a big, grinning hello with a hint of a laugh to it, and the first thing I couldn't help but notice was how astoundingly short she was (about five feet tall). It was a true surprise, because her height made absolutely no sense: How could this pleasant, squat lady looking up at me contain the *largeness* of Pauline Kael?

Pauline was far from beautiful, but her face, with its wise eyes and warm smile that could, at moments, stretch into a slackly knowing leer, had so much personality that there was a kind of beauty to how fully it expressed *her* at every moment. She looked a lot like Rachel Dratch (who, in fact, once played a Paulinesque critic on *Saturday Night Live*). As I entered her suite, I noticed a fresh copy of *The National Enquirer* and several other tabloids on the nightstand, and Pauline rolled her eyes and said, "Oh, a silly friend of mine gave these to me!" It was a curious comment, because I sensed that Pauline had, in fact, bought them herself, and that she wasn't so much embarrassed about it as she was play-acting at being embarrassed. (It made total sense to me that she'd read the tabloids; I looked at them all the time.) The TV was on, and she took a moment to mock a commercial for Tegrin medicated shampoo; it was the name of the product that got her ("Tegrin!" she giggled, as if relishing the market-tested foolishness of it). She asked me how long I'd be in town, and since she was still on hiatus, I asked her what she was doing in New York. The hotel-room setting didn't necessarily make me uncomfortable, but I have to admit that the question at least wafted through my mind, for a split second, of whether I had wandered into some surreal film-critic equivalent of a Mrs. Robinson situation—or, given that Pauline was 60 years old, a *Harold and Maude* situation. The thought faded away as soon as Pauline said that she'd come to town for the annual meeting of the National Society of Film Critics, who would be voting the next day. Attempting to chitchat, I asked what movie she thought would win, and she locked eyes with me, her head bowed slightly down with purpose, and said, "Well I hope to God it's not *Kramer vs. Kramer!*"

I had seen *Kramer vs. Kramer* on opening day, just a couple of weeks before, and I had loved it. Which produced a slight discomfiting feeling. How should I reply? My reptile brain quickly told me that the words "Really? I thought it was fantastic!" were not the precise thing I wanted to be saying at that moment. Yet I didn't want to lie, either. So I tap-danced, saying rather sheepishly, "I thought it was pretty good. What did you not like about it?" I figured, correctly, that it was the kind of middle-class weeper that Pauline had no soft spot for, but she added something quite interesting, complaining that the film was selling the idea that "fathering ennobles." I'd never heard the word "ennobles" before (very Pauline), but turning that phrase over in my head (*fathering ennobles...*), I thought to myself: Well, *doesn't* it?

At the time, I had no idea that Pauline's own relationship to parenthood was marked by a rather disquieting possessiveness. As a single mother, she had never completely let go of her daughter, Gina (then 31), and used her as a kind of personal assistant. There was a tangled aspect to their relationship: Gina was there to *serve* Pauline—to serve the higher cause of writing and fearless truth-telling to which Pauline had dedicated herself. The noble side of motherhood this most definitely was not. So it's no wonder that Pauline was hostile to a movie like *Kramer vs. Kramer*—a drama of divorce, starring Dustin Hoffman as a newly abandoned and unequipped single parent, that movingly caught the cultural moment when fathers, for the first time, were now going to be expected to be warm-and-fuzzy nurturers, just like women. Milan Kundera, in his novel *Identity*, used one of his characters to complain that the new fathers weren't really fathers at all—they were soft paternal Teddy bears, mere *daddies*. To the extent that this was becoming true, my God, Pauline must have hated it! Yet with a brusque jerk of a father like mine, the notion of being a good daddy couldn't help but look, to me, rather noble. Still, I decided to leave that discussion off the table.

It was time to have dinner, so we went out and walked a few blocks, and Pauline took us to what seemed to me to be the swankiest Chinese restaurant in Manhattan. It was a Szechuan place, and I let Pauline do the ordering, even though she said, "I usually skip the appetizers, I think they're a drag!" That was a disappointment to me, because appetizers like egg rolls and dumplings tended to be my favorite part of a Chinese meal. But Pauline got you right on her wavelength, and after a few moments I started to think, "Hmmm, maybe the appetizers *are* a drag." Pauline's conversation was a lot more relaxed than her writing, yet in a way it had the same excitement, the same what-will-she-say-next drop-dead analytical verve.

Over dinner, Pauline talked about movies she'd seen recently, like *Star Trek: The Motion Picture* ("*So* bad, but not as bad as *The Black Hole*"), and she was eager to know which critics and writers I liked. She shared her own tastes (she thought the film critic David Ansen of *Newsweek* "does a very good job," and, like me, she was mostly a fan of the kamikaze-genius rock critic Lester Bangs; she had major problems with the feminist dogma of *The Village Voice*'s Ellen Willis, who of course had once been the rock critic of *The New Yorker*). Mostly, though, Pauline liked to gossip, and her inside-the-bubble view of famous names awed me with its salacious knowledge and judgmental kick. Just the night before, she had been to a New Year's Eve party that was also attended by Mick Jagger, Woody Allen, and Norman Mailer (I tried to wrap my head around what that party looked like), and Mailer had asked to butt heads with her. When the subject of Woody Allen came up, she put her fork down and said, "Everyone thinks Warren Beatty goes off and fucks all these beautiful women. Well, he does. But so does Woody!" Her favorite word, at least on this particular night, was "whore." Her former acolyte, the writer-director Paul Schrader, "goes around with expensive whores." I honestly didn't know if that was metaphorical or not (was she saying that he liked prostitutes? Or trashy Hollywood gold-diggers?), and when she said of John Simon, the infamously vitriolic film and theater critic, "He's such a *shameless* whore," it truly confused the issue. Whore, for Pauline, seemed to be a powerful catch-all phrase that covered a wide litany of sins.

One filmmaker who I could tell had become a whore for her was Bob Fosse. *All That Jazz* had just come out (I'd seen it in New York and thought it was overblown), and Pauline was fixated on the outrage of what she took to be a direct (if coded) message in the movie to her from Fosse: When Roy Scheider's Joe Gideon releases the film he's made about an edgy stand-up comic, it's trashed by a female film critic on TV, and that review spirals him into a heart attack. "That was supposed to be a version of me," Pauline said, "because I panned *Lenny*. But dear God, to be accused of causing his heart attack..." She flashed a rueful smile. Insane as it may seem, what hit me most about Pauline's comment is that she used what sounded to my ears like trade-paper jargon—"panned"— to describe her review of *Lenny*, which I thought was one of her greatest pieces. Yes, she'd had mixed feelings about the movie, but what she'd written was so much more than a *pan*. I sensed that she was truly bothered by Fosse's accusatory reference to her (if that's, in fact, what it was), and I also sensed just how much she wanted me on her side.

She also spoke of Francis Ford Coppola, and how she'd gone to visit him with the prospect of making him the subject of a *New Yorker* profile. But that fell apart, she said, because he turned out to be "crazy." She shook her head disparagingly, as if she didn't want to go into it, but with the suggestion that "crazy" was the tip of the iceberg. She had harsh words to say about Coppola's extramarital flings. I was intrigued, because I'd had my own mini glimpse of the Coppola "craziness." At the tail end of my Wichita internship, I finagled an invitation to the New York press junket for *Apocalypse Now*. It was the early days of movie junkets, but this was no ordinary Hollywood/media circle jerk—it was the most anticipated American movie premiere in years.

At the screening of *Apocalypse* at the lush Ziegfeld Theater on W. 54th St., I thought the movie was so monumental that just about the only way I can capture the experience is to resort to a Wayne-and-Garthism like *It was awesome.* The movie left me stunned, an experience I attempted to replicate over the autumn months by going back to see it four or five times, getting as high as possible before each viewing. The more I went, the more I saw the beauty of even the controversial ending, and the more I came to believe—as I still do—that Brando, so mocked for his self-indulgence at the time, gives a memorable performance in it. He makes Kurtz a wormy sly philosopher of death. Unlike Pauline, I thought *Apocalypse Now* was a masterpiece, but at the press conference the morning after the junket screening, Dennis Hopper seemed like even more of a drug casualty than the stutter-brained photographer he plays in the film, and Coppola, scratching his beard as if flies from the Philippine jungles were infested there, was on a manic, babbling high. He made one statement that haunted me: that the '60s revolution was over, but we were now on the verge of something bigger—what he called "the communications revolution." And, of course, he was right; he was miles ahead of the curve, talking about the new age of technology that was then only gestating. I hung on every word, even if he did seem like a possessed semi-lunatic. And I could see how the visionary filmmaker monomaniac and the skeptical critical deity might not have hit it off. But naively, all I could think was: How I wish they had.

Dinner ended with lychee nuts (which were…strange), and as we began our way back to the Royalton, Pauline, feeling stuffed, undid the top button of her pants to make the walk more comfortable. At the hotel, she made a beeline for the payphone and said, "I'm going to call Jim Wolcott. He's usually at CBGB's, but maybe he'll come meet us." James Wolcott, the 27-year-old television critic of *The Village Voice*, was someone I and my college arts-writer friends all worshipped. Outside of Pauline, there was nothing as electric as his column. I had no idea that the two were friends, but it made sense, and after a brief spell, Wolcott, with lowered eyebrows and long hair, came by Pauline's room, toting a fresh copy of the *Voice*. I was struck by how Pauline took the paper and immediately flopped her body, face down, onto the bed, to dig into his column. I thought: She really lives for writing. The three of us then headed across the street to the plush couches of the Algonquin, which should have been a college film critic's high-toned dream date. But Pauline, ordering Rémy Martin cognacs, and Wolcott, a straight-edge sugar junkie slugging down Cokes, took off into literary and journalistic gossip that left me way behind. After a while, I didn't know who or what they were talking about, and I clammed up, drifting out of the conversation. I figured my part of the evening was over, and it was. As the three of us walked out, Pauline said goodbye, and asked me to stay in touch, and I strolled to the corner of 44th and Broadway with Wolcott, who did his best to be friendly to this 20-year-old nobody. And that was that.

Meeting Pauline had been a trip, but not, perhaps, in the way that I expected. She was dazzling, scathing, challenging, and hypnotic. She was a ton of fun, and to use one of her favorite "polite" words, she was more than *generous* in devoting most of an evening to me. But before I met Pauline, the image I had in my head of her was that of a penetrating yet saintly guru of the mind; up until that moment, she was still a glorified version of my mother. And the Pauline I'd met was haughty and worldly and imperious in a more than intimidating way. Her casual opinionizing was entertaining as hell, yet it carried an implicit threat: How would she judge *you*? Pauline was still my enchanted critical deity, but after just one evening, she was no longer, perhaps, nearly so Godlike. I saw and felt her humanity, and to my surprise, that made her scarier.

CHAPTER 7

YES, I CAN WATCH MOVIES FOR A LIVING

I'm looking to hire a film critic." Really, are you kidding? Well, okay. Done.

That's not what I said, but it's what I thought—and who wouldn't have? The voice at the other end of the phone sounded exceedingly relaxed and cheery and lightly corporate. It belonged to someone I didn't know: Stephen Schiff, who introduced himself as the film editor and lead film critic of *The Boston Phoenix*, a paper I had never heard of. My first thought was: He sounds way too unruffled to be a film critic. "My second-string critic, David Chute, just got a job in Los Angeles," he explained, "and I need someone to take over for him. I got your name from Pauline Kael. I'd be interested to have a look at your clips." That made sense of it all: If Kael was the voice of God phoning me out of the blue, then this was God's messenger, offering me the prospect of a job that, in a sense, I was already doing, and that I was more than happy to keep doing. At the moment, I didn't realize I was the luckiest dude on earth, though the timing was almost karmic.

I got Stephen's call in late October 1980, when I was in the middle of finishing one extra fall semester to complete my BA. To compensate for having been the university's most delinquent Honors English major (Thackeray! Eliot! Hardy! Sterne! All the novels I hadn't read!), I had decided to apply myself with dire seriousness to the task of writing my senior thesis, which was a stoned analysis—I didn't call it that, but that's what it was—of Norman Mailer's 1965 novel *An American Dream*. The truth is that I felt virtually no kinship with the literature of the 17th, 18th, or 19th centuries, but I had become a Mailer fanatic. And though I knew in every bone that his nonfiction (*The Armies of the Night, The*

Presidential Papers) was infinitely superior to his fiction—the nonfiction was the essence of Mailer, the *real* Mailer—*An American Dream* was the one transcendent act of Mailer's early moonstruck literary imagination.

I consumed the entire book in one into-the-night sitting in a closed-door Undergraduate Library cubicle, stepping outside the building just twice to toke up, and I thought that it was the greatest "movie" I had ever read. It was like a homicidal noir penned by a poetic psycho-analytic sociopath, and somehow it seemed to elude every critic who ever wrote about it that the entire book was a confessional manifesto: Mailer's way of explaining to the world how and why, in 1962, he had descended into the abyss by drunkenly stabbing his wife with a penknife. I wrote about it all—the novel, the stabbing, Mailer's destructive bad-boy compulsiveness—and I also read everything Mailer had written, smoking dope each day, not doing a hell of a lot else, generally enjoying my semester-long existence as a slacker stoner monk. Here's how much thought I put into figuring out what would come next: zero. It was the end-of-college extension of my basic drifting nature.

I collected my small handful of presentable *Daily* clips, which included reviews of *Being There*, *Coal Miner's Daughter*, and Herzog's *Nosferatu* and also an unfashionable swipe at Lester Bangs (I tore apart his book about Blondie), and I sent them off to Stephen. A few days later, he called back and said that he liked them, explaining to me: "You're a college writer, and you write like a college writer. You need to learn how to be a professional. But that will happen. And I can teach you." Then he added, "When could you start?" My soul took a leap, and I said: "How about February?" I arrived in Boston on Feb. 22, 1981, two days before my 22nd birthday. The weeks in between rolled by in a blur, except for the earthquake that was John Lennon's assassination; it was like hearing that a planet had been knocked out of the solar system. There was a going-away party for me, which I have no memory of, but I do remember saying goodbye to my father. I told him that I loved him, because I thought it's what I should say (and also because I realized, as I was saying it, that I meant it), and he said, "I love you, too," and I couldn't tell if he meant it or if he was just saying it because... how else, really, could he reply? It was the only time the two of us ever spoke those words to each other.

I took an overnight train to Boston, and the next morning, when I wandered into the terminal of South Station, groggy and a little nervous, I looked around for a newsstand, and when I spotted one the first thing I noticed was a pile of *Boston Phoenix*es, which looked not at all like newspapers but like a stack of two-inch-thick white bricks. I picked up a copy, and it seemed like serendipity that the cover of that week's Arts section was devoted to an interview with Mailer. I'd already read several issues of the *Phoenix* that Stephen had sent me, and I read *The Village Voice* devotedly each week, but the *Voice*, the granddaddy of alternative weeklies, was still wearing its avant leftist boho roots on its smudgy sleeve. The *Phoenix* looked and felt different: clean, elegant, upstanding, a bit flush. It wasn't a more successful paper than the *Voice* (the economies of both were built, to a degree, on a cornerstone of sex ads, which no mainstream paper would run), but the *Phoenix* had already crossed the line into seeing itself as an arts-fixated consumerist bible rather than a consciousness-raising "underground" paper. The politics linked up with that: A number of the *Voice* writers—like the Marxist muckraker Alexander Cockburn—were still trying to "change the world" (and would despise anyone who put quote marks around that phrase), but the writers at the *Phoenix* were, by and large, enlightened liberal level-heads, and that suited me fine, since that's more or less what I was. Some might have called that view complacent, but the way I would put it is: We had already absorbed the lesson that The Revolution was over, that the counterculture had been incorporated (in every sense), and that things weren't, in any essential way, going to change. America still needed to evolve, and would, but the template of the 1950s now seemed to be its unshakable bedrock.

Stephen, my new editor (my first boss, really), struck me as the perfect embodiment of this post-radical world. He was an avid conversationalist and a writer of nimble brilliance in love with audacious ideas, and he had packed in more than his share of sex-drugs-and-rock-&-roll, yet the way I saw him, he was basically a tastefully fashioned suburban married guy (I would have said *yuppie* if this was two years later), and that spoke to me: In the new world, audacity wasn't about middle-class-baiting lifestyle choices—it was about the power of what you thought and wrote.

The evening of my first day in Boston, I ventured out and was waiting for a subway in Harvard Square when a fur-coated young woman, with a mouth like wax lips, smiled right at me, which I wasn't used to. I said hello, and she said her name was Dora, and I realized that she was tipsy in a slightly kooky carefree way. I took her back to the room where I was staying, and the two of us fell into bed. Picking up strangers has never been my forte, yet she had the silkiest skin imaginable, and I was able, for the first time, to have sex while feeling comfortable in *my* skin. I considered her an apparition, a sign from above that Boston was the right place for me.

I rented a room in a sprawling tunnel of a Back Bay apartment with four roommates, one of whom was an aspiring stand-up comedian named Lauren. Comedy was already big in Boston (the city was instrumental in launching the stand-up boom), and Lauren's boyfriend was a comedian as well, a quiet straight-shooter I knew simply as Denis, who a few years later would turn out to be Denis Leary. (A decade after that, once I'd built up a track record of panning his movie performances, he threatened to beat me up.) I got along with everyone, but I'd already had more than my share of roommates, and I was instantly weary of the whole setup. I spent the heart of my time burrowed in my cramped bedroom, drinking gin-and-tonics and sinking into the Beach Boys and the Doors—the light and dark sides of California dreamin'.

My apartment was a few blocks from the *Phoenix* along the grimy bustle of Mass Ave., and the first time I went up the elevator to the paper's pleasantly ramshackle second-floor editorial office, which consisted of exactly one room of about 40 x 40 feet, with a modest row of cubicles for the editors, I'd never felt more in my life like a kid impersonating a grownup. It was far from a fleeting sensation—for in more ways than not, that's what I was. Watching movies, the thing I was now going to be paid to do, was still, to me, a womblike activity: curling up, by yourself, in the dark and floating into someone else's dream.

The *Phoenix* had already become a kind of hallowed grad-school academy for film critics. Stephen Schiff had been hired by David Denby, whose heady and eloquent reviews I was only just starting to consume in *New York* magazine. At times, I found Denby as exciting to read as Pauline, and the fact that he often disagreed with her was an ongoing source of fascination. Denby had first worked at the *Phoenix* after Janet Maslin, who had gone on to become the second-string critic for *The New*

York Times, and between Maslin, Denby, and Schiff, that was an extraordinary pedigree. I realized that I was now an apprentice to that legacy. There were other legacies in Boston, like the legendary Orson Welles Theater, a three-screen venue devoted entirely to art films. Every time I passed it on a bus, it gave me a reassuring rush, as if I were a young priest and the theater a stately church. If there was a movie-buff equivalent of rosary beads, I would have caressed them.

I met the fellow whose position I would be taking over: the bearded, tweed-jacketed David Chute, who had landed a critic post at the *Los Angeles Herald Examiner* and was about to be married (to Anne Thompson, the future film-industry reporter and blogger). Chute had just written the *Film Comment* cover story on John Waters, and the first day, when we were sitting at Chute's desk and he got a call from Waters, I was in a state of unmitigated shock and awe: Being on personal terms with a film director seemed the epicenter of cool. Chute showed me the logistics of putting out the *Phoenix*'s monster-size section of movie capsules, a mix of revivals and current releases. It sprawled over 12 pages, and the capsules could be indulgently long, making the section more than just a consumer guide—it was an ad-hoc weekly encyclopedia of film. That was the key reason that my gig at the *Phoenix*, while technically freelance, fulfilled the base requirements of a job. I got $125 a week to assemble and write that capsule section, and that, plus the money I made from reviews, added up to something approaching a salary (at least, for a 22-year-old). Almost anything at the *Phoenix* could run very long, and did. Each week, Stephen's lead review was a spirited magnum opus done in the lofty exploratory mode of Pauline. In film criticism, this had become the new normal.

My very first piece was a review of *American Pop*, an attempt by Ralph Bakshi, the naughty-urban-sleaze cartoonmeister of the '70s, to tell the story of America through the history of popular music. It was an unbearably tinny movie, and I said so, with a fair degree of awkwardness. When I sat down at Schiff's desk to edit the review, the first thing he said to me was, "You're going to be fine." Then he added, "Pauline's a great critic, but you have to try to write a *little* less like her." Coming from someone as influenced by Pauline as Stephen was, that meant: "You're really overdoing it." He was right. The influence of her prose on me was profound,

but I was already discovering that the temptation to write—and think—
like her could be a slippery slope.

I'd visited Pauline the month before I arrived in Boston, going for
the first time to see her at *The New Yorker*, now that she'd resumed her
post there. I was shown to her office, and when I appeared at the door-
way, she was hunched over the proofs of her review of *Altered States*,
making changes and corrections, and I remember, before she had the
chance to look up, that I could feel the intensity of the fixation—head
cocked, pencil poised—with which her body language connected her
to the page. She complimented me on my look (I was wearing a black
turtleneck, a wan attempt at style), and I could see, in a way that surprised me, that that was important to her. She spoke disparagingly about
some of the films she'd been writing about, like the "ungodly dreary"
Kagemusha, and I expressed my gratefulness to her for helping to hook
me up with the *Phoenix*. "It's a very lively paper," she said, grinning her
approval, though when we spoke of the film section, she struck a slightly
discordant note, saying that Stephen's reviews, while she admired them,
struck her as being "a touch rabbinical." She said she actually preferred
the work of David Chute. I found this curious, since Chute was a fine
critic, but Stephen's writing just about popped off the page. It's the first
time I would encounter the side of Pauline that seemed a little happier
when a film critic was in a lesser position of power.

It didn't take long for my opinion of a movie to get me into trouble,
or at least create a problem. That happened during my second week at
the *Phoenix*. I'd been assigned to review *Gates of Heaven*, the first film
directed by Errol Morris; it was made in 1978 but had barely been
released, and was now getting a second chance. It was at that screening
that I met the rest of the Boston film commentariat, which included
Gerald Peary, the charmingly self-righteous left-wing *echt*-boomer critic
of *The Real Paper* (the *Phoenix*'s much thinner rival alt weekly, which
would fold that coming summer); David Brudnoy, the smirk-mouthed
gay libertarian radio talk-show host and TV critic; and Michael Blowen,
the lead critic of *The Boston Globe*, who was my first experience of the
regular-guy daily-newspaper prole-reviewer—the on-the-beat movie fan
who prided himself on being smart but not "intellectual," who viewed
himself as a reporter more than a critic because that was more manly. We

all sat down inside the Nickelodeon Cinemas to watch *Gates of Heaven*, and from the moment the movie started, I hated it. Shot in the Napa Valley, it was an ironic documentary about pet cemeteries that featured a parade of stuffed-shirt "eccentrics," and the film's wry misanthropic joke wasn't just that they loved their pets more than they did people; it was that these Middle American drones who longed to meet their dogs and cats in the afterlife were already dead. I could tell that Morris, fixing his camera with a stately precision that turned it into a weapon, was gifted, yet the faux-wide-eyed snark of *Gates of Heaven* was stifling to me. And I couldn't wait to say so. But as soon as the screening ended and we all trickled out into the lobby, I realized that I was the only one who felt that way. Everyone stood around, breaking into conversational rhapsodies about what an amazing movie it was. I finally piped up, telling the handful of critics who were standing near me that I thought the film was patronizing and monotonous. I was mocked (in a friendly enough fashion) for the wrongness of my opinion, and in the end the review was taken away from me and reassigned.

I think I was perceived as too untested a critic to be pushing this idiosyncratic a judgment. I wasn't angry; I realized that I *was* untested. And had I been allowed to write that review, I don't think that I possessed the writing skills, at the time, to do my opinion justice. I probably would have fallen on my face. Another critic ended up writing a rave review, and I didn't have any major objection to that. But I did have a lingering sensation of thinking: *I'm being cut off because my opinion doesn't "fit in."* It was a tad disquieting, and having seen *Gates of Heaven* since then, I don't think I was wrong.

In the weeks following, I got used to the exotic ritual of going to screenings—which was, of course, the most ridiculous pure-cake aspect of my new job. To sit in a screening room, or in a mostly empty theater, watching a movie with a handful of critics and editors was to realize that even though you weren't making a million bucks, you had won the lottery. That's one reason why, as the '80s rolled on, I never coveted the kind of job (Wall Street, etc.) that so many people seemed to be wanting. Money, if you have a lot of it, can buy you luxury, and I was not spartan—I was a material sensualist who liked to feed my appetites. But nothing seemed more luxurious to me than getting up in the morning and knowing that the first official thing I had to do was attend a 10:00 a.m. screening of a movie I was avid to see. Being a film critic made respectable the essential pathology of my moviegoing habit: watching films as a way to hide from the world and spy on it at the same time. There were moments I felt a rush of shame at the easy pleasure of it, aware that so many people who earned honest livings would kill to be doing this. I knew from the outset that the living I'd stumbled into was barely honest. But I also considered film criticism, as Pauline's writing had taught it to me, to be a kind of mission, and my way of giving back was to bust my nut to do it as scintillatingly, and honestly, as possible. I always carried a notebook, and taking notes on movies in a barely legible hand (you couldn't look down at the page, since you'd miss something up on screen), which resulted in my being able to decipher maybe two-fifths of what I'd scrawled, served several functions at once. It was a way to recall what I'd seen, but it was also a way to remind myself that I wasn't *just* having fun, that watching movies was now...a responsibility.

Pauline's writing had taught me most of what I knew about being a critic, but the worst habit I absorbed from her was already showing itself, and it wasn't the temptation to mimic her prose tics. It was the knee-jerk tendency to hold back praise in the face of doubt. Pauline, for all her passion and movie love, was a skeptic about so many films that going negative seemed the safest way for a young critic like myself to resolve unresolved feelings into a response that would win her praise by suggesting sophistication. The first time I did that for the *Phoenix* was when I was assigned to review *Thief*, the debut feature of Michael Mann. I was impressed by the burnished elegance of Mann's style, and by his invention of the genre of what I called "the high-tech heist," but I treated the film's human story with derision, writing of James Caan's hardass hero: "There's something half-admirable about the way Frank flouts the rules, but his fantasy about settling back with wife and kids is just a token character touch, designed to tone up the action-movie clichés." When Pauline weighed in with her own withering review, tweaking Mann for his existential macho bluster, I felt vindicated. But during a visit to Ann Arbor a few months later, I had dinner with my friend Hugh Cohen, my most cherished film professor at U of M, who I considered a kind of sage for his blend of cutting perception and absolute populist openness. He loved *Thief* for the Caan character's hard-knuckle code of honor, and he took issue not so much with my opinion as with the grudging, churlish tone of my review: "You looked at the glass and fixated on the part that was empty," he said. "The way you wrote that review, it's as if you were punishing the film for not being a masterpiece. It's a *good movie*. And that's all it has to be." I knew, in that moment, that there was truth to what he was saying. I had staked out a position on *Thief* that I trumped up into something "righteous" but that was actually rather facile. (Why was the hero's fantasy of settling back with wife and kids "a token character touch"? I had no idea.)

Deep down, I *did* want every movie to be a masterpiece, to be right up there with *Carrie, Nashville, Mean Streets*. It was an outwardly noble wish, but it violated the nature of what movies were. That said, the first review I wrote for the *Phoenix* that connected as writing was about a movie I hailed as "a shoe-string masterpiece that reaches new peaks of barbaric dementia." *The Texas Chain Saw Massacre* had first been released on the drive-in circuit in 1974, and I had seen and loved it in college, but it was now being given, for the first time, a national re-release, and its status as a touchstone of modern horror was just beginning to take hold. This time, I found it even more terrifying, writing that "the butcher-shop madness explodes with enough incongruous force to evoke the terror of real-life violence. Leatherface is one of the few characters in movies who seems both an 'inhuman' demon and a man—in this case, a big fat maniac with a toy that maims." Months later, when I met another young critic at the *Phoenix*, David Edelstein, who was writing theater reviews and would soon become my fellow second-string movie critic, he told me how much he liked that review. From the start, the two of us shared an immersion in horror, and that rooted our friendship—at least, for the few years it lasted.

Horror films have always dug deep into the pangs of adolescent sexuality (the furtive lust of Dracula, the hairy palms of the Werewolf), but it was my luck—or not—to kick off my life as a professional film critic at the moment when a grisly new kind of return-of-the-repressed thriller was starting to stalk the culture. It all began, of course, with *Halloween*, the 1978 John Carpenter shocker that was greeted as an instant "classic," though that's not how I saw it. In college, I got a few good scares out of

Halloween and recognized Carpenter's gliding-camera finesse, but I was already a *Chain saw* believer, and the masked figure of Michael Myers was an obvious—and depressing—mechanized knock-off of Leatherface. The essence of my gripe was that Myers, like the movie itself, delivered the jolts without the dread-draped mystery.

I couldn't fathom why so many people viewed *Halloween* with a reverence that was worthy of a latter-day *Psycho*, and by the time I got to Boston, the film had already begun to spawn its industry of multiplex gore: the *Friday the 13th* films, the *Halloween* sequels, and a hundred other anonymous ax-murder videogames masquerading as suspense films. The slasher movie had arrived! As a second-string critic, I had to review a ton of this crap (that and cheesy T&A-fixated *Animal House* clones were the compost layer of the new teen cinema), and it put me in the odd position of being a zealous young horror maven who already felt like he was outgrowing horror. With my drive-in roots, I was an ardent advocate of extreme violence in movies, yet I didn't like what horror was becoming, and was deeply suspect of the way that slasher films turned fear into something as formulaic as a crossword puzzle.

It wasn't until I caught a rowdy matinee show of *Friday the 13th Part 3* in the summer of 1982 that I realized what was going on. Near the end of the movie, Jason, the hockey-masked Myers/Leatherface psycho, was taking an unusually long time to finish off some comely victim. When he finally did, with a decisive disembodying knife thrust, one of the jokers who had been barking out comments near the front of the theater, like a low-rent Richard Pryor, took an artful pause and yelled, "Good night *Irene*!" The whole crowd erupted into laughing jeers and cheers. At that moment I realized: Jason, meting out his deranged violence, was no longer someone to fear—he'd become, in effect, the hero. Viewers still liked to quiver at his wrath, but the drumbeat of murder and sadism had nudged audiences to the point that they were now, in effect, on the other side of that *Psycho* shower curtain. The whole grisly joke of slasher films was that they no longer asked you to give a fuck about the bimbos and hunks who got slaughtered. The characters were fresh meat, for the killers and for the audience. Overnight, I felt as if I was seeing my beloved genre of horror turn into something that was numbing the world.

Edelstein had that same trepidation, and the two of us shared more than that. We were both born in 1959, were both outré-egghead film fanatics, were both prematurely losing our hair (David had a small bald spot—though I would ultimately surpass him), and both of us greatly enjoyed taking the piss out of our editor, Stephen, mostly because we admired him so much. David and I became drinking buddies, spending many an hour in the watering hole favored by *Phoenix* writers and editors, a tavern just across Mass. Ave. called the Eliot Lounge, where the bartender, Tommy, looked at you as if staring through the Black Irish mist, and the jukebox blared Stevie Nicks' "Stop Draggin' My Heart Around" at least six times a night. The two of us would order pints of Bass Ale, talk movies, and play videogames, first Asteroids and then the trip-wire acid-head funbox that was Donkey Kong. I had friends I was closer to (Edelstein as well), but I'd never had a *film geek* buddy I could lock sensibilities with like David. It's not just that we shared the obsession; it's that we both *got* movies in the same way. We went to a lot of them together, like *48 HRS.*, which we loved, and a sneak preview of *E.T., The Extra-Terrestrial*, which provoked an endless discussion of whether it was sublime or cloying or somehow both at once, and also a rare showing of Andy Warhol's four-hour-long *Chelsea Girls*, which was so torturous that David walked out at the halfway point, while I stayed to the bitter end simply so that I would always be able to say: I sat through all four hours of *Chelsea Girls*.

Despite the ardent movie chatter, my friendship with David never blossomed into a bromance, because it was too laced on either side with a spiky skepticism. Edelstein was still very clubby with his Harvard pals—they organized boutique beer tastings, which I thought was kind of lame—while I was the Midwestern rube, which meant that I lacked a certain jaded flair. The contrast was enough to fuel a tension in our camaraderie, though it was never one that couldn't be doused by a pint of Bass Ale.

If you were as hungry for masterpieces as I was, the early '80s was an ironic time to be launching a career as a critic. The age of high concept—bad sequels, Mike Ovitz, Sly and Arnold, *Porky's* and *Police Academy*, the dumbing down of everything—was just kicking in. No one had figured out how to reduce movies to popcorn sensationalism and to do it with any finesse. Most of the films with numbers at the end of their titles

(*Jaws 3-D! The Sting II! Amityville II: The Possession!*) were transparently reheated leftovers, usually of stuff that was fake calories to begin with. Hollywood was turning into the big-budget version of a grade-Z factory. The thing is, it worked. Schwarzenegger hit paydirt with the solemnly bombastic *Conan the Barbarian*, Stallone became a bigger star each time he made a *Rocky* film that further degraded our affection for the original, and *Superman II* was a mishmash of caped-demigod charm and special effects so rickety that they now look less convincing than those of a Broadway show. And yet, I found this weekly parade of trash oddly comforting. It was like living in a circus of stupido fantasy, and my job was that I got to stand to the side and comment on it. At the *Phoenix*, I was honing my chops, and the fact that so much of what I was seeing made so little claim for itself helped to empower me.

Besides, there were nuggets of gold glinting out from the new schlock culture. I relished Bill Murray's antics in *Stripes*, I grooved on the mainstreaming of John Waters in *Polyester* (I did an interview with him, making journalistic hay out of his then-novel gifts as a raconteur), I reveled in the stark gutter tragedy of *Pixote* and the sublime talking heads of *My Dinner with Andre*, I ate up the new-fangled old-fashioned corn of *An Officer and a Gentleman*, and though I thought *Halloween* had come close to wrecking horror, I was bowled over by the bad-acid-trip imagination of what John Carpenter—and his special-effects colleague, the twisted Rob Bottin—brought off in the 1982 remake of *The Thing*.

I was no basher of the Lucas-Spielberg axis, having liked *The Empire Strikes Back* even more than *Star Wars*, and I felt a deep kinship with Spielberg, who I viewed as a my-generation genius (even though he was 13 years older than me). Yet a film I didn't much care for—I found it one-third exciting and two-thirds exhausting—was *Raiders of the Lost Ark*. I saw it at a sneak preview, an experience that filled me with an agitation I would feel echoes of years later, after I entered the magazine world. The agitation came from this: I saw that the very thing I didn't like about *Raiders*—that it was one high point after another, that it rushed by but didn't breathe—was exactly what the audience reveled in. It was a film programmed to create the impression that if you didn't enjoy it, that meant that you didn't like "fun." *Raiders*, I would argue, became the single most influential movie of the last 40 years—more than

Jaws or *Star Wars*. The pop-zap ideology had already entered Hollywood's bloodstream, but the visionary (numbing) influence of *Raiders* was the full-throttle pace, the defiant lack of narrative ebb and flow. All-climax-all-the-time became the new template, to the point that no one, anymore, would even think to notice it.

The movies that got my bloodstream churning the way *Raiders of the Lost Ark* did for others were *Mad Max* and *The Road Warrior*, and they became my raging cinematic obsession. They were the greatest action films I'd ever seen—the fastest and the cruelest, the most casually rooted in sudden death—but it was more than that. The way director George Miller kept his camera at speeding-tire level, mounted on the front of the cars' bumpers, turned the films' aggression into something nearly metaphysical. In their cinematic language, all burnt rubber and hurtling metal, they seemed to be the first films to capture what the world looked like when God was no longer around, when speed was the only force left. What made them so deathlessly transfixing is that Miller wasn't mourning the absence of a higher power; he was getting off on it. Mel Gibson's Max—still with his baby fat in *Mad Max*, and with that atrocious dubbed he-man voice—was a badass in chaps who was really a nastier fuel-injected Dirty Harry. If he didn't get as ugly as possible to protect the good folks around him from the Toecutter, played by Hugh Keays-Byrne like the Shakespearean version of a Hells Angel, then no one else would. *Mad Max* and *The Road Warrior* were nihilism on wheels, turning the cinema into pure kamikaze poetry. I used to ask myself which of the two films was greater, and the answer was: whichever one I happened to be watching, often with the accompaniment of a few beers I'd smuggled into the theater.

Too often, though, I wasn't writing about the movies I loved. I was writing about a film like *Tender Mercies*, which got me into . . . not trouble, exactly, but the kind of situation where the editor of the newspaper lets it be known, through channels, that a film has deeply moved him, and that my review, which combined respect (for Robert Duvall) with a touch of mockery (for what I thought was a pleasantly pious ramble of a movie), was a review he wasn't happy with.

I thought something was lacking in *Tender Mercies*, and 30 years of Duvall performances in far greater films like *The Apostle* have made it clear what that something was. Mac Sledge, Duvall's broken-down country singer, is a recovering drunk with a selfish streak of violence in him; he abandoned his daughter, and once tried to kill his wife. Yet every single thing about the character that's less than noble takes place before the film even begins. The Mac we see is basically a low-key Christian gentleman with a craggy smile who heralds from the "Yes, ma'am" school of monosyllabic Texas manners. The scene in which he gets baptized is redundant—he's already a saint. And given that the great Duvall performances (the moody corporate consigliere in the *Godfather* films, the jaw-thrusting napalm jock in *Apocalypse Now*, the killer evangelist in *The Apostle*) have almost always showcased a touch of sin, *Tender Mercies* needed at least a hint of that sinner's honesty. But the film's dry-goods sentimentality wound up winning Duvall his only Oscar. He sent me a note about my review. It said:

> *Dear Mr. Gleiberwitz,*
> *If you had spent less time in a synagogue and more time in the world of the south, I might understand you better. Acting you know nothing about.*
>
> > *Sincerely,*
> > *Robert Duvall*

My first thought was: If only Mac Sledge got to say a couple of lines like that in *Tender Mercies*, I would have liked the character a lot better! (He certainly would have been more interesting.) Until the Internet, with its let-your-id-rip exhibitionism, this was the first and last time I ever got a letter quite like that, and it didn't offend me, since apart from the fact that I had never set foot in a synagogue (and found his prejudice laughably quaint), I appreciated what an exuberant scoundrel Robert Duvall is. I still do.

For a second, I wondered if Edelstein had sent the letter as a joke, since it seemed like a Harvard prank, and David's nasty sense of humor was his defining feature as a writer. But the wording—and the handwriting—was all wrong. A seed of discord, however, was about to be planted between the two of us. David and I, for all our differences, weren't oil and water. We were more like two magnets pointed in the same direction who pushed each other away when a difference got heightened. In the spring of 1983, we went to an opening-weekend show of a movie that had received a staggering orgy of praise from the New York critics. Pauline had raved about it ("So good it's thrilling"), David Denby had raved about it, and just that week, Stephen, in the last review he wrote for the *Phoenix* before moving to New York to join the 1983 startup of *Vanity Fair*, had raved about it. On a Saturday night, David and I stood together in the packed lobby of the Nickelodeon, preparing for a cinematic feast. The movie was called *The Night of the Shooting Stars*. It was directed by the Taviani brothers, Paolo and Vittorio, and it was about a group of Italian villagers fleeing through the wilds of Tuscany near the end of World War II.

Neither of us liked the film. I had never seen a movie by the Tavianis before, and it was obvious that they were impeccable craftsmen, but maybe too impeccable. For all the artistry of their images—close-ups of ears listening to bombs, sloping wheatfields out of Bruegel—their pristine pictorialism had a bordering-on-impersonal quality. It was like watching a film about 37 supporting players, none of whom attain a dramatic life that transcends their place in the mosaic. You could almost feel how the double perspective of the Tavianis' decision-making distanced the action. (In filmmaking, two heads may not be better than one.) *The Night of the Shooting Stars* was trying doggedly to be a great film, but there was something quaintly artisanal and monotonous about it. It was like a Rossellini movie on sedatives.

Afterwards, David and I tried to figure out what was wrong with the film, and it was a tough one to pinpoint; we simply agreed that there was an irksomely detached quality to it. And that it had been overpraised. We then moved on to what was going to happen with the *Phoenix* film section now that Stephen was leaving. I said that I was tempted to apply for the lead critic position, and David urged me to do so, saying that the job wasn't for him. He said that he'd begun to feel like checking out of the *Phoenix*. (It turned out that he already had one eye on New York City.) I did apply for the job, but never stood a chance of getting it. I was too green, too naive and unpolished in my writing, and I knew it. The position wound up going to Michael Sragow, then the film critic for *Rolling Stone*, and though Michael proved to be a peach of an editor, he would be my first experience of getting to know a "Paulette." That is, one of Pauline Kael's fervent, true-believer, she-can-do-no-wrong acolytes, who mirrored virtually every opinion she had of any contemporary movie. Given what a nice guy Michael was, it was an extremely uncomfortable experience.

About a week after I'd applied, I ran into David at the *Phoenix*, and we chatted about this and that, and then he mentioned that he had gone to see *The Night of the Shooting Stars* again. I was surprised: Why go back *so* soon to a film one hadn't liked? I asked what he thought, and he thrust out his lower lip with a look of knowing approval and nodded sagely. It was a gesture that said: "Yes, it really is great. We fucked up. *They* were right." I had certainly changed my mind about a movie before; the ability to do so was, to me, a sign of open-mindedness. Yet what my gut told me is that David had rushed back to see the movie because he'd been a little anxious about being so out of step with the critical establishment. And lo, he now agreed with them!

What I knew is that our original, underwhelmed response to the movie was genuine. It wasn't right, and it wasn't wrong; it was what we thought and felt. And I couldn't shake the feeling that David had made an effort—too studious a one—to remold his opinion. In the guise of open-mindedness, he was genuflecting. He had a right to think what he wanted, but the whole experience made me wonder: What do all these opinions even mean if they're ours and then, a moment later, they're not ours at all?

CHAPTER 8

THE PERILS OF PAULETTE-ISM

She would forever be my muse, but I was never sure of how truly I could call Pauline Kael a "friend." For me, our relationship was a camaraderie dusted with the sweet coating of idol worship, which was starting to congeal a bit. After I landed at the *Phoenix*, I would see Pauline once in a while, during occasional trips to Manhattan, like the day I visited her at *The New Yorker* just after she'd come back from an afternoon screening of *Richard Pryor Live on the Sunset Strip*, a follow-up to the greatest recorded stand-up-comedy performance of all time, *Richard Pryor Live in Concert*. She liked the new movie more than she didn't, but she could hardly conceal her disappointment in it, due mostly to the sudden appearance of the Pryor character known as Mudbone, who Pauline said "bored the bejesus out of me."

Mostly, I chatted with Pauline on the phone, the conversations circling around the movies we'd seen. I tended to let the exchanges drift toward films we had the same basic view of, which wasn't hard to do. My reverence for the weekly amazements of Pauline's writing remained undiminished, and I could always count on a lively conversation with her about why *Reds* was overblown, or *My Dinner with Andre* was marvelous, or *Return of the Jedi* was junk. (It was the first *Star Wars* film I ever reviewed, writing: "The movie veers dangerously close to the wooden outer-space adventures that *Star Wars* so gleefully transcended. It's all flash and no feeling…Trying to cleanse Luke of vengeance, Lucas has made him into a wimp. And so the man who created the new era in movies has now seen his empire turn into the status quo. He needs to rejoin the rebel forces.") And Pauline continued to be encouraging about my reviews. She particularly liked a piece I did for the *Phoenix* about the works of director Jacques Tati, and her praise left an imprint of warmth. It was addictive. I felt colder without it.

Yet I also felt like there was an invisible third rail running down the middle of our conversations. It pertained to those films I disagreed with Pauline about yet felt that I couldn't broach, because they were so clearly movies she was passionate about that had become central to her identity as a critic. One of them was *Dressed to Kill*. After the emotional orgasm I'd had seeing *Carrie*, Brian De Palma had became a directorial superstar of mine. I caught up with his films from the early '70s (I relished *Hi, Mom!* and the tawdry *Psycho* knock-off *Sisters*, starring a demented Margot Kidder), and after badgering a studio publicist during my senior year at U of M, I'd managed to talk my way onto the set of *Dressed to Kill*. One freezing January night, from midnight until around 3:00 a.m., I stood on the corner of Broadway and 53rd St., across the street from the Sheraton Hotel, and watched De Palma film a stunt double in a blonde wig hopping into a cab. At one point there was a break in the filming, and De Palma went inside the lobby of the Sheraton, sitting down with a thermos of coffee. I wandered up and asked if I could talk to him for a few minutes, and when he gave me a curtly glowering "No," I didn't mind. It was all part of the aura of intensity De Palma gave off.

Then, that summer, *Dressed to Kill* came out, and for Pauline it was a defining film. She treated it like it was *her* answer to *Psycho*, saying that it went further than Hitchcock had ever dared. Given my lifelong propensity for the dark and the forbidden, plus my own feelings about *Carrie* and *Psycho* and the claims that Pauline was now making (*Brian De Palma outdoes Hitchcock's most mythic film!*), *Dressed to Kill* sounded like a movie that was born for me to love. So imagine my shock when I caught it on opening day and found it to be a tacky and borderline nonsensical pastiche. The opening sequence set in an art museum, which was De Palma's high-camp riff on the swooning voyeurism of *Vertigo*, undeniably held you with its whooshes of luxe camerawork. Yet once the movie proper began, the dialogue had a hideous tinniness about it, and the whole thing played like a bad thriller you were watching on television spiked with little spurts of ultra-violence that woke up the proceedings without necessarily making them any more convincing. To me, *Dressed to Kill* wasn't a knowingly overwrought knockout; it was simply over-the-top in the worst way. The film wasn't tethered to the real world, as *Carrie* and *Psycho* had been. It seemed to unfold in a junk-movie hall of mirrors that was all lurid, patched-together gestures.

Which, to me, made it the ultimate can of worms I didn't feel like opening up around Pauline. It was starting to seem like her reverence for De Palma was compensating for something—maybe her own lack of worship for Hitchcock, which was a pretty lonely island to be on. There were moments in her reviews when she seemed to draw a line in the sand, as when she declared Walter Hill's *The Warriors* to be a fearless piece of "visual rock" that the viewers she derisively called "the *Masterpiece Theatre* generation" were too soft and complacent to embrace. Actually, I'd thought *The Warriors* was harmless and a bit lame—a movie clearly conceived to be an inner-city gang-war film, yet by the time it reached the screen it had been racially defused and turned into a goofily diverting yet rather toothless fluorescent comic book. (The one element of danger left was David Patrick Kelly's witchy-chinned hostility as the villain.) Kael, however, treated *The Warriors* as a pop event, and for her Brian De Palma had clearly become a *cause*. She would occasionally tease me, with grandmotherly affection, about liking *Dawn of the Dead* or *Pink Flamingos* or *The Texas Chain Saw Massacre*, none of which, in my book, she really got, but somehow it just wouldn't do for me to say something like: "How could you have fallen for *Dressed to Kill*? It's a badly made piece of shit." That was a conversation I did not want to have. And I think that's because Pauline, with her whippersnapper belief system, let me know between the lines that it was not a conversation she wanted to have. Our friendship existed with an asterisk of dishonesty that I didn't know what to do about.

It also contradicted one of the prime reasons I'd fallen into the critic game in the first place: to spend my life talking, in the most open and freewheeling way possible, about the movies.

Of all the fun aspects of being a film critic, the fact that watching movies is your job is certainly number one. You can always find critics, of course, who will try to ease their guilt over the profession's basic lassitude by denying it outright, usually with the "bad movie" defense. It goes something like this: "You may *think* sitting through these movies is fun, but if you had to watch as many bad films as I do, you'd change your mind." Yeah, right! This is nothing but a shameless canard, as if enduring two boring hours at the movies were the equivalent of hard labor. "I just had to endure the new Adam Sandler movie! The agony!" The real lie, of course, is that with very rare exceptions, even bad movies carry a certain baseline amusement factor; you're still there, in the dark, in the funhouse. For a true pop critic, anytime you're watching anything, you're probably gaining a grace note of insight into *something* about the culture that produced it. And that in itself—at least to me—is its own (fun) reward.

But if one of the main reasons I fell into this absurd profession was to soak up my time as a good old slacker film junkie, there's a second reason that, I came to realize, was nearly as central: Becoming a film critic solved the problem of having to talk to other people. It did so by allowing me to gas on, whenever I wanted, about the subject that possessed and tickled *me* the most, and to do so under the cover of gratifying *other* people's curiosity. If I'd been a sports fanatic, that would at least have required the company of other sports fanatics. If I'd been a stamp collector (like my dad) or a computer geek, that would have required seeking out an even more specialized colleague to bounce my passion off of. Movie buffs, in their way, *are* collectors, even if our collections aren't physical (we itemize the experiences of the movies we've seen), but the difference is this: *Everyone loves movies!* They're not just the universal art form; they're the universal conversation piece. And so becoming a professional film buff transformed my single-minded obsessiveness into a perverse social asset. Or, at least, I could always make it look that way.

Whatever the setting (the office, a dinner party, a rock club), I suddenly had a subject that people were dying to talk about, and what they wanted to hear most was *my* opinion. But it never worked that way until I started reviewing movies for a living. In college, if you wanted to talk about a movie at, say, a keg party, you certainly had the right to point the conversation that way, but at the expense of looking like a pathetic dork. ("So, do you like Sam Peckinpah?") On the level of flirtation, it was sheer toxicity. But once I became a critic, I could allow the conversation to steer itself in the direction of my favorite topic, so that it looked like I was being nudged into it. When people have just been introduced, "What do you do?" is the most common question they come around to. The moment I dropped those magic words "I'm a film critic" into the exchange, just about anyone I ever said the phrase to acted as if they'd hit the conversational jackpot. It was my eternal lazy ice-breaker.

I had, at long last, gotten my first man-cave apartment, after discovering that one of my roommates had refilled the kitchen dish-detergent container with shampoo. The fact that she honestly believed that was a good substitute somehow, for me, became the last straw in enduring the habits of others. It was time for my own place! I took over a one-bedroom roach motel in the student ghetto of Allston from Jim Sullivan, a rock critic for *The Boston Globe*. Jim knew everyone on the local music scene, and I was proud to learn that the ancient scuffed furniture I bought from him had previously belonged to Peter Prescott, the drummer from Mission of Burma. I felt that gave my new place cred.

The Boston rock scene was becoming a hangout for me, not because I liked most of the music (I thought it was dreadful), but because it had a downbeat anti-social vibe that fit with my own slightly depressive style. Around that time, Jim took me to see a Jerry Lee Lewis show at the Channel (usually the home of postpunk bands), and we got to go backstage afterwards, which resulted in a close-up glimpse of the great Jerry Lee, who was grizzled but lithe, still with an ornery youthfulness. He had his latest bottle-blonde up-from-jailbait wife with him, and when we entered the dressing room he was pissed off about something or other and was literally throwing a chair around the room, doing classic rockstar damage. (It was like seeing the tantrum equivalent of a golden oldie.) We all stared, dumbfounded. But I must have been staring a little more intrusively than most, because at one point Jerry Lee halted his tantrum and stared right at me for about five seconds, then said, in a suddenly quiet drawl, "There's somethin' strange about you, boy." I still don't know for sure what he meant, but I think what he'd registered was my critical remove, my way of being inside a situation and outside it at the same time.

I moved into the roach motel near the end of 1983, and to mark that pivotal moment, I got cable TV (not *such* a late adaptation—in those fledgling cable days, all I really wanted was to watch my MTV), and I.

also purchased my first VCR, which *was* a rather late adaptation, at least for a film critic, though I've always been slow to embrace new technology. I was still writing my reviews, as I would until the middle of 1985, on the clunky imitation-Smith-Corona-by-Sears electric typewriter that my parents had gotten me for college. And since I've always been an obsessive re-writer, this meant that each page of my copy, when I was finished with it, would consist of line after line x-ed out, with the redone copy typed in patches above or below the rows of black x's, until the whole thing looked like a heavily redacted CIA document redone as a Japanese woodblock print. I would then take the pages, indecipherable to anyone but me, into the *Phoenix* office, where I retyped them into one of our glowing-green-screen Epson PCs.

I'd abandoned series television in college, and didn't return to it until the dawn of *Miami Vice*, which I thought of as more exciting than most movies (it was the *real* kickoff of the age of quality TV). But whenever I was home, I nurtured two yin-and-yang small-screen fixations. I gorged on MTV, addicted to the ADD surprise of never knowing which four-minute cheesy seductive promotional rock nugget was coming next, and grooving on the essential paradox that the bad videos, like Gary Numan's "Cars" or Rockwell's "Somebody's Watching Me," were as arresting to watch as the good videos, like "Owner of a Lonely Heart" or "Take On Me" or ZZ Top's supremely salacious "Legs." My other fixation was taping and watching, with daily devotion, what I came to think of as a new virus in the cosmos, a show called *Entertainment Tonight*. It seemed like a bulletin beamed in from some Hollywood version of the Death Star: a command center that manufactured advertising that pretended not to be advertising. I was possessed by the way that Mary Hart, with her Miss America dimples, and John Tesh, with his blond geek enthusiasm, were harmless drones, but on another level they seemed like they were running for king and queen of the new Happy Talk America, something I was only too glad to study on a nightly basis, since the virus, at that point, seemed so reassuringly contained, restricted to just half an hour of hype a day. I found *ET* strangely gripping, having no idea that it was an early version of the monster that would eat pop culture (and, in the process, give me a career).

The VCR was, of course, a pure toy. And though I became an

obsessive video-store maven, I found that in my desire to increase the adventurousness of my movie-watching habits, my principal strategy was to tape old movies, almost at random, off the television, relying on the caprice of obscure cable and network scheduling to see things I wouldn't have thought of otherwise, from obscure biker movies to *Lilith* and *D.O.A.* and *The Tarnished Angels* to the complete works of Michael Powell and Emeric Pressburger (a PBS festival!) to a movie that haunted me when I saw it in grainy black-and-white at 4:00 a.m.: Carl Dreyer's *Ordet*, an eerie rural passion play that was the most exciting religious film I'd ever seen. It was a movie about love and madness and adultery in which a key character dies, and is then resurrected, and sitting there watching it on my cruddy rock & roll furniture in the middle of the night, the mysticism of it seemed so real that the movie left me shaking, as if I had beheld an actual miracle. It was the first Dreyer film I ever saw (I would soon catch up with the spooky death poetry of *Vampyr*), and he became one of my favorite filmmakers, a magician of the spirit world.

It was around then that an opportunity came knocking that proved pivotal in my relationship to Pauline. I was sitting in the computer corridor of the *Phoenix* (i.e., four PCs stuck in a gloomy walkway), and the phone extension I was hooked up to for the afternoon rang. The voice at the other end said, "Hi, this is Clay Felker." Yes, it was the former editorial maestro of *New York* magazine, but in just a few years, the once-mighty Felker had become a shadow of his former power self, a fallen legend on the comeback trail. He told me he was starting a new publication called *The East Side Express*, and that he'd seen some of my reviews and was interested in me possibly becoming its film critic. Would I be interested in talking to him? I said sure and flew to New York the following week.

Felker's apartment was the hugest I had ever seen (the ceiling seemed to loom up about three stories, though it was probably only two), and I liked how he sat back in his plush chair, looking like a New York Jewish version of Ben Bradlee, draping one leg over the armrest in a disarmingly casual way. We talked movies for a bit (he wanted me to justify why I thought David Lynch's *Eraserhead* was a great film), and he explained that this was probably not the sort of reviewing gig one would need to move to New York for. It didn't pay enough, but it was a freelance position I could do from Boston. There seemed to be no downside; I agreed to take the position. And for the next six months, I wrote reviews, every other week, for *The East Side Express*, which turned out to be a quirky, short-lived Upper East Side tabloid-straining-for-class, printed on crisp bright white paper, that was sort of the early, embryonic version of *7 Days*. The extra cash was fine, but the main thing the paper did for me was to give me a chance to write about the major movies of the week on a regular basis. For the first time, I stepped out of the second-string role and reviewed films like *The Right Stuff* and *Star 80*.

I was dazzled by the former, experiencing Philip Kaufman's rangy astronaut epic as a mesmerizing fusion of liberal and conservative values. And I was blown away by the latter. Except for *Cabaret*, I'd always had mixed feelings about the work of Bob Fosse, yet *Star 80*, his scalding docudrama about the rise and murder of the *Playboy* Playmate Dorothy Stratten, struck me as the movie he'd been working toward, almost subconsciously, for his entire career. It had showbiz, it had sleaze, it had psychopathology, it had the siren song of feminine beauty. But like a contempo *Cabaret*, it was also about the degradation of the entire culture, about something happening right here and now, that I probably related to more than most: the pornification of America. And only Fosse could give that kinky rot a kick of confessional vitality.

Fosse, I wrote, "understands that in an America locked into a love-hate affair with celebrity, wealth, and the images of perfection that bombard us from every newsstand, Stratten is already a myth—her story might have sprung full-blown from a collusion of our national obsessions." I said that in its characterization of Paul Snider, Stratten's flesh-peddling Svengali and killer, the film exploits "the familiar *Star Is Born* formula, with a once-proud man slipping into the gutter as his wife sails toward fame and glory, but here it has an unusually feverish sting, since Eric Roberts lets us see how Paul is driven by his fear of humiliation, of being one-upped." I linked *Star 80* to *Taxi Driver*—and I still think it's the one film of the period Scorsese *didn't* make that's comparable to his sin-soaked fever dreams. Yet the fact that Fosse asked you to sympathize not just with a killer, but with a badly dressed pimp vulgarian who idolized the values of *Playboy* magazine, brought out the class snob in too many critics. The film was lambasted; it was accused of reveling in the sordidness. (Kael: "Fosse shoots skin and sleaze from fancy camera angles.") But the way I saw it, reveling in the sordidness was what the power of *Star 80* was all about. Paul Snider may have been a despicable killer, but in the movie he was the lusty sap antihero of film noir all over again, now plugged into a cheesecake nightmare.

I knew that I related to Snider's obsession (not the violence, but the lust-as-worldview). At the same time, my interest in porn was on the wane, a casualty of the turn the triple-X industry was taking, the one that wound up being chronicled 15 years later in *Boogie Nights*: the changeover from 16mm to video. Dumb as it sounds, the films no longer had plots! They were just people fucking in white rooms, and without that corny glint of fake situational reality, porn suddenly seemed soullessly naked, an effect enhanced by the newly minted look and demeanor of the actresses, who all suddenly seemed to be robo-sexy 36DD platinum blondes out of metal videos. I still dipped occasionally into porn videos, though there was nothing left to discover in them. But the porn *vision*—the one from the '70s, the image of life as an unbuttoned shaggy bacchanal—lived on in me, even as I'd evolved into that creature who was trying, really *trying*, to be an addict of respectable sensuality. I had become a serial monogamist.

Whoever invented that phrase deserves the Pulitzer Prize for snark. For, of course, to be a serial monogamist is basically to be a failed Lothario operating in slow motion, gliding from one "committed" relationship to another, each grounded in the loyalty of devotion...until the next one comes along. It's no accident that the first word of serial monogamist is a word that links you to the behavior of compulsive homicidal maniacs. In this case, what you're bumping off, with the demise of each relationship, is any chance of intimacy. And, of course, it's required that you take an incredible amount of shit for it. In 2008, when I saw that instant-classic *Sex and the City* episode commonly known as "He's Just Not That Into You," which spun around the notion that not *every* relationship ends because the man simply isn't up to it (some of them end because...well, *he's just not that into you*), I thought: "Wow, if only I'd had that episode around when I was the official asshole trashing the promises of eternal commitment." It wouldn't have altered my behavior one iota, but I might have felt just a little less guilty.

My serial monogamy began the year after I arrived in Boston, when I met Christina (at a showing of John Cassavetes' *Shadows*), a beautiful and rather nervous Hispanic-American middle school teacher who, at 29, was six years my senior, and therefore seemed an impossibly exotic "older woman." It proved a more prototypical relationship for me than I could have guessed at the time: We shared movies and music and food and a rather wholesome erotic playfulness that I was, for the first time, more relaxed about than not, and with a girlfriend I enjoyed and was proud to be seen with, everything seemed right with the world...until I hit, for the first time, the wall that I would hit over and over and over again. It was called: dating the same person for four months. It was *always* the four-month mark, as if my entire system had been set to some slow-acting relationship alarm clock. At that point, it would start to feel as if I'd been involved with the person for four decades. I was spent, I was done, I was bored, I wanted out. I would fight that feeling, but after a while I couldn't deny it: My hunger for experience—i.e., having sex with somebody new—would overtake my being. It would seem like the oxygen I was being denied. And that's when I had to get all serial on the monogamy, a debauched repetitive cycle that saw no end. It was my laid-back form of sex addiction, and I think one of the reasons I fell into it is that, with my neurotically cerebral nature, I was a tricky person to interface with ("There's somethin' strange about you, boy"), and a great many women wouldn't give me the time of day, but the ones who *did*, who for some reason had no problem with my detached personality, tended to let down their guards and go all the way with it. And so I was drawn, almost symbiotically, into letting hookups flower into "serious" relationships.

One relationship flowered only because it literally twisted my insides in knots. I met Caroline at a movie screening, and the fact that she was there alone, sitting two rows behind me, made me feel like we were in communion before we'd even begun to talk. She later told me that she felt the same way. She was a graduate student in poetry, a year younger than me, and alluring in a slightly repressed angular-WASP way. She was the first girlfriend I ever had who was a total heart-and-mind companion, though I did learn one lesson I would draw upon often in the future: When dating a poet, *refrain from expressing analytical thoughts about her poetry.* Impressionistic free verse does not take well to criticism.

Caroline was a dream girl to me, but a month into the relationship, we were about to have sex on a chair in her living room, and I could tell that she was trying hard to be "naughty," which in theory was just what I wanted, but the fact that she was so obviously *trying* only revealed her essentially demure nature. If she had been a prude, I would have written her off, but she was a sexually eager person with an innocent kind of sultriness. It was clear to me at that moment that she could never match my appetite for depravity, and so even as I found myself in the honeymoon stage of an idyllic relationship, I was already, in some basic part of my being, glimpsing the end of things. And since this was just starting to come into focus as a disquieting pattern, I felt like my life was already being squashed by my hunger. I knew, sadly, that Caroline wouldn't be enough for me.

My body knew it too, and was in turmoil about it, because it was only a day or two later that I began to feel the knots in my intestines, and found that I couldn't go to the bathroom, which should have sent me to the doctor. But instead, being scared of doctors (all because my father, who *was* a doctor, never took us to one), I began to buy laxatives, and was able to go to the bathroom at least intermittently, and did so for weeks, but something was clearly wrong, the cramps in my stomach region returning periodically, and after a while I began to run a low-grade fever, which I couldn't kill with aspirin (it just ran, 24/7, week after week, at about 99.6). When I finally did amble into the walk-in clinic at Beth Israel Hospital, they took one look at me and admitted me then and there, explaining that I had an abscess in my intestine, and the reason that had happened was that I'd had an attack of Crohn's disease, a potentially devastating syndrome in which the gut lining becomes inflamed.

There are many theories as to what causes Crohn's disease (as well as its sister syndrome, colitis). It's an autoimmune disorder, which means that the immune system is attacking itself, and some have speculated that too much exposure to antibiotics at a young age can play a part. Crohn's disease also seems to manifest itself quite often in ambitious, tightly wound, driven people. (John F. Kennedy had colitis.) But I knew *exactly* what had brought on this attack: Torn between love and desire, between the power of romantic yearning and the imperative of dirty-dog lust (and fearing that those two things would forever be opposed in me), my gut had an existential breakdown. My inner conflicts had set my plumbing on fire.

I had no health insurance, but the caretakers at Beth Israel kept me in the hospital for seven weeks, putting me on hyperalimentation (a feeding drip that's sewed right into your vein), trying to heal my infection without resorting to an operation. Ultimately, I went under the knife and had a 10-inch chunk at the tail end of my small intestine chopped out. During the two months I spent in the hospital, Caroline stayed with me, and was so caring that the experience extended our bond beyond my usual neurotic four-month deadline. That summer, the two of us would travel up to the gorgeous white sands of Crane Beach, then drive around sharing a six-pack, talking about things like how the line "Out on the road today, I saw a Deadhead sticker on a Cadillac" from Don Henley's "The Boys of Summer" was the biggest "Whoa!" line we'd ever heard. *That's* how novel the money culture was in the '80s. (A wealthy Deadhead? *Not fucking possible!*) The night we went to a sneak preview of *Back to the Future* was glorious to me, because the film was so thrilling, in such a brazen commercial way, that just like *Saturday Night Fever*, it revivified my belief in the beauty of the new mainstream culture, which somehow fused in my mind with the sort of ""mainstream" relationship I was having.

Unfortunately, the four-month deadline hadn't been eliminated. It had simply been delayed. A few weeks later, when I sat in my recently purchased 1982 yellow Toyota Celica with the tiger-striped seats and explained to Caroline why it might be good for us to "see other people," she responded by banging her head on the dashboard as hard as she could for about 30 seconds, shouting, with each violent forehead smash, "Blonde...*pussy*! Blonde...*pussy*!," as if to say: *That's all I ever was to you!* (And also, perhaps, that that was the curse of *being* an attractive blonde.) Actually, it was the curse of dating me. The truth is that Caroline had never just been "blonde pussy" to me. If anything, it was the dream of blonde pussy that had wrenched me away from her. I thought of myself as a romantic, but the truth was that I was a slave to my unfulfilled horny dreams. I was 26, and my deepest romance *was* with sex.

Maybe because I became a critic at such a young age, it placed me in a role of solemn "maturity" that I was scarcely ready for. It also left me profoundly confused about how to react to things like John Hughes movies, which I was basically in the demo for, yet I watched them straddling the contradictory roles of jovial teen-movie consumer and trenchant know-it-all adult. I had fiercely divided feelings about *Sixteen Candles*, loving the eye-rolling jadedness of the Molly Ringwald heroine but wishing that Hughes had extended the same sympathetic understanding to everyone on screen. The film struck me as a fresh high-school vision spiked with too much misanthropic arsenic. I don't necessarily think I was wrong about how Hughes' cartoon aggression got in the way of his humanity, but at the same time, I couldn't let myself experience *Sixteen Candles* simply as a lark, a piece of hip product spiced with postpunk-bubblegum thrift-shop 'tude—which is how an entire generation, just two or three years younger than me, consumed it. It was the first movie to make me feel that the people who would soon be branded Generation X were on the other side of a divide from me. I vastly preferred the old-school, well-made-play virtues of *The Breakfast Club*, which in that beautifully realized Saturday-morning library-as-concrete-detention-bunker setting kept striking the notes of witty and light-fingered emotional honesty I craved—and that Hughes' films never did again.

I disagreed with Pauline about a lot of youth movies. She, for instance, preferred *Sixteen Candles* to *The Breakfast Club*, taking what I saw as Hughes' sincerity to be sentimental claptrap. And I'd grown so accustomed to disagreeing with Pauline that the limits it put on our interaction were starting not to bother me. It just seemed like the way that things had evolved. But then came the moment that broke open the piñata of our relationship, and emotions came spilling out that I knew I had to deal with.

I'd put myself up for membership in the National Society of Film Critics, turning in a package of clips for each of the members to read. The group admitted new members (or voted them down) at their year-end awards meeting, and on this initial try, I wound up being turned down. It bothered me a bit, but I was told that it was common for critics not to make the cut the first year they applied, and I really didn't sweat it. Until many months later, that is, when I was talking to Pauline on the phone. "I think a number of the members saw the stuff you were doing for *The East Side Express*," she told me. "And frankly, those pieces weren't as good." (The reviews I'd submitted had all been *Phoenix* clips.) I didn't know how the system worked, but at that moment, every bone in my body told me that it didn't work the way that Pauline was saying. And, in fact, once I did become a member (the following year), I saw exactly how it worked: You evaluated potential new members by looking at the clips that you'd been sent. No one had the time to bother about anything else.

But more than that, I was a little disturbed by Pauline's assertion that my reviews for *The East Side Express* weren't as good as my *Phoenix* reviews. It's not that my feelings were hurt; it's that my common sense was insulted. At the *Phoenix*, my editor, Michael Sragow (a close friend of Pauline's), scarcely edited me at all. My writing went into the paper basically as I wrote it. Whatever one thought of my *East Side Express* reviews, they weren't qualitatively different from my *Phoenix* reviews. A few of them might conceivably have been better: They were about more important movies, and therefore included bolder claims. Yet they were the first pieces of mine that Pauline had *ever* put down in a blanket, dismissive way. And I realized that that was because of what they represented. Pieces like my review of *Star 80* had outed what a different critic I was from Pauline. And the claim that she made about the members of the National Society of Film Critics—that *they* hadn't liked those reviews either—was clearly a preposterous lie. I didn't know what to say to Pauline, so I said something like, "Oh, that's interesting." But what I thought was: "Okay, Pauline, I get you. If I'm not in line with your opinion, you obviously have a problem with it. But what the fuck is that about?"

It was, of course, about something that I'd always sensed. It was why I hadn't told Pauline, within the first three minutes of meeting her, that I loved *Kramer vs. Kramer*. But now I knew what was happening beyond the shadow of a doubt. I had broken ranks, and Pauline, I realized, was willing to deceive and manipulate to get me in line. She was a compulsive truth-teller in her writing, and maybe that's why she felt that she could afford to lie in life; she didn't take deception that seriously if it wasn't cast in the stone of her critical art. I confess that I didn't tell her how I felt. But what I knew is that our friendship, in any meaningful sense, was over. I could no longer go on enabling Pauline's "belief" in me. Yet the fact that I didn't want to continue the slightly haughty mutual admiration society that our friendship had been didn't, ultimately, amount to a rebellion against her. All I was really doing was deciding to be my own self.

The one who taught me to do that was Pauline.

CHAPTER 9

THE GREATEST YEAR IN MOVIES IS...1986!!

As terrible as it is to admit, the Golden Globe Awards have gotten to be nearly as respectable as the Academy Awards (or maybe it's the other way around: that the Oscars are now just about as disreputable as the Globes). That's why there's so much more coverage than there used to be of the Hollywood Foreign Press Association and what this international racket of hack entertainment journalists is really all about. No one knows who they are, of course, but there's now a routine overflow of chatter about all the things that movie stars have to do to court their favor. The celebrities, with glued-on rictus grins, attend lavish publicity dinners at which they agree to get their pictures snapped with their arms curled around their new best buds, the HFPA voters. It's a ritual of hype. And it's a lot less exotically under the radar than it used to be, considering that pretty much the same stroking of the press goes on each year at Comic-Con, and on an almost weekly basis at Hollywood movie junkets. Yet there was a time back in the '80s when junket culture was only just becoming the norm. And that was the moment I chose to tap back into my eighth-grade power-to-the-people self and get all huffy and righteous about it, never suspecting that my rebel snit fit would do my career at *The Boston Phoenix* serious damage.

Anyone who's ever been fired knows that before you officially get into trouble on the job, there's often an incident that gets the whole shit-can ball rolling, a possibly trivial event that plants the seeds of your demise long before they flower. That's what happened to me at the *Phoenix*, and the incident was totally my own damn fault. But I still blame the junket.

The first major movie junket was in 1978, when Columbia Pictures had the bright idea to fly journalists from around the country to a special preview screening of *Close Encounters of the Third Kind*. They were put up in a swank hotel and given limited access to the stars, and they also received pre-goody-bag perks like tape recorders (all to assist the journalism!), which were a super-cheap form of payola. The junket for *Apocalypse Now* that I attended in 1979 was an early follow-up to that *Close Encounters* bash, and since both films were undeniably special—droolingly awaited, and with good reason—it seemed almost appropriate that critics and entertainment journalists had been given a privileged early look at them. The junkets, in their way, were spreading genuine news.

But the studios quickly figured out that the junket template could be applied to almost any movie. It didn't matter if the film wasn't "special." The point was to give members of the press a weekend jaunt (cool hotel, nice meals, free trip to New York or L.A.), to let them meet and greet and briefly interview the filmmakers and stars—and, more than any of that, to flatter the hell out of the press corps by treating them, in some cut-rate way, as if *they* were stars. The first junket I went on at the *Phoenix* was for *Stripes*: I flew to L.A., saw (and loved) the movie, and landed myself a technically not allowed one-on-one interview with Bill Murray by leaving a scrawled note in his hotel-room box that, in his words, was "so sloppy and arrogant" that he couldn't not honor the request. Getting the chance to talk to Murray in his hotel room, even with a couple of publicists hanging around, made me feel like I was doing something right. When I went on another junket a month or two later, for *Cheech and Chong's Nice Dreams*, and it turned out to be one of the worst films I'd ever seen, I didn't mind. I ate up the perks (this was my first real chance to get a taste of Los Angeles), and the whole junket experience seemed like a harmless lark.

In the fall of 1985, I was promoted to be the *Phoenix*'s lead critic (Michael Sragow, who hated the paper's skinflint management, left after only two years), and it took me a while to find my footing. Personally, I don't think I wrote my first truly vibrant, forceful, inspired review until I'd held the post for close to a year. It was mostly out of habit that I kept going on the occasional junket, even though the drill was so clearly third-rate: You saw the film the night you arrived, and then, the next morning, you participated in a series of "round-table interviews," which meant that you and four or five other entertainment journalists would be seated at a circular table, with the film's talent—stars, director, writer, producer—moving from one table to the next, giving each group about 20 minutes apiece. I had a few vital experiences. I loved talking to the pensive-but-slightly-devilish Ben Kingsley on the *Gandhi* junket; on a junket for *The Mosquito Coast*, I got to watch a visibly surly Harrison Ford get more and more apoplectic with each question he was asked. Ford, in this case, had a point. It was hard not to notice that the junkets were becoming insufferable infotainment love-ins in which the "interviews" consisted of newspaper and TV reporters trying to look in the know by pelting movie stars with questions like, "So, how's the new baby?"

I was fast losing interest, but in the spring of 1986, when I made the mistake of attending the junket for *Short Circuit*, the movie that tried to replicate the charm of *E.T.* with a cuddly robot in place of an alien, I exploded, quietly, in disgust. I despised the movie; it seemed not just awful but an excruciatingly perfect metaphor for what was happening to Hollywood—replacing a movie with soul, like *E.T.*, with the machine-tooled version of same. I think I was also more than a little angry at myself for having flown all the way to L.A. to see this piece of trash on a major movie studio's dime. What kicked in for me was how badly we journalists were allowing ourselves to be used. The next morning, I suffered through two of the round-table interviews, with Ally Sheedy and director John Badham, and though I knew that Badham was basically a gifted commercial journeyman, he had still made *Saturday Night Fever*, a film that meant so much to me, and I found his genial embrace of a project like *Short Circuit* too much to stomach. I skipped out on the other interviews, figuring that I would blow off the feature article you made a deal to write by attending the junket. I figured no one would even notice.

But, of course, they did. After I got back to Boston, I was called on the carpet by the editor of the *Phoenix*, the sharp-witted and blustery Richard Gaines, who told me that I had messed up badly, offending many powers that be, and that to make things right, I needed to write a letter of apology to the publicity department of Paramount Pictures. At that point, I still thought of Paramount as the evil corporate studio that had made *Short Circuit*. To me, walking out on the junket hadn't been a matter of boredom; it was a matter of principle, a kind of statement (albeit a naive one). So I wrote the note of apology, but made it as perfunctory as possible. Gaines wasn't satisfied. He was a veteran reporter on state politics who now saw himself as a mainstream activist and me as the loose-cannon youth he needed to tame. He ordered me to write another note (he wanted a far more obsequious one; he wanted me to *grovel*), and when I did, it still didn't satisfy him, so he ended up writing his own note, which *really* groveled, and I signed it. At that point I realized that placating Paramount Pictures had become Gaines' excuse for taking me out to the woodshed. It was a classic case of office politics gone Oedipal.

Gaines and I never got along after that (I think he'd looked at me warily ever since *Tender Mercies*), and I don't think I helped my case any by behaving badly at a party thrown in the posh North End apartment of A. Alan Friedberg, the chief executive of Sack Theaters, the city's monopoly of multiplexes. Friedberg was like a pompous parody of someone out to prove he was a highbrow. He spoke in William Buckley Jr. 10-dollar words and liked to carry a duck-headed walking stick, as if he were some long-lost British gentleman. But he wielded power in the Boston movie world (he once had to be argued out of pulling Sack Theaters' advertising from the *Phoenix*, all because *Chariots of Fire* had gotten a mixed review), so being at this party was nothing if not a political situation for me. And what did I do? Shortly after being introduced to the girlfriend of Friedberg's twentysomething son, I attempted to pick her up (to be fair, with a bit of flirtatious encouragement on her part). The attempt was not successful, but as I learned later on, I certainly succeeded in pissing off the host. I'd had my job for a little over six months, and somehow I was acting as if this gave me license to do whatever I wanted. Actually, I hardly thought it out that much. I was still the bored hedonist wandering the halls of high school, living by the notion that acting on impulse was probably the right thing to do.

I mostly stopped going to junkets, though I did attend one in 1987 for *The Untouchables* and one in 1988 for *The Unbearable Lightness of Being*. I think the reason I blew a gasket watching *Short Circuit* is that as a movie it was beyond trivial, but as a symbol of what movies were *becoming*, it was a good candidate to disturb a young critic who'd stumbled into the greatest job in the world, but that job now threatened to become a parody of itself if what I was reviewing was contemptible big-budget dross. I'd become a critic because I wanted to write about great movies, and they were the fuel that sustained me. Yet I was less head-spun than a lot of critics by a movie like *My Beautiful Laundrette*, a skillful but overdetermined underbelly-of-London curio. *A Room with a View*, which sent audiences into spasms of delight when they saw how startlingly different Daniel Day-Lewis' fop with the candy grin was from his raccoon-haired punk in *Laundrette*, was the film that really planted the "*Masterpiece Theatre* movie" on the commercial map, and I thought it was fun in a quaint, obvious, sex-versus-uptight-prudery way (gee, which side of that debate are we on?).

As for Jean-Luc Godard, I did not share the rhapsodies of boomer nostalgia that drove the praise for *First Name: Carmen* and *Hail Mary* (reviewing the latter, I wrote: "Godard's films aren't just chilly and intellectualized, they're psychotic—mosaics of alienation devices designed to keep throwing you out of whatever reality has just been established, so that pretty soon there's no reality left, nothing but the clink of dialogue that has no connection to the sound of people talking and every connection to the hyperactive voices Godard must hear in his dreams. In *Hail Mary*, the children of Marx and Coca-Cola have given way to the children of IBM and Thorazine, and you watch them in vain"). I did find flashes of excitement in Oliver Stone's first major film, *Salvador* ("It's to Stone's credit that his El Salvador makes your senses tremble"). And I felt like I'd stumbled onto a real discovery when I saw Shohei Imamura's *The Ballad of Narayama* ("There's something shocking about witnessing a culture in which mysticism is bound up with the most casual acceptance of barbarism and death"). These were the best films I'd written about, yet I yearned for more. I hungered for something shatteringly intense, for an audacity that could match the fabled '70s, for danger made alive. Fortunately, it turned out that I was living in the greatest year for movies *since* the '70s. God fucking bless 1986!

It's long been gospel among a certain breed of vintage-movie fanatic that the greatest year in the history of the studio system was 1939, the year that Hollywood gave us the unreasonable bounty of *Gone with the Wind*, *Stagecoach*, *Ninotchka*, *The Wizard of Oz*, *Mr. Smith Goes to Washington*, *Dark Victory*, and *Wuthering Heights*. In truth, that's an arbitrary list of great movies, but it stands as a convenient symbol of the multiple glories of Old Hollywood. As someone who worshipped the New Hollywood '70s but was born too late to experience them as they were happening, I found that *my* 1939 was 1986, because the three greatest films of the '80s were all released that year—and in some darkly linked cinematic coincidence, they actually came out within three months of each other. The movies, in no special order (because ranking them would be like ranking one's children), are *Blue Velvet*, *Sid and Nancy*, and *Manhunter*.

The first thing to say about my claim is that most people would not agree with it. David Lynch's *Blue Velvet* is certainly thought of as an extraordinary achievement; the other two, not nearly so much. But that just goes to show how the pantheon of official cinema, and the conventional taste of the critical establishment, is so often wrong. These three movies are the masterpieces of their time, and they became, for me, a kind of unholy trinity, a testament to why cinema had ever become my faith. They showed me why I was a critic.

Blue Velvet is a spine-tingling demonstration of how the greatest modern movies make every moment a supreme voyage into the unknown. When Kyle MacLachlan's Jeffrey, who wears his wholesomeness like a disguise, watches Isabella Rossellini's bare-backed, harlot-wigged Dorothy Vallens sing "Blue Velvet" in what looks like a cabaret from the afterlife as lit by Douglas Sirk, he's in thrall to a sensation so toxically alluring that it's almost beyond love. It is, perhaps, the dark side of love, and the itchy hook of *Blue Velvet* is that Lynch turned this dread-fueled desire into something perilously *romantic*.

Then Dennis Hopper, in his slicked-back hair, skin-tight leather, and bolo tie, makes his malevolent grand entrance, and from that moment on the cinema was never the same. It's hard to describe just how shocking it was, in 1986, to watch Frank Booth spit out the word *fuck* like a bullet and then reach for his gas mask, getting himself higher and higher on... *something*, all to heighten his sinister lust while shooting volts of hatred out of his forehead. At first, he simply seemed to be the ultimate psychotic greaser perv, a villain whose sickness had nothing to do with *you*. Yet the way the scene played out, Frank's fetishes and perversions—his moans of angry pleasure as he stuffs the sash of a blue-velvet bathrobe into his mouth—became a stand-in for all kink and perversion, for the hellbent compulsion of any desire that is willing to take itself over the edge. Frank was the villain, but even his evil disease was touched with humanity. Just check out the tormented mood ring of Hopper's face as he watches Dean Stockwell's Ben—a "suave" Andy Warhol on downers— lip-synch to "In Dreams." Frank is in a heaven and hell at the same time. He's in a place we can only dream of.

"In Dreams," of course, was the film's mesmerizing high point, and what defined its indelibility is that no matter how many times you saw it, you could never quite say *why* it was one of the greatest scenes you'd ever seen. The scene just sort of... *existed*, as if it had ripped itself out of David Lynch's unconscious. It was there because Lynch felt compelled, by the nearly carnal logic of moviemaking, to put it there. *Blue Velvet* was a Hardy Boys mystery turned into a film noir of decadent proportions, yet the whole movie was entrancingly emotional (*"And I still can see blue velvet through my tears"*), and that, in the end, was its true shock value. It left you just about weeping for the robins of love to save us from the temptations of the damned.

A few years later, in 1989, the myth of the American independent film revolution centered on one cool, small, kinky, out-of-the-box movie that, as the story goes, changed everything. That movie was Steven Soderbergh's *sex, lies, and videotape*. I myself have repeated the myth—in reviews, in history-of-the-indie-movement pieces—many times. I knew, of course, that American independent film had started in 1959, with John Cassavetes' *Shadows*. And that it then blossomed into a movement of films that tried to reveal dusty human truths of existence between the cracks of Hollywood gloss. And that by the 1980s, it had devolved into a borderline irrelevant school of monosyllabic dramas about wheat farmers that got shown on PBS. At that point, the American indie movement that Cassavetes had kicked off didn't just need to be reinvented. It needed to be resuscitated.

Here, though, is why the myth of *sex, lies* misses as much as it captures. The film was distributed by Harvey Weinstein's Miramax, a company whose devotion to taking indie film into the big leagues marked a paradigm shift, and a much-needed one. Yet the reason we date the kickoff of the revolution to *sex, lies* has to do with more than Harvey Weinstein. Soderbergh overthrew the wheat farmers and tapped into something (seemingly) new: a desire on the part of the indie audience for sensation and suspense, for the adult excitement that lousy '80s Hollywood high-concept movies had abandoned—for everything that was promised by the words "sex, lies, and videotape." And *that* American independent film movement—the revolution in tone and subject matter—didn't start with *sex, lies* at all. It started in 1984, with the Coen brothers' *Blood Simple*. *That* was the original indie upstart, the "small" film that reclaimed the ticklish pleasure of the forbidden for a new generation of outside-the-system filmmakers. And the movie that elevated the spirit of the Coen brothers' achievement into a revolution was *Blue Velvet*. It didn't have videotape, but in a more brilliant and influential way, it had sex, it had lies, it had the feeling that every single moment in the movie had been created by a director who couldn't *not* create that moment. And *that* was the spark that spawned Quentin Tarantino. No *Blue Velvet*, no *Pulp Fiction*. This was the revolution.

I went back to see *Blue Velvet* repeatedly, in part because I loved experiencing the queasy shiver that Frank Booth sent through an audience. But I lacked the skills to write about it, and I made a real mistake in reviewing it after I'd seen it only once. I hadn't fully taken the movie in, and I treated it far too intellectually, as an "avant-garde" crossover fluke rather than the powerfully accessible and Hitchcockian bugs-wriggling-into-the-mainstream vision it was. But a little over a month later, I saw another movie that pierced my soul, and now—for the first time—I was ready.

I'd been deeply curious about *Sid and Nancy*, because I was a fan of Alex Cox's nihilism-on-happy-pills L.A. punk burlesque *Repo Man*, and I knew that the British punk scene of the '70s was a true insurrection that was also pure barb-wire theater. The question that tantalized me was: How could you possibly make a dramatic feature in which a walking disaster like Sid Vicious was the main character? And in which the central relationship, between Sid and his dilapidated girlfriend, Nancy Spungen, culminated in his (probably) killing her? What would that *look* like? But as soon as I saw *Sid and Nancy*, I knew it was a movie of such scathing majesty that it was worthy of being hailed as a safety-pin cousin to *A Hard Day's Night*. Sid Vicious and Nancy Spungen were stunted, strung-out, half-crazed junkie misfits, but the movie gave you an overwhelming sense that despite (or because of) their complete and total dysfunction as human beings, they loved each other, and clung to each other, with a wasted sensuality and devotion that was about as real as love gets. *Sid and Nancy* was one of the most scandalously joyful movies ever made.

For most of 1986, I'd been writing reviews that got the job done, occasionally a little better than it needed to be done, often a little worse. David Edelstein, who'd gone on to become a critic at *The Village Voice*, was still technically my friend, but more and more our connection came down to David leaving long messages on my answering machine that ridiculed the pieces I was writing. He had a particular fixation on the fact that I'd liked *About Last Night...* and—God help me—Demi Moore's performance in it, and that review inspired a good two minutes of David's derisive laughter. It would take me another year or so to figure out why he had developed such a hate-on for my writing (and my basic critical character), but he was correct about some of the prose, which was still awkward. When I wrote my review of *Sid and Nancy*, I was 27, and it had been 10 years since I'd read Pauline Kael's review of *Carrie* and began, in my college-blunderbuss way, to try my hand at doing what she did. But now, for the first time ever, I felt like I delivered a piece that could stand.

"The beauty of the movie," I wrote, "is that it lets us revel in the abrasive, fuck-everything exuberance of punk even as it shows Sid and Nancy's lives sliding into the gutter." Inspired by the awesomeness of the lead performances, I finally figured out how to evoke what actors were doing: "Sid, a tall, gangly carouser, stands with a permanent, flaccid tilt that makes the sheer act of his walking around unexpectedly graceful. [Gary Oldman's] face has the same angular planes as Vicious's, the same thin, goofy-protruding lips, and he gives Sid a blankly happy stare that neither lets much out nor takes much in. What attracts you to Sid is that he's so utterly himself; he's so genuine—that is, unpremeditated—in his stuporous narcissism and his willingness to destroy anything in his vicinity, notably his own body, that there's something almost pure about him." I took the opportunity to gas on about punk, something that was a lot more fun for me than actually going out to the clubs—though I did my share of time there—and enduring the endless sets of squalid threadbare music along with the limpidly ironic attitudes. Punk fit snugly into my movie freakdom: It was something I reveled in the aesthetic of but vastly preferred to experience...vicariously. "On some level," I wrote, "[Cox] understood that to make a true punk movie, one had to confront not just the angry, moralistic, I-am-an-anarchist part of the culture but the Sids and Nancys, the goofball anarchists who were really just selfish, pissed-off kids, who pushed nihilism over the edge, who were to the rest of punk what punk was to the rest of society.... It's our investment in the most squalid aspects of their lives that finally redeems them for us." *Sid and Nancy* was *about* punk, but to me it was never just a punk movie. It was closer to an act of skewed classicism—*Romeo and Juliet* with syringes and razor-blade flesh carvings. It was Gary Oldman's first film, and his evocation of Sid's eyeballs-into-the-forehead performance style was sheer demented bliss. Chloe Webb's performance, beneath its caterwauling comedy (*"Si-i-i-i-d!"*), carried the high emotional wreckage of a Vivien Leigh or Liv Ullmann.

Tellingly, the night I finished editing and closing my review of *Sid and Nancy*, I went home and realized that I was exhausted, but I knew the piece was a breakthrough for me, and I wanted to relax and celebrate at the same time, so I made one of my favorite home dinners—El Paso tacos, with the *so*, so tasty chemical seasoning—and cracked open a beer, and finished it pronto, and had another, and by the time the evening was done, I realized that I had drunk the entire six-pack, which wasn't, of course, all *that* much beer, but it was the first time I'd ever slugged down a six-pack on my own, and I knew that you weren't supposed to do that, that it was official alcoholic behavior, but since I was doing it out of writerly exhilaration rather than despair, I figured it was okay. But it was a watershed moment: I began to have a lot more of those evenings after that.

I went to New York to interview Alex Cox, and he struck me as very straight-up and diligent, buried in work when I entered his hotel suite. But he had an anti-social side—at one point he picked his nose, rolled it around for about a minute, and ate it—and when he began to harangue Hollywood executives, talking about how they would "lie, and cheat, and steal," he was rather inspiring to me. As it turns out, though, Cox was *so* ruthless in his idealism that he would soon rebel against the entire Hollywood game, even the independent side of it, making wacked "anarchic" trifles like *Straight to Hell* and *Walker* (the latter practically designed to waste millions of dollars and piss off its studio). He started speaking cinematic gibberish to power, and that became a lesson to me, and a tragedy: Cox was gifted enough to make one of the most thrilling pieces of cinema I had ever seen, and he threw it all away for some dolt-ish high-and-mighty Marxist-British notion of "integrity." He made the bloody flameout of a punk like Sid look purposeful.

It wasn't hard for me to understand my consuming identification with *Sid and Nancy*. I framed a copy of the film's one-sheet poster, a beautiful dark-toned shot of Sid kissing Nancy while leaning up against a Dumpster, with garbage falling from the sky, and the way that image made true love seem the answer to a degraded world spoke to the anni-hilating sexual romantic in me. *Blue Velvet* dove into the same inky res-ervoir of desire as intoxicating pleasure tinged with decay. But the third film in my dark trilogy of '80s transcendence drew me into its web in a different way, and the connection I formed to it grew so intense that I didn't even try to interpret it. It just was. The movie was *Manhunter*, Michael Mann's thriller about three startling characters: an FBI detective who empathizes his way into the feel-bad thoughts of killers; a puckish evil genius named Hannibal Lecter (spelled "Lecktor" in the credits), who eats his victims to consume their identities; and an unspeakably warped serial killer who could be. . . anyone. Anyone under the sun, or moon.

To convey what *Manhunter* meant to me, let me pose a simple ques-tion: How many times have you sat through a drama about cops and criminals and mystery and murder? The answer, of course, is every day (or close enough to it). From Hitchcock to noir to any grade-B piece of pulp, the crime thriller is kind of the quintessential *movie*. And *Manhunter* was—and is—the greatest thriller I'd ever seen: the most ingenious and fascinating and terrifying, the most authentic in its under-standing of what those on the side of law and order actually do, the most rooted in the demons that infuse men with the compulsion to kill.

The film was released in August, a month before *Blue Velvet* (and two before *Sid and Nancy*), and it was treated as a late-summer throwaway by its studio, the De Laurentiis Entertainment Group, whose executives first signaled their lack of belief in the film by insisting that its title be changed from *Red Dragon*—the name of the 1981 Thomas Harris novel on which it was based—to the vague, generic, *avoid-this-piece-of-shit* title *Manhunter*. I first saw the film at a word-of-mouth screening in a multiplex, knowing nothing about it beyond the fact that it starred William Petersen, an actor who'd held his own with a hammy bravura in *To Live and Die in L.A.* I was possessed by the film's key early shot, taken from the POV of an intruder who's creeping up the stairway of a house shrouded in bedtime darkness, the carpeted stairs lit only by the murky beam of his flashlight. The shot didn't look like something out of a movie. It looked like home-video footage, and there was something unique embedded in that image, which seemed to be saying: *This movie is going to show you what murder really looks like. And what it* feels *like.*

And that's just what *Manhunter* did. Mann waited close to an hour before giving the audience a glimpse of his monster, and it scared me more than anything I'd ever seen. Drugged and kidnapped, a sleaze-hound reporter for the *Tatler* (the film's fictionalized version of *The National Enquirer*) wakes up to discover that he's been epoxied to a wheelchair. The lights are low, the decor is drab (except for a poster of the lunar surface), and a maniac with a nylon stocking over his face talks to him in a voice so casual and halting it doesn't sound like the voice of a killer in a movie. He's got a harelip, and you notice he's murmuring things about how he's going to "staple your eyelids to your forehead," and it's clear that the scene is just going to get worse, trapping us in a vault of fear. The reporter has to read a printed statement, like an ISIS victim who's about to be decapitated, and Stephen Lang, the actor who plays him, reads it trembling with so much repressed hysteria that he can barely sputter the words out. If you were a prisoner in a concentration camp about to be experimented upon by a Nazi doctor, *this* suggests what you might be feeling. Tom Noonan, the actor who plays the killer, is a tall, bald spectre with a freakish leer who used his stilted, slightly-too-rapid speaking style to suggest the personality of a man who can't express the depths of the horror he feels except by cutting into the bodies of others until their blood washes away his indifference. He's the greatest psycho since *Psycho*.

There were many things that kept bringing me back to *Manhunter*, to the point that it became the film I've seen more than any other, around 40 or 50 times. It was the first forensic thriller, and there was a layered intricacy to seeing how clues like the infra-red scan of a felt-tip pen on toilet paper could be held up to the light and solved. Brian Cox's performance as Lecter, so magnetic in it smugness ("Operator, I don't have the use of my arms"), established the character as a scene-stealing know-it-all gargoyle-you-love-to-love 15 years before Anthony Hopkins basically riffed on what Cox did in *The Silence of the Lambs* (a great movie, though not as great as *Manhunter*). And Mann's direction, which re-created Harris' story with surgical deftness while synching it to a glorious synth-pop knockoff of Pink Floyd's "Comfortably Numb," turned horror into slasher poetry.

Yet what ultimately addicted me was the way that Agent Will Graham's attempt to solve a chain of crimes too ugly for words becomes a kind of *quest*. More than the heroes of Sidney Lumet's great underworld dramas, more than Jack Nicholson in *Chinatown*, Graham solves the heart of darkness by knowing it himself, by seeing it from the inside out. Petersen's performance has a few dated inflections of Mann-ly macho, but it's still a fantastic piece of moody noir Method acting that shows you the hidden contours of a detective's *mind*, so that by the end, when he's figured out how a cache of seemingly random home movies reveals the killer, you feel as if you've experienced a process of understanding that merges the moral with the insane. Watching *Manhunter*, I came to feel a singular and almost embarrassing symbiosis with Graham. The more I saw the movie, the more I indulged in the fantasy that what I was trying to do, as a critic, was Graham-like in its mission—I was trying to unlock the secrets of the darkness. But this is the kind of thought you can have at 1:30 a.m. watching the greatest contemporary thriller for the 27th time.

Blue Velvet, Sid and Nancy, and *Manhunter* are all tales of addiction and violence and desire and taboo, and getting hooked on those films, I was like a '70s teenager hunkered down in his bedroom under his headphones, wearing out copies of albums by Dylan or Kiss or the Velvet Underground. For many months, or even a couple of years (in the case of *Manhunter*, about five years), I swirled those movies around in my soul, carried away by the link they made between the torment of their heroes and what I experienced as my own luridly hungry and desperate nature. What I didn't expect is that my father would provide me with a slice of truth-is-stranger-than-fiction drama that was like an added chapter to the dark-side trilogy I'd been living in.

It began in New York, where I decided, after my interview with Alex Cox, to look up my father's brother, Mel, who I hadn't seen in a number of years. He and my father weren't quite estranged, but they didn't speak much, and that was too bad, because Mel was like a softer, warmer version of Eli, and I always liked him. On a whim, I called him, and he said he would pick me up in the city and drive me back to his place on Long Island. When his car pulled up at a downtown street corner, I jumped into the passenger seat, gave him a quick embrace (he hadn't changed, which tends to happen when you're already pot-bellied and bald), and noticed that there was a girl of about eight in the back seat. "This is my daughter, Judy," said Mel, with a wavery grin of pride. "Wow," I said, not knowing what to say. "Did you know that I have two daughters?" he asked. "I didn't even know you were married," I replied. (Mel had been hitched once before, but that marriage had crashed and burned in about a year.)

"Do you have any idea who I'm married to?" he asked.

"I have no idea," I said, at this point rabid with curiosity.

"I'm married to Laura White."

Okay, now *that* was a jaw-dropper. Laura White had been an acquaintance of my father's, a polite and pretty shrinking violent who sometimes babysat for us and used to occasionally travel up with me to the U of M School of Music. I didn't understand: What was the connection? Mel, who was never one to explain much, said simply: "A little over ten years ago, she was coming to New York for a visit, and Eli gave her my number and told her to look me up. She did, and the two of us hit it off." Mel shrugged, in his *what the hell else is new in Brooklyn?* way. I guess weirder things had happened.

But in this case, they truly had. About a month later, when I went back to Ann Arbor for Christmas, I told my parents that I'd looked up Mel and "discovered" his heretofore hidden life. He had two daughters! He was married to Laura White! I thought I would be congratulated on my family detective work. Instead, my parents looked at each other with a glance of rueful scorn. What the fuck was going on? "Yes," my dad said. "I know."

Here's what *I* didn't know. That afternoon, my father took me out for a drive, and we wound up in our old neighborhood, the one with the overly cramped schoolhouse-red home we'd once lived in, and he told me the story of who he was. "Almost twenty years ago," he said, "I had a passionate love affair with someone. And it nearly destroyed your mother." I went numb with shock, but trying to think of something to say, I was able to put two and two together.

"It was with Laura White, right?" I said.

"Yes."

"So how did she end up married to Mel?"

"Our affair had ended," he explained. "I loved her, but I didn't want to marry her. I didn't want to break up the family."

"Why not?" I said. "You were never there for us, anyway."

"Maybe not," he said with his customary indifference. "But that's how I felt. She was desperate for me to leave Lillian. So I had to end things. I gave her Mel's number, and she looked him up. And the rest, as they say, is history." My father liked to talk in clichés, because they were so good at camouflaging emotion, and now that he'd told me about himself and Laura, it seemed awfully...pat. But it also seemed a little sick: My father couldn't bring himself to marry his mistress, so he "gave" her to his brother, who married her instead, and *she* got...the imitation Eli. Very, very fucked up. "I'll tell you," my dad said, "the first time I made love to her..." and he just shook his head, as if he were talking about some ultimate deflowering that still gave him the shivers. I had never heard him say anything like that before.

You could say that I was suddenly glimpsing a new side of my father, but that's not how I saw it. *This* side, the side of him that "made love," that sounded mournfully romantic, didn't complete him so much as it filled in a man who had never been there. I realized that if he *had* left my mother and married Laura White, he would have been one more meaningless divorce statistic. But I couldn't keep myself from saying, with more sympathy than anger, "You know, Dad, if you *had* left, I bet it would have been a good thing, not just for you but for me. I could hardly have had less of a relationship with you than I did. If you'd gotten divorced, we probably would have talked more."

"Maybe so," he said, in his noncommittal way.

"Does Mom know about all this?" I asked.

"She knows about Laura," he said. "What she doesn't know, and what you can't tell her..." he said, pausing, as if to ask for my confidence. "Okay," I said cautiously. "I won't say anything. Go on."

"Mom has no idea how many women I've been with."

"How many was it?" I said, as I felt myself turning red.

"A lot. Remember Deirdre Connolly?" That was his physician colleague, who I'd met a couple of times as a boy. "I fucked her in a hospital closet." Okay, my father did not just say that; that was a sentence I now wanted out of my head. "I slept with a lot of nurses, a lot of divorcés."

"Well," I said, not trying to be funny, "now I can see why you were never home."

I turned to him, and I was sad, but I wasn't angry—far from it. Because even though my father had just told me that he was a scoundrel, that he'd betrayed my mother and my family, he had also never seemed like less of a scoundrel. For most of my life, he had treated me harshly. This didn't change that, but it showed me a side of him that I'd always longed to see was actually there. He had desire, he had love inside, he had passion. He fully *existed*, for me, for the first time. And maybe that's because in everything he was confessing, I saw my own self. My own erotic compulsiveness—the porn, the bad-girl fixations, the serial monogamy that was really my civilized form of bed-hopping—hadn't come out of nowhere. I was my father's son, all right. Only now I understood him. He wasn't crying (at least not literally), but for the first time, I thought I could see blue velvet through his tears.

CHAPTER 10

WHY IT'S IMPORTANT FOR A FILM CRITIC TO DATE AT LEAST ONE SEXUALLY UNHINGED COKEHEAD

When someone asks me what the job requirements are for being a film critic, I tend to respond with a curt, "There are none." Which is mostly true. You have to love movies! And see a truckload of them! And acquire a ton of knowledge about them! A decade and a half into the 21st century, that describes a great many people who have no real life apart from consuming films and television shows and spewing their opinions about them into the blogosphere. (I'm not being condescending; minus the computer part, I basically started off as one of those people.) Of course, the whole "knowledge" thing can cut a few ways. You can be an encyclopedia of fanboy scholasticism and still not touch the psychological layers of how even a lot of popcorn films work. To really understand movies isn't just to take them, good or bad, at face value, or simply on their own terms. It's to look behind the face, to fuse those terms with your own highly charged responses and—yes—values. (A lot of people can probably tell a good *X-Men* movie from a bad *X-Men* movie. The question is: Is a good *X-Men* movie...actually a good movie?)

For a critic, passion and insight and a backlog of thousands of films in your brain are a major requirement, and so is a knowledge of how the real world operates: politics, sports, real estate, crime, media, religion, the stock market, divorce...everything. Each movie is an opportunity for immersion, a way to try to view a subject in three dimensions.

Yet once I'd been on the job a while, I began to meditate, half-seriously,

and then a little more seriously, on what I decided was a secret requirement for any vibrant and discerning critic: *You need to be a happy person.*
I realize that sounds like the dippiest thing ever stated, and that it con-
tradicts the essential perception most people have of critics. I don't mean
the fizzy "Check it out!" fake reviewers on local TV. They, of course,
are smiley-faces-for-hire, paid to put a rubber stamp of enthusiasm on
whatever it is they're reviewing. Real critics, however, are not generally
thought of as a peppy or happy bunch, and they will often joke about it
at their own expense. The image of the critic as walking pill was locked
down for all time by Addison DeWitt, the legendary theater critic played,
with dry-martini charisma, by George Sanders in *All About Eve*. He was
the destructive fascist bitch-snob swanning into rooms, spraying his opinions around like slightly stinky perfume—and always ready to pounce, to
come up with a caustic observation at someone else's expense. The mythological upshot of a suavely negative personality like Addison DeWitt is
that the critic, deep down, is *not* a happy camper. He's noxious and spite-
ful, using "opinion" as an excuse to purge his bile. Writing reviews is his
way of getting even.

It's always amazing, to me, how much this myth persists. In the '70s,
the Eurocentric movie and theater assassin John Simon gave it vicious
new blood (he was like a Gestapo aesthete squinting at his typewriter
through a monocle), but it was also common to take the relentless judgments and barbed wit of Pauline Kael's writing as a sign that she, too,
was one of the Dyspeptic Ones, a bully with indigestion who got off on
putting others down. A movie like *Birdman* features a retro-fitted version
of Addison DeWitt: a vengeful *New York Times* theater critic who gets
sloshed to stay in touch with the dismal spirit of her inner executioner.
I certainly think there's a dark art to writing a scathing review, and I've
gotten off on the icy hostile pleasure of it many times, but the whole reason movie reviewing sucked me in in the first place was not about that.
It was about a gnawing desire to figure out and express why I loved the
things I loved. And as I fell into the weekly groove of being an on-the-
beat critic (where most of what you're writing about *isn't* worthy of love),
I grew obsessed with the mission of trying to capture the uniqueness of
each movie. I can be as nasty as the next critic, and occasionally delight
in doing so, but to me there's a Zen to criticism. It's not about being

mean: It's about getting to the mean truth, to the inner reality of what each movie is.

And that's where the happy part comes in. If you're not a happy critic, then you're doing your job with a faulty barometer. Let's say that you go to a movie one night, and you don't respond to it, it leaves you restless and a little annoyed, but you're basically a prickly, dissatisfied person to begin with. How are you going to tell where the inadequacy of the movie leaves off and your own irascibility begins? You can't. And that, really, is the whole rap on critics: that they're panning this and that, but they're really writing about *themselves*, their lack of inner satisfaction.

But consider the following scenario: If you go to a movie within a state of well-being, and *that* movie leaves you restless and annoyed, then you know, deep in your cellular protoplasm, that it's the movie's fault. It's not a projection of your inner grump. Tough critics are seen by the culture as if they were taking revenge, but the reason I came to be viewed as a tough critic is that I love movies to death, and they possess me, but if a film *doesn't* do a good job of occupying my imagination, I have little use for it. I don't *need* it. I'm much happier when the end credits roll and I—finally!—get to leave. The world outside the theater will seem more interesting (will seem, in a way, like a more interesting *movie*) than what was up on screen. I admit that I bore faster than almost anyone I know, but I believe the reason for that is that I usually want *more*. And I think that's a healthy thing.

I got happy working at the *Phoenix*, and a state of well-being started to shine through my reviews. Not that I was suddenly in any possession of the secret of life. I was tormented by the romantic barrenness of my existence; the fact that I'd never been in love with anyone made me feel like a thirsty man in the desert. I desperately yearned, hungered for, *craved* that connection, sometimes imagining—cringe alert!—that the pillow I was lying next to at night was my beloved, who I could turn to kiss (a thought I often had even with my arms around the person I was sleeping with). I had absolutely no doubt that the acuteness with which I experienced the absence of love in my life was *some* sort of reflection of the pain I felt in my inner primal-scream John Lennon–on–*Plastic Ono Band* self at having grown up with a father who was the affection equivalent of a black hole.

I of course saw a shrink, a 40ish mensch named Jay who wore tasseled loafers and a fuzzy-wuzzy Jewfro and had a tranquil office overlooking Boston Harbor. He and I shared an obsession with *The Morton Downey, Jr. Show*, and we would spend the first 10 or 15 minutes of just about every session dissecting the antics of the previous night's episode, which may have indicated that I didn't take therapy seriously, though in fact I did. Morton Downey, Jr. struck me as a profound figure, a trash ringleader presiding over the vulgar human comedy. It made sense to talk about his show in therapy—the show was pure id. And once we'd gone through the weekly ritual of deconstructing Downey, I pummeled away at my daddy issues like a boxer in training.

Yet I remained a creature of faith, my optimism—indeed, my happiness—stoked by the intertwined balms of art and addiction. I wasn't in love, but I was, in effect, having a love affair with sexuality. It *was* my mistress and, along with movies, my faith. Sex (as Norman Mailer might put it) was the life force, just waiting to be lifted up by love, to become (as Steve Winwood put it) a higher love. But until that happened, the lower love would do. I was never haunted for two minutes by the Woody Allen problem—the feeling that life has no "meaning." No meaning? I had no idea what that *meant*. To me, every moment erupted with meaning, so even in a bad moment (of which I had countless), the potential for happiness always stood right in front me.

And as someone who was basically being paid to write about his faith, I knew I was on a roll. I was wriggling out of the skin of my callow youthful judgments, and the fusion of opinion and analysis began to pour out of my head with liquid ease, in a way that was now fun to read—even if you didn't agree with me—because I was so obviously having fun doing it. I reveled in the sheer cornucopia of what movies are.

I wrote happily about John Waters' miraculous crossover into the mainstream ("Waters is as fascinated by the yummy-synthetic as that kid next to you in grade school who ate library paste. In *Hairspray*, he melds romance and camp—he finds something heartfelt in the garish fakery") and about how synthetic and tedious I found the faux-Waters outrageousness of *Heathers* ("After a while, you may find yourself worn down by the sarcastic relentlessness. There isn't a moment that breathes").

I wrote about the zingy depravity of *RoboCop* ("A smashingly nihilistic thriller. It's set in that most dilapidated of American cities, Detroit, sometime in the 1990s—a world of decayed buildings and clogged skies, of scummy psychotic thugs who roam the streets like terrorists and malevolent executives living high off the corruption below. In other words, things haven't changed much").

I wrote about Tom Hanks in *Big* and the new generation of arrested adults ("Hanks purges himself of any nastiness or cunning, until he's as clear-eyed as a pup—triumphantly guileless. The filmmakers have taken a gimmicky idea and treated it artfully. They've made a delicate satire of the 30ish adults who, no matter how successful or worldly, will always find the idea of being 'grown up' a trifle weird, since part of their legacy as children of the counterculture is to hold on, and proudly, to childish things"). And I wrote about the movie that anticipated *GoodFellas* and *The Sopranos*, Jonathan Demme's *Married to the Mob* ("Demme humanizes the mob. He gives us a Long Island underworld that's a clan of backyard-barbecue suburbanites swimming in kitsch. It's like an extension of Middle America, but a bit more vulgar, because the characters have a little more money, and also because so many of their home furnishings are stolen").

I went to New York to see Martin Scorsese's *The Last Temptation of Christ* at the Ziegfeld Theatre on a sweltering opening day, braving a four-block line, a tattered brigade of placard-wielding fundamentalists, and a vague anxiety that a bomb of protest might go off in the theater. But *Last Temptation* turned out to be the furthest thing from blasphemy ("One feels closer to Jesus than in perhaps any other Biblical movie. It's the Christ story as a mythic psychodrama; it's about a Jesus burdened with self-consciousness—a Messiah who stands back and watches himself save mankind").

I tried to explain why I loved Robin Williams as a stand-up comic and hated him as actor, a feeling that, as the years went on, I never shook ("On stage, his fantasies and impressions appear to escape uncensored, as though his mind were a video collage of references beamed in from the cosmos. As an actor, though, he sculpts his characters, using the external approach of the comic; he does bizarrely kinetic *impressions* of them. He gives you tragedy with blips").

And in a triple review of *Rambo III*, *Willow*, and *Crocodile Dundee II*

("Paul Hogan is the superhero as handyman, greeting each new danger with a laid-back, Mr. Fix-It smile, and always with the perfect utensil"), I riffed on the still early days of the new blockbuster culture: "That these movies exist purely to make money is hardly a shock (or a crime), yet the way they choose to make money is by seconding what the audience already brings into the theater. When all you're seeing is what you came to see, the thrill of what it means to go to a movie is diminished, trivialized. The lust to fulfill expectations has become the psychosis of the American film industry—and part of the way it's killing off our movies is by killing off the demand that they do anything more."

Blockbusters, it must be said, didn't dominate the culture as relentlessly as they do now. And when it came to the excitement that a great film could give you, no movie of the '80s—apart from *Blue Velvet, Sid and Nancy*, and *Manhunter*—poured itself into my imagination like Stanley Kubrick's *Full Metal Jacket*. The irony is that I'm a Kubrick fanatic, the kind of person who could watch *2001: A Space Odyssey* or *A Clockwork Orange* or *Barry Lyndon* any night of the week, yet my reverence for *Full Metal Jacket* felt a little off-kilter to me, because I came to believer that it's Kubrick's greatest film, yet you'd be hard-pressed to find a Kubrick cultist who feels that way. It's as if the very universe of people the movie was made for couldn't see it for what it was.

When *Full Metal Jacket* came out, I could always tell I was talking to someone who didn't get it if they chose to go on and on, with a knowing grin, about how cool the opening Marine boot-camp sequence was. True, it *was* an amazing sequence, as R. Lee Ermey pelted his recruits with obscenely jaunty verbal hand grenades ("You had best un-fuck yourself or I will unscrew your head and shit down your neck!"), but the reason I developed a bug up my ass about the boot-camp sequence is that people were getting off *way* too much on what a foul-mouthed misanthropic comedy it was. The bravura thing about *Full Metal Jacket* is that it *isn't* a comedy—it's not some derisive *Strangelove*-goes-to-'Nam piece of hip mockery. It had a few moments like that, but they paved the way for the most intimate war film ever made. What Kubrick captured is a truth that our culture basically keeps trying to cover up: that in the slaughterhouse of modern combat, the soldiers rarely know—I mean really *know*—"why they're there." It doesn't matter if the cause is noble (World War II) or corrupt (Iraq). Once the boots are on the ground, the cause the soldiers are fighting for is survival, the cause is one another, the cause is never... the war's cause.

I got so possessed by *Full Metal Jacket* that I wrote two long reviews of it several weeks apart. The scene that really lit my fuse came 20 minutes after the film landed in Vietnam, when Matthew Modine's Private Joker is wandering with his platoon through the remains of Hué, and "Woolly Bully" is playing, and they come across a dead Vietnamese soldier, and one of the Marines, holding a hat (for a while) over the dead face, does a sinister monologue about how it's the soldier's "birthday," and Kubrick holds the shot for *so* long, with the music and the whole death-trip freakiness building, that every time I saw the film I felt the sequence come close to getting me stoned. *Full Metal Jacket* was a down-the-rabbit-hole war film. Kubrick gave you a view that was sheer vertigo—a world falling apart—and it was rooted in his extraordinary vision of Hué as a moonscape of wreckage, a spectacular colossal *ruin*, like something abandoned a thousand years ago, with black smoke flowing out of the concrete rubble in choking plumes of death. Inside the wasteland, there was no order, no enemy you could even see. There were just bullets from a sniper's gun that tore into soldiers' bodies with cruelly random horror.

Kubrick's message was elemental: War is its own separate reality, with its own slang and brotherhood, its own cult of life and death. At the same time, the movie asked: Once a soldier is *inside* war, what creates his identity there? The answer was that it could only be the impulse to act, to repel the fear, to learn to kill. Joker spends the film standing apart, outside the kill zone. When he at last stands tall and, with a squint of agony, pulls the trigger, he finally exists. When *Full Metal Jacket* came out, I went to see it every day for a week, hooked on the *journey* of it. No war that you'd ever believed in, or didn't, would ever look the same.

I was caught up in a few combat skirmishes of my own. Now that I'd hit my stride as a critic, I felt it was my turn to be one of the three Arts writers the *Phoenix* traditionally submitted as potential nominees for the Pulitzer Prize in criticism. It's not that I thought I had a chance of winning. But I wanted my shot, and I wanted to know that the paper believed in me. By 1988, I'd been the paper's lead film critic for three years, and I felt I'd earned it. But Richard Gaines had other ideas. He decided to submit the names of just two Arts writers, neither of which was me. He could have included one more; he decided not to as a slap. So I went into his office and complained. He told me that I wasn't ready to be nominated, and then said, with a taunting grin, "What are you going to do, Owen? Are you going to *rebel*?" He was still punishing me for that *Short Circuit* junket. Gaines pushed my buttons, so I said: "No, Richard. To be honest, it feels like you're the one who's rebelling. But I can't say this does any wonders for my loyalty to the paper." It was the single stupidest thing I ever said in a workplace setting.

The other skirmish was with David Edelstein. For all his answering-machine critiques of my criticism, I didn't realize my friendship with David had crumbled into dust until I bumped into him after a New York all-media screening. Outside the theater, people were gathering, and I found myself standing next to David and another familiar face, my former editor Michael Sragow, who was now the film critic of *The San Francisco Examiner*. David made a point of ignoring me, and then, to my surprise, he looked over at Michael and gave him a fraternal bear hug and a big, eager, smiling hello. I didn't relish being treated that way by someone I considered a friend, yet the reason I wasn't just annoyed but shocked is that Edelstein had worked under Sragow for only about four months (before going off to the *Voice*). During that time, David and I agreed on two things about Michael: that he was a super-nice guy, but also that there was something absurd about the way that he mimicked Pauline Kael's opinions. David and I both liked Michael, but we made constant sport of his Paulette-ism, often predicting what he would say about a movie, our workplace conversations salted with eye-rolling comments like "Of *course* he thinks that." That didn't mean it was wrong to now give Michael a hug. But as I stood there, taking in David's snub of me coupled with his whole "Hello to my new critic BFF!" vibe toward Michael, it suddenly hit me what was going on: David, a comrade whose writing I respected beyond measure, was now one of *them*. He had become a friend of Michael, because he was now a Friend of Pauline! And I was now the enemy. I felt like I was standing in the middle of *Invasion of the Critic Snatchers*.

In case I needed any more confirmation of what had happened, I got it during one of the most uncomfortable sitting-around-having-a-drink evenings I could conceive of. It was right after the January 1989 voting meeting of the National Society of Film Critics. The movie that had won was Philip Kaufman's *The Unbearable Lightness of Being*, a picture that Pauline had championed (and rightly so, since it turned Kundera's novel into a hauntingly wise and sad and rapturous big-screen exploration of love, sex, oppression, and transcendence). After the voting was over, a handful of Pauline's critical friends trooped over to her hotel suite, and I tentatively joined them, having never declared any kind of war on Pauline, because I didn't feel that in my heart. The two of us ran into each other once a year, at these critic powwows, and we would exchange a few amiable trivial words. But we both knew that we were no longer friends.

Once inside the suite, Pauline found Philip Kaufman's phone number, gave him a call to tell him that he had won (news like that traveled a little less fast pre-Internet), and then insisted that each of her acolyte chums get on the phone and congratulate him. I noticed a bit of comedy that I don't think anyone else did regarding Terrence Rafferty, who I considered the most gifted of her disciples. Terry, with flyaway hair and a professorial gleam, was a nervous, at times visibly antsy chain-smoking type—the sort of intensely private, bookish person you could still get away with calling "neurotic"—and for one of Pauline's followers, he had a way of occasionally straying outside her critical orbit. It was clear to me that he did *not* want to get on the phone to offer his personal congratulations to Philip Kaufman; it was clear that he thought it was kowtowing (which, of course, it was). But in the end, he did. It was like a ritual each of them had to go through to satisfy the Khmer Rouge.

Afterwards, I went out to a bar with Terry and a handful of Pauline's other friends. Hanging out with these folks, listening to them crack wise in the quippy knowing brain-food language of *film criticese*, hearing them spout one proudly enlightened opinion after another that always had a way of mirroring exactly what Pauline thought (Meryl Streep is a virtuoso stiff! Hollywood won't let De Palma be De Palma! Paul Schrader used to be a bad director! Now, suddenly, he's good!), I found myself wondering: How could people this intelligent and compelling believe so totally in what they're saying…when it's so often not coming from them? I realized this wasn't a question, ultimately, about movies or film criticism. It was about identity, about the mysterious ways that role-playing could become real. I knew that the Paulettes were copping out, but the way they blended the assertion of fearless opinion with hidden subservience to the mind of Pauline made my head spin. I couldn't begin to fathom it.

Edelstein was there, and the two of us, seated on opposite sides of a large round group table, never spoke, but when it came time to order drinks, I asked for a Rolling Rock, and this so offended the beer snob in David that he kept muttering about it for the next 10 minutes ("How could anyone drink *Rolling* Rock? It's shit..."). In hindsight, he was right about my selection of tasteless brew, but of course he wasn't really talking about Rolling Rock. I knew *that* wasn't what the crash and burn of our friendship was about. It was that I was outside the cult. And he was now in.

• • • • • •

Back in Boston, the *Phoenix* had a new arts editor along with the rumblings of a new agenda. The editor, Peter Kadzis, didn't strike me as the sort of guy who would be hired by the *Phoenix*. A former editor at *Forbes*, he still dressed in pin-stripe suits, and he had recently been found guilty of plagiarism (that's why the *Phoenix* could hire him for cheap—he was damaged goods). He spoke in the yahoo version of a Boss-town accent and had the blunt-wittedness of a daily beat reporter. He also wasn't above running fawning articles as favor trading (like when he billed the forgettable ersatz-cult movie *Tapeheads* as...the cult movie of the year!). He told me, right after I closed my review of *Bull Durham*, that it was "very long," in an I've-got-a-problem-with-this way. He also introduced a new feature, a horizontal movie chart called Flicks in a Flash, in which assorted critics' opinions would be represented by one of three images: a star (meaning that the movie was recommended), a pair of dice (meaning it was so-so, a crap shoot), or a turkey (you get it). Say this for Peter Kadzis: He saw the future.

He certainly saw my future. At the end of January '89, he called a series of one-on-one meetings with the arts-section editors, and when the time for mine arrived, I could feel the hollow tension in his office as soon as I walked in. I sat down, and Peter fixed me with his owlish stare and said, "I have to tell you, Owen, that I'm starting to look for someone to be film editor." Someone besides me. I could feel my stomach drop right out of my body, but I mustered the presence to say, "I don't understand. Do you have a problem with my work?"

"It's not that," he said. "You're a very talented guy. But I'm going to be taking the section in a different direction."

At which point my attention faded away. I knew what had happened. This wasn't Peter Kadzis' decision; it was a Richard Gaines hit. He had never liked me, and he had now finally fucked me. Or, in fact, I had fucked myself. But it was done; it was over. Kadzis was quite decent about letting me stay on for a while as he searched for a replacement, on the condition that I didn't tell anyone (I wound up remaining on the paper until the end of April), and by that point I more than saw the largeness of what had happened. I hadn't just lost my job. I'd gotten tossed off the film-critic train. It's the only train I wanted to ride, but I wasn't sure if I would ever get back on.

Over those next three months, I proved to myself that I could compartmentalize by doing some urgent writing, like my riff on the re-issue of *Lawrence of Arabia* ("Perhaps it took an English director, a *civilized* director, to make the ultimate desert movie, to glimpse such panoramic drama in the visible absence of society"). In February, for my 30th birthday, I decided to throw a party—the first time I had ever put one together—and considering how nervous I was that no one would show up, it worked out well. The night crested into a buzzing hive of party energy, and I noticed at one point that there were several dozen people I didn't know, a sign of the six degrees of separation in the Boston arts journalism–meets–punk club community. To me, though, the most indelible event of the evening happened before the party even began. I was all set up and ready to go, the living room cleared, my pop-meets-hip-hop party tapes (Run-DMC, "Major Tom," Pet Shop Boys, Public Enemy, "Smooth Criminal") meticulously chosen and recorded, and, of course, no one began to arrive for well over an hour. I had nothing to do, so I figured I would finally check out a videotape that someone had given me of an odd-sounding little undergroundish movie that was only 43 minutes long. It was called *Superstar: The Karen Carpenter Story*, and it was made entirely with Barbie dolls, which sounded like the definition of an overly cheeky stunt.

I put the VHS tape on and quickly forget about my party, because I was transported. Yes, the characters were dolls, but the film was written and shot in a remarkable simulation of a live-action disease-of-the-week TV biopic. It told the story—with teasing candor—of Karen Carpenter's anorexia, which it presented not just as an "eating disorder" but as what it was: an addiction. The story was horrifying, a real descent, yet the way the movie juxtaposed it with the music of the Carpenters reminded me of *Blue Velvet*. The whole decaying-American-doll premise of *Superstar* seemed a postmodern soufflé of kitsch semiotics, yet I could see that the person who made it, Todd Haynes, was breathtakingly sincere, and it was clear that he was as much of a fan of the Carpenters as I was—that he took in the full dark-honey swoon of Karen Carpenter's voice. In the climactic scene, Karen passed from anorexia to bulimia, drinking down two containers of ipecac (shown from her guzzling-the-bottle POV), accompanied by a dreamy-nightmare blur of Carpenters songs that made me feel like I was inside Karen Carpenter's head. The movie ended and I thought, "That's the greatest film about addiction I've ever seen." It showed you what addiction was, not just a bad habit but a belief system, an alternate existence.

Still shell-shocked at having been cut loose from the *Phoenix*, I made two hapless attempts to break into the New York media world, both of which did little more than take my ego down a notch. The fledgling upscale weekly *7 Days* needed a film critic, and when the editor, Adam Moss, ignored my inquiry and chose Richard T. Jameson, a writer based in Seattle who knew a lot about movies but wrote about them in the most dusty, rambling folksy-boomer style imaginable, I thought: Man, this editor truly hates my stuff! (I found out through channels: He did.) I also landed a lunch with the arts editor of *Vogue*, James Truman, who was part of the first battalion in the new British blitzkrieg of Manhattan media. Over sushi, we came up with a column idea for me to do: about how villains in the movies were becoming more and more extreme. I wrote the column and sent it to him, and he sent back two pages of single-spaced typed editor's notes that were longer than the original piece, so I rewrote the column and sent it back, and he sent me *another* single-spaced epic, so I rewrote it again (at which point I thought the piece was actually pretty good), and then I heard nothing, and more nothing, until I finally called *Vogue* and learned that I was getting a kill fee. It seemed the New York magazine world did not want me.

I began to ponder a Plan B, and about the only one I could come up with was to go to bartending school. It would have been a self-destructive, path-to-nowhere mistake, but I spent the next six months with that plan lodged in the back of my mind. In what turned out to be a stroke of dark karma, though, I also spent the next six months living out a movie I had long fantasized about starring in. It was my *Last Tango*, my *9½ Weeks*, my *Basic Instinct*, my *Fifty Shades of Grey*. As it turns out, it could not have happened at a better time. Decadence and work don't mix well, but with nothing to do (and as I saw it, possibly no future), this was the perfect moment for me to dive off the cliff of an affair that consisted of sex and cocaine and absolutely nothing else. It was my six-month Lost Weekend, and for a while it made staring into the abyss look like fun.

I'm not exaggerating when I say that 10 seconds after being introduced to Valerie, a friend of one of my ex-flames, I knew that our relationship would be different from anything I had experienced. She was short and slender, her tangle of jet-black hair streaked with magenta, and she talked, for some reason, in the faux-aristocratic purr of a Hollywood starlet of the '30s—a borderline ludicrous affectation I assumed she would soon drop, but never did. It was the voice equivalent of a retro thrift-shop wardrobe, and it made her seem like a *character* in a way that didn't draw me at all. What drew me is the way she fixed her heavily mascara'd eyes on mine and just... *stared*, resting her gaze as if she were Carole Lombard and had found her Clark Gable. I would have been even more flattered if her adoring look hadn't come out of nowhere and wasn't so completely incongruous with... every other moment of my life. I had no illusions that I was attractive enough to merit this level of instant come-on (most women looked right past me, regarding me as a standard specimen of *dorkus Americanus*). But as we began to converse (about movies, of course), and her raccoon-eyed laser beams maintained that high sparkle of intensity, I realized that Valerie had already *decided* something.

She lived in Providence, Rhode Island (about an hour away), and we made a date for the following week. I met her for a drink at the Rat, the vintage '80s rock dive (it was the CBGB of Boston), where I had spent many an evening of discordant semi-musical diversion and desultory semi-human contact. Only now, on a Wednesday at 7:00 p.m., the upstairs bar was empty. It was just me and—yes, there she was!—Valerie, entering the place like a punk waif channeling Jean Harlow, the two of us drawn together by what already felt like an obsession, which made the pretense of small talk seem almost ludicrously beside the point. We left after 15 minutes, drove to my place, and began our torrid exertions the moment we got inside.

Valerie, I soon learned, liked to explain things. She saw sex as a drug, pure and simple, and thought that was the most enlightened way to view it. She was a weekend cocaine addict. And she was an ardent sadomasochist— a submissive who got off on being spanked, but was only too eager to be used in any way that I deemed fit. "As soon as I saw you," she said in her weirdly breathy faux-Brahmin way, "I could tell that you had it."

"Had what?" I said.

"The *desire*! That whole fucked-up sex thing."

I figured I'd gone too far to turn back, and didn't want to anyway. "Yeah," I said. "I guess I do." And I did. "I've just never known what to do with it."

"Well," she said with a smile, making me see for the first time, beneath the stylized artifice of her personality, that she was rather pretty, and also a few years older than I was. "Now you do."

It already felt like I was caught in some drama of kinky compulsion, and that's because Valerie, like so many devotees of S&M, approached pleasure in a way that was reckless but hermetic, *organized* and sealed off from the world. She was proposing that the two of us form a kind of playpen for adults, a place that would be liberating yet comforting because it said, "You don't have to worry about anything. Everything you need is here." It was the drugs that sealed that feeling.

I had done coke now and then throughout the '80s, occasionally buying a quarter of a gram myself, and it was a drug I made a point of using sparingly, because I knew how much I loved it. With Valerie, I let myself go. Each week, she drove in from Providence early on Friday evening and took out her small tinted vial, and we would do a few lines to get started, and then just *go go go* all weekend, staying up most of the two nights, doing the nastiest things we could think of.

I knew I reveled in cocaine because, despite my basic well-being, I lived with an underlying passivity that was folded into my nature; that's why I liked spending my life watching movies. Yet the mainstreaming of psychotropic drugs—the Prozac era, which was only just kicking in— was something that I considered to be an insidious corporate conspiracy, and still do. Personally, I knew I was self-medicating, but the way I saw it, I wasn't altering my personality *permanently*. That struck me as pure sinister *1984*. The glory of cocaine is that it knocked away the cobwebs of depression that were floating around in any civilized person's emotional ecosystem. It allowed the euphoria you carried around inside you to flourish, and then returned you to earth. (The crash, of course, could kill you. It was like the beginning of a death cycle.)

With Valerie, I experienced raw excitement and irresponsibility elevated to bliss. Each weekend, she and I would sit around in my darkened apartment, on my terrible furniture, doing lines (the adrenalizing effect of which I balanced out with sips of fresh-from-the-freezer Stoli vodka), working our way through my hundreds of albums, with sex breaking up the evening like a theater performance that arrived in isolated acts. Valerie's basic drill was to get spanked, and as the one who did the spanking, I felt utterly silly at first, as though I was playing the headmaster in some cheesy '20s stag film. I loved the notion of breaking boundaries, but the solemn ritualized *strictness* of S&M wasn't really in my blood. Yet corporal punishment, the more brutal the better, didn't just turn Valerie on—it carried her away—and the desire to jolt her into that faraway place, and to join her there, stoked my lust too. The turn-on was experiencing the full ferocity of her desire—a movie that I was at once watching, performing in, and living in. She liked other things, like getting dripped with molten candle wax, and once I was high enough, I entered her fantasy, role-playing with a dominance that began as acting and became real. It was a catharsis of badness—at last, the life-as-porn freedom zone I had longed for. Apart from sex and drugs, though, my alliance with Valerie was chatty but cold. There was no love in the room. We'd agreed to use each other.

Between weekends, I recovered, stayed away from cocaine, and kept on drinking. What kept me away from the coke was that I tended to wake up after our benders with phrases like "*I hate myself and want to die"* ricocheting around in my head. I knew in some part of my brain that I didn't truly feel that way (I never had those thoughts at any other time), but then, this was why the crash from cocaine could kill you.

I landed a handful of local freelance assignments, and I went to every movie that came out, including two that defined the summer. When I saw the opening-day crowds for Tim Burton's *Batman*, with half the kids already wearing their Batman T-shirts, I got a wave of *Star Wars* déjà vu, and it was jolting: Somehow, Hollywood had figured out a way to pump up the volume on marketing yet *another* couple of notches. It was now turned up to 11. This might not have seemed so depressing if *Batman* had been better, but though I was entertained by Jack Nicholson's demonic camping and the occasional gothic Wagnerian swooping-through-the-urban-canyons camera dive, I thought that the movie, at heart, was trash. In hindsight, the franchise era was all there: the overbright lighting of sets that looked like sets, the hero who felt like a stand-in (Michael Keaton had a suave first scene and then got lost), and, most of all, the feeling that nothing—*nothing!*—was at stake. *Batman* was hailed as a quasi-outré Burton crossover, but the movie had way too little Burton for my taste. It should have been called *The Dark McKnight*.

But then there was *sex, lies, and videotape*, which opened a little over a month later. On the Saturday afternoon I went, there was a major crowd, only this one radiated a healthy power. They had come to see something *new*, and you could tell that they wanted it and needed it. As did I. The film had a saturnine playfulness that tapped the audience's voyeurism. It was about *secrets*—the secrets of sex—and it seemed to nod toward a new era in which men and woman would now be viewed as occupying vastly different spheres of expectation and experience. That's what the audience was alive to.

Watching *sex, lies, and videotape*, I realized that my own sordid exploits with Valerie had started to enhance the way I watched certain movies. So many films were based on elements of vicarious fantasy: the gangster living the life, the gods-at-play hedonism of beautiful people fucking other beautiful people, the whole lure of the kinky and the forbidden and the damned. I now felt like I was on the other side of all that, that I had passed through the looking glass of pleasure. I never again had to watch a scene of crazy horny ecstasy and think, in my hidden heart,

"Hmmmm, I wish I could try that." Now I knew what it was to smash those boundaries.

But I was starting to risk breaking my own self. After close to six months, the coke high wasn't as high—more and more, it was just manic. I knew I'd done my version of hitting bottom on the night I suddenly got the idea, at around 4:30 a.m., that Valerie and I should drive to her place in Providence (she was talking about some leather outfit she had there that I suddenly *had* to see her in), and we did, with me at the wheel, higher than a kite, averaging around 90 miles an hour on the freeway. That we weren't stopped by the cops was a stroke of luck, but of course the really fortunate thing is that we made it there in one piece. When we arrived, I saw why Valerie had never invited me to her apartment: The place looked like it hadn't been cleaned in a year, and it smelled as if it was drenched in cat piss. I thought: "My functional-cocaine-addict fuck buddy is a semi-derelict of dysfunction." After seeing her in the leather outfit (and, tellingly, being way too high to fuck), I then drove myself *back*, this time at the relatively sedate speed of 80 miles an hour, and when I got home, now coming down from the coke, I realized that I was, in my thoughtless way, courting destruction. I needed an intervention, a savior, a new road.

I got the rumblings of one just about a week later.

The phone rang.

"Hi, is this Owen?" the voice said, speaking the words with a certain agitated quickness.

"Yes, it is."

"My name is Jeff Jarvis. I'm starting a magazine called *Entertainment Weekly*."

CHAPTER 11

PRETTY WOMAN AND ITS DISCONTENTS

It seemed a real "Isn't it ironic?" coincidence—or, just maybe, a sign. *Maybe this was meant to be.* When I ambled into Jeff Jarvis' office in the Time & Life building, walking over to his desk to shake hands, the first thing I noticed, apart from the fact that Jarvis was a total visual oxymoron (he looked like a neatly groomed computer scientist who had somehow stolen Abraham Lincoln's beard), was a piece of paper on his desk, half-buried under a pile of other papers. It was a photocopy of Flicks in a Flash, the movie-rating graph introduced the year before by Peter Kadzis, the editor who had fired me. I knew its being there had no connection to me, because I didn't send it, and the page was all marked up with light-blue highlighter. Jarvis, it was clear, had gotten hold of Flicks in a Flash because he was *studying* it. I'd learn, soon enough, that that's where he lifted the idea for Critical Mass. The irony was 200 proof: The most catchy, reductive, dumbing-down-the-world gimmick in all of *Entertainment Weekly* was ripped off...from *The Boston Phoenix*.

Jeff, as I'd noticed on the phone, spoke very quickly—compulsively fast, rushing to the ends of his sentences as if he was taking part in a speed-talking contest. It was his way of demonstrating how smart he was. The other person in the room, who introduced himself as *Entertainment Weekly*'s film editor, also struck me as an oxymoron, because I associated words like "film editor" with stringbean geeks like myself, and Peter Hauck was a blondish giant of a fellow, with an aging bodybuilder's physique and the moustache of a '70s porn star.

The two wasted no time letting me know that they liked the clips I'd sent, and given that I didn't have the job yet, they were surprisingly fixated on whether I was even available. (Yes, I was available. To put it mildly.) Jeff wanted to know if I would have any problem assigning letter grades to movies. I said no, I'd basically done a version of that at the *Phoenix*, where the capsule section included star ratings. We wound up focusing on what it would be like to write shorter reviews than I was used to. I put it to them like this: "If you already know how to write a long review, one that has insight, it's no trick to write a shorter one." Then Peter Hauck said: "The question is, can you make that shorter review every bit as rich as the long one?" I replied, "I think I can," but my real reaction was to do an inner cartwheel. "Amazing," I thought. "They actually want reviews that are...rich." I liked the sound of that word. It was not dumb; it was resonant.

The last thing Jarvis said, almost as an afterthought—but it was like the last thing you say in a therapy session that winds up being the most significant thing uttered all hour—was that he'd been impressed by my review of *Three Men and a Baby*. He said, "I just really, really liked that piece." I said, "Thanks, I had fun with that one," but on the way out I was shaking my head at the irony. I'd tried to send Jarvis my most heady, eloquent, *epic* reviews; I'd also included a few short throwaways to show him my range. My sarcastic dismissal of *Three Men and a Baby*—a high-concept Hollywood remake of a mediocre French farce—was one of those. I did vaudeville riffs on its utter predictability and landed with a vaudeville riff on Ted Danson's hair ("Is it a weave job or the result of five hours' daily blow-drying? A small turtle could live in there"). But Jarvis, the former TV critic of *People* magazine, was looking for someone who had mastered the trick of responsible whiplash snideness.

I left the interview with good vibes, but Jarvis kept me hanging for over a month. During that time, I continued my now-bordering-on-joyless bacchanals with Valerie (just because I needed an intervention didn't mean I was about to give myself one), I shot a lot of pool, and I attempted to figure out what *Entertainment Weekly* was going to be, based on the ad campaign for it that I'd begun to see popping up in places like *New York* magazine. The campaign was so nerdishly enthusiastic it induced a quiver of embarrassment. It announced, with different setups (one said, "Just because you won the rat race doesn't mean you're not a rat"), that the greed decade was over, and that the time had come to obey a new mantra: "Kick Back, Chill Out, Hang Loose, Have Fun." My reaction was that this sounded like a magazine that was going to be put out by *SNL*'s Wild and Crazy Guys. ("Do you... *swing*? Do you enjoy the *kicking back* and *hanging loose*?") The first time I laid eyes on that ad, I almost gagged. But the more I thought about it, the more I realized that there was a method to its cluelessness. The ad campaign, like *Entertainment Weekly* itself, was about the launch of not just a new magazine but a new state of mind. It announced the arrival of Couch Potato Nation. And that was more than a sales pitch. My reaction was to think: "I get what they're doing. The counterculture is over. Punk and new wave are over. The glitzy huffing and puffing of the '80s are over. Bohemia is over. *Everything* is over. It's all been eaten by The System. What is there left to do but sit around and be... entertained?"

In the end, I approved (sort of), but of course I was also *desperate to land the fucking job*. I wanted it, needed it, prayed for it. I got on my knees, every night, and begged God to make me His bitch. I felt as if this was the fork in the road of my life. And maybe it was. When Jarvis finally called me, the day before Thanksgiving, and said that he'd like me to be *Entertainment Weekly*'s film critic, I knew that I no longer had the right to complain about anything. (Not that that would stop me.) I'd had the best job in the world, then I lost it through my own volition, and then, seven months later, on the week my Massachusetts unemployment checks were due to run out, I landed the dream version of that job. I realized from that moment that any issue I would have to deal with, short of a critical health crisis, no longer amounted to a hill of beans.

I arrived in New York City on Dec. 1, 1989, the kickoff to the last month of the 1980s. Personally, I was more than ready to let the '80s go. I had no hatred of money, but the new mood of wealth fetishism did seem to be sucking up everything in its path. What eight years of Reagan delivered wasn't so much the triumph of right-wing politics as the ultimate ascension of the advertising culture, with Reagan himself as the spokesmodel for his own presidency. The sizzle was becoming the steak. And what was the blockbuster mentality but Hollywood's own version of *follow the money*? When I moved to New York, my turning of the page—on my sexually desperate twenties, on my life as an alt-weekly critic—aligned almost spiritually with the feeling that "morning in America" was played out, and that the dawn of something more honest just had to be on the horizon. In movies, at least, that's exactly what happened.

On that first afternoon, I went to my first screening in my new capacity as *EW*'s critic. It was for *The War of the Roses*, and it was being held at Magno, a singularly perverse New York institution: It's the most actively used screening room in Manhattan, yet it's a terrible place to watch a movie, with a screen that sits so low that despite the slightly banked seating, the sightlines almost guarantee you'll be tilting your head at some point to see around the person in front of you. After a few minutes, Rex Reed came into the room, in his Blanche DuBois-with-a-hemorrhoid way, whining about the holiday movies that he was already being subjected to ("Did you *see* that piece of swill?"), and I thought: Rex Reed! The television-age Addison DeWitt! A once powerful and now diminished icon, to be sure, but today, for the first time... he is my colleague! I went to a second screening early that evening, this one for *Leatherface: The Texas Chainsaw Massacre III*, and a few minutes before the movie began, who should come barreling down the aisle of the cruddy theater we were sitting in but Al Goldstein, the rumpled king of New York smut, looking like a short, white-bearded Jewish Teddy bear in a spiked leather jacket. I wasn't a reader of *Screw* magazine, but on my stray visits to Manhattan, I'd already become a casual fan of *Midnight Blue*, Goldstein's salaciously warped Friday-night public-access cable show, which was the most unhinged hour of TV mishegas I'd encountered since *The Ghoul*. Each week, Goldstein did a "Fuck you!" into the camera, viciously dissing his ex-wives or some gadget from the Hammacher Schlemmer catalogue that failed to work, and before the Internet there was almost nothing you could find to match this hilariously boiling monologue of off-the-cuff venom. Watching Goldstein saunter into that *Chainsaw* screening, I thought: If Rex Reed is my new colleague, Al Goldstein is now my fellow New York trash-movie maven! I had arrived.

That night, I wanted to celebrate, but me being me, I also wanted to hang back and meditate, to wander the halls, to drink in the reality of my good fortune. So instead of making a plan with one of my handful of New York friends, I left the company apartment on W. 57th St. that Time Inc. was letting me stay in for a month and went out solo to have a martini, a drink I'd only recently discovered, but one that would figure prominently in my life over the next decade. Or two. Or three. (They're hard to give up.)

I found a comfortable-looking fake Irish bar on Eighth Ave., where I got agreeably stoned on gin, and then, as I transitioned to a couple of glasses of wine, I began to think about my father, now considering him through the lens of the career I was about to try to launch. In the close-up clarity of my alcohol haze, I took a sci-fi glide right into my father's head, and what I saw, swimming around there, was not just his hostility but the intense anxiety that I now realized had ruled him. I saw how the shit way he'd treated me was driven by fear. At bottom, he was too frightened to connect with anyone around him. And having this first moment of total empathy, *ever*, for him, I began to weep—not quietly but *convulsively*, as if volts of electroshock were shooting through me. In that moment of catharsis, which made everyone in the bar turn and stare like I was some blubbering derelict, I realized that the whole problem with my father was his lack of faith (in every sense of the word), and that the only way for me to nail my new job was to do it with the faith that he never had. It was my sloshed, exhibitionistic, est-therapy way of saying: Thanks, Dad! In a strange sort of do-the-opposite-of-what-I-do way, he had shown me the path.

The sleek new offices of *Entertainment Weekly* were a few blocks from the Time & Life building, and that was done by design: Jarvis wanted the magazine to be away from corporate central, so that it would have a different feel—more designer, less Time Inc. cookie-cutter. When I arrived on the 28th floor and saw that most of us on staff had our own offices with doors we could close, creating the kind of privacy zone I craved, I strolled around like I was walking on air, but the place also made me nervous, because I thought: The potential to fuck up here is major. What had happened to me at the *Phoenix* boiled down to my being too naive to play office politics because I was too arrogant to think I needed to know what office politics was. Getting fired was my crash course; I would not let it happen again. Yet how that would translate into behavior remained vague. In those first days, I worked hard to be "nice" to everyone, but my basic personality is shoot-from-the-hip and not all that social. I found it hard to conceal my daily irritation at a feature writer two doors down from me named Ned, who had come from *People* magazine and who made a point, every time I walked through the office's glass doors, of assaulting me with a big, grinning, ever-so-slightly assholically condescending *"Whadja see?"* As if the fact that I was a film critic meant that I was this... *character*, that I never, ever went out to go to the bank or grab a bite or meet with someone from a studio: I *must* be coming from a movie! My office overlooked W. 53rd St. (years later, I was able to stare down and watch people getting shot out of cannons during tapings of *Late Show With David Letterman*), and the person who had the office across from mine was a curly-haired young writer named Jess Cagle, also from *People*, who served up shrewd observation with a quizzical mockery that I mostly appreciated.

What was happening is that *Entertainment Weekly* was a hugely expensive—and risky—startup, with a lot of media wags licking their chops over its predicted demise (*Spy* magazine had already christened it "the doomed *Entertainment Weekly*"), and the mood around the office was a visibly nervous esprit de corps. We'd been thrown together like kids at summer camp, and the question that hovered over all of us was: Would the magazine be a leaky lifeboat or a powerful ocean liner? Strange as it now seems, the idea that one general-interest magazine could, and should, cover every single form of pop culture struck many observers as a bad and even bizarre idea. It cut against the specialized aesthetic people were used to from *Rolling Stone, Creem, TV Guide, Premiere*, and a hundred more obscure fanzines. (The real truth, though, is that *Rolling Stone* helped to pioneer the concept of *EW* back in the '70s, when it began to feature movie stars, stand-up comedians, and other subjects just as avidly as it did music.) I felt like I was in a different position from most, because I was coming from having no job, and therefore I had nothing to lose. But that was just my defensive short-term logic. Now that I'd landed the gig at *Entertainment Weekly*, I had a great deal to lose.

When I met my two fellow critics on the magazine, I could tell how private and anxious both of them were. Ken Tucker, the TV critic, had left a solid job at *The Philadelphia Inquirer*, although I knew his name from my college years—to me, he was still part of the elite brigade of

Rolling Stone music writers that included Cameron Crowe, Ken Emerson, Stephen Holden, and Charles M. Young. I met Ken the first day I was there, and he struck me as a recessive professor: amiable and a bit diffident, almost invisibly droll, a more avid listener than talker. We had more common interests than we did chemistry. (That's how it would stay.) Greg Sandow, the music critic, was a real song-of-himself eccentric. His background was in classical music, and he'd decided to become a pop-music writer in a topsy-turvy time-warp way: He wrote about everything from Prince to Journey as if it were *new* to him—and indeed, most of it was. Greg, with flowing gray hair and a jutting chin, looked like a "longhair" musician from the 19th century, and the first time that he, Ken, and I sat around together (it was in my office), I realized that the three of us—Sandow the slumming highbrow, Tucker the acerbic WASP minimalist, and me the comparatively youngish downbeat whippersnapper—added up to Jeff Jarvis' deeply unglamorous idea of a superstar backfield of pop-culture critics. "I'm going to make you *stahs*," Jarvis joked, as if he were some '50s agent from Brooklyn, but what he meant was: Tucker, Sandow, and I were projections of his dweeb-pest vision of what a critic should be. After working inside the machine of *People*, Jarvis was eager to push buttons. He was the last man in America who still wore Wallabees, but he was the kind of *echt*-nerd who fancied himself a closet rebel. As a TV critic, he took pride in the fact that he despised *thirtysomething*; he told me that he thought Steven Spielberg was a hack. He wanted the critics at *EW* to be gadflies, to be free to stir up trouble, and he knew—though he wasn't telling us—how much of a challenge that was going to be for the suits at Time Inc.

I went to a few screenings with my new office mates, and I quickly learned that this was *not* the most fun way to see a movie, due to the nattering annoyance of the entertainment media–meets–movieland politics one had to deal with. I got introduced to all this the first time I went to a screening with the other members of the film section. It was for *Blaze*, Ron Shelton's drama about the tempestuous relationship between the stripper Blaze Starr and the '40s and '50s governor of Louisiana, Earl Long. The two were played by Lolita Davidovich and Paul Newman, and the material sounded "juicy," but most of the movie just sat there, with Newman phoning in a rare bad histrionic-peacock performance.

None of us cared much for it, but when we got outside the theater, the first thing that Peter Hauck said was, "I don't think it's going to do very well," and a writer named Melina piped up with a feisty, "I don't either," and now that I thought about it, I guess I didn't think the film would do well myself. I instantly grasped—and accepted—that the editors and feature writers of *Entertainment Weekly* were obligated to try to figure out which movies would be hits and which wouldn't be. But what struck me about the conversation is the degree to which the box-office assessment *became*, in effect, the judgment—or, at least, got all gummed up with it. The tone was very high school, very in-crowd: *I didn't like this movie, and I bet no else is going to either!* (I flashed on all the good movies that had been box-office failures. As I would during these dialogues for years to come.) We each had our own opinion of *Blaze*, but there was another *presence* in the conversation, unseen yet powerful, like the Wizard of Oz—it was the nearly compulsive interest in whether the movie would be *popular*, and how that influenced what everyone would say, like a magnet that could bend opinion. It was my introduction to a language I would ultimately have to know how to speak with fluent flippancy: the metaphysics of *EW* box-office-tea-leaves bullshit.

I'd been hunting for an apartment, but when I emerged from the subway at 7th Ave. and W. 12th St. and began to stroll south in the glowing January sun, I knew, at that moment, that this was home, that *this* was the place I was going to live. Not just in the West Village but near Sheridan Square, home of the sawdust-floor bar Chumley's, the Ridiculous Theatrical Company, and the legendary gay-liberation riot site the Stonewall Inn. It wasn't just a gay neighborhood anymore, but forty years of gay liberation had mellowed the area to a supremely festive laidback vitality. It's the one part of the Village that truly felt to me like a *village*, and when I found a high-ceilinged one-bedroom apartment on Barrow St., right above a grandly cavernous bar on the corner of W. 4th, I felt, after six years in the Boston roach motel, that everyday life was looking like a mirage.

As it turned out, I now lived right around the corner from James Truman, my nemesis of over-editing from *Vogue*, who was just starting his ascension at Condé Nast. He and I passed each other on the sidewalk about once a month, but he never acknowledged my presence, so I never acknowledged his. My favorite ritual was stopping with my *New York Post* each morning to eat at the Bagel, a breakfast place the size of a tiny studio apartment (the entire "kitchen" was tucked inside the front window), where everything you could order—omelettes, pancakes, grits— was dunked in butter and tasted like the most heavenly cholesterol bomb of your most scrumptious 1950s fantasy. How seductively unhealthy was the food? I learned, after a time, that the Bagel played a small role in movie history: It was the place where Robert De Niro ate every single day to bulk up for *Raging Bull.* So this was legendary grease.

My first review for *Entertainment Weekly* was of *Men Don't Leave*, an ambitious Jessica Lange weeper that I fell for, perhaps a bit too much, getting a little enthused about my own enthusiasm. Directed by Paul Brickman, the *Risky Business* screenwriter, it was a rare honest tearjerker, but I poured on the affection for it like organic maple syrup ("Brickman gazes at his characters with a mixture of compassion and pure delight— even when their hearts are breaking, they tickle him"), and I don't think I was wrong, but I was still trying too hard. My first grade for *EW* turned out to be a straight A. What an upbeat, movie-loving guy! But it didn't stay that way for long.

On a Monday night in March, I went off to a screening of a movie I had to return to the office that night to review, filling up a lead space of just 375 words. (It was shorter than my review of *Three Men and a Baby*.) The film was called *Pretty Woman*, and it was an early entry in the still not completely official revival of the Hollywood screwball comedy—that wisecracking romantic form, by and large uncommercial since the '50s, that back in the studio-system days had given us some of the jauntiest, most casually enchanting big-screen love stories ever made. The genre had been slingshot back into orbit in the summer of 1989 with *When Harry Met Sally*, a comedy I sat through with a fair degree of hostility, because I experienced it as the insidiously watchable version of a fake Woody Allen movie. It was *Annie Hall: The Sitcom*—or, more precisely, *Annie Hall* meets Sam and Diane from *Cheers*, with Billy Crystal and Meg Ryan mismatched in such a perfectly diagrammed "*Look!! Pastrami on white really works!*" sort of way that it drove me a little nuts. I was far from a classic-old-movie nut, but I still didn't like to see the worm of network television burrowing its way into the magical landscape of Gable and Colbert.

About 20 minutes into *Pretty Woman*, when I realized it was going to be another version of what I thought of as plastic screwball, I turned on it. I had no problem with the "sexist" premise: a rich guy hires a hooker because he's lonely and wants someone to spend time with. But I had little response to the interplay between Julia Roberts and Richard Gere, and when I returned to the office, I let fly with invective. What I'd love to be able to say now is that *Pretty Woman* was a bad movie, and that in issue #6 of *Entertainment Weekly* I nailed what was wrong with it, and what a dogged fearless straight-shooter of a critic I was!

But that's not really what happened. My review was churlish and sniping and not very well written. The dazzle of Julia Roberts' wide-screen smile wasn't lost on me, but her antic sweetness was (although two years before at the *Phoenix*, I'd raved about her in *Mystic Pizza*), and my lukewarm response turned to angry ice in the scenes set at a Rodeo Drive boutique, where Julia is humiliated and then, armed with a credit card, returns for her indulgently vengeful Cinderella-goes-shopping spree. I watched that scene and thought: Bad! Corrupt! The values of the 1980s! Returning from the grave! Reeling in outrage, I slapped *Pretty Woman* with a grade of D.

I should have left my high horse in Boston. There was exactly one line of insight in my review, and that was when I said: "Yet the movie may catch on. With its tough-hooker heroine, it can work as a feminist version of an upscale-princess fantasy." If I'd written a compelling piece, I would have fleshed out that theme with greater flair, with more understanding of *why* that fantasy might speak to empowered women. For as it happened, *Pretty Woman* became not just a smash hit but the rare film that marked a paradigm shift in American life. It helped to usher in the rise of princess feminism: a return to the primal notion that the way women look—the clothes, the cosmetics, the high heels, the tattoos, you name it—can operate as an uncompromising enhancement of their intelligence and spiritual power. If you put it that way, it can still sound like a radical notion—or, in the eyes of some (like the corporate-media conspiracy theorist Susan Faludi, author of *Backlash*), a retrograde one. Yet

Sex and the City helped massage it into respectability, and *Pretty Woman* was close to being its genesis.

But okay. I panned the movie, and it became huge. So what? So this: The executives at Time Inc. wanted my head.

It's a lucky thing I didn't learn until later that my nickname, on Time Inc.'s 34th floor, became Owen "He Must Be Fired." Yet little by little, the spirit of that antipathy came trickling down. It wasn't just about me, either: The whole magazine was perceived as being too snobbish, too elite, even—God forbid—too "downtown" and "highbrow." The alarm bells went off from the first issue, which featured a cover image of k.d. lang smirking into the camera, looking not like a luscious entertainment babe—no pretty woman this!—but like the return of Julian Lennon. In terms of what k.d. lang embodied as an entertainer, she was a perfect choice for the debut issue of *EW*: a symbol of the new rise of country music, and also a symbol of how the new pop culture was different from the old. But to the Time Inc. brass, the magazine's editors had surveyed the entire galaxy of pop and movie stardom and decided to symbolize their mission by going with...an unknown brush-cut lesbian with razory cheekbones. The cover set off an instant mainstream-vs.-edge culture war, one that *EW*, to this day, has never shaken off. That helped to lend my trashing of *Pretty Woman* an aura of controversy, and as I realized before long, that review quickly came to define what people thought about me. Wherever I went, I was "the guy who panned *Pretty Woman*." It became a Symbol Of My Integrity. In general, there was a lot of hostility toward the movie (and still is), much of it for the wrong reasons—it glorified a woman playing a hooker! it fueled "objectification"—and so people welcomed my debunking of it. But more than that, they welcomed the notion that a wanna-be showbiz bible like *EW* would pan it. *Pretty Woman* became the cornerstone of my brand before I even had one.

I guess I wasn't all that nervous about it, because exactly one week later, I wrote three reviews—of *Teenage Mutant Ninja Turtles*, the Dana Carvey comedy *Opportunity Knocks*, and a pair of lambada movies, *Lambada* and *The Forbidden Dance*—and handed every one of those films a grade of F. I had not, to put it mildly, mastered the nuances of the grading system. The F, make no mistake, is a wonderful grade to give:

It attracts readers like a heat-seeking missile, and coming at the end of a review, it's like a little exclamation point of hate. But while it's not as if four Fs in a single issue wasn't allowed, there was a lack of perspective there. To me, the F means, and always has: *could not possibly be more excruciating to sit through*. I was bored by *Teenage Mutant Ninja Turtles* ("They're certainly fun to look at. They would have been even more fun had someone bothered to give them personalities"), but before handing it the ultimate damning grade, I should have taken into account a *little* bit that it was action fodder for 4-year-olds.

The editors at Time Inc. didn't like me or the other critics; they didn't like the k.d. lang cover; they didn't like *EW*'s Tinkertoy version of a modular design; they didn't like the magazine, period. But they weren't the only ones. Industry analysts and advertisers hated the magazine. At one point, a couple of people from the publishing side took Jeff Jarvis to lunch along with a prominent advertiser, and after Jeff explained with breathless enthusiasm that he was planning to run business articles in *EW* just like the ones they did in *Fortune*, the advertiser leaned over and said, "I don't think you understand the problem, Jeff. Your baby is *ugly*." It was. That's why the readers didn't like it either. And the shit all came raining down after issue #13.

On a sunny day in May, the magazine's editors, along with a handful of writers, were summoned to a meeting in the Time & Life building with the company's three editorial top dogs. We had no idea what it was about. During the minutes of meet and greet, I noticed there was a bar, and though I never drank during the day, I was still so mindlessly exuberant about my new circumstances that I thought, *Why not! This looks like fun! I'll have myself a bloody Mary!* The trio of Time bosses all gathered around me, and I thought they were just being nice, but really they were checking me out, like mafiosi. They wanted to know, up close and personal: Who *is* this critic loser who's been ruining our investment?

We all sat down at a circular table that sprawled around the conference room, and Jason McManus, the editorial director, said in his dry avuncular way, "Let's not waste any time; this is a serious lunch," and then, after eyeing the rather fancy-looking hamburger on his plate, he picked up a copy of *EW* and said, "We have a serious problem with this magazine." A chill went through me, as I presume it did through everyone in the room. He explained that *EW* was failing, big time. It was generating terrible newsstand sales, but more than that, it was alienating readers.

"The problem," he said, "is that people aren't connecting to the magazine. It's not a club they want to belong to. It doesn't make them feel good when they hold it in their hands." I had to admit, right there, that McManus *did* nail what bonding with a magazine is all about. And it occurred to me that he might be right.

The other two Time bigwigs spoke their piece. Gil Rogin, who had the rather ominous title of corporate editor, looked like a leathery carp, with a gluttonous gleam and longish salt-and-pepper hair slicked back from his forehead. He was the most sardonic of the three, and he made the point, more harshly than McManus had, that the magazine was simply not "mainstream" enough. (I thought to myself: *Really?* We're covering everything that's out there.) Rogin took pains to let us know that he *did* get pop culture, recalling a highway drive during which he felt compelled to pull over to the side of the road because it was the first time he'd ever heard Peaches & Herb's "Reunited," and he knew that he was witnessing the rebirth of soul music. I found the fact that he told us that a little pathetic, and also a little touching. Joan Feeney, the *EW* editor who was Jarvis' number two (whenever she passed two of the critics talking in the hallways, she made a point of saying, in a '50s-robot drone voice, "*critical mass*"), wound up posing the key question of the day: "We were *told* to put out a magazine for smart connoisseurs of pop culture. We thought we were doing that. Isn't that what you asked for?"

That's when McManus' second-in-command, Richard Stolley, piped up. Stolley, the founding editor of *People* magazine, was visibly older than the other two, with a crown of grayish hair, but still impressively handsome, and he spoke in a tone of slightly wavery aging authority that conveyed deep power. To me, he seemed like a veteran Republican senator, the sort that even Democrats feel compelled to respect (or did back in the Nixon era). "The problem, Joan," he said, "is that *that* universe isn't large enough to support this magazine." So what exactly does that mean, I thought. Are we now supposed to aim for a bigger, broader, lesser demo?

EW did, in fact, have a major problem, but the problem had been misdiagnosed. In actuality, the magazine wasn't snobby at all. (Jeff Jarvis, who thought *thirtysomething* was too intellectual, hated snobs.) Just about every article and cover story was thoroughly mainstream. But if the magazine wasn't snobby, it wasn't sexy, either. And Jason McManus had put his finger on why: *Entertainment Weekly* was supposed to be a magazine that celebrated pop culture—but it wasn't channeling the *joy* of pop culture. It was too stodgy, too earnestly wonkish; you couldn't feel the joy on its pages. The covers looked like covers of *Popular Mechanics*. And Jarvis, in his critic-centric naïveté, had spread the reviews throughout the book, which actually made the critics too central; it robbed the structure of any flow. The magazine *had* no center. As a basic recipe, *Entertainment Weekly* was close to perfect, but it needed a new chef.

From that point, it was decreed that every one of our pieces would be given an edit from the top, a highly unusual act of micro-managing that meant that each week, I received print-outs of my reviews with notes in the margins written in green felt-tip pen (those came from Gil Rogin) or red felt-tip pen (Richard Stolley). The first week, my lead was a review of *Bird on a Wire*, a godawful Mel Gibson–Goldie Hawn action thriller directed by John Badham, and Rogin must have thought it was *Pretty Woman 2*, because he greeted my trashing ("When a director as talented as Badham reaches this state of empty craftsmanship, who can say whether he's working out of boredom or cynicism? At this point, there may be very little difference") with the comment: "This is a movie that people will enjoy!" I toned it down a bit, but there wasn't really much I could do.

Dick Stolley wasn't as negative, though one of his comments presaged the battle for column inches that I would carry on at *EW* forever. I was writing about one of the biggest movies of the summer, Warren Beatty's Day-Glo version of *Dick Tracy* ("It's as if a '30s gangland melodrama had been colorized by Andy Warhol...Beatty plays Tracy as a charming, polite nothing, a Clark Kent with no Superman inside him. He's such a gentle actor that he all but disappears inside that trench coat"), and Stolley wrote at the bottom: "Quite lively! But still too long. I think our readers are looking for a quicker fix." I thought: *If you find it lively, why is it long?* It seemed almost too perfect a comment to get from the man who invented *People* magazine.

The air was clogged with rumors that *Entertainment Weekly* would fold. Those rumors would float around for years. Yet even before the cavalry was sent in to save the magazine, *EW* had a secret weapon. Time Inc. had been humiliated by the 1983 failure of *TV-Cable Week*, a television guide that lasted all of five months, and then, in 1986, by the implosion of *Picture Week*, a downmarket prototype that managed to consume $30 million without ever getting off the ground. The last thing the company needed was another high-profile debacle, and as I began to suss out just how much money had been spent on the launch of *Entertainment Weekly* (some estimates had it as high as $150 million), I realized that *EW* was a bit like the Vietnam War: The powers behind it *couldn't* get out—they'd already spent too much. They did not want to pull the plug.

It was around six weeks after that meeting that the word came down: Jeff Jarvis was getting yanked out of his job. He would be replaced by... who? No one knew, not even the Time Inc. executives; they just knew that they wanted Jarvis out. He had created and shepherded the magazine (and if you look back at its earliest issues, it's clear that he really *did* forge its DNA), but in their eyes he was not the right person to captain the ship. And history would prove them right.

Before long, we began to hear chatter about the editor who would replace him: Jim Seymore. He was the number-two editor at *People* magazine, and that gave most of us pause. It's true that *Entertainment Weekly* had been spun, like Adam's rib, out of the Picks and Pans section of *People*. Yet from Jarvis on down, all of us who worked there saw *EW* as the anti-*People*. We wanted to make it smart, witty, and elegantly written where *People*, in its buzzily reported way, was written by committee and blandly processed. The obvious worry was that the new leadership represented a takeover of *Entertainment Weekly* by "*People* magazine values."

A few days later, we all gathered in the art department, which doubled as an impromptu staff meeting space, and in walked Jim Seymore. I'm not sure what I expected, but whatever it was, he didn't resemble it. He was soft and stocky, with a friendly round face and thinning hair he wore a bit longish, and the way he was dressed, he looked like a banker out of Dickens on casual Friday. He was 47 years old, and to the youthful staff of *EW*, that made him seem like he'd just stepped off Starship Ancient Generation. There were rumors that he'd pushed Jarvis out, and he started by dousing those. "I want you all to know that I didn't campaign for this job," he said, his voice surprisingly gentle. Though he didn't speak with a Southern accent, he was from Richmond, Virginia, and you could hear it in his courtly cadences. "I do think, though, that we have the chance to do something very exciting. I think this can be the news magazine of entertainment." A seemingly simple idea, but I heard it and thought: "Yes, that's the way to own this field." Seymore continued: "A lot of you are probably worried about your jobs. Don't be. I'm not here to get rid of people. I want to give everyone in this room a chance. After a while, if for some reason we aren't working well together, you may have to move on. But that's not what I'm hoping for." And that, more or less, was the meeting.

The words were reassuring, but more than that, the *tone* was reassuring. It sounded like he meant what he said. But apart from being briefly introduced to him in the hallway afterwards, that was the last contact I'd have with Seymore for some time, because I spent the next few months dutifully writing my reviews and keeping my head down. Seymore, as I later learned, had been advised to get rid of me. But when he became managing editor of *Entertainment Weekly*, he was wily—and independent—enough to look around and see that the guy who panned *Pretty Woman* wasn't the problem. The only people he had a problem with were those who had a problem with him. A few of Seymore's early covers were terrible, because they were—yes—too *People*-ish, and one that sticks out was his whim of iron that the magazine should do a cover on Cybill Shepherd pegged to *Texasville*, the 20-years-after sequel to *The Last Picture Show* that no one in the known universe was hankering for. The notion that Shepherd would be a "hot" subject seemed stuck in the paleolithic era, and there was pushback from the staff. Jim, however, during a cover meeting, announced that we were going ahead with it, at which point my editor, Peter Hauck, yelled "*Sucks!*" from the back of the room. He thought *EW* had just surrendered in the culture war (actually, Seymore just needed to get a few stodgy, old-school bugs out of his system), and that outburst cost him his job.

I was far more political. In October, when Seymore reorganized the magazine, grouping the critics' reviews in the back where they belonged, I sent him an inter-office e-mail telling him that I thought the new structure was "a triumph." I meant it, and he sent me back a surprisingly grateful note of thanks that began, "Owen, my friend..." I realized, at that moment, that he might be a touch insecure. I was eager to keep my job, but he seemed eager for my approval. Not that any of this would stop him from giving me mountains of shit in the future.

Fueled by that note, I continued to write reviews just as I would have for the *Phoenix*, without worry. I dismissed the "beautiful and soft-headed" *Dances with Wolves* as "*Robinson Crusoe* with a tribeful of Fridays," and I despised *Home Alone*, accusing John Hughes of "pulling our strings as though he'd never learned to do anything else." (The original line I'd written was "yanking our chains like a cheap hooker." There are moments when you *do* need editors.) *Home Alone* became the biggest hit of the year, but there were still major movies to get excited about. I loved Tim Burton's *Edward Scissorhands* ("It's no coincidence that this strange and sorrowful boy, this Pinocchio with Freddy Krueger's hands, has grown up with such a saintly demeanor. If he allowed himself the tiniest bit of aggression, he might maim or even kill someone... Edward is, of course, Burton's surreal portrait of himself as an artist: a wounded child converting his private darkness into outlandish pop visions"). And my movie of the year was *Reversal of Fortune*, which turned the tale of Claus von Bülow, the sinister Eurotrash aristocrat accused of attempting to drug his wife to death, and Alan Dershowitz, the publicity-nut lawyer who defended him, into a playful tragedy that presaged the era when tabloid voyeurism would become a sick art form of its own.

"This was the closest the liberal, Jewish Dershowitz was ever going to get to defending Hitler," I wrote. Yet in Jeremy Irons' portrayal of von Bülow, the film lofted into a strange sort of monstrous humanity. "His Claus is the aristocrat as rotting Victorian ghoul, a man so hemmed in by his snobbery, his suppressed rage, his twisted Continental elegance that he has turned the life-denying mannerisms of the uppercrust into a ghastly form of style." By the end, "whether or not Claus did the deed almost doesn't matter. Simply by staying in this hellish marriage, he was committing a civilized, passive form of murder." One of Jim Seymore's executive friends at Time Inc.—I don't remember who—loved my review of *Reversal of Fortune*, and when Jim, late in December, made a point of telling me, I was introduced to one of the essential rules of the critic/editor-in-chief power dynamic: When it comes to evaluating your opinion, editors will, of course, listen to themselves—but not nearly as much as they heed the opinions of others.

In January, I went to see a comedy called *Scenes from a Mall*, starring Woody Allen and Bette Midler, at the Broadway Screening Room, the most comfortable and elegant of Manhattan's Midtown film-screening facilities. It's located on the sixth floor of the Brill Building, the fabled Art Deco song palace where Top 40 composers from Goffin and King to Burt Bacharach knocked out incandescent hits in bare-bones offices (the beautiful gold-leaf elevator doors look like they haven't changed since 1955). The screening room itself evokes everything you think of when you hear the words "screening room": a plush, compact, womblike space with deep chairs. For some reason, I got there 20 minutes early, and when I walked in, I saw that there was just one small figure in the room. It was Pauline Kael.

Despite the pleasantries we'd exchanged at meetings, we hadn't really *talked* for years. But now it was just the two of us, and to my slight surprise, the conversation began to flow. Without ever revealing what she thought of *EW*, she asked me how things were going at the magazine, and I said, with some euphemism, "A little rocky, but good." Then I asked her if she'd seen *The Silence of the Lambs*, which was due to be released later in the month. She said, "Yes. It's Jonathan Demme doing what everyone else is doing—something he doesn't believe in."

I'd loved the film, but more than that, with my *Manhunter* obsession, I couldn't have been more of a "believer" in the artful spell cast by Dr. Lecter, Clarice Starling, and Thomas Harris' shock-theater psychopaths, so I said, "Why don't you think he believes in it?"

"It's very well done," she said. "But he's at a tough point in his career, and this sensational trash came along. He saw an opportunity."

I felt as if Pauline was treating Demme, one of her favorite directors, like a pet critic who had left the fold. "I dunno," I said. "I don't think it's trash just because it's sensational. I think there's an artistry to the material. But I have to ask: Didn't you like Anthony Hopkins?"

I knew Hopkins was not one of Kael's favorites. But still, I thought...

"How can you *like* Anthony Hopkins?" she said. "He's so slimy."

"Well, yes," I replied, "but that's kind of the point." I paused and said, "Do you think it'll be a success for Demme?"

"Are you kidding?" she said. "I think it's going to be the *Psycho* of the '90s." It was, of course. But at the time I wasn't so sure, and later I marveled at the way that Pauline, for all her objections, had grasped that a lot more clearly than me.

She shifted gears. "You look well," she said with a smile. "More handsome than you used to be. Success agrees with you."

It was an extraordinarily gracious thing to say. At that point, a couple of other people filed into the screening room, and we both said that it was good to see each other, and we took our seats a few rows apart. For all our differences, it felt lovely to bask in Pauline's energy again.

It was the last time I ever saw her.

CHAPTER 12

MAKING THE GRADE AT
ENTERTAINMENT WEEKLY

By 1991, the American independent film movement was like an exotic hipster houseplant that was growing one quietly flowering bud at a time. Few, including me, had any notion that it was about to turn the movie world upside down. It would be a year before Quentin Tarantino unveiled his debut feature, the cunningly booby-trapped torture-porn heist thriller *Reservoir Dogs*. It would be three years before the release of Kevin Smith's naughty-boy talkfest *Clerks* and five years before Todd Solondz's squirmy suburban nerdfest *Welcome to the Dollhouse*. The debut features of Paul Thomas Anderson, Darren Aronofsky, Spike Jonze, Mary Harron, Wes Anderson, Alexander Payne, Doug Liman, David O. Russell, Sofia Coppola, and Christopher Nolan were all years away—at that point, barely a gleam in their creators' eyes. Independent film was still standing on the sidelines. But I got to write about a great deal of it for *Entertainment Weekly*, carving out space to review films like the startling drag-queen documentary *Paris Is Burning*, which I called "a tale of dispossessed youth taking refuge in their own narcissism" ("They want to be beautiful and they want to be rich, and the way they see it, the two states have become virtually inseparable") or Sean Penn's *The Indian Runner* ("Penn is trying to get at gritty American 'truths' about love, brutality, and blood ties. Somehow, though, it's all a bit pat. By now, even these stark themes have the ring of movie conventions").

One week, I grabbed the chance to nudge a movie on the extreme margins into the spotlight. It was the first time I realized that my critic's perch might just be a bully pulpit. Todd Haynes, the creator of *Superstar:*

The Karen Carpenter Story (which had stuck in my head ever since I saw it on VHS the night of my 30th birthday party), had made his first movie that was actually going to play in theaters, a cutting-edge queer triptych called *Poison*. I was eager to see it but didn't care much for it; it felt like a calculated act of subversion—a kinky academic's "outlaw" thesis film. I knew the movie was just going to be a dry drop in the ocean, but I wondered: Was there a way I could use it to draw attention to *Superstar*? And it occurred to me that there was.

Superstar was literally an underground film, since Haynes had made it without securing the rights to the Carpenters' hits, almost all of which were featured in the movie. Legally, this 43-minute Barbie-doll masterpiece couldn't be shown. The rights were held by Richard Carpenter, and he wasn't about to give permission to Todd Haynes any more than he would have sanctioned the vandalization of his home. As a sidebar to my review of *Poison*, I got the idea to write an open letter to Carpenter in the pages of *EW*, asking him to give Haynes permission. It was just a stunt, but it was my way to sneak in a review of *Superstar*. Amazingly, the editors agreed.

"Dear Richard Carpenter," the letter began, "Would you please allow people to see Todd Haynes' *Superstar: The Karen Carpenter Story?*" I went on to say, "I can see why you might want the movie under wraps. You probably think that it's some sort of exploitative joke, and that you personally don't come off that well in it. (Let's be honest: You don't.)" And yet, "the movie is more than a case study: It's also a supreme tribute to the music that you and Karen created. Haynes counterpoints Karen's private horror with the rapt beauty of her singing—the melancholy warmth and *smoothness* that turned songs like 'Rainy Days and Mondays' into soft-pop epiphanies. By putting the light and dark sides of Karen Carpenter together, *Superstar*, like David Lynch's *Blue Velvet*, says something powerful and haunting about America." The letter caught the attention of a producer at *Entertainment Tonight*, and the following week the show did a feature on *Superstar* and the whole issue of the music rights, featuring an interview with yours truly (though not with Richard Carpenter, who refused to appear) in what turned out to be my fabulous *ET* debut. By which I mean: My hair looked relatively okay, and I remembered to smile.

I flattered myself, for a moment, that I'd snuck a movie this out-rageous into the most mindless of infotainment formats. But then I real-ized that *Entertainment Tonight* was just a giant maw that needed to be fed, and endlessly. For three minutes, I had provided Carpenters nos-talgia mixed with a revival of an old tabloid chestnut and a one-sided celebrity pissing match. *ET* had used *EW*, and *EW* had used *ET.* It was your basic act of synergistic log-rolling. And it clarified something about *Entertainment Weekly*: We were an independent magazine, but in story after story, we needed to dip into the same pool of publicity that every-one else did. It wasn't a choice—it was survival. That's why all the specu-lative chatter that went on for years about whether *EW*, as a unit of Time Warner (the merger cemented in 1989), ever got coerced into providing favorable coverage to Warner Bros. product was almost always beside the point. We weren't asked to pimp for Warner Bros. Why would we be? The whole premise of the magazine is that we pimped for everybody. And no one grasped that principle better than Jim Seymore.

When Seymore came over to *Entertainment Weekly*, he was a middle-aged martini-at-lunch guy stranded in an office of relatively straight-edge *yoots*, and the culture clash was more than an issue of contrasting—or even conflicting—styles. It was a metaphor.

Jim was a product of the old Time Inc. culture, one that had held sway since the *Mad Men* era (the Time & Life building was the key inspiration for the stodgy grandiose white-collar premises of Sterling Cooper). That way of existence at Time was in the midst of doing a slow fade, but it was still hanging on, due entirely to the presence of old-school figures like Jim. Only recently, we learned, had Time Inc. abandoned the ritual of late-night liquor carts, which got wheeled around the offices of magazines like *Time, Sports Illustrated,* and *People* on closing nights, so that the writers and editors could enjoy a whiskey or two or three, imbibing their way toward placing the proper seal of satisfaction on their pages. The liquor carts were gone, but that only meant that the editors, if they chose, could now provide their own bottles, which Jim always did.

The *EW* offices were dotted with other Time Inc. relics. Seymore had his own shoeshine guy, who lugged his equipment up to the office every few weeks, and Jim also brought in two stodgy, traditional Time Inc. editors as deputies: Don Morrison, a fortyish straight-arrow who was like a middle manager out of the military bureaucracy, and Dick Lemon, a sweetly goofy *People* veteran who'd been around long enough to hang photos in his office of himself interviewing the early Beatles. Morrison and Lemon were there to make sure that *EW* didn't stray too far from The Tastes of Normal America, but with these two as "top editors," every day was sure to include at least one moment when you felt like you were explaining pop culture to your uncles at Thanksgiving.

As a born-again martini man myself, I, unlike the vast majority of those at *EW*, didn't look askance at the Time Inc. drinking culture. Yet the drug we were all addicted to at *Entertainment Weekly* was pop culture—consuming it, parsing it, deconstructing it. The office was like a Petri dish of fan geekdom. To Jim, this seemed every bit as outlandish and removed from his experience as the corporately approved WASPs-in-shirt-sleeves alcoholism of Time Inc. did to most of us. During his first year, Jim would sit at meetings and talk about how, exactly, we were going to go about the business of covering "entertainment," and he would literally enunciate that word as if he were referring to some hobby that was perfectly benign yet slightly removed from him. (He would have felt much more at home if the word was "golf.") It didn't take long for Jim to figure out that at *EW*, everyone in the room grasped infinitely more about pop culture than he ever would. How was that a formula for leadership?

It turned out to be the perfect one, because Jim, with no hope of competing against the insane pop wisdom of people who knew every episode of *Saved By the Bell*—or every Scorsese movie—by heart, elected not to compete. Instead, he would orchestrate that knowledge by listening to what everyone had to say and making key judgment calls. He didn't have to be the expert, the tastemaker; he just needed to be the magazine-maker, the invisible master of the mix, the delegator who could make a glossy book flow. At meetings, Jim encouraged everyone to speak up, and what he did was to channel the raw enthusiasm of the staff. But he did it with a directive that related to the original *EW* culture war: He was going to make *EW* a *fun* read. He did it by saying: We can't put out a successful entertainment magazine by shunning the hype-industrial complex. We've got to *hype* the hype, to embrace the sex appeal and the glamour, to cover Julia and Tom and Madonna and everyone else, by playing the publicity game that the studios and record companies want us to play. If we do *that*...we can also do what we want. (Not that we shouldn't also want to do *that*.)

There were moments in Jim's first year when merging the two sensibilities—the populist-mainstream and the pop-geek—was rather awkward, and watching the sausage of *EW*'s celebrity coverage get made was not always pretty. At one point, the magazine got a chance to do a major exclusive interview with a seismically beloved center-of-the-cosmos entertainment figure; it was a scoop and a game-changer, helping to enhance the magazine's identity, establishing it as a real player. What no one knew is that the handlers of the star in question were losing their shit over the fact that she'd become a heroin addict (a fact that was not, to put it mildly, in keeping with her image), and they were desperate for some major confectionary journalistic diversion to keep *that* story from leaking. The softball interview we did was a major propaganda coup. It was highly planted spin control, but it helped *EW* to stay afloat and gain power.

At one point, Jim summoned me to his office to talk about the review I'd just turned in of *The Marrying Man*, a lousy Neil Simon romantic comedy that starred Alec Baldwin and Kim Basinger, who were still—if such a thing is even possible to imagine—in the honeymoon stage of their off-screen relationship. Jim called me in at around 8:00 p.m., which meant that he'd moved on to his evening bourbon phase, and watching him sit there with that glass of golden-brown elixir in front of him, I felt a touch of envy at how the Time Inc. lush life extended several levels beyond mine. I thought: Man, what a great comfort!

I had trashed *The Marrying Man* and given it a C, and Jim had no problem (well, not much of one) with that. But I'd written harshly about Basinger's performance, and *EW* was in the midst of trying to wrangle a feature on the couple that Jim thought was crucial to the magazine's momentum. "It's not her I'm concerned about," he said. "It's Baldwin. He's incredibly protective of Kim, and if he reads that, he's going to blow his stack, and the whole feature could fall apart."

"Okay," I said. "So where does that leave us?"

"Is there a way you can say what you wanted to say but tone it down?"

I thought about it for a second, and my thought was, "This is terrible!

I'm on the slippery slope!" Then I thought about it for a second more, pondering Jim's words, and I sensed that he was being honest. He thought the magazine *did* need that feature. And I thought: "Who gives a damn? It won't matter." I said to Jim, "Yes, I can do that. It's not a big deal." He gave me a hearty thanks, and, in fact, it didn't matter. Jim never asked me to do anything like that again. I wrote with filed-down teeth about Basinger's performance, making it sound like it was half my problem ("Basinger, who raises hormone levels in just about everyone I know, continues to leave me cold. There's something petulant and detached about her that prevents her sexiness from leaping off the screen. I always get the feeling she isn't really *enjoying* herself"), and the world kept spinning. Politically, I'd made a smart play: I'd compromised (a bit), but I'd let Jim see that I wasn't some sort of high-maintenance blowhard purist. What that did, going forward, was to create an opportunity for me to compromise less.

Jim asked me to go to lunch with him, as he was doing with many members of the *EW* staff, so we went to '21' and sat there, politely and awkwardly, in the darkened windowless dining room with the checkerboard tablecloths, sussing out how little we had in common. Richard Gaines, the *Phoenix* editor who'd fired me, was the rumpled, avid, pot-stirring leader of an alt-weekly, and Jeff Jarvis was a former critic, but until Seymore, I'd never had a boss who seemed to call up some slightly last-century country-club idea of interaction that made me feel like I didn't relate to his mode, his rules, his values. I could, at least, join him in a martini, and I think I scored a few points by making a fellow drinker feel comfortable. We didn't talk about movies, or being a critic, or anything too *EW*-related. Instead Jim told me, with an almost confessional aura, how he once nurtured literary ambitions and felt guilty, at first, about joining a magazine as mass-market as *People*. He started to feel differently when he was at a party and it suddenly struck him that he was in the kitchen talking to all the women, who were hanging on his every word, while the men were in the living room talking sports. I could see that Jim, in his courtly way, was a guy's guy who appreciated women, and that working at *People* functioned for him as a kind of connector. What was left of the old Time Inc. culture gave him clubbiness, safety, power. I envied that feeling too. Because I was having some connecting issues myself.

If you worked for a media corporation in the early '90s, a role you probably didn't want to be caught dead playing—though it's frowned on even more today than it was then—is office horndog. To have a fling with a workmate isn't a sin, but it's one thing when gossip gathers around an isolated affair; it's another when it coalesces around your identity as a reckless walking hard-on. There is, however, a role that falls even a notch below office horndog on the totem pole of respectability. And that's the office horndog who's no damn good at it. That was me.

I've described myself as a geek, a dweeb, and other words that call up that familiar species. But it's worth taking a moment to note what, exactly, those terms really mean, since so many of the geek images in pop culture (Terry the Toad, *Revenge of the Nerds*, *Freaks and Geeks*) are decades out of date, especially in this century of geek chic. In my case, geekdom has never been primarily about fashion—though I wouldn't offer much of a defense of my MOR utilitarian wardrobe—but, rather, about the way I converse. It doesn't matter what the subject is. I could be discussing a movie, a restaurant, a presidential election, the subway, the weather, or the musical guest on last week's *Saturday Night Live*. Whatever the topic at hand, it's programmed into my cerebral cortex to serve up a miniature analysis of it. Regardless of how laidback or friendly I'm trying to be, my mode of thinking—and talking—is earnest, idea-driven, compulsively logical, and argumentative in a rather nagging Talmudic way. No matter how I try to tone it down, I speak in the voice of a critic, 24/7. It's a voice that enough people find tolerable, and even interesting, that it hasn't cut me off me from the rest of the human race. But it's a mode of discourse that is almost metaphysically designed *not* to be a form of flirtation.

The way I converse descends from how I grew up talking to my mother, a brilliant and beautiful woman who didn't know how to flirt, either, and it descends, as well, from how I grew up *not* talking to my father, since he barely even listened to me. My conversation, at its child-like heart, is a constant and compulsive attempt to make myself "interesting," and that's not a model of how to impress women. It's a model of how not to do it. That's why I'm the last person on earth who could ever pick up a woman at a bar, or get a phone number at a nightclub. I don't function in those settings, because I'm too didactically self-serious.

In many ways, the conversational flow in the halls of *EW* was my speed exactly: a babbling brook of pop chatter, one that you could dip into just about anytime you wanted. But since I felt I knew the subject as well as anyone, that gave me the confidence to be myself—and, in the twisted logic of the nervous narcissist, to spend as much time as possible hitting on women in the office. In the early '90s, especially after the Anita Hill hearings (October 1991), this kind of thing was just starting to provoke grumbles of ideological contempt, and I knew that, but the way I saw it, there was also a bit of a double standard at work: If you were a *successful* office lothario, then the sin was far less objectionable. In a funny way, striking out was the real crime.

One's looks, of course, are not incidental to the equation, and part of what drove me is that I'm one of those men who just missed out on being good-looking. Viewed from the front, my features are more than pleasant, with a smile that twinkles in a way that can light up a moment, but my profile undermines the hint of handsomeness. The overbite I inherited from my father was a lot more genetically restrained in him—it nudges my grin into a gawky leer—and the whole shape of my head resembles an oblong coconut. There's an interactive issue as well: When I look at someone, I tend to come off as if I'm *studying* them, which I probably, in fact, am. In sum: I was not put on earth to be a seducer or an office stud. Yet I kept on trying. And since I was basically a strikeout king (interrupted by the very rare infield double), I fell into a far more egregious role. I was the office creep.

Not that my behavior ever crossed the line into the officially inappropriate. I was canny enough to know that down that path lay oblivion. There was a writer at *EW* I'll call Ashley, who every guy had a crush on (she had a '60s-pinup figure and the Walter Keane eyes of a dewy ingenue), but she was extremely self-possessed, and also married, and she didn't have to fend off too many advances. But there was one incident that became a part of *EW* lore: A senior editor, newly divorced and on the prowl, held a meeting in his office attended by Ashley and a handful of other writers, and when the meeting ended and she left, there was no one in the room but a few other guys, and the editor said, "I can't help it: Whenever I look at her face, I see a wet, open, glistening vagina." He obviously thought he was speaking in confidence, but the Code of Guys is one of many things that collapsed during the '90s, and the story of his comment got around. He wasn't fired, but his eventual departure from the magazine was certainly prodded along by this instructional video out of Rules of Sexual Harassment 101.

I was enough of an evolved male to abhor such behavior, but that's part of why I felt so trapped in my critic's personality. I believed in the chivalrous codes of our office. I just wanted to have a mad consensual fling! A quietly decadent one! I did have one ongoing relationship with someone at work, an editor named Marta who looked like a very pretty owl, and who I was basically pals with but found a little too snippy to develop romantic feelings for, so we became fuck buddies. But my other forays were mostly a series of dead ends. The comely music assistant I managed to get to go with me to an Aretha Franklin concert (because Aretha was her favorite), which turned out to be a real *wow! we're just friends* kind of evening. Or the cute television writer I thought I connected with on a lot of levels yet couldn't begin to land a date with—and then I learned, of *course*, that she was sleeping with Max, the feature writer who *was* the office stud, because he was cute as fuck and not disadvantaged with an Antsy Critical Brain. There was Donna, the researcher who looked like a saucy Native-American warrior and liked to spar, which I did too…only my form of sparring sounded like I was studying for the law finals. (She slept with Max too.) I didn't want to be with a fellow geek (like Marta), yet those were the women I chimed with. My six-month lost weekend with Valerie in Boston had been an anomaly. You could say that I was trying to be someone I wasn't, yet I was willing to make a fool of myself in the office because of the depths of my desire to transcend geek connection and the vanilla sex that too often went with it.

One reason I was turning the office into a singles' bar is that the real reason I was there—to write movie reviews!—was stuck in a holding pattern. More and more, the studio films (*Backdraft, Hudson Hawk, Father of the Bride, Star Trek VI: The Undiscovered Country, Robin Hood: Prince of Thieves*) seemed like overscaled yet lightweight packages with nothing inside. I went to the gargantuan Loews Astor Plaza for a midsummer screening of *Terminator 2: Judgment Day*, a film I found at once exciting and de-sensitizing (those two things were starting to go together a lot at the movies), and during the closing credits, I turned to the friend next to me and said, only half-jokingly, "Well, I think the '80s are now over." I meant that *T2* seemed like it might be the last, straggling hangover of an iconic '80s blockbuster. But what I *really* meant—and almost believed—is that now that the films of the '80s were officially sequeled out, perhaps Hollywood's endless loop of post–Lucas and Spielberg indulgence was over. Maybe things would now go back to normal! In *EW,* I said that James Cameron "has become our reigning master of heavy-metal action," noting that "reckless indifference to human life is, of course, intrinsic to the appeal of *Terminator 2.* The movie is a great big feast of wreckage." I turned in that review at 1,200 words, and when Seymore read it, he blew a gasket and sent an irked e-mail to myself and the film-section editor, saying, "Do we really need a four-column review of *Terminator 2*? Please cut to appropriate length." It was my first skirmish for space in *EW,* and though I knew the review didn't have to be that long, I was dismayed at the hypocrisy of how we'd given the film a lavish cover story and treated it as maximally important... until it came down to actually writing about *what was up on screen.* At that point, *T2* became another a piece of product that wasn't important at all.

I still carried a major tinge of *Pretty Woman* paranoia, so when I saw the year's biggest Christmas release, Steven Spielberg's *Hook,* and found it to be awful to the point of ghastliness, I had a wave of anxiety over the prospect of trashing yet *another* Julia Roberts movie (she only played Tinkerbell, but still, the film would be sprinkled with Princess Julia fairy dust!). I felt like I couldn't sit down and write, word for word, the damning review I had in my heart. Yet I didn't want to compromise my feelings. So I came up with...a strategy. I would lead the review by talking about the one thing in the film I sort of enjoyed, which was Dustin Hoffman's performance as Captain Hook. I awarded the picture a grade of B-minus, which I knew was much higher than it deserved. I included the craven sentence, "*Hook* is jam-packed with 'entertainment value,' enough to give you your money's worth, and to guarantee (in all probability) that Spielberg earns his." But right after that weaselly line, I summed up the film with more honesty than not: "Something has clouded this director's vision. Except for Hoffman's performance, the movie is so frenetic, so bursting with movement and rowdiness and special effects, so drenched in gooey, mythic sentiment about the child within, that nothing in it quite gels. The problem isn't that Spielberg has lost his gift for fantasy. It's that he no longer seems to know (or care) about anything else." Spielberg, in hindsight, had binged out on fantasy; it's no coincidence that he was already starting to prepare for the starkly monumental *Schindler's List*. And though my review of *Hook* was good enough to get by, I hated myself for softening it. It was an experiment that taught me a lesson.

Things would go better with my next piece. I didn't have towering expectations for Oliver Stone's *JFK*. Yet when I saw it at a screening room with half a dozen other critics, I felt like I was at some sort of motion-picture black mass. The film hypnotized me—and not because I necessarily believed in its conspiracy theories. I thought it was more profound than that. Arguing that "Stone's instincts as a filmmaker transcend his glibness as a moral inquisitor," I wrote, "If Stone hasn't exactly solved the Kennedy assassination, he has captured—with a dark cinematic flair that leaves you reeling—why it still looms like a sickening nightmare." I said that Nov. 22, 1963 "disturbs our dreams because it seems to exist in some netherworld at the dawn of the media age. That day mocks our desire for certainty. It tells us that even in an era when everything is recorded, the more we see the less we know. This, far more than any cooked-up, all-encompassing conspiracy theory, is the true subject of *JFK*. The movie is about the way we see the assassination, about the way it lives inside our minds."

The day my review of *JFK* was closing also happened to be the day of *Entertainment Weekly*'s Christmas party. When I got to the ballroom on the east side of Times Square where the drunken office revelry was already unfolding, I went in and grabbed a cocktail, and I noticed a telling visitor to the party: Richard Stolley, the Time Inc. executive who, one year earlier, looked like he was getting ready to deliver the eulogy at the magazine's funeral. I knew that Stolley's career featured a legendary coup: In Dallas on that fateful day, he was the man who bought the Zapruder film, literally out of the hands of Abraham Zapruder, for *Life* magazine. Amazingly, the film was *still* the property of Time Inc. At the party, I tried to steer clear of Stolley (as is often my wimpy way), but after about 15 minutes, I turned around and there he was, looking right at me, so I stuck out my hand and re-introduced myself, and he clasped it and said, "I just read your review of *JFK*. It was brilliant!"

I said, "Wow, thanks so much!" (I tend to say "Wow" when I'm flustered), and then I tried to think of something political to say, so I blurted out, "I just read the review by Richard Corliss [the critic for *Time*]. He did a fantastic job."

"His piece was good," said Stolley. "But yours was better. You really grabbed hold of what it all meant." I was, of course, intensely flattered, but beneath the swell of ego, I felt a deeper boost of satisfaction, one that could be described as a catharsis of reassurance. *Dick Stolley... the man who bought the Zapruder film... has just told me that my review of* JFK *nailed it.* There is nothing in the world like the kind of compliment that carries the suggestion of job security. In Stolley's endorsement, I felt that the *EW* culture war—mainstream vs. edge! smart vs. dumb!—was perhaps finally entering a period of détente. The lavish party swirling around me spoke to the magazine's potential for success.

That night, I reconnected to a feeling I'd had in an airport months before, when I stopped at a newsstand, as I had done so often, to leaf through the latest issue of *The New Yorker* because I was *that* eager to see what Pauline Kael had to say about whatever movies she was writing on. I skimmed through the column—I would read it properly when I got home—but the tail end of it caught my eye: a little squib under the byline that said that after this issue, Ms. Kael will no longer be reviewing. Pauline was retiring! This would be her last column! There would be no more Pauline Kael reviews to read... ever! I later heard through channels that the film that finally broke her spirit was *Scenes from a Mall*—the very screening where I'd last spoken to her. I put the magazine down and shuffled through the airport in a daze, thinking about everything that Pauline had meant in my life, and I said to myself, right there, practically voicing the words out loud: *I will stay true to you, Pauline, by doing what you taught me. I will say what I think, straight up.*

I'd violated that oath at *Entertainment Weekly*. I would try not to do it again, even if I sometimes had to bend over backward to smooth feathers simply to write a basic, unremarkable, honest piece. When the basketball comedy *White Men Can't Jump* came out, I was mixed about it, which seemed like no big whoop, but *Entertainment Weekly* was doing a silly cover story on the movie that insisted, in every paragraph, that its stars, Woody Harrelson and Wesley Snipes, weren't just playing buddies—they were *rilly rilly* big buddies off camera, too. The feature played up this fact so much that it was obvious to me the two had probably never even met before, but it was one of those cases where the magazine *allied* itself with the movie. When I pulled no punches in my review, my editor, the normally cordial Jim Meigs, walked into my office with a Church Lady pucker on his face, holding up the printed-out pages of my review, and announced, "I don't like this piece." He explained his objections—I didn't make the case, blah blah blah—but I knew that his real problem was: *You weren't enthusiastic enough!*

As I sat down at the computer to try to deal with his complaints, I was pissed off, and decided to go into his office and tell him that the review was fine as is. Standing up, I knocked over the cup of coffee that was sitting on my desk, and it spilled right onto my keyboard: a total fucking mess. It took a split second for me to realize that I'd done it on purpose, in a Freudian there-are-no-accidents sort of way. I'd vented my anger and gotten myself to take a breather; I decided in that instant *not* to go into Jim's office and throw a fit. Instead, I diplomatically redid a few passages and saved the essential criticism. I thought about that spilled cup of coffee for years afterwards, because it was really a message I was sending to myself for the new corporate era. The message was: "Don't get angry. Get creative. Or you will not last."

Though *Entertainment Weekly* wasn't out of the woods, I felt safe in the office, because it was the best corporate atmosphere imaginable: an elegant physical space with all the privacy a writer could want. The workday started late (if you got in before 10:00 a.m., you were probably the first one there), and on closing nights it extended into the wee hours with a cozy communality. I did almost all my writing at home, and felt that a review was more or less done by the time I turned it in, but once I'd shepherded it through the editing process, I loved staying at the office until 1:30 a.m. on a Monday or Tuesday to make obsessive changes—or "tweaks"—on my copy. I developed a reputation as someone who would engage in midnight battles with copy editors, over comma placement or the word coinages that one of them dubbed "Owenisms," and I usually got my way by keeping the fights almost painfully diplomatic. (I used that Talmudic personality of mine to wear people down.) It also seemed a trivial yet right-on blessing to work at the heart of media central in an age when you didn't need to shave (thank you, Don Johnson!) or even wear a tie.

I made a couple of close friends at the office, like David Browne, the music feature writer who would soon become the lead music critic (as well as my closest confidante), and George Pitts, a photo researcher about 10 years my senior. George, a dandy who dressed in ties nearly as wide as they were long, was a serious and gifted painter who considered Time Inc. his day job, and he introduced me to enclaves of downtown Manhattan that reminded me, in a funny way, of my wide-eyed seventh-grade voyages into the hippie utopia of Ann Arbor. The two of us would hit the East Village hole-in-the-wall shops that seemed to be hawking the secret detritus of the 20th century, and it was on one of those outings that I first saw photographs of Bettie Page, who I had never heard of. I became obsessed with her, because in addition to finding her the most delectable goddess of flesh I had ever encountered, her effect on me was mind-opening: Here, smack in the middle of the black-and-white, buttoned-down 1950s, was an image of sexuality as radical and joyful, as dark and light, as any that I had imagined. It told me that my lust for sinful transgression wasn't so off-base—that this had always been there, not just in me but in the world, and that it was beautiful and eternal.

George boxed open my perceptions in other ways. He was the first friend I'd ever had who was African American, a fact I tried to approach with an attitude of "post-racial" enlightenment that George had little patience for. He thought middle-class white people like myself were more or less blind to the experience of black people, and we fought about it a lot. George's tastes were promiscuously unpredictable in a way that I found galvanizing even when I disagreed with him (he thought Scorsese was a genius but a male fascist; he thought Prince's greatest album was the *Under the Cherry Moon* soundtrack), but our debates about movies and music cued me to see how obscenely regimented pop culture still was. I had long believed that going into a record store and seeing the last 50 years of music neatly divided into "rock" and "R&B" was a form of musical apartheid. But that applied, in a subtler way, to movies too. It began to occur to me that carving up cinema into categories like *black film* or *movie by a woman director!* was every bit as despicable. My friendship with George reminded me, in the midst of all the greasy popcorn I was reviewing, that movies were supposed to be a thing of purity. But could those movies survive in a *T2* world? I started to think they could the day I saw *Reservoir Dogs*.

By the time I made it to a screening of Quentin Tarantino's first film, in early October of 1992, it was already heating up New York movie conversations like a sizzling piece of gossip, and the talk was all about the ear-severing scene; people shook their heads with a grin of disbelief when they spoke about it. Since I ate movies that perched violence on the edge for breakfast, I was incredibly keen to see it. But none of the chatter prepared me for what was thrilling about *Reservoir Dogs*.

The opening few minutes, in which a group of crooks sat around a restaurant table debating the meaning of Madonna's "Like a Virgin," served no visible purpose beyond the fact that the people on screen *totally fucking wanted to say these things*, and the director *totally fucking wanted you to hear them saying them*. The astounding thing was, that was enough. And that was the sensation that coursed through the entire movie. The credits sequence, with the characters skulking toward the camera in their skinny-black-tie suits and "Little Green Bag," with its herky-jerky ska groove, sounding like the coolest song you'd ever heard... that was pure pop. But then the film leapt to the chaos in the back of a getaway car, with Tim Roth, his shirt drenched in tomato-red blood, acting up such a storm that you could just about feel the bullet that was ripping into his guts.

By the time the torture scene arrived, I was braced for it, and it felt like something I'd never seen: psychotic violence staged by a true artist for sheer kicks. The giddiness of it is that even as Michael Madsen's performance was chilling, the movie, with a wink, wanted you to *share* the delight of his kicky little dance to "Stuck in the Middle with You." Whose side was Tarantino on? He was on the side of the victim, the torturer, the noble police rat, the honorable comrade he was ratting out... he was on everyone's side, and no one's side. The movie, unlike most pulp, invited our empathy, then dissolved it in the acid bath of macho bluster. *Reservoir Dogs* was a vintage heist movie—*The Asphalt Jungle* or *The Killing*—done by a new Scorsese. It was the old Hollywood meets the new, the past converted into the future.

I knew it was major, but it took one more movie for me to realize just how big the thing that Quentin started was going to be. That film was

The Crying Game. It's not that I saw Neil Jordan's lyrical thriller about a femme fatale who's not what she appears to be as the complete and total game-changer that *Reservoir Dogs* was. (Though once Harvey Weinstein figured out how to sell its secret, *The Crying Game* did become—to quote *Anchorman*—kind of a big deal). It's that *The Crying Game*, like *Reservoir Dogs*, merged the soul of an old Hollywood movie with a spirit so new it was transformative. When I put those two films together, I saw the light: The independent film movement was going to be about nothing less than a *reinvention* of movies. It had the chance to be a revolution, to be a second coming of '70s Hollywood. It had the chance to resurrect the whole reason I'd ever become a movie freak.

I celebrated this perception by focusing my joy on the title song to *The Crying Game*, a percolating bauble of melancholy that Boy George sang with such hard-won transcendence that I sat at home late at night, cranking up the song on my earphones, sipping vodka gone syrup-thick in the freezer, and somehow took the lyrics—"I know all there is to know about the crying game,/I've had my share...of the crying game"—to be not about the plight of love in the age of free sex (which, of course, is what they were about) but about the plight of movies in the age of blockbusters, when it looked like *real* movies might be going away, forever. *Reservoir Dogs* and *The Crying Game* told me: They are not going away.

The movies that were turning out to be my touchstones all glorified the allure of bad behavior, the thrilling rightness of actions that were wrong. So maybe it was a coincidence, or maybe it wasn't, that around this time I did the worst thing I'd ever done.

When I didn't have a girlfriend (which was roughly two-thirds of the time), I never knew what to do with myself over the 10-day holiday break. So as 1992 came to a close, I spontaneously asked Marta, the office pal I sometimes hooked up with, if she'd like to go with me to Key West, a spot I'd discovered and fallen for the year before. I loved the historic eccentricity of it (what could you say about a place whose two most legendary residents were Ernest Hemingway and Jimmy Buffett?), the slightly curdled viny American beauty. She said yes, and we took a vacation down there for a week. The second night of our trip, we were feeling good, having a drink, and who should we spot across the rattan-walled bar but Becky, who worked on the advertising side of *Entertainment Weekly*. It's a small world after all!

In this case, the coincidence was not a happy one, because the fact that Marta and I were sleeping together was something we had taken pains, for reasons of office politics, to conceal. Now, having been spotted on vacation together by someone from work we didn't know well (and therefore couldn't rely on), the cat was out of the gossip bag. What could we do but go over and say hello, act absurdly casual (of *course* the two of us are down here together in Key West!), and have a friendly drink. Since all of us were on vacation, the drinks turned into shots of tequila.

If you drink enough of it (which isn't very much), tequila really can make life seem like a movie—a slow-motion car crash you're sitting and watching, even as you're in the middle of it. I don't remember how we all started dancing. I just remember the music, the crowded dance floor, the *scene* I was in the middle of as Becky and I locked eyes. And just because tequila melts away your control doesn't mean, exactly, that you have zero control. The truth is that I was so *flattered* that this girl from my office I barely knew was coming on to me that any other consideration—like the fact that I happened to be, you know, *on vacation with someone else*— ceased to exist. Without a thought as to what Marta would think, or even where she was, I snuck off with Becky and went back to her room, fooled around with her, though didn't sleep with her (she wouldn't let me). It was my own personal Spring Break moment of deplorable male shabbiness.

Becky didn't want me to stay over, so in my lurching it's-only-a-movie sloshed haze, I found my way back to the place where Marta and I were staying. She was waiting in the dark when I arrived.

"I want you *out* of here!" she screamed.

This was no crying game. More like a dying game.

CHAPTER 13

DAZED AND CONFUSED

A colleague at *The Boston Phoenix* once said that he saw me strolling toward the office one morning, carrying, as I usually did, absolutely nothing—no briefcase, no man bag, no backpack—and with a chuckle he thought, "That just defines why Owen has such a perfect job. Of *course* he doesn't carry anything. It's all in his head!" That may be a slight exaggeration of reality, and at *EW,* I did start to tote around a nice smooth flat leather folder, to store the books and papers I needed for research (and also because I thought it added to the illusion of my adult professionalism), but essentially, my *Phoenix* chum had a point: When you're a film critic, the movie at hand, and the swirl of thoughts and feelings and words and reactions it triggers within you, is 90 to 100 percent of the relevant material. In contrast to, say, a reporter or feature writer (who's always beholden to interviews), you don't have to rely on anything else. Once you've seen the film, it's all *you.* And that self-contained aspect of the job has always suited my slightly insular, self-oriented, inside-the-head personality.

It's also made me feel like I don't need editors—even though, of course, like every writer under the sun, I do. With one or two exceptions, every editor I ever worked with at *EW*—they seemed to rotate in and out of the movie section about every two years—helped make my writing better, not worse. But when it came to dealing with the top-dog editor, Jim Seymore, I knew that whenever I was summoned into his office, the odds were it was for something I did not want to hear. I've never had much of a knack for cozying up to the boss, and certainly not Jim. (I liked him, but couldn't make small talk with him; we were way too different.) So I was more than relieved when I got called in one day by his longtime assistant, a wry Jewish den mother named Rita, and Jim told me that the publishing side had a junket in store for me: Did I want to go to San Diego to appear on a panel at an advertising conference? It seemed like an excuse for a trivial, amusing two-day escape. And that's all it was, really, except for the fact that it was on that trip that I first met Gene Siskel and Roger Ebert and got to see them in action away from the cameras.

Gene and Roger were there because they had their own rather lucrative gig at the conference: an hour-long "seminar" in which they reviewed (and gave thumbs up or down to) a series of television commercials, so that the advertisers in the room could ostensibly learn from their insights about what it takes to create a good one. My panel, something to do with blockbusters, would be the usual blab-a-thon with zero import, moderated by an L.A. talk-radio host.

I first spotted Siskel and Ebert in the lobby of the hotel, and when I walked over and introduced myself, they looked just like they did on TV, though in person the contrast between them wasn't so much The Bald One In A Sport Coat vs. The Fat One In A Sweater as it was their dramatic difference in height. They were like Laurel and Hardy, and it was instantly clear how much their personalities emanated from that. The tall, gangly Siskel loomed over me and had a confident, easygoing Jimmy Stewart cordiality, while Ebert was shorter than I was, which made him pretty short—a snowman with the combative demeanor of a firecracker. Both of them complimented me on my work, with Gene trotting out the then relatively new L.A. catchphrase *"I like what you do,"* but he said it sincerely, whereas Roger, once he'd gotten the back-scratching formalities out of the way, immediately turned cracklingly intense in his withering observations about the hotel, as if he was daring me to keep up with him. I also met Ebert's wife, Chaz, who struck me as a world-class diplomat, a quality that probably came in handy given how much time she had to spend dealing with not one but two monster-truck egos.

Roger, Chaz, and Gene did not ask me to go to dinner, but at the hotel restaurant, where I wound up dining with a film-journalist acquaintance who was also on the panel, the three of them walked in and wound up being seated just a few tables away, and that meant that I got to overhear... not so much their conversation as the jockeying and arguing that seemed to erupt between Gene and Roger about every five minutes, over everything from where they would sit to what they should order. Roger was the happy provocateur, turning everything into a contest, and Gene was the eye-rolling oh-my-God-gimme-a-break enabler who was just competitive enough himself to rise to the bait. The lights in the restaurant were low, and this was no preening, camera-ready shtick. It was the real S&M marriage of S&E.

I was excited to meet Siskel and Ebert (especially now that I considered myself a peer of theirs), because I've always been childishly susceptible to the lure of celebrity, and these were the two most famous film critics on the planet. In terms of iconic visibility and influence, they dwarfed every other reviewer and always would. But I should point out something that it would never have even occurred to me to say back in the early '90s: If you had told me then that over the next decade or so, a growing horde of younger movie buffs—and some older ones, too—would come to regard Roger Ebert as the greatest film critic of all time, my response would have been a simple *"Are you fucking serious?"* Next to Pauline Kael or Andrew Sarris, David Denby or David Ansen, or a handful of other venerable reviewers, like the crusty, fearless *New Republic* stalwart Stanley Kauffmann (who I'd only just begun developing a friendly bond with), Ebert struck me as an intensely gifted yet problematic populist. I had watched Siskel and Ebert throughout the late '70s and '80s, and I always found their show to be enjoyable and infuriating in equal measure. They were good talkers (especially Roger, who was actually a great talker), the fireworks were fun, and during any given segment, you might even see a trenchant nugget or two of film criticism. But you also, just as often, might not. The thumbs-up/thumbs-down format was, I felt, inherently corrupt—not because it was a dumbed-down quantifying "system" (like, you know, grades), but because it gave the two of them the stark choice, every time, of either endorsing a movie or condemning it, which falsified the experience of way too many movies you could name.

I recognized that Ebert was the more brilliant of the two (though I often thought Gene showed more common sense), and certainly the better writer. Ebert's prose, to me, was a minor wonder of tossed-off facility. Yet if his thoughts were eloquent, they were seldom *gripping* (they had a way of evaporating once you'd read them), and the skill of his writing only made it all the more frustrating that his judgments were so often indiscriminate in their enthusiasm. Simply put: Ebert was far too perceptive a man to give a tongue kiss to as many mediocre movies as he did. I decided that he was a little like the Cookie Monster: so happy to be sitting there in the aisle seat, scarfing yet another cinematic confection, that it didn't matter that much, in the end, exactly how it tasted. Just watching it tasted *goood*!! I had admiration for Ebert's mind, his prose, his incredible knowledge—not to mention his baroquely inspired screenplay for *Beneath the Valley of the Ultra-Vixens* (penned under the pseudonym R. Hyde), which I actually thought was a better movie than the turgidly clever *Beyond the Valley of the Dolls.* Yet I couldn't take him that *seriously* as a critic. It's not that Ebert—or Siskel—was on the take. It's that when you saw them on their show, the two, while great Punch-and-Judy entertainers, were intelligent yet arbitrary enough that it sometimes seemed *as if* they were on the take. And that was almost worse.

I had my own minor experience of trying to be a critic on national TV a couple of years later, and it was illustrative. The E! channel was trying out a half-hour weekly show devoted to movie critics and asked me to join its rotating bullpen. The program would be modeled on E!'s *The Gossip Show*: It would feature film critics spouting their opinions, in unbroken two-minute segments, directly into the camera. We did a handful of shows, and I was part of about half of them. I remember taking a special delight in reviewing Jim Carrey's *The Mask*, because it gave me the chance to go on about how vivacious—and sexy—its unknown female costar, Cameron Diaz, was, in a way that I couldn't have at *EW,* where it would have been flagged as inappropriate male-gaze stuff. The whole rhythm of the show was relaxed enough to let you be sincere. I had hopes for it, but then, like that, it was canceled, after half a dozen episodes. I assumed the plug was pulled for low ratings, but I later learned that the ratings were not the problem. The show had, in fact, been killed because of pressure from the studios, who didn't want that kind of shoot-from-the-hip opinion bumping up against the round-the-clock promotional gloss that was E!'s bread and butter. I learned a lesson: The kind of criticism that's accepted in print seems harsher, and ruffles more feathers, when you say it out loud on television.

After my panel, I stayed around to see Gene and Roger's duelin' duet of advertising criticism, and it turned out to be an extremely funny and entertaining testament to what spontaneously embattled showmen they were. The big moment occurred when they watched a slick patriotic commercial for the U.S. Army, which Gene found very effective and Roger thought was awful, and for the rest of the hour, Roger kept returning to it, at one point interrupting a completely different topic to say, "I can't *believe* you fell for that stupid Army spot!" It was shtick, yet it revealed not just how competitive Roger was, but how invested in the idea that *his* opinion was the *right* one. Believe me, I know that mindset all too well, because I share it. (Any good critic does.) And Roger was certainly not guilty of buying into the myth of his own critical omnipotence any more than, say, Pauline Kael. The difference is that Kael, with her lacerating sharpness, was right about things five times as much as Roger Ebert ever was.

After I got back to New York, I was called into Jim's office yet again, and this time, sure enough, it was for something I was not pleased to hear. "I want Ty to start doing some movie reviews," Jim said in his quiet, no-big-deal drawl manqué, and every bone in my body was saying, "No!" Ty was Ty Burr, the magazine's video critic, who had been shadowing me for what felt like a few years. After I got fired from the *Phoenix*, Peter Kadzis offered him my job there, but Ty didn't want to leave New York. Now, the two of us were colleagues, though he was on the second-tier beat of reviewing the same movies I did several months later, when they came out on VHS. I had respect for Ty as a critic; he was a whip-smart writer, with tastes that frequently overlapped mine. But that's just why I didn't want him in the movie section. I'd grown intensely territorial and had no desire to share the real estate. I wanted to be *Entertainment Weekly*'s one and only film critic. It was obvious, however, that Jim had made up his mind, and I couldn't really mount a good argument against Ty coming in, so I more or less had to say yes. For a while, Ty became *EW*'s second-string movie critic. But I defeated him in the most ironic way.

I felt that Ty, as a critic, was kind of like a WASP version of me, and within the evolving political atmosphere of *EW* that was threatening. Though I'd never had a Jewish upbringing (despite Robert Duvall's assertions, the first time I ever set foot in a synagogue was at a friend's wedding, when I was in my early thirties), my parents were born-and-bred

New York Jews, and I had a certain antic verbal New York Jewish mojo wired into my synapses. I'd never given much thought to having a "Jewish identity" before I worked at Time Inc., but once there, at my paranoid worst, I had moments when I felt as if Jim, my country-club WASP boss, though he had saved my job, still viewed me as the pesky, intellectual, overly negative bar-mitzvah-boy outsider he had to deal with. Whereas Ty, I felt, seemed less odd, and maybe less intimidating, to someone like Jim. Ty had gone to Dartmouth and looked like the quirkiest member of the glee club, and he was a better schmoozer than me, with a lighter happier touch, and as a critic he was less prickly. I felt that, frankly, he was more disposed to go with the flow.

Lucky for me, the person in charge of the movie section was David Hajdu, a highly acerbic and lofty editor who was just enough of an eccentric brainiac that he and I got along famously. He had worked with Ty before, and had a bug up his ass about him. David relished my prickliness; he thought that Ty, for all his talent, was too slick and accommodating a writer. And so he kept him in a low-profile position, giving him minor assignments and maintaining my role as the star of the section. If Ty had just waited it out, I think that the history of movie reviewing at *EW* might have been different. I suspect that with Jim's support, Ty would have risen. But instead, Ty felt stymied and frustrated and even angry (he had a right to feel those things), and after a number of months, he left the section in a huff. Not long after that, he went over to *People* magazine—a big mistake for a writer of his quality—and I had the movie section back to myself.

My prickliness expressed itself in various ways, one of which centered on the issue of which movie was going to be selected each week for the lead review: the first, longest, and most defining piece of the section. I accepted that on certain weeks, the choice was a no-brainer. Now that the summer of 1993 was upon us, nothing was going to elbow *Jurassic Park* out of the lead spot—and that was a case where the biggest film was also the most enthrallingly artful, since Steven Spielberg, working with the just-busted-out toy of CGI, tapped deeply into our primal love of dinosaurs.

But a couple of weeks later, for our summer double issue, we were juggling two major releases, *Sleepless in Seattle* and *What's Love Got to Do with It,* and there was pressure from above to feature the Nora Ephron romantic comedy as the lead. I argued against it once I'd seen both films, because I thought *Sleepless* was just a sad-sack greeting card ("It's bound to be hailed in some quarters as corny, romantic, and old-fashioned, and for good reason: The movie is so prefab, so plastically aware of being 'corny,' 'romantic,' and 'old-fashioned,' that it feels programmed to make you fall in love with it…It's like a '50s tearjerker synthesized by microchip"). Whereas I loved the Tina Turner biopic for its wrenching dance between Angela Bassett's volcanic rock-siren-as-victim performance as Tina and Laurence Fishburne's mesmerizing menace as Ike Turner. I got my way; *What's Love Got to Do with It* was the lead. But *Sleepless* wound up being the far bigger hit, and it kicked off the coronation of Tom Hanks as the new king of Hollywood.

From that point on, it became harder for me to push back against whatever movie The System had basically directed us to place in the lead spot, either because it had the biggest star or was going to make the most money. (The two tended to go together. And they *always* did in the eyes of The System.) I resented the notion that as *EW*'s critic, I didn't have more clout in deciding which film, on any given week, was the most important. After all, isn't that what a critic *does*? I also resented that as journalists, the review-section editors at *EW* didn't feel the full freedom to make those decisions—they were expected to get with the program, to play up the movie that had already, in essence, been chosen for them. By now, this way of doing things is so routine that it's simply the old new normal, even at a magazine as independent as *The New Yorker.* But in 1993, it was part of the early screwing in of the nuts and bolts of a structure designed to make criticism function as marketing.

Going from the *Phoenix* to *EW,* I never consciously altered my writing style, and was never asked to; if anything, I felt like my prose got tighter and more polished. But there's no doubt that I was now, on a weekly basis, parsing issues of art vs. commerce and authenticity in criticism that I had never spent much time pondering at the *Phoenix,* where I could afford to be a casual purist. And that whole mode of proactive, high-minded vigilance began to seep, in small ways, into my personal life, resulting in one break with my past that seemed cataclysmic but that needed to happen.

My mother had come to New York for a visit. The two of us had our disagreements, but we'd always gotten along; I viewed her as a comrade, and she was proud that I'd made it to a major magazine. For lunch on a Saturday, I took her to a swanky spot in SoHo, and though she was not the pathological cheapskate my father was, she was still relatively neurotic about money. When she saw the bill (which I guess I expected her to pay), she groused, suggesting that I was living a lifestyle that threw cash down the drain. The argument we had, which wasn't about who would pick up the check but about the "extravagance" of it, should have been a tempest in a teapot, but at that moment it hit a raw nerve of underlying issues—not just of money, but of how we treat ourselves and of what it means—that I felt I'd been fighting in my parents for too long.

For years, when I discussed my parents in therapy, I explored—that is, griped about—concrete things that were right in front of me: my father's brusque selfishness, the fact that in my family there were countless more debates than hugs. (Cue the world's tiniest violin!) But I was now seeing that the real problem was something it was nearly impossible for me to get my head around. For when there *isn't* enough love in a family, enough unconditional affection or mirroring, the problem has the odd effect of being invisible. The feeling of too little love isn't a problem that's "there," standing right in front of you; it is, almost by definition, *not* there. That's one of the reasons, perhaps, why I cleaved to movies. They *became* my mirror, my third parent. The rest of the visit with my mother was tense, and when the two of us said goodbye, I'd already made the decision that I was not going to see her, or my father, for a long time, and maybe a *very* long time. (As it turned out, it was seven years.) The issue wasn't so much that I was angry (I was, but I don't believe in holding on to festering resentment). It's that I now realized I needed to get as far away as possible from my parents' karma, so that I could stop interacting with the world in a way that rhymed with how I interacted with them. I needed to create a new karma, to be out there alone, to feel the ache of my alienation all the more and, in doing so, to heal it.

The healing would take a long time. But perhaps the green shoots of it showed themselves in September, when I had the liberating experience of seeing a movie I felt had been made for me. I also thought it was the greatest achievement the independent film revolution had yet produced.

That was Richard Linklater's dizzyingly authentic all-night-long '70s high-school drama *Dazed and Confused*. It was shot in Austin, one of the sisterhood of American college towns that included Ann Arbor, and the opening title read "Last Day of School, May 28, 1976, 1:05 p.m.," which blew me away, because I graduated from high school in 1976, and though the film revolved around characters who still had another year to go, if I hadn't skipped kindergarten, that would have been me. As Linklater, born one year after me, understood all too well, 1976 was a state of mind, one of those unspoken transitional moments—in this case, from the druggy scruffy aimlessness of the post-counterculture, post–Watergate and Vietnam, post-everything mid-'70s to whatever came next, something less definable but a lot straighter. Here, for the record, is how 1976 I am: In my senior year of high school, I played bass and keyboards in a band called Marbles (we did Zeppelin and Aerosmith, Kiss and Zappa, "Whipping Post" and "Color My World"), and when we were chosen at the last moment to play the junior prom, we had to spend the entire day learning every track on *Frampton Comes Alive!*, which had only just erupted.

Dazed and Confused is a time-machine miracle, and here's why I still have no idea how Linklater brought it off. It's one thing to get every detail right—to nail the cars (those awesome slope-backed Chevys and Plymouths), the clothes (the flat jeans as snug as corsets and the cork-wedge heels), the hairstyles (shaggy disco rebel, and for the girls still some major ironing going on), not to mention the lingo (the stoned "*Man!*"s and early "*Whatever*"s). But when filmmakers go back into the past, even when it's their own, they almost never succeed in capturing the *vibe*, the way an entire era felt. There was an ethereally morose, hanging-in-the-air stasis to the mid-'70s, and the eeriness of *Dazed and Confused* is how completely Linklater tapped into the feeling of *nothing happening* in the midst of everything that was happening. It was the last moment before the ascendance of technology, and that's why it now looks like the Stone Age (no pun intended). The opening shot, of an orange Pontiac GTO slowly arcing around a parking lot to "Sweet Emotion," caught the dilapidated aimlessness, and Linklater never deviated from that; he made a teen comedy about the lowly, lovely splendor of going nowhere fast. The spirit of my favorite filmmaker, Robert Altman, hovers over *Dazed and Confused*, and it remains the greatest Altman film that Altman never made.

I immediately saw myself in two of the characters: the talky dweebs played by Anthony Rapp and Adam Goldberg, always standing on the sidelines, commenting rather than participating. It's not just that I did that a lot. I really was *those two guys*, with a bit of the head-shaking, knitted-eyebrow moralistic sputter of Goldberg's Mike, though I was a little more self-possessed than that, with medium-longish hair and an amused dismissive manner very much like that of Rapp's Tony. He, however, was more advanced with girls, and in its sly depiction of boy-girl sexual politics, *Dazed and Confused* became a profound glimpse into the pivot-point weirdness of the '70s. Parker Posey's mock-military bitch princess, who at times seems certifiable, might be the patron saint of every sorority of the future, and Jason London's Pink, a football star who's expected to carry himself like a jock king, is also a mellow stoner who bristles at signing an Orwellian drug pledge. Can he be both at once? The movie's wistful joke is that this might have been the last moment when you could.

Dazed and Confused was all about the meaning—the feeling—of freedom. It was there in the ramshackle glory of the film's slacker sprawl, in the way that Wiley Wiggins' man-in-the-moon-faced Mitch feels like he's crossing over into adulthood just by entering a foosball bar, in the way that a woodland keg bash, with beer and dope as elixirs, had the transformational wonder of a teen-burnout *Midsummer Night's Dream*. In my review, I wrote that the movie immerses us in "that singular moment in the 20th century when getting high, dressing in whatever was handy, saying whatever came into your head, and, in general, not doing much of anything somehow passed as righteous behavior." I said that *Dazed and Confused* "may be the most slyly funny and dead-on portrait of American teenage life ever made."

A couple of months later, I received a long, gracious, and highly enlightening letter from Linklater. "Dear Owen," he said, "I'm just writing to let you know how much I appreciated your kind words and support for *Dazed and Confused* (and also for *Slacker* a couple of years ago). It was so exciting to read your piece: an intelligent film critic who just so thoroughly 'got it.' One always hopes to connect with people but you never really know...." He went on to excoriate Universal Pictures and its independent arm, Gramercy, for the way they handled the movie, watering down its ad budget and never getting it out to more than 250 theaters: "Studio heads have gotten wiser and very subtle about how to sabotage a film in order to not look bad. You don't *NOT* release it (*Brazil*), but you actually support it in New York and L.A. so as to give the appearance of support. Then the filmmaker can't bitch. Then you dump it everywhere else and say the film just 'didn't perform like we'd hoped.' Basically, none of the big boys were behind it. It was truly the worst of both worlds: all the bullshit of a studio production and all the cheapness of an independent release. My most paranoid, but perhaps most lucid conclusion is that they snuffed *Dazed* because a victory (in their only terms—$$) would have been a vindication of the individual filmmaker against the committee studio system. I had ruffled some feathers there in making this film, and they didn't mind proving a point at the expense of their shareholders. 'If Richard had just done it a little more our way,' they can dangle over the next guy." He ended the letter by saying, "Our country needs more tough critics like you who don't just swallow the hype like everyone else. So many writers might as well be on the payroll—be it entertainment industry or government. Happy Holidays! Best always, Richard."

At first, I was surprised that the experience of *Dazed* had left Linklater so embittered. Inside my critic's bubble, I thought he should just be glad he'd made such a great film! But, of course, once you've sweated blood on a movie to bring it to life exactly as you want, it's going to tear you up if the film isn't given a chance to find its audience. This was my first halfway intimate peek into the personality of film directors, who can afford to be aesthetes, but only because they're icy generals, control-freak businessmen, and—when they need to be—ruthless assholes. I was gratified, of course, that Linklater thought I'd nailed his movie. Yet when it came time a week or so later to start compiling my 10 best of the year list, I unconsciously didn't go with my heart in a way that haunted—and educated—me for years.

I knew, at the end of 1993, that I loved *Dazed and Confused* more than I did *Schindler's List*, because even though Spielberg's Holocaust spectacle had a dark virtuosity, a few aspects of it nagged at me, notably the tone-deaf ending, in which Oskar Schindler weeps with regret as he fingers some precious trinket and says things like, "With this, I could have saved eight more Jews!" (I thought that made him sound like more of a Nazi than Ralph Fiennes' commandant.) I wound up choosing *Dazed* as my number three film of the year, and *Schindler's List* as number four, a juxtaposition I was asked about for years, as in, "How could you *possibly* rank *Dazed and Confused* ahead of *Schindler's List*?" What I've always said is that Linklater's film did an even more remarkable job of the exact thing that *Schindler's List* did: Both were visionary historical re-creations. In the first two slots, I chose Jane Campion's *The Piano* and Robert Altman's *Short Cuts*, a pair of large, sweeping, swing-for-the-fences art statements, both of which churned up my emotions. But when it came down to it, I had simply balked at placing a movie like *Dazed*—a movie about teenagers, a *stoner* comedy—ahead of all that heavy-duty haute cuisine. It took more than a year to hit me that *Dazed and Confused* really *was* the best movie of 1993, and that I hadn't known it because, deep down, I lacked the courage to say it.

CHAPTER 14

NATURAL BORN THRILLERS

Just before noon on June 13, 1994, the flight I was on touched down in Los Angeles. I rented a car and drove over to Book Soup, the fabled West Hollywood bookstore where I was scheduled to meet Katie, whose apartment I would be staying at for the week. She was a journalist I'd slept with exactly once, but after that, the two of us became film buddies, and she'd recently moved from New York to L.A. to take an entry-level position with *The National Enquirer*. When half an hour passed and Katie didn't show up, I had no way to get in touch with her (the pre–cell phone epoch!). So I waited in front of the store for another 15 minutes and was just getting ready to leave when I looked up and saw her, in her frosted short hair, rambling toward me on the sidewalk. "I'm so sorry!" she said. "There's this huge story. O.J. Simpson's wife got murdered. And they think maybe he did it."

"You're kidding," I said.

"They need me to help cover this. So I've got to leave right now." Okay, I said, I'll fend for myself. With Katie assigned to round-the-clock O.J. coverage, I spent my vacation week in L.A. hanging out and doing nothing too remarkable. At one point, while having a drink with an aspiring film-editor pal, I got introduced to her friend Todd McCarthy, the stalwart film critic of *Variety*, who had just come from a screening. "I saw Oliver Stone's new movie," he said, and then he shook his head, miming a "whoosh!" of befuddlement. "I still don't know what to make of it." In my experience, when a critic says he doesn't know what to make of something, it means he didn't fully care for it but is weighing the politics of his response.

I'm not overstating it when I say that it was surreal to spend the kickoff week of O.J. madness in Los Angeles, crashing with someone who was covering the case. At one point, Katie was assigned by the *Enquirer* to sneak into Nicole Simpson's wake, which she did with no problem. "How the hell did you manage that?" I asked, impressed at her undercover acumen. "Nothing to it," she said. "I just dressed like one of the mourners, and I was in." On Thursday, as the slow-mo highway chase that shook the world was unfolding, the cars traveled under an overpass right near Katie's apartment, and though I was of course watching it on TV, I felt so dead close to the action that it was almost as if I could physically touch the fear, fascination, excitement, and dread.

Whether or not it was due to that proximity, I experienced the O.J. Simpson case as a rip in the fabric. It marked the culmination—or perhaps the true beginning—of an age in which the seamier sides of fame would now feed directly into people's identities. Almost literally overnight, the Simpson case became part of what Norman Mailer once called "the dream life of the nation." It was a celebrity slasher nightmare that colonized our fixations, and so, in a horrific way, it also qualified as a new form of entertainment. It was only one double homicide, but it became the game-changing big click in our de-evolution into Tabloid Nation.

When I returned to New York, things felt different, and the whole atmosphere of O.J.—the way the crime didn't just shock and appall but, in effect, merged with us—came to seem a ghostly premonition of the greatest film I'd seen in a long time, certainly since the launch of *EW*. That was *Natural Born Killers*, the Oliver Stone film that a lot of people, in addition to Todd McCarthy, would not quite know what to make of. The first movie I had to see when I got back, though, was a new-fangled version of the old-fashioned treacle called *Forrest Gump*, and to this day I can't believe there was a critic in the country who fell for it. But I knew as I was watching it that audiences would get sucked in (the film was dishonest in just the right catchy, profound-beer-commercial way), and that perception gave rise to what was starting to feel like a familiar sensation of irritating anxiety. As I walked out of the Paramount screening room, I said to myself: *Get ready to be an enemy of the people again!*

My readers must have begun to think I hated Tom Hanks, but that wasn't the case at all. I was a big Hanks fan, going all the way back to *Bachelor Party*; I just didn't like the calculated, both-eyes-on-the-crowd message movies he was now making, like *Philadelphia*, which dribbled him with downtrodden nobility. *Forrest Gump*, a theme-park ride through history in which Hanks' Forrest, with his idiot/saint '50s flattop, was digitally inserted into iconic moments, is, I wrote, "a technically amazing pop stunt. It is also glib, shallow, and monotonous, a movie that spends so much time sanctifying its hero that, despite his 'innocence,' he ends up seeming about as vulnerable as Superman... The movie suggests that Forrest, rather than living through history, is triumphing over history, like a slow-brained Ferris Bueller. He's making the last 30 years feel good again." There was a soft-edged boomer didacticism to *Forrest Gump*; if you didn't like it, the film implied that you were on the wrong side of the historical looking glass. But it was really the movie that was on the wrong side.

I knew all of this would make Jim Seymore grumble, but it's not like I was going to pull punches. Having made a couple of lame nods— like my *Hook* review—in that direction, I knew it wouldn't work. It just made me sound like a dumber version of myself. But I won't deny that saying exactly what I thought about a movie like *Forrest Gump* left me feeling a little uneasy. The essence of the anxiety is that it was vague and free-floating. Did I think I'd lose my job? I knew that Seymore had protected me, so the answer to that was no. (But maybe, deep down, yes.) My real concern, in some inchoate way, was about losing *power*. There were perpetual whispers that Jim wanted the lead movie reviews to be shorter, and since they were, on balance, longer than the reviews in the other sections, that worry seemed real enough. Then there was the turf war. Once Ty Burr abandoned the movie section, I didn't have it all to myself for very long. It was decided that I still needed backup, and the section editor, David Hajdu, came up with the idea for who that should be: Lisa Schwarzbaum.

Lisa had been a feature writer at *EW* since 1991, and I first sat up and took notice of what a superb writer she was because of two pieces she'd done. One was her 1993 cover story on Daniel Day-Lewis. She had traveled all the way to his hideaway in Ireland, and given that access, the profile she came up with was one of the rare *EW* features that felt like a flowing, eloquently full-scale portrait of an artist. The other article Lisa did that spoke to me in a rare way was, believe it or not, her feature on

The McLaughlin Group. I'd become a fanatic for this Sunday-morning TV ritual of gloriously disputatious political chitchat (I told people that I loved it because it reminded me of my family), and Lisa's piece was a deep dive into McLaughlin mania. I realized, in reading it, that she and I were kindred spirits, and the Day-Lewis piece showed me that she had the sensibility of a movie critic, even though she had never been one. But that didn't mean I wanted her in the movie section! I accepted her presence, but my territoriality remained on full alert. For a long time, I maintained a cordial but distant relationship with Lisa, not talking to her much beyond the times we ran into each other in the halls. In the office, she cut a distinctive figure: tall, a little severe, with a brisk and highly purposeful *strut*, which a lot of the younger writers found intimidating. But I glimpsed the insecurity beneath the bravado, in a takes-one-to-know-one way.

One of the many reasons I felt at home at *EW* was that so many of the writers and editors thought just like critics. Even the researchers, copy editors, and designers did; that's part of what gave the magazine its pizzazz. *Entertainment Weekly* still had yet to turn a profit, and financially it wasn't out of the woods yet, but something extraordinary had happened. It had jelled into a buzzy, exciting magazine, its cookie-cutter modular design refined into something playfully elegant. That growth, at least in theory, portended a happy future for the bottom line. The magazine wasn't simply catching the mood of the '90s. It was starting to help define what the '90s were: an American decade that was hopeful and eager and flush, with the whole culture now oriented toward obsessive, enlightened commentary about a subject as disposable as entertainment—but not because people were looking to pop culture to escape their desperate, wretched lives, as they did in the '30s. Quite the contrary: Now, it was more like people felt they could *afford* to while away their time consuming and thinking about trivia. About *nothing*. *EW* had come up with a great cover image—still perhaps my all-time favorite—that pictured the four faces of the *Seinfeld* cast against a black background, in a nod to the cover of *Meet the Beatles*. That image represented a perfect alignment of not just two but three icons, à la the sun, the moon, and the earth: It was the Beatles, *Seinfeld* . . . and now *EW*.

There was a new and enlightened hierarchy at the magazine. In the

early days, it often felt like Sheriff Jim Seymore and his Time Inc. deputies vs. the rest of the staff. But several of the original editors had left
(voluntarily), and Jim, in replacing them, had made two significant hires.
He recruited Maggie Murphy, the wife of my *EW* buddy David Browne
(who had moved into the role of lead music critic), to oversee the News
& Notes section at the front of the magazine, and Maggie turned out
to be a sharp-eyed observer of pop trends who reveled in the allure of
celebrity without a glimmer of shame. Her unapologetic fixation helped
to give *EW* more of a starstruck sheen, but it was also under Murphy's
influence that the magazine found a mass-audience way to showcase
inside Hollywood information—the kind of reporting that, up until
then, had been available only in the trades. She liked to feature "trouble
on the set" stories, like a piece about the chaos that was bedeviling the
shooting of *The Crow*. Just as the story was ready to hit newsstands, the
film's star, Brandon Lee, was killed by a prop gun with a real bullet in
it, making *EW* look astonishingly prescient. The magazine's readership
scores began to rise in tandem with the rise of News & Notes, vindicat-
ing Seymore's vision of a "news magazine of entertainment."

Jim also hired the brash and feministic Mary Kaye Schilling, from
Sassy, and what she brought to the table was an appreciation for the
cool/niche/alternative side of things that would prove way ahead of the
curve once she took over the magazine's television coverage. She was a
formative champion of shows with rabid fan bases, like *Buffy the Vampire Slayer* and *The X-Files*, which for the first time were making the
landscape of TV seem hip. Rounding out *EW*'s new power structure
was the deceptively boyish, bogglingly brilliant Mark Harris, who had
begun, back in 1990, as the magazine's most gifted feature writer, and
then became the editor overseeing its movie coverage. I was in awe of
how Mark could turn out a wizardly piece of writing—like his cover
story on *Wayne's World*—virtually off the top of his head, and he had
an uncanny ability to draw people to him with his charismatic alternat-
ing current of personality: He was earnestly friendly and supportive...
and also a grandmaster of snark. He had a rarefied aesthetic and critical
mind...and also computer-level knowledge of everything from mystery
novels to soap operas to Hollywood's most intricate executive shuffles. I
nicknamed him, only half-jokingly, The Smartest Man in the Universe,

and Mark became a mentor for many writers, raising the game of *EW*'s feature-writing capacity.

At meetings, Maggie, Mark, and Mary Kaye became something like the junior Joint Chiefs of Staff. They made the case for adventurous ideas, presenting them to Jim in the best possible fashion, but they often disagreed with one another, which made for juicy theater, since it was like seeing *EW*'s three ninjas of pop knowledge square off in the ring. If any two out of three of them agreed on a cover idea, the chances were it could be sold to Jim. It was amazing which stories sometimes required the hard-sell. The week that Kurt Cobain killed himself, the magazine was all set to do a cover story on *Mad About You*, and the debate that ensued about which cover should prevail looked like it could go either way, until Cobain (duh!) ultimately wound up on the cover.

The reason even that choice wasn't so clear related to a guideline that had, in my opinion, hobbled *EW* from the earliest days. The original concept of the magazine was that it should cover, in Jeff Jarvis' words, "the product, not the people." *EW*, in other words, would be about the *content* of entertainment, as opposed to the gossipy sideshow of celebrity. The main reason for that mandate—and the reason it exists to this day—was that the executives at Time Inc. decided that *Entertainment Weekly*, if it wasn't bridled in that way, would begin to edge onto *People* magazine's terrain and, potentially, cut into *People*'s profits. They didn't want *EW* and *People* as rivals. But when you buy an entertainment magazine that features a movie, TV, or music star on the cover, there's simply a natural inclination to want to read about that person's *life* as well as that person's *art*. It's not as if the two can really be separated. From the start, *EW* wasn't allowed to venture out nearly as much as it could have into the lives of the artists it covered—not in a tawdry superficial way, but to show us who they were as human beings. And that gave the magazine, for all its addictive wit and passion, a certain airless quality.

Within those strictures, however, it was becoming one of the most avidly beloved magazines of the '90s (though no one there, including me, knew it yet). I loved going to work, even if I often felt like a member of the club who was standing a little on the outside. I'll confess—though it's one of the dorkiest things I've ever said—that when I got out of the subway at the corner of 50th St. and Broadway on Monday mornings, there were moments I wanted to toss my hat in the air (if I'd had a hat) just like Mary Tyler Moore. That's how much I relished working at *Entertainment Weekly*. It felt like the only office in the history of American corporate culture where carrying on the proverbial water-cooler conversation about a movie or TV show you just saw wasn't just a waste of time. *It was your job.* I wasn't that much of a TV head myself, but *Seinfeld* was the first show since *Miami Vice* that became appointment viewing for me, and deconstructing the episodes on Friday, with whoever was around, was a deeply pleasurable ritual. As was, of course, talking about every movie under the sun.

Much as I cherished the casual fellowship of the pop-culture cultists I worked with, there was a side to the *EW* staff I did think was stodgy and reactionary. The day after Madonna's infamous March 1994 appearance on *Late Night with David Letterman*, everyone gathered in the conference room for a video replay of the outrageous talk-show encounter. It was obviously great television, because Madonna, openly taunting Letterman, escalated it into one of those priceless moments of star-trip psychodrama. Still in the prime of her *Sex*-coffee-table-book/"Justify My Love" outré-erotic mode, she came on like a high-school dominatrix making merciless sport of the innocent uptight jock. Letterman got in some good jabs, but he was clearly hostile to who and what Madonna was, and when the replay was over, I was dismayed to see that same level of hostility toward Madonna on the part of everyone in the room. They all "sided" with Letterman, the straitlaced good boy, but I felt this was incredibly hypocritical, given that the whole reason we were sitting there and re-watching this showdown in the first place—something I don't ever remember happening before—is that Madonna had made a strategic decision to go "too far." It was self-promotion as postmodern showbiz, and the simultaneous attraction to it and rejection of it reflected a symbiosis that was going on at *EW*: If Jim Seymore, after four years, had grown attuned to the hipper sensibilities of the staff, the writers, in turn, were beginning to show the influential mark of Time Inc. They worked for *Entertainment Weekly*, but I wondered if they understood that pop culture wasn't just supposed to be entertaining or even artful. There were times it was supposed to be radical.

The first time I saw *Natural Born Killers*, it was in the Todd-AO

Screening Room, right across the street from the old Studio 54. The room was a giant box, wired for stupendous sound, with large leather couches in the back, and from the opening images, shot on contrasting film stocks—a wolf, a tongue-flicking rattlesnake, an ancient roadside diner sign, a TV set with channels being flipped through *Leave It to Beaver*, Nixon's resignation speech, and maybe the devil—I knew exactly what to make of it. Or close enough. It's a film I would end up seeing probably around 40 times, but that first time, around 10 minutes into it, I thought, "This is the first movie I've ever seen that looks like the inside of my brain."

Sitting at the diner counter, Woody Harrelson's Mickey, his back to us, his blond hair in a long ponytail and his voice smoothly sinister, asks a depressed-looking waitress which pie she recommends, and she drawls, "Well, the key lime's great, but it's an acquired taste," and just as she says "taste," in cuts a black-and-white image of her saying the same thing (*"acquired taste!"*), only this time with a broad flirtatious smile; then the film snaps back to color and her morose look. The movie is teaching us how to watch it, with the jutting-in-and-out black-and-white images as psychological X-rays of what's happening in the scene. They're more real than the reality. From the start, there was an over-the-top quality to *Natural Born Killers*, but the gravelly grandeur of Leonard Cohen singing "Waiting for the Miracle" under those opening minutes (*"Baby, I've been waiting, I've been waiting night and day"*), like some jaunty funeral march, told you that everything you were about to see was dead-serious as well.

Seconds later, Juliette Lewis' Mallory is at the far end of the diner, in pigtails and hip-huggers, with a swiveling bare midriff that looks nearly as long as she is. She's gyrating like some snake-charming stripper to a dirty rock boogie when a couple of rednecks come in. One of them, uninvited, starts to dance with her, or maybe *at* her, and just before the jukebox flips on a new 45, he flashes a lascivious grin and says, "*Beep-beep!*" Did he forget that Wile E. Coyote never caught his prey? The next song isn't ancient rock anymore, it's L7's "Shit List," a grunge feminist rant at old bad discarded lovers. When Mallory starts to kick the living shit out of her harasser, it's not only what he deserves; it's guy power giving way to girl power. It's the birth of a new world.

That's what *Natural Born Killers* was about: a new world. One in which lives melt into media and media melts back, and all the old rules are gone. The credits sequence, with its pile of stock images (getaway cars, a fake Hydra out of a B-horror movie) woven into a flickering outlaw collage, with a caterwauling soundtrack laid on top of it ("Leader of the Pack" downshifts into Patti Smith's "Rock 'n' Roll Nigger"), is infused with a half century's worth of youth rebellion and film-noir danger, and even after the film settles down (a relative settling, in this case), those images, and a hundred others, keep biting back into the texture.

When *Natural Born Killers* came out, critics who didn't get the movie made a point of sneering at its most obvious layer of meaning: that Mickey and Mallory, who go on a three-week murder spree that turns them into infamous media stars, become celebrities because they're killers. Wow, big irony! What the film knows all too well is that mass killers have been an iconic (and ironic) part of pop culture for a very long time—a point made definitively in the 1967 New Hollywood classic *Bonnie and Clyde*. The tingly audacity of *Natural Born Killers*, and the addictive pleasure of watching it, begins with the far bolder perception that Mickey and Mallory experience not just their infamy but *every moment of their lives* as pop culture. Their lives are poured through the images they carry around in their heads. The sequence in which they meet and become a couple sealed in blood is done as a vile, scum-dripping sitcom, with Rodney Dangerfield—in a shockingly scary performance—as the abusive slob dad who's been sneaking into Mallory's bedroom since she was a young girl. What the sequence communicates, in a hypnotically funny and compact way, is: *This is our lives now. Family craziness. Hate and dysfunction and violence. Leading to great pain. And, inevitably, to more violence. All of it recycled into entertainment. A vicious circle of media-endorsed insanity.* But which came first, the sitcom or the egg?

It's this dynamic that connects Mickey and Mallory to the audience. Our identification with them as killers, each acting out a vicious vengeance rooted in their childhood, works in a basic, mythic, pop-badass *Bonnie and Clyde*–meets–*Badlands* way, but what's really going on is that the two of them enact a heightened version of a world in which all of identity is increasingly becoming a murky, bundled fusion of true life and media fantasy. It works something like this: You are what you watch, which is what you want to be, which is what you think you are, which is what you really can be (yes, you can!), as long as you... *believe.*

When the screening of *Natural Born Killers* ended, I emerged and literally felt like my entire body was humming, as if it had been irradiated. I rode the subway downtown, went into a bar near my apartment, and ordered a beer, and I realized, sitting there in the middle of August (usually the dog days for movies), that the film had gotten into my system, imprinting itself on my senses kinesthetically, more than any film I'd seen since *Nashville.* It now owned me, and that kind of experience is so rare that I was only too happy to give myself up to it. I consider it religious—a movie as conduit to something mystical. I saw the film a second time before writing about it, and saw it once again the Sunday night of opening weekend (I was eager to observe how it would play with an audience, and the crowd I saw it with went wild). But my true addiction to *NBK* began months later, when it came out on video. I had watched a handful of films obsessively before, notably *Manhunter,* but this was different: I didn't just watch *Natural Born Killers* again and again—I *played* it, like an album I couldn't stop listening to. I saw and heard and experienced it as an opera of scandalous amazements.

The screenwriters of *Bonnie and Clyde* had once approached Jean-Luc Godard to be their director, and what they wanted was the Godard of *Breathless.* But *Natural Born Killers* was like *Bonnie and Clyde* made by the Godard of *Weekend,* crossed with Kenneth Anger's *Scorpio Rising* and with some witches' brew that Oliver Stone had devised in his fever-dream daring. He'd reworked a Quentin Tarantino script, and you could hear glimmers of Tarantino in the baroque nihilism, but Stone, pouring on images so that Mickey and Mallory seemed to be watching themselves, transformed that into pop poetry. The story, the more you watched it, expanded into three dimensions, or maybe four. *Natural Born Killers* seemed to be making a vicious mockery of media, as embodied by Wayne Gale, the Aussie tabloid-TV host played as a spectacular weasel by Robert Downey Jr. But the deeper mystery of the film is that it's about real demons: the ones that slither up out of families and the landscape and history. Woody Harrelson, in what may be the most underappreciated piece of great acting in the '90s, plays Mickey as a good ol' boy with a sick gleam and a hint of terrified depths beneath his coiled-cat cunning. At the climax of his jail-cell interview with Wayne Gale, his words inspire a prison riot, and it's staged by Stone as a melee of apocalyptic deliverance, whipped along by a song—"Nusrat 1083/Nusrat"—that sounds like it's foreseeing the rise of radical Islam. *Natural Born Killers* is about the birth of a new world that blasts the old world—ours—apart. The end of the movie is sealed by Leonard Cohen singing, "I've seen the future, brother, it is murder."

The appearance of a movie as lethally mesmerizing as *Natural Born Killers* loomed so large for me that it didn't bother me when the film wasn't widely recognized as the landmark it is. It's healthy when some works exist outside the official academy of taste. A small handful of critics did grasp the film's power; they included Roger Ebert and, God bless him, *The New Republic*'s 78-year-old Stanley Kauffmann. At my office, very few people did, but I was drawn into enough water-cooler conversations about *NBK* to last for months. That the film was a late-summer hit allowed my raving about it to seem less controversial than it might have otherwise, though the film crystallized a developing category at *EW* known as The Movies Owen Likes—i.e., dark, weird, violent, intense, and out of the mainstream. Okay, those *were* movies I liked, but I knew my sensibility wasn't really all that extreme. Because I knew that this *was* the new mainstream.

The high of *Natural Born Killers* fed into a fall release schedule that mirrored, in an uncanny way, August through October 1986, when my three crowning masterpieces of the '80s—*Manhunter, Blue Velvet,* and *Sid and Nancy*—were all released within three months of each other. In 1994, that more or less happened all over again, the trio in this case consisting of *Natural Born Killers* (August), *Ed Wood* (September), and *Pulp Fiction* (October). To be fair, I wouldn't quite rank *Ed Wood* as the third best film of the decade; more like #6. But still! For movies, what a cultural hinge moment.

Ed Wood suffered a trickier fate than *Natural Born Killers*—it was highly acclaimed, and also a high-profile commercial bomb. In essence, it was an indie film marketed by Disney; no wonder it fell through the cracks. Yet the small handful who saw and cherished it recognized that Tim Burton, making his most personal statement, had turned the life of the worst filmmaker of all time into a uniquely ticklish celebration of what movies really are. In the '50s, Edward D. Wood Jr. churned out grade-Z sci-fi and horror films so scrappy and awful that watching them, one can't begin to suspend one's disbelief. The rich comic beauty of *Ed Wood* lay in how much *he* believed in them. Played with a mysterioso perky grace by Johnny Depp, Wood, an impassioned no-talent, unapologetic transvestite, and holy fool of cinema, became nothing less than the spirit of art, and Martin Landau's performance as the washed-up, morphine-junkie Bela Lugosi, wrapping his legend around him like a rat-eaten cape, completed the film's winking vision of Hollywood as a place of gleeful ghosts. As haunting a job as Burton did directing *Ed Wood*, it was the screenwriters, Scott Alexander and Larry Karaszewski, who were the film's real auteurs. By inventing the whole topsy-turvy notion of making a biopic about a person no one in his right mind would ever make a biopic about, they helped to nudge movies into the reality-is-more-gripping-than-fiction era.

Then again, fiction was about to be reborn. It would now (once again) be called "pulp," and what that meant was: something so raw and tawdry and outrageous and tempestuous and taboo that it popped your eyes open with astonishment to watch it. That was the Quentin Tarantino revolution. He invented a new kind of movie, but only to return us—and by "us," I mean the whole world—to what movies had been, and no longer were. A spectacle so complete, so full of cinematic and human surprise, that it had the magical effect of taking you out of yourself. Once again, the primal movie question (*"What's going to happen next?"*) seemed to carry the weight of existence: *I learn what happens next, therefore I am.* In the final moments of *Pulp Fiction*, when John Travolta's Vincent Vega saunters out of a diner in a slovenly track suit, we already know that he's been killed, but thanks to the film's pretzel-logic time sequence his presence counts as nothing less than a resurrection.

Jim Seymore had major problems with *Pulp Fiction*. At the weekly staff meeting, he drew a line in the sand on Tarantino. "He's bringing sadism into the mainstream," Jim declared. You could feel everyone in the room thinking, *"And your problem with that is...?"*

Pulp Fiction and *Ed Wood* both played at the New York Film Festival, and on Saturday night, about a week into the festival, there was a party for *Ed Wood* that turned out to be the most intoxicating movie bash

I'd ever been to, the kind that tapped deep into my inner 12-year-old gawker-fan. It was held in a jazz club called Iridium, which had the feel of a basement cave. Quentin was there, looking chiseled and humble, still feeling out the new role of director-as-generational-superstar; he even danced a bit. Then Johnny Depp and Kate Moss walked in—they were at that point the It Couple of all media—and they happened to stand right next to me, so I turned and drank in their faces for about a minute, and I thought Moss was pure ivory angelic splendor, and that Depp, because he was adjacent to her, was revealed to be the single most beautiful person I had ever seen, like some high-cheekboned superman gigolo sheik who merged the masculine and the feminine. I knew at that moment, because it hadn't totally happened yet, that he was going to be a very, very big movie star.

And then, just when I thought the galaxy couldn't get much brighter, in walked someone who trumped everyone in the room, because he seemed to have entered from a different dimension. He had three body-guards with him, and he was tall, and bulked, and a little hunched over; stretched over his torso was an ugly tropical polyester shirt that somehow, on him, looked like Technicolor. It was Mickey Rourke, who was officially a has-been, a trashed reject of the system. But for that very reason he now seemed cooler than ever, like Elvis rising from the grave. He went to a booth in the back, settling in there with his boys, flashing white Tony Robbins teeth and a smiling semi-mashed pink face that looked about halfway down the road to ruin of what it would eventually come to be. He sat there all night, and each time I looked over to spy on him for a second (which, like everyone else in the room, was about as often as I could), I got zapped by his presence in the same way. Now *that*, I said to myself, is a fucking *star*! I felt like I'd made it to the chewy center of the movie universe. It was sweet and tasty and good.

CHAPTER 15

"IT IS WHAT IT IS"

Film festivals are buzzy, sprawling, neck-craning, party-and-conversation-packed hives, but the first time I ever went to the Sundance Film Festival, I got lured in by the snowbound quiet of it all. There was a majestic hush blanketing Park City, Utah, an old mining town dotted with rustic-modernist hillside homes and boutique silver-and-turquoise jewelry shops, all of which made it look like the glittery stage set for some art-directed Western musical *set* in an old mining town. I was too late for phase one of the festival's rise: *Reservoir Dogs* premiered there in 1992, *Clerks* in 1994, and my virgin visit took place in 1995. So this was already a Sundance that had morphed into an off-Hollywood colony, besieged by movie stars, agents, publicists, directors, producers, models, musicians, and, of course, the whole eager sharky apparatus of the indie world. Yet Sundance was a *lot* smaller than it soon would be. The Eccles Theater, which became the central place to see movies starting in 1999, seats 1,270 people, and the dull roar of the audience there before a movie starts is a very defining Sundance din. In '95, the year that I arrived, the main venue was still the Egyptian Theater, a cozy-crumbly "movie palace" near the top of Main Street that seats all of 282. Back then, that was about as big as a Sundance mob could get.

After checking into my hotel, I took the shuttle bus to Main Street, the long, sloping, climb-to-the-top-and-the-thin-mountain-air-will-wind-you street where the festival was centered, and when I got off, the light was crisp and sun-streaked, the caked-on snow still pristine. As I made my way to the festival headquarters, I spotted Julie Delpy, who I'd been writing about in *Before Sunrise* just a few days earlier (it was the festival's opening-night feature, and was set to open theatrically the following Friday). Watching her stalk down the street, in what looked like a bit of a huff, I had a star-sighting sensation very different from the usual one: Delpy was a minor celebrity, but I got a tingle from seeing her because she was just... *there*, in her beige down jacket, like someone you might have spotted on the first day of camp. I'd come to see movies, but I already felt like I was playing a bit part in *Sundance: The Movie*.

That afternoon, I went to my first screening, and it turned out to be the perfect Sundance ice-breaker: a nifty little comedy called *Party Girl*, starring Parker Posey as an anonymous latter-day Edie Sedgwick who spirals down into too many druggy good times. I thought it was a great role for her—and to this day, the film remains a neglected gem in the Posey canon, especially given that the actress, who I was already a fan of, never did land the defining star role that might have taken her postmodern sauciness and flashing-eyed Katharine Hepburn beauty to the next level. I got introduced to the film's first-time director, Daisy von Scherler Mayer, and I was struck by how much she—sort of like Julie Delpy—came off as an ordinary person, not some intimidating high-powered Filmmaker. It had something to do with the heavy winterwear and how that democratized everything in a kind of furry frosty Soviet way. If Sundance was winter camp, then this was the camp uniform.

I'd lucked out with *Party Girl*, but having been to only one other film festival before (the Montreal Film Festival, which is basically four days of the drabbest Canadian wallpaper you could imagine), I didn't quite know what I was doing. *Entertainment Weekly*, at that point, didn't run festival coverage from me, and I lined up for one random disposable movie after another. I didn't keep my ear close enough to the ground to tease out a higher quotient of the better ones, which is why I wound up not even seeing *The Brothers McMullen*, the Ed Burns movie that took the Grand Jury Prize. Yet there were a handful of moments that wowed me. The record producer Don Was had directed a documentary, *I Just Wasn't Made for These Times*, that was a musicological meditation on Brian Wilson and the Beach Boys, and Wilson, still crawling out from his years of "recovery" with the charlatan shrink Eugene Landy, showed up to support the movie. At the Riverhorse Café, a lodge-like restaurant perched over Main Street that doubled as the festival's key party venue, he sat at a piano one late afternoon and performed a couple of songs. He was choppy and out of tune, but no one cared. That night, I went to a party at Don Was's rented condo high up in Deer Valley, and Brian Wilson was there. I desperately wanted to say a private hello-and-thanks-for-being-the-genius-you-are, and I did, but he was still clearly in bad shape, struggling to put the words together, at one point just zoning out.

Every encounter I had that year was more muted than I expected. I relished the chance to meet Richard Linklater, especially after the letter he'd sent me, but as soon as I shook his hand, he turned away with a too-cool-for-school vibe that said, "You're not special, you're just a critic," which is the vibe I've gotten from him ever since. As far as I was concerned, our "relationship" ended before it had a chance to begin. A couple of days later, in the mostly empty press lounge that was set up in an old vintage hotel lobby–turned–tavern called the Claim Jumper, I was reading a newspaper, and I glanced over at the woman sitting kiddie corner from me and thought that she looked familiar. Seconds later, I realized it was Kim Cattrall, and I thought, "Holy shit, the girl from *Mannequin*!" I couldn't pass up this rare chance to strike up a casual conversation with an actress who had been such a figure of '80s adolescent male fantasy. We talked about was what she was working on, and a little about what I did, but what surprised me—especially when I thought back on it three years later, after *Sex and the City* began—is that Kim Cattrall was so serious and demure that she seemed like some very shy high-school English teacher.

The film I most wanted to see at Sundance was *Crumb*, Terry Zwigoff's documentary about the legendary underground cartoonist, and when I did, the experience was transformative. I saw what I'd always known in my bones but had never quite put together, which is that R. Crumb was one of the defining artists of the 20th century (in the movie, *Time*'s art critic, Robert Hughes, compared him to Bruegel, which I thought was a fantastic insight). The film did his life and art full justice; it was a staggering portrait. Yet what hit me most about *Crumb* was how incredibly personal my connection to Robert Crumb turned out to be on almost every level. The fearlessness with which he plucked his visions right out of his acid-head id made him seem like the original bard of political incorrectness, and I felt an intense identification with his hunger to depict the truth as he saw it. When I'd read his comics during the days of my teen counterculture romance, I never knew what to make of the fact that I found some of them rather arousing. But *Crumb*, as a movie, was all about a geek's mad-dog sexual obsession. That was the fire that fueled Crumb's art, and it still fueled him as a person. I felt like the very existence of a movie like *Crumb* dignified my own obsessions.

The movie also shed astonishing light on where those obsessions can come from. *Crumb* contrasted Robert Crumb with his two brothers, who were also gifted artists, but they, unlike him, emerged from their traumatic '50s home life as human wreckage: Charles, a recluse with pedophilic tendencies, still living at home with his mother, marinating in his sardonic bitterness like some bookish Norman Bates; and Maxxon, an admitted sexual molester who led the existence of a masochistic hippie monk. Robert escaped this level of fate, but just barely, his success having lifted him out of purgatory. Like Crumb, I tended to think of myself as a horny deviant, and within my own unhappy family I also had two brothers, both of whom arguably suffered more than I did: Erik from an extended battle with depression, which kicked in when he was in college, and Stefan from the massive burden of his Tourette syndrome. I, too, had escaped and been "saved" through my success. Or had I? Watching *Crumb*, I saw that erotic compulsion and repression, the twin-headed demon of the Crumb family, was also the demon of mine. And I saw how that demon had the power to destroy.

I knew that *Crumb* was opening in April, and back at *EW*, I began a campaign in the middle of February to do it as a lead review. The film became highly symbolic for me: If the astounding crossover success of *Pulp Fiction* was like the war of independence declaring victory, *Crumb* incarnated the still-dangerous soul of the indie movement—the vitality of the real, the need to go deep into the darkness. I knew that any serious publication would play up its importance, so I saw the issue of *Crumb* as lead review as a major test case. We simply *had* to do it. I lobbied and lobbied, making myself annoying, planting the seed so early that it came to seem a fait accompli...and lo and behold, I won. We did *Crumb* as the lead, at 900 words.

Though I didn't declare it outright in my review, my identification with Crumb the nerd libertine avenger was hiding in plain sight: "In *Crumb*, the man himself, wearing oversize spectacles and a porkpie hat that give him the look of a grocery-store clerk from the 1920s, turns out to be a gangly, rather talkative chap with sharp eyes and a whiplash wit that's almost scary in its acrid detachment...Crumb's words, like his cartoons, amount to an ongoing confession—of compulsive erotic longing, or near-metaphysical paranoia about his inability to fit in." The movie was "a portrait of the artist as misanthrope, as bad-boy visionary, as joker and sex maniac and, finally, as hero." My piece, I felt, was a small victory for everything R. Crumb stood for.

In Crumb's life, as in his comics, there was an intertwined agony and ecstasy of longing that I also felt defined my existence. Desire so consumed me that it was like a curse I never wanted to have lifted. I felt like I had the revved emotions of a sex addict, if only on occasion the self-annihilating behavior. I believed in monogamy, but my civilized form of "cheating" was to break up with someone, and I'd been a rapid-turnover ADD serial monogamist for so long that the patterns were starting to look like reruns: the restless hunger for *more* that was always the monkey wrench thrown into my relationships; the way I chose girlfriends I had affection for, and even cared about, but that only made me wonder why I had never—ever—fallen in love with a single one of them. Maybe love was standing right in front of me and I just didn't know it. Yet my piggish slow churn through women appeared to have no end. The slinky right-wing essayist, the whiskey-sipping law-firm publicist, the featherheaded dental hygienist, the playfully sparring BBC producer: Each turned into a seduce-and-grow-close-and-break-up "drama" that was really a tempest in the relationship teapot. The truth is that my partners were rarely crazy enough in bed for me. Or on the rare occasions they were, they would turn out to be too crazy *out* of bed.

Like Brandi, who I met at a screening of *The Quick and the Dead*. She was a children's-book-publishing assistant who moonlighted as a dominatrix. She looked like a tall, lascivious Paula Abdul, and in her private life what got her off was playing at domination, only to have the tables turned on her. There was a combustibly arousing drama to that, and for a while it became addictive. Our switchback role-playing heightened the *collision* of sex, made it feel more real to me; it was as if we were lifting each other, through borderline hateful teasing, to higher and higher levels of depraved intensity. At the end of a wild night with Brandi, I would feel cleansed, almost holy, yet I didn't like her as a person, and the feeling was mutual. It didn't take long for me to realize that the main reason she worked two nights a week at an S&M dungeon in Chelsea was to act out her contempt for men. She began to turn vicious about my being a film critic, calling my career "ridiculous," and that wounded me, because on some level I felt she had a point. I knew I couldn't be with someone like her, but our viciousness was the mud in which our sex games took root.

In the spring of 1995, *Entertainment Weekly* won a National Magazine Award for General Excellence, which was like winning Best Picture at journalism's Oscars. It was an ecstatic moment for all of us, one of several signs—the first being ad sales, the second being the general anecdotal level of buzzy relevance—that the magazine was really, truly going to stick around. I thought, "Cool, *now* I can relax." The truth, though, is that doing my job was stirring up more and more feelings of subtle tension. I first really noticed it after a screening of *Die Hard with a Vengeance* at the brand new Sony Lincoln Square Theater, a corporately stately megaplex on the Upper West Side that soon became the top-grossing movie theater in the United States. The Lincoln Square marked a new era in what a typical "all-media" screening of a popcorn movie would be: bigger, more boisterous, more stuffed with "fans," more popcorny. All of which was designed to make critics think: *Look around you! This is the reaction you're supposed to be having!* The third film in the *Die Hard* series teamed Bruce Willis' John McClane with a buddy/adversary played by Samuel L. Jackson, and it was really just a series of set pieces slam-banged together, but it flagged a telling moment. At *EW*, Mark Harris and I often talked about the rather startling way that the original *Die Hard* looked like a totally different movie than it had in 1988, when it first came out. Then, it had been the definition of over-the-top—a thriller so entertainingly preposterous that it played like some shameless inside joke of Hollywood action decadence. But just a few years later, the exact same movie looked tight, rigorous, disciplined; much of it could even be called *slow*. And that, of course, was a measure of how action films had speeded up, had lost all restraint and become badly scripted Cuisinart jamborees, full of wisecracks and fireballs and fragmentary editing (all together now: *"These are a few of my favorite things..."*).

Die Hard with a Vengeance was *that* kind of over-the-top—the slovenly, cynical kind. The day after I saw it, I ran into Steve Daly, an *EW* writer I was friendly with who had gone to the same screening. Steve was a true film buff with a treasure trove of historical and technical knowledge, but after I took a dig at the movie, instead of piling on as I expected, he offered a weary grin and said, "It is what it is." Meaning: It's junk, but it's not trying to be *more* than junk. I got a bit irritated and said, "What does that mean? That we shouldn't call it a piece of shit?"

"You can call it that," he said. "But you're out of the loop."

"I'm not sure," I replied. "The loop you're talking about is commerce. And who cares about that? Who cares if it's a hit?"

"A lot of people *do*," he said, striking a note of jovial wariness that indicated he didn't necessarily side with those people.

In a way, he was talking about the paradigm that had kicked in after *Star Wars*: Don't just go to a movie—join the club of a movie along with a great big bunch of other people. The actual product is of secondary importance. I knew what it was to have that feeling. It was there almost anytime you went to a movie on a Saturday night: The movie "was what it was," and it was the act of going out to the movies that was fun. Yet one of the reasons I evolved into a critic is that, going all the way back to high school, even when I found myself in that situation, if a movie was bad, I still experienced it as…bad. Period. The context didn't really alter anything for me. My trashing of *Die Hard with a Vengeance* was done with an appropriate lighthearted sneer ("Willis and Jackson are turned into 12-year-old boys on a play date, desperate to come up with a new game every 10 minutes"). Later on, though, Steve's words came back to haunt me more than I ever expected.

But not as much as I was haunted by the reaction to *Apollo 13*.

In June, *EW* always put out a special double issue that was on the stands for two weeks, giving everyone a week off. It started as the What Is Cool issue, then evolved into The Must List, then The It List, then the Here's a Big Bunch of Shit We'd Like You To Buy list (*kidding!*). In the days before the Internet, doubles issues really were God's gift—in essence, a free week of vacation. In this particular issue, my lead review was of *Apollo 13*, a movie I'd been excited to see but thought was far from a home run. I'd enjoyed many a Ron Howard film, and his direction of *Apollo 13* was outwardly admirable: The film truly placed you back in 1970, and it put you right aboard that desperate wounded lunar spaceship. On paper, it was my kind of terrific—an avidly authentic white-knuckle docudrama. But as much as I respected the effort, the film was dogged and repetitive, and the suspense flagged. I gave *Apollo 13* a grade of B and wrote, "Most of the action hinges on the technical maneuvers of the astronauts: the way they get the capsule to dock with the lunar module, or pilot the ship in a fuel-saving trajectory around the dark side of the moon...The revelation of the movie is how low-tech much of their activity seems, as if they were '50s mechanics in a 21st century vehicle. Yet Howard's decision to let the inherent drama of the mission dictate his entire scenario has a downside. In a sense, he hasn't done enough shaping himself. He has made a movie of objective events—an epic of tinkering."

I didn't think twice about writing a respectful but dismissive review of *Apollo 13*. But in the middle of my vacation, I was sitting on a Long Island beach reading a copy of *Esquire*, which had a small review of the film that made it sound like the *Citizen Kane* of space-voyage thrillers. I thought, "Hmmmm..." Then I began to see other reviews, and the tone was one of universal rapture. It was quite unsettling: I had no problem with any critic loving *Apollo 13*, but the collective hosanna of praise left me feeling like I had seen a different film. I didn't doubt my opinion. I knew in my heart that *The Right Stuff* (which had received mixed reviews) was a far richer and more dramatic NASA saga. But then why was everyone anointing *Apollo 13*?

When I got back to the office, I spoke to David Browne about it, and he said he'd noticed something similar happening in music criticism, with praise shoveled almost by fiat onto an album like Radiohead's *The Bends*.

"It's like people aren't allowed to dislike it," he said.

"Exactly," I said. "The same way that you aren't allowed to think *Apollo 13* is anything less than a masterpiece. And it's just not that fucking good."

He said, "It's like there's some microchip that's been planted in everyone's brain."

"Yeah," I said, "or some guy sitting there in a little room surrounded by computer consoles, with a microphone in front of him, and he tells everyone exactly what to think."

David, without missing a beat, said: "His name is Media Mike."

From that moment on, David and I would always refer to Media Mike—not as a running joke, but as a running metaphor. He was the dweeb Buddha of groupthink, and he practically became a real person to us. "Media Mike is not wild about R.E.M.'s new album," we would say. "But for some unfathomable reason, he suddenly loves Mariah Carey." "He thinks Will Smith is cool now." "Mike is deeply suspect of how *Reality Bites* got sold to Gen X. In the case of that movie, he wouldn't stand for any of that marketing crap." "He's decided that *Showgirls* is so bad it's good." "He says you can't like *The Cable Guy*." "He says you aren't allowed to dislike Arcade Fire." And on and on and on. Let's be clear: It's not as if David or I never had an opinion that was part of the majority. Of course we did! All the time. And it might sound like I'm saying that a Media Mike opinion was *any* group opinion that I happened to disagree with. Yet the difference between an honest majority and a Media Mike majority was like the old definition of pornography: hard to define, but you knew it when you saw it. You could just about smell when there was an overly collective, from-the-top-down agreement about something in pop culture, and an honestly diverse range of opinion was suddenly deafening in its absence.

Then again, there were moments I almost longed to be on Media Mike's side. As the end of the year approached, it was time to choose the best film of 1995, and I knew that I wanted mine to be *Crumb*. The only real competition thus far had been *Toy Story*, the miraculous, screwball-nutty Pixar debut that I adored and still think is the greatest of all Pixar films. "What *Bambi* and *Snow White* did for nature," I wrote, "*Toy Story*, amazingly, does for plastic—for the synthetic gizmo culture of the modern mall brat. The film's wit (and resonance) is that it brings toys to life exactly the way children do in their heads." *Toy Story* was a marvel, but *Crumb* touched a deeper chord. When I floated my choice of *Crumb*, I heard that there was some grumbling on Seymore's part, but that was about as far as it went. The choice wasn't questioned, and the design department went to work commissioning a *Crumb* illustration (or illo, as it's known in the trade) from an artist who was an associate of Crumb's, and it was a beautiful evocation of the Crumb universe. In the five years of *EW*'s existence, my most idiosyncratic choice for best film of the year slipped by without turbulence. Which made it more than a bit ironic that I then had to go and fuck it up big-time.

The major Christmas movies were being wheeled out, one by one, and I didn't think any of them were all that good, but the last one to screen was *Nixon*, Oliver Stone's three-hour poison passion play of a biopic. I saw it the second week of December, and again a week later, and I knew almost immediately that it would unseat *Crumb* to become my movie of the year. When I said so, at least two members of the *EW* design department were incredibly pissed off at me. I had messed up the deal they made for their precious piece of Crumb art! But that was the least of my problems.

It was a rough choice. *Crumb* was a tantalizing work of documentary brilliance ("A nightmare and a party at the same time," I'd written), and it was a movie I felt thrillingly close to. But *Nixon* got inside my bloodstream like heroin. It had to do with the furious synchronicity of Stone's filmmaking, with all the levels he was working on at once: personal, political, historical, mystical. He surveyed the rise and fall of Richard M. Nixon with a karmic sense of how America had been altered by the aggression it turned on the world. Anthony Hopkins, while his Welsh vowels occasionally glimmered through, gave the rare contemporary performance that could truly be called Shakespearean. He showed you Nixon's twitchy ambition and despair right along with the fulminating obscenity of his anger. The movie had the vision to see that even at his worst, Nixon was a damaged idealist, the first president to take the full measure of Eisenhower's famous warning and grasp that the system put in place after World War II had taken on a life of its own. To lead the octopus state that America had become, you were now channeling forces beyond your control.

If the defining line about Watergate is that the cover-up was worse than the crime, the upshot of *Nixon* is that cover-up, when it comes to the issue of national security, had now become the condition of our politics. The movie viewed Watergate as an electrifying cloak-and-dagger expression of Nixon's cloistered paranoia, but it also saw the scandal as more than a Nixon phenomenon. (Hello, Iran-Contra! Bush and Cheney's clandestine global torture chambers! Obama's *I'm shocked, shocked* ratcheting up of the Orwellian NSA!) If you watch *Nixon* today, it looks not so much historical as prophetic. To borrow a line from Pauline Kael's review of *The Godfather, Part II*, it's an epic vision of the corruption of America.

The week after I first saw it, I was walking through the office when a trio of *EW* editors got off the elevator, having just returned from the screening of *Nixon* that had been set up for them. Still wearing their winter coats, they trooped in through the door, one by one. The first one I saw was Mark Harris, who was always a powerful advocate for protecting my critical space. Mark and I were friends, but he flashed me an unhappy look and just said one word: "No." He was followed by George Bloosten, an honorable but slightly prickly dude who was now the editor of the movie section, and he picked up on Mark's comment by saying the exact same thing: "No." Then came another editor, who completed the depressing verdict: "No." Let's be clear: No one was saying that *Nixon* couldn't be my movie of the year. That "no" meant: "Sorry, Owen, *Nixon* is not the movie you think it is." All three had major problems with it, beginning with the issue of Hopkins' impersonation, which they found distracting and unconvincing. I respected these editors, and this wasn't something that we were going to have a fight about. But what the collective glower I'd been given told me was that the politics were shifting. *Nixon* wasn't just *my* movie of the year—it was the magazine's. To a degree, I was representing, and in this case the folks I was representing hated how I was representing them. I thought that *Nixon* might be hailed as a new classic, but for me it turned out to be a thornier, more eccentric and out-of-the-mainstream choice than *Crumb*. Audiences had no real desire to see it. The disgrace of Watergate was seen as very old, tired news.

"A man watches a movie," wrote Robert Warshow, "and the critic must acknowledge that he is that man." That's one of the most famous quotes about film criticism, and it's always been one of my defining favorites, right along with a quote from Pauline that I had tacked up on my office bulletin board: "In the arts, the critic is the only independent source of information. The rest is advertising." You could disagree with Pauline's statement, but no one could really claim that they didn't know what it meant. Yet what, exactly, did Robert Warshow mean? What does it mean for a critic to "acknowledge" that he is just a man (or a woman) watching a movie? There are several ways to interpret that statement, and one of them strikes me as potentially corrupt: If your role is that of the critic-as-ordinary-man, then you may think your job is to try to think exactly like "the mass audience." But all that would mean is that you're mindlessly anticipating or mimicking their opinions. And that can't possibly be what Warshow meant.

I think what he meant begins with the idea that a true critic knows he isn't above the audience. He's a *member* of the audience. The fact that he does this for a living, and sees a great many more movies than other people do, doesn't—or shouldn't—turn him into an elitist. Ideally, he should be a kind of enlightened populist. But many would say that if you're a professional critic, you are, by nature, an elitist. You have all sorts of opinions that are not typical of the mass audience. To pretend otherwise is to be...well, a poseur. A snob who takes on the pose of being an anti-snob.

I think the trouble with that argument is that it sells the mass audience short. A critic's point-of-view may be rarefied, cultivated, unique. But that doesn't make it "elite." On the contrary: It's precisely through his willingness to be all those things that a critic comes closest to acknowledging—in Warshow's words—that "he is that man." Because the inner essence of the mass audience is that it is *not* one thing. It's a collection of individuals. The box office is a crude rendering of their collective verdict; many people in the audience may, in fact, be just as idiosyncratic, at any given moment, as a critic. Their point-of-view may be just as rarefied, cultivated, unique. The critic's job is to be who he or she is, and in doing so to echo the powerful individuality of each and every member of the audience. That's the spirit of aesthetic democracy. The belief I had finally evolved to was: When you're a critic, you are never closer to being part of the audience than when you're willing to be your honest, pure, individual, out-there self.

But—and this is a major but—the movies were changing. Almost exactly one year after I saw *Die Hard with a Vengeance*, I went to another screening of another brutally schlocky, banged-together early-summer action thriller. This time it was *The Rock*, which yoked together Nicolas Cage, in a performance that felt like he'd already cut right to the high middle period of his narcissistic-shouting-as-I-take-the-money-and-run era (though, in fact, he had only just won the Academy Award for *Leaving Last Vegas*), and Sean Connery, compressing his graying magnetism into the kind of macho-dick role that made even Sean Connery look a little used. *The Rock* was the last "adrenalized" testosterone machine to be produced by Don Simpson and Jerry Bruckheimer before Simpson's death, and the bad joke of it was: It assaulted you with all this pumped-up puffery about breaking into Alcatraz...but really, it was just *Die Hard* all over again! Another hyped-up hostage thriller, this time with two guys instead of one crawling through catwalks to stop a crazed mastermind. That *The Rock* was the final Simpson-Bruckheimer opus should have marked it as the end of an era; on that night, though, it felt more to me like the end of movies. I hated every minute of it, and if I'd been in a more clear-headed mood, I would have recognized, without much angst, that it was simply a lame movie, even though it had "crowd-pleaser" written all over it. It was nothing but thriller logistics, a laborious exposition that never seemed to end.

Here, however, was the rub. To the extent that I had a criteria for what distinguishes a good movie from a bad movie, it came down to something fairly simple: Did what was happening on screen have an essential human quality you could connect to? To me, the criteria applied to everything from the loftiest of art films to the scuzziest of B-movies—which is why, of course, there were plenty of popcorn films that were better than art films. It all came down to the human connection. The action genre had started as a humane form. The grand seed of it was the crop-dusting sequence in Hitchcock's *North by Northwest*, which paved the way for the exhilarating life-or-death set pieces in the early Bond films, which established the template for all contemporary action. In those movies, the wild extravagance of the chases and hairbreadth escapes played as a dreamscape projection of the anxieties of modern life. To be an ordinary person was never to be hanging off the edge of a helicopter like James Bond, but it was, in the heart of one's mind, to sometimes *feel* that way, maybe when you were just walking down a crowded street. Our lives had the illusion of safety and control, but our fears and fantasies knew no boundaries, and that's what the action film expressed.

But in *The Rock*, the action was no longer expressing anything; it was just a formulaic drug designed to pound and stimulate worn-out sensory muscles. And the night I saw it, what got to me was how much *The Rock* seemed to be not the exception but the rule. In the year since *Die Hard with a Vengeance*, there had been dozens of overwrought and uniformly mediocre (or worse) action extravaganzas, and that was business as usual. Movies like *Bad Boys*. *GoldenEye* (the Bond series at its deadliest). *Mortal Kombat*. *Judge Dredd*. *Virtuosity*. *Congo*. *Assassins*. *Under Siege 2: Dark Territory*. *Just Cause*. *Money Train*. *Desperado*. *Sudden Death*. *Highlander: The Final Dimension*. I had to ask myself: Was this what popcorn cinema was becoming?

As a critic, of course, I had the right to pan any of those movies, including *The Rock*. (The one thing I wasn't allowed to do was ignore them.) But the trouble was the criteria. It was starting to become oppressive, if not a little impossible, to write in review after review after review: *"This movie is dehumanized...," "This movie is dehumanized...," "This movie is dehumanized..."* To make an analogy: A food critic has the right (and the responsibility) to occasionally review a fast-food restaurant, and maybe to pan it on the basis of its processed grease-and-fake-meat calorie-bomb tastiness. But if a food critic were suddenly told that all he or she was going to be reviewing from now on was McDonald's and KFC and Taco Bell, could he or she legitimately write that negative review over and over again? It would bloat readers more than the fast food! As a critic, I found myself between *The Rock* and a hard place: I wanted to keep writing exactly what I thought, and no one was telling me, in so many words, that I couldn't, but the whole system seemed to be rearing up and saying: "No."

CHAPTER 16
MY BOOGIE NIGHTS WITH OLIVER STONE

Alfred Hitchcock used his weekly TV series to market himself as a tongue-in-jowl icon of the macabre ("Good *eeeve*-ning!"), a slow-talking butler from hell. He set the standard for how a Hollywood film director could become not just a behind-the-scenes name but a star image in his own right. Over the decades, a small handful of directors (Scorsese, Spike Lee, Coppola, James Cameron, Spielberg) have attained that level of celebrity visibility, but it's actually more rare than it used to be to see a filmmaker who's just as famous as the films he makes. Quentin Tarantino may have been the last one. You can still imagine Quentin getting harassed for autographs during a casual walk down the street—but seriously, how often is that going to happen to Paul Thomas Anderson or Alejandro G. Iñárritu or J.J. Abrams or Judd Apatow? They're heroes to many, and recognizable to a few, but none of them have that added iconic dimension of mediagenic star quality.

In the mid-to-late '90s, however, Oliver Stone had that dimension to a degree that surprised me. And I only learned about it at around 2:00 a.m. when I went into a nightclub with him.

The club was a new place downtown, nestled behind an anonymous gray steel door somewhere in the MacDougal/Bleecker Street nexus of the West Village, and Oliver knew about it because he was always heading to some new place, where the bold-face names pop up, so that he could be part of the scene. All that meant, usually, was getting a table in the back, where we would sit and continue the conversation, now with the dance track pounding and a complimentary bottle propped up on the table. On this particular evening, as we entered the club, I saw that everyone there looked 25 or younger (when you get to be in your late thirties, you really start to notice stuff like that), and my first assumption was that this was already the *post*-film generation: the sort of kids who probably felt a deeper connection to *Beverly Hills 90210* than they ever did to movies. I didn't think most of them would know who Oliver Stone was. But Oliver had a presence—he loomed, tall and pensive in a shaggy way—and as soon as he appeared that night, something startling happened. The crowd parted, *literally*, as if it was the Red Sea made up of NYU trust-fund hipsters. As we made our way through the parted waters, I saw two dozen people gawking and saying some variation on, "*That's Oliver Stone . . . ,*" and I was honestly amazed that he held that kind of currency. Did they know him from *Wall Street* and *Platoon*? From *Born on the Fourth of July*? Or had the Oliver moment that had made a Stone believer out of me—the head-trip trilogy of *JFK, Natural Born Killers,* and *Nixon*—now won over this generation as well?

Oliver, a sensation junkie, liked a lot of the same things I did (alcohol, drugs, women), and with the exception of drinking, he excelled at them in a way that left me at the starting gate. Normally, I would have been paralyzed with insecurity at the thought of trying to keep up with a celebrity who was a bit of a wild man, who radiated the aura of being on the prowl, even when he wasn't. (Oliver didn't necessarily go to nightclubs to pick up women; he just liked the vibe.) But where he and I had common ground, apart from the obvious fact that I was a critic who revered his films, is that Oliver, beneath his shit-kicking bluster, had a strikingly solemn and reflective temperament, a furrowed seriousness about whatever he was discussing. His voice would grow quiet, so that you were forced to lean in, and he exuded an aura of searching for answers, and maybe of imparting a few secrets along the way. He seemed to have spies in a lot of places, as well as dense thickets of information at his fingertips about everything from the World Bank to the World Cup to the CIA (arcane bureaucratic details, recountings of black ops). I'd had just enough adventures that I now thought of myself as a dweeb in recovery; he was an ex-jock and combat veteran driven by an intellectual curiosity—a hidden dweeb—at his center. And so we connected.

We often talked about movies, but our tastes were quite different, because Oliver reveled in high-powered pulp trash, stuff like *Rush Hour* and—yes—*The Rock*, which he thought people like me were too uptight to enjoy. "It's a high," he'd say in his calm, light singsong bass tones. "It's meant to be over-the-top. You critics don't know how to relax, how to go with the flow of the action." You'd think that would have annoyed me, but he'd say it with a wink, his gap-toothed smile telling you that he was giving you shit because he knew it would annoy you. He liked to knock you around in a paternal way. And the truth is that Oliver valued and understood critics as much as anyone I've ever met in Hollywood. He respected how when a good movie came along, critics, at their best, could shape and drive the conversation. At first, I wondered about his movie tastes, but then I saw that apart from his penchant for mainlining action films, he had a giant competitive streak. He was more comfortable praising Jerry Bruckheimer than Steven Spielberg because that was his version of a pattern that existed in a great many directors, who have a way of diminishing the people they're really measuring themselves against.

I met Oliver in the fall of 1996, after a few notes had passed between us via his assistant. In my review of *Nixon*, I'd written that "Oliver Stone has become the most exciting filmmaker of his time," and after my impassioned responses to that film and *Natural Born Killers*, it suddenly dawned on me that I'd become Stone's foremost critical champion. It wasn't just about the level of praise. It was a critical/journalistic rite of passage in which I now saw, for the first time, that with *Entertainment Weekly* as my bullhorn, my opinion could have weight and influence. My voice might just create and signify something. That sounds pompous (or, given that I'd only just become aware of it, self-deprecating in a convoluted way), but you have to understand that when I started at *EW* in 1990, I thought of the New York media world as a cacophony of voices. It was hard to stand out (and I loathed hipper-than-thou reviewers who made a point of doing so). My honest embrace of Stone's films was, at last, a phenomenon that *defined* me.

Oliver and I arranged to meet at the Four Seasons Hotel on W. 57th St., where he was staying for a few days, and one night after work, I walked over there, knocked on his room door, and wound up chatting with him for the next few hours as we had a few drinks and he watched a pro football game, which I didn't even pretend to be interested in, since my indifference to sports is almost phenomenological. Of course, I'd learned over the years that sports betting is the secret engine of a great deal more sports mania than one might guess, and Oliver, sure enough, had money on the game. At a couple of key moments, when his team scored or halted an offensive drive, he stood and jumped up and down with lighthearted glee, and the boyishness of his enthusiasm was infectious. It made me wish, as I often did, that I could stand the boredom of convincing myself that I really cared about which franchise of corporately traded multimillionaire brand athletes known as a "team" would wind up defeating the other one.

Oliver, who'd just turned 50, said that he'd recently come back from shooting a movie he described as "a film noir in sunlight," and I thought: What a smart change of pace—just the kind of serrated entertainment he should be applying his newfound kaleidoscopic skills to. The movie, which came out a year later, was *U Turn*, and though it was clever and watchable in a hermetic way, the disappointment of it is that it *wasn't* really a noir, like Oliver said—more like an arch comic nightmare, an *After Hours* with greater grunge. It was the first film of his I'd reviewed since I'd gotten to know him, and already I saw the potential conflict: I didn't believe in pulling punches, but as soon as you were tempted to phrase even a minor criticism a little less harshly than you might have, that's what you were doing. It was hard to see how that wouldn't at some point happen. When you're friendly with a filmmaker, there's just a natural human temptation to take ten percent off your fastball.

"I liked your review of *The Fan*," said Oliver, in a nod of approval to my penchant for the disreputable and the low-down. I was one of the only critics to give the late-summer baseball remake of the 1982 stalker thriller a halfway decent review ("Robert De Niro has spent so much of his career playing cold-eyed psychotic freaks that you'd think by now he'd have run out of variations. He hasn't, of course... We keep watching, because we want to see how far he'll go this time"), and it was a movie that Oliver thought was underappreciated. It was the first indication of his own low-down movie tastes.

I had just seen *The People vs. Larry Flynt*, which Stone produced, at the New York Film Festival, and I thought it was a brilliant film, spun by the screenwriters of *Ed Wood* out of the same skewed biopic aesthetic of anti-heroic tabloid irony. I congratulated Stone on the movie, but he took no credit for it. "It was all Milos [Forman] and the writers," he said. "But without me, they couldn't have cast Courtney Love. That was really the thing I did. No studio would go near her, because the bond companies refused to insure her. Too unstable, too much risk. I used my pull to nail down the coverage, which was a good thing, because she's great in the movie."

"She really is," I said. "She's so electrifying. The same way she is on-stage." I told him about how I occasionally liked to stop conversation at parties simply by offering up my honest assessment of Hole's *Live Through This*, which I believed to be a greater album than Nirvana's *Never-mind*. "When you say that," I chuckled, "especially to a certain kind of Gen X dude, they always look at you like they want to hit you. Of course, there's also the theory that Kurt Cobain actually wrote the album. But I think that's newfangled sexism."

"They can't deal with a woman that powerful," said Oliver as he knitted his brows, suddenly quite serious, which is the way he got. "It's very threatening, as it always has been." He'd been on the receiving end of spitballs for his own portrayal of women, and back in the *Wall Street* days, the grousing was justified. But though a lot of people didn't realize it, he had turned over his version of a new leaf. In *Natural Born Killers*, Juliette Lewis made Mallory a vibrantly wounded homicidal ragdoll, and Joan Allen's performance as Pat Nixon was a revelation, melting the infamous ice queen into a figure at once wily and empathetic. Whether or not Stone "got" women, he was more oriented than ever toward capturing their complexities.

After the football game ended, we chatted a bit more, but it was time to go. I didn't necessarily think the evening would lead to further contact, but Oliver was both more prickly and more likable than I was prepared for—in his half-frame reading glasses, with his soft-spoken provocations, he seemed a quietly mad professor more than the aging bad-boy power player he was. Meeting and hanging out with him felt good.

A bit of film-nerd confessional: I'm as starstruck by actors as anyone, but ever since my college movie-maniac days, it was *directors* who were always the awesome gods to me, the magical thinkers, the artist-superheroes who my existence spun around. The opportunity to spend quality time with them had always been a dream of mine, a kind of holy grail. I can't say they were the people I wanted to *be*, exactly, yet in an imaginary sense they were. The essence of watching a movie, especially a great one, is that your point-of-view becomes rivetingly *aligned* with that of the filmmaker, so that you almost seem to be living for a couple of hours in his head (and he, by turn, uses the movie to enter yours). And that lent a unique quality to the relationship between someone like me, who basically spent his life reading directors' minds, and the filmmakers themselves. The truth is that in getting to know them as friends, I think I fantasized that I would finally be rising up to fly over the wall of my father's indifference.

The chance to get to know directors presented itself at film festivals. At my second Sundance in January 1996, the most amazing film I saw was *I Shot Andy Warhol*, the first feature directed by Mary Harron, who did her version of the ironic biopic by dramatizing the life of Valerie Solanas, who had fired a bullet into Andy Warhol's chest in 1968, nearly killing him. Solanas had always been a fascinatingly unexplored pop-culture footnote: Aside from the Warhol shooting, all anyone really knew about her is that she was a lesbian and radical feminist who had written something called the *SCUM Manifesto* (SCUM stood for Society for Cutting Up Men), which I'd always assumed were the ramblings of a hateful lunatic. Harron's vision was thrillingly double-edged: Lili Taylor played Solanas with a squirrelly rage that was often quite funny, but the film also saw that she was a crackpot ahead of the curve. Her violence was indefensible, but her ideas had force, and in the Warhol shooting something larger was being played out. Harron gave it context with her stunning re-creation of the Warhol universe—the chic sleaze of the Factory, and Andy himself, nailed with blasé exquisiteness by Jared Harris. *I Shot Andy Warhol* stunned me, and as soon as I met Mary, I felt she was a kindred spirit. A former rock critic (and a longtime friend of Jim Wolcott's), she had a nervous, crunched way of talking that chimed with my own restless analytical nature. We hung out at Sundance during a rather dreadful one-man acoustic concert by Beck, and she gave me a homemade bound copy of the *SCUM Manifesto*, which I read on the plane back to New York and found shocking in how its paranoid fury anticipated the world that was coming. By the time Sundance was over, I felt Mary was already a friend.

Later that year, shortly before I met Oliver, I got together with Steven

Soderbergh at the Toronto Film Festival, having a breakfast with him that lasted into the early afternoon. He was finally just emerging from his post–*sex, lies* "I'm a failure!" moment, going to work on *Out of Sight* (a movie he already seemed to know would rescue him), and he was spiky and direct, though with a shield of cynicism. When I told him how much I'd liked his 1995 thriller *The Underneath*, which *was* a noir in sunlight, he waved away the compliment. "I hated the film, and I hated making it," he said. The look that crossed his face let me know how depressing the act of shooting a movie could be (I'd always fantasized it was automatic fun, like running a giant toy train set). *sex, lies* had defined the indie world, but when it came to the priorities of the industry, Soderbergh thought the whole system was rigged. The subject of Tim Burton came up, and he said with a grin, "It must do a real number on you when your worst film is your biggest hit and your greatest film is your biggest bomb." He was referring to *Batman* and *Ed Wood*, and I agreed on both counts, though I suspected that this kind of thing might do a bigger number on Soderbergh than it did on others. His neuroticism seemed to emerge from an overdeveloped sense of fair play. We also discussed celebrity magazine profiles, and he cued me to what he saw as their intricately confected layers of artifice. He was highly amused by it all, referring to a recent scandal by observing, "You know what they say: When something embarrassing about a star comes out, it usually means the story has been planted to cover up something even *more* embarrassing." Accurate or not, I've weighed many a scandal since against that statement.

In the '90s, each year minted a mind-boggling bumper crop of directors: either those who made a debut film that blew people away, or those who made a second feature that was really the first to bottle the immensity of their talent. Imagine, for instance, that you went to sleep on January 1, 1996, and woke up one year later. Here are some of the filmmakers who would have sprouted onto the radar like mushrooms. Todd Solondz ruled Sundance with *Welcome to the Dollhouse*, which seemed a classic debut film but actually wasn't (Solondz had first tried to cram his downbeat squirminess into a late-'80s comedy called *Fear, Anxiety & Depression*, which played like bad student-film Woody Allen). Stanley Tucci and Campbell Scott proved brilliant collaborators with *Big Night*, the most succulent of all food-porn movies, and Danny Boyle, who'd made the overly synthetic and bumptious *Shallow Grave*, unveiled the exhilarating Welsh rock & roll drug-rotter fantasia *Trainspotting*.

At the Toronto Film Festival, Doug Liman declared himself with *Swingers*, that instant touchstone of new male courtship rites, and Robert Duvall directed *The Apostle*, in which he cast himself as a Pentecostal preacher full of lordly rapture and violence. It was the performance of his life, and the movie was a staggering work of art: the full vision of "the world of the South" (to quote Duvall's letter to me) that *Tender Mercies* was not. Also at Toronto, Christopher Guest revealed that he'd now become the slyest of filmmakers, with a movie I consider to be the comedy gem of the decade: *Waiting for Guffman*. It was the first of Guest's mockumentaries, and he turned the travails of a local theater troupe that stages an original musical into something worthy of Preston Sturges. I would argue that Guest's performance as Corky St. Clair, the small-fish-in-a-tinier-pond theater bug who was as closeted as he was flaming, marked a transitional moment in consciousness regarding gays in pop culture, and maybe the culture at large. Corky's mincing mannerisms, hideous bowl cut, and edge-of-tears narcissism came close to being the gay equivalent of blackface, but that's exactly why the comedy was so liberating. The movie was saying: Even the enlightened can now revel in this stereotype... because it's both with us and blessedly behind us.

Then there was the greatest film of 1996, the one that heralded the arrival of, potentially, the most important filmmaker to emerge from Europe since the glory days of Bergman, Bresson, and Fellini. That was *Breaking the Waves*, the sophomore masterpiece of Lars von Trier. It saddens me to write that sentence, because in the two decades since, I have very much become a non–von Trier believer. I think he quickly turned into a vainglorious conceptual showman, an annoying and often tedious highbrow sensationalist, and a director who forgot almost entirely how to stage a convincing scene (oh, that!). If you watched movies with a Geiger counter that detected fraud, it would click away like crazy through most of *Dogville* and *Melancholia* and *Nymphomaniac, Vol. I and II*. But *Breaking the Waves* has an organic sublimity that leaves the indulgent theatrics of the rest of von Trier's career in the kitschy dust.

It may be the only period piece set in the early '70s that never announces that fact (apart from fragments of glam rock, which are used

as momentary cantatas), and the effect of that slight temporal disloca-
tion is to say, almost between the lines: "This was a time before the clut-
ter and the noise. And that allowed it to be a time of *belief*." The believer,
played with a beam of manic-depressive luminosity by Emily Watson, is
Bess, who lives on a remote Scottish island and is leaning away from her
strict Calvinist sect—elders in long beards, an Amish kind of feeling—
to marry an outsider, an oil-rig worker named Jan (Stellan Skarsgård).
She gazes at him with the purity of true love, but there's a danger to her
devotion. She has essentially made Jan her new church.

Like such high dramas of divinity on earth as *Diary of a Country
Priest* or *Ordet*, *Breaking the Waves* is a movie in which God is very much
a character, even though you can't see him. Bess is desperate for Jan to
return from a job, and so she talks to God: soberly, calmly, rationally,
madly. At first we think, "Hmmm, what a disturbed girl." Then again,
this is what prayer *is* and always has been. When she asks for Jan to be
sent home, and the film then cuts to a terrible accident in which he's
struck on the head by an untethered construction pipe, von Trier is telling the audience: This was no accident. God has answered Bess—he has
granted her wish. Be careful what you pray for.

Breaking the Waves is a shattering parable of devotion. It's as solemn as Bergman, as achingly attuned to the vibrations of feminine
strength and masochism as *The Passion of Joan of Arc*, and as haunting
as the early-'70s rock snippets (most gorgeously, Deep Purple's "Child
in Time") that introduce each chapter on top of spangly tinted photographs that have the effect of psychedelic stained glass. What draws it
all together is the transcendent sincerity of von Trier's filmmaking. He
wants the audience's connection to Bess to be consuming, a total mind
and spirit meld, and Emily Watson's performance lets that happen. Her
Bess is locked into a faith that's too extreme to be fully sane and too
soulful to be *in*sane. She teeters on that place the Western world has lost,
where we can still hear God speak because His voice is part of us. When
Bess climbs aboard the ship of Udo Keir's evil captain, then emerges after
what he has done to her, the degradation of her sacrifice pulls us toward
something holy and ancient.

I mounted the same campaign to do *Breaking the Waves* as a lead
review that I'd done with *Crumb*, only this time I lost. I got a page for it

(a livable compromise), but it bothered me to see how the decision was weighed as if what I was suggesting wasn't even in the playbook. In the end, the movie that displaced *Breaking the Waves* was *Daylight*, a lousy Sylvester Stallone disaster film that, even given the magazine's basic commercial priorities, hardly needed or deserved the showcase. It was fourth-tier schlock. The message was: We'll put *any* movie in the lead spot but that weird-ass art thing that Owen likes. A few weeks later, after Emily Watson took the New York Film Critics Circle award for Best Actress (and *Breaking the Waves* itself narrowly missed winning Best Picture), Mark Harris, who was almost always on my side in these matters but had to negotiate everything with Jim Seymore, told me, "I'm glad she won. It really helps." He meant the words to be reassuring, and since *Breaking the Waves* was my movie of the year, I admit that I, too, was relieved at how the politics of awards season were playing out. Of course, the downside was, What if they hadn't played out that way? At a party, I spoke to Seymore and his wife, Joyce, a bubble of perkiness who I was always friendly with, and they told me that they had tried to watch *Breaking the Waves* one night on a video copy at home. They were not fans, though I was grateful they made the effort. But the most telling comment was Joyce's: "After a while," she said, "I just couldn't watch that actor [Stellan Skarsgård]. I'm sorry, but he looked like he needed a bath."

One person who was impressed by *Breaking the Waves* was Oliver Stone, although he indicated to me that it wasn't really his kind of movie. "I could see what you loved about it," he said. "It had a rough passion. It was uncompromising."

"It sounds like you didn't totally relate to it," I said.

"It was a bit heavy on the martyrdom," he said. And then, with a quick flash of his delinquent smile, "That was too much for the Catholic in me." I didn't push the issue, but I sensed there was another barrier—that in his current context, Stone couldn't help but regard *Breaking the Waves* as outsider art. As it happens, though, that context was now rapidly shifting sand.

I got to know Oliver at a paradoxical moment. The movies of his that enthralled me, whatever you thought of them, had found a place in the culture. *Natural Born Killers* was loved, hated, fiercely debated, and widely seen. It made ultra-fans, like me, as well as people (including many critics) who despised every frame of it. But Oliver held his place at the center of the action, where he was addicted to being. It was intensely ironic to me that at *EW*, where I'd spent the '90s coloring in my identity as a critic mostly through my reverence for the independent film movement, the director I now felt closest to was from the old school. More than even Scorsese, it was Stone who struck me as the Last '70s Filmmaker. By which I mean that *his* independent, at times radical vision was all churned up with the DNA of Hollywood. He was a *studio* filmmaker. But the world had changed. *Nixon* was a major commercial dud, and that crystallized a turning point in the industry, because as Stone put it to me less than two years later, "I couldn't get that film financed today. What's coming, what's already happening, is the death of the mid-budget film. The drama for adults. The major studios don't want it anymore, because the way they see it, even when it works, there isn't enough payoff." The indies, of course, were designed to fill that gap, and that's just what they were doing. But Oliver couldn't bring himself to think like an "independent filmmaker." He thought that was small potatoes (which it wasn't), and he wanted to touch the world.

After meeting Oliver, I'd gone along to a few dinners he organized with a handful of journalists, producers, and other cohorts. The first was at Indochine, a restaurant just north of SoHo that was still clinging by its fingernails to a glimmer of its late-'80s/early-'90s cachet, and the fact that the dinner was there struck me as borderline kitsch: It was a Vietnamese place, with French-Colonial design—and so it was Stone choosing a spot that glancingly alluded to his legend. (Or maybe he just really liked the spicy crab dumplings.) Stephen Schiff, my former mentor from *The Boston Phoenix*, was one of the guests. Stephen had recently taken the leap—which so many try and fail at—from journalism to screenwriting, penning the script for Adrian Lyne's *Lolita*, but before that he had written a terrific profile of Stone for *The New Yorker* pegged to *Natural Born Killers*. Oliver, it's clear, found a place at the table for writers who liked and understood him. On this particular evening, Stephen sat kiddie corner from Oliver, up at the power end of the table, and I was about halfway down, talking to the amicable Michael Mailer, an aspiring producer who was one of Norman Mailer's sons and had clearly inherited little of his father's bellicosity.

As the months went by, the evenings took on a more exotic flavor. I'd have dinner with Oliver at Balthazar (where, being the raw-meat kind of person he was, he got me to see that steak tartare isn't quite as scary as it seems), or I'd be invited to a restaurant bar to meet him at 9:00 p.m., and he'd be about an hour late, but meanwhile, the table he'd reserved would already have seated four or five women who were obviously models (they had that remote alabaster hauteur that was more *there* than their beauty), and they'd all been invited as...what? Decor? Potential hookups? Oliver never did go home with any of them, and neither did I, because I never had any idea how to relate to them. I was some breed of womanizer, but I was the opposite of a modelizer, because I didn't know how to make the small talk, that very *phrase* being a thousand years moldy-old in a way that indicates the genetic deficiency that would not allow me to send out a psychic laser beam of invitation to a woman I had so little in common with.

Then Oliver would show up, sometimes with his date for the evening (usually very tall, often black or Asian), and we would sit around and talk, drink, eat some sushi, and go out to a club. There were sometimes other writers there, like my friend the brilliant *New York Press* critic Godfrey Cheshire, and early on, before I knew enough to anticipate the wall-candy ritual of the models, I brought along my girlfriend, a bookish sort named Sandra, and since our communion was comfortable and rather staid, Oliver would later make a point of referring to her as my "wife," as if to say: Why are you in a relationship that's *already* as boring as marriage? (The more I thought about it, the more I realized he was right.)

When you're friends with a filmmaker, there's one topic of conversation that always changes, but it really stays the same, and that is: his ongoing report on the movie he's making, or getting ready to make. During the period I was hanging out with Oliver, that was two films: *Any Given Sunday*, the smash-and-grab gridiron epic that established Jamie Foxx as a major movie star (I thought it was decent and said so), and *Alexander*, his post–*Lord of the Rings* attempt to make a serious but actiony ancient-world blockbuster that fitted into what Hollywood was now becoming (I thought it was abysmal and said so). At first, the *here's how my project's going!* conversations can be fascinating, in their mixture of grand ambition—Oliver was obsessed with football as the modern gladiatorial arena—and the daily accounting of directorial headaches. But they can also grow wearying in their one-sidedness. Directors, or at least the great ones, are all monomaniacs. It's the nature of the beast; it's the only way to get done what they do. And though Oliver was generally a give-and-take conversationalist, there were moments when the dictator shined through.

I remember actually being a bit nervous the first time I got together with him after the release of *Saving Private Ryan*, because at that point, having known him for a couple of years, I just *sensed* that he was going to have a major bone to pick with that movie, since it drastically took away from his star (or, at least, I suspected that he would feel that way). *Platoon*, which had swept the Oscars, had been the one Vietnam film that Hollywood had chosen to coronate. It was a new classic, celebrated for its grunt's-eye-view realism—and, of course, what Stone brought to it that no other great director (Coppola, Kubrick) could have was that he was *there*, not just in Vietnam but in war, period. He was the one giant contemporary American filmmaker who had been in the shit. He ripped *Platoon* out of that experience. Now, here comes Steven Spielberg, who was a nice Jewish boy, not a warrior; he had probably never even been in a fistfight. And *he* was being lionized for making the ultimate film to capture the devastation of combat.

As soon as Oliver showed up that night, I could tell that he was in a surly mood, and since I was on the record as hailing Spielberg's World War II movie as "a masterpiece of blood, terror, chaos, and death" (I thought it was a much greater film than *Platoon*), I was on the receiving end of some of the surliness. Stone picked away at what he saw as the film's inaccurate details, but ultimately, what he had a problem with was Tom Hanks: He never, for one minute, bought that this man was a soldier. (He also made a few acerbic comments about what a joke it was to buy that Tom Hanks was a nice guy.) I defended the film. I said, "Isn't the whole point that he's just an ordinary guy? I mean, in World War II, everyone got drafted. What's so unbelievable about him?"

"What's unbelievable," said Oliver, "is that he ever would have survived that war."

"Maybe so," I said, not exactly having my own experience in the rice paddies that I could draw on to make my case. "But I never felt like he did anything too heroic. It was plausible. And I thought Hanks was amazing. He had a resonance to me."

We argued back and forth a bit, getting nowhere, and I probably should have just let it drop, because after I'd offered one defense of Hanks and *Ryan* too many, Oliver, getting steamed for the first time, slammed his fist down on the table and yelled, "He would have been fuckin' fragged!" Oliver now looked like he wanted to frag me, and I knew that when a Vietnam veteran starts talking like's he's still in the war, the time has come to shut the fuck up.

There was an image of Oliver in the popular culture, one that he himself, knowingly or not, helped to shape: the zealot devoid of a sense of humor about himself, the brooding conspiracy theorist who was ultimately a kind of simplistic finger-pointer. Actually, Oliver liked to poke fun at himself. After tossing off some intricate explanation of, say, what was really driving the Clinton policy in the Middle East, he would suddenly laugh and say something like, "It's all part of the conspiracy." The truth is that he was a mindful observer who always searched for shades of gray; he had too fine a grasp of the dynamics of power to do otherwise. What I saw—and identified with—in Oliver was really his Jungian search for the hidden patterns in things.

But when it came to the JFK assassination, I tried to steer clear of talking about it because of the way my own ideas had developed, and because I knew it was an article of faith for him. For most of my life, I'd assumed that there was probably *some* kind of conspiracy to kill JFK. But it was Stone's extraordinary head-spinning movie, paradoxically, that reopened the issue for me in a way that slowly changed my mind. I read Gerald Posner's book *Case Closed*, written in response to *JFK* (it was published in 1993, two years after the film), and I found it to be a staggeringly insightful, multi-faceted argument against conspiracy. (Its portrait of Oswald is the single most convincing thing ever written about him.) Stone, naturally, thought the book was hogwash, and I confess that I avoided getting into a discussion about it, because I knew I didn't have either the mind or the stomach to debate JFK assassination arcana with Oliver Stone. At one point, though, I finally nudged my thoughts into the room, telling Oliver that I was starting to come around to the belief that Oswald had acted alone. We were both a bit drunk, and he took it in stride, saying with a shrug, "That's what they want you to think," which I recognized was a closed circle of a statement. I sensed his disappointment, but I could tell that he'd had this argument way too many times, and I think he chalked up my comment to what he saw as the safe, conventional side of myself. I *did* have that side; to me, though, conspiracy had become the new conventionality—it may not have been "safe," but it was all too easy. And that's as far as the conversation went.

A little later, we said goodbye on an empty downtown sidewalk, doing the man-hug thing, Oliver with his silent extravagant girlfriend of the evening next to him, and me by myself. I thought, "It's 3:00 a.m., and I'm ready to crash." But I had no idea if Oliver was, as I stood there for about half a minute, watching him walk into the night.

CHAPTER 17

FESTIVAL FEVER

I can't say for sure, but I do believe I'm the first person who ever compared the experience of being at a film festival to that of living inside the movie *Groundhog Day*. At a festival, the drill is pretty elemental: Get up early, go to a movie, then another movie, then another movie, and then there are people who just keep going from there, as if to prove that they're the Olympic Energizer Bunnies of cinemania. Not me: With rare exceptions, three films a day is my limit. (I will discuss this a bit later on, since some people think it's a scandal; for me, it's simply self-preservation.) At night, go to a party, maybe a nice civilized cocktail-size one where you can have a lively conversation about the industry or get introduced to the indie It Girl of the moment (Parker Posey, Patricia Clarkson, Vera Farmiga, Elizabeth Olsen—the role gets rotated annually, like a beauty-pageant tiara), and then go to another party, perhaps one of those hellacious overstuffed ones with a glow-in-the-dark bracelet as entry token and music provided by a reunited two-hit-wonder band from 20 years ago, the sort of event I refer to as a "rat fuck." If you're at Cannes, get lured into having *another* drink outside the Petit Majestic bar, where people gather on a winding, otherwise deserted shopping-zone backstreet for a casual nightly wee-hours bash that's only just kicking into gear at around 1:00 a.m. Each night tell yourself, *"Don't do it! Don't go to the Petit Majestic! You need some sleep!"* And each night get sucked in all over again, because the transcendently welcoming dawn-of-summer all-night-party movie vibe is just too sweet to resist.

Whether you're at Cannes or Sundance or the Boise Film Festival (at this point, there must surely be one), drink free drinks, chat with publicists and distributors and reporters and fellow critics, exchange warm greetings with folks you haven't seen for a while, who then instantly mesh into the mob you're seeing every day. Talk about the movies you're watching. Then talk about those same movies again. And again. If you're willing (and I always am), get into an in-depth analysis and debate about one of those movies. Then, assuming you're one of those people who, like me, is rarely smooth enough to get laid at a festival, return to your hotel, go to bed, wake up with what you hope is only a modest hangover, and begin the ritual all over again. Warning: Conversations the next day may be a little less fun than those same conversations were the day before.

At a festival, the repetition-with-small-ripples-of-variation produces a giddy comfort-food feeling, kind of like a cross between *Groundhog Day* and *Super Size Me*, the Morgan Spurlock documentary that pretended to be a science experiment in the health factor of eating McDonald's every day (surprise! not good!) but that was really a fantasy of what it might actually be *like* to eat McDonald's every day (first good, then less good, then like swallowing a grenade of cholesterol). When I first show up at a festival, nearly ravenous with anticipation, I always feel like I want to move in and stay at movie camp for about a month. The feeling doesn't last. After six or seven days, I'm sated, bloated, reduced to the movie equivalent of a food coma. Yet if there's such a thing as healthy overkill, then surely this must be it. At a festival, even the annoying and/or disappointing moments have a way of being somehow redemptive; even the boringness is weirdly fun. Here are two snapshots that evoke, by turns, the insanity and the majesty:

The imperfect storm. It's January 1997, and I'm finally about to see the Sundance movie that has been on everyone's lips. It's called *Hurricane*, and the chatter about it is electric. When you start hearing about a festival film, it's usually one of several that have been elevated, through word of mouth, to must-see status; making room for each of them is the scheduling equivalent of filling in a crossword puzzle. I wasn't able to catch *Hurricane* until the very end of the week, at a Friday afternoon showing in the Library Center Theatre, a creaky homespun venue with ancient fold-up wooden seats that occupies the third floor of the Park City Library. (It's an odd building: In all my travels through its hallways and stairwells, I have never once glimpsed so much as one room that held a single book.) On this day, the "line" is four people thick, with everyone shoving and pressing forward to make sure they don't get shut out of a movie so anticipated that it now feels like it should be called *Citizen Hurricane*. By the time I'm jammed onto the third floor, I start drifting to anxious thoughts of the lethal audience sardine smoosh at the 1979 Who concert. I notice a shock of straight tan hair to the left of me and realize that it's Jodie Foster, who looks a little pale, as if her delicate bones were about to be pulverized. As we're squeezed like toothpaste into the theater, I grab a seat in back, ready to watch a movie worthy of this explosion of Sundance buzz. *Hurricane*, however, is not that movie. It's a cliché-flecked coming-of-age trifle about a 15-year-old ruffian who hangs out in the hood, dreams his little dreams, gets drawn—wait for it! a story arc!—into petty crime, and then comes out okay. I'd seen infinitely better movies all week, like *Go* and *Chasing Amy* and *Sunday* and *Gridlock'd* and *In the Company of Men* and *Prefontaine* and *Star Maps*; I'd seen a much better movie earlier that day (the extraordinary documentary *Sick: The Life and Death of Bob Flanagan, Supermasochist*). *Hurricane* turns out to be a big zero (though it does win three awards). But this was my first experience of a Sundance bubble, a glistening globule of hype with nothing but hot air inside.

Season of the witch. It's January 1999, and I have a choice to make. I can go to the Sundance awards ceremony and gawp at the winning filmmakers, or I can go to the final screening of the festival: a horror film I've been hearing about for the last two days called *The Blair Witch Project*. Since my festival wrap-up for *Entertainment Weekly* is priority one, that tells me: Don't miss what could be a defining festival film. So I skip the awards and wind up at the Eccles Theater, which is filled to capacity. The movie begins, and the terror felt by just about every member of the audience, including me, weaves together to form a crazy-quilt of jitters that eerily echoes what's happening on screen, until it seems less a movie than a séance. *Blair Witch* is about the fear of things you can't see, because they're hiding—not just in the dark or in the shadows, but in the genuine godforsaken *night*. The screams from the audience come in waves, not the way they do at slasher films, where the basic rhythm is scream/giggle/scream/giggle. Here it's closer to scream/murmur/suck-in-breath-and-hold-it/scream again. (That, of course, is how screams *used* to come at slasher films. Before they got megaplexed.) *The Blair Witch Project* is like MTV's *Road Rules* with the annoying shot-on-the-fly videotape infiltrated by the devil. It's the most artful horror film I've seen in years, and where it's also ahead of the curve is that it plays as a devious satire of a generation too busy recording every moment of their lives on camera to notice when they're about to die on camera. It's that rarity, a real popcorn catharsis. At the end, when the filmmakers come up on stage to answer questions, the first question is just one guy standing up and saying, "*Oh, my, God!*" At which point everyone in the theater collapses into laughter, deflating the tension, ecstatic to have seen a film that somehow seems to reconfigure—as a good Sundance movie can do—the whole reason this festival exists.

Of course, when *The Blair Witch Project* opened in theaters six months later, it provoked a reaction divided enough to be called schizophrenic. It became the most successful independent feature of all time, grossing $140 million (that's $32 million more than *Pulp Fiction*). One assumed that the wild-fire spread of popularity had *something* to do with word of mouth that said, in effect, "*You gotta see this!*" Yet three out of every five people who did see it seemed to think that it was the unscary/tedious letdown/ripoff of all time. Was everyone even watching the same film? Yes and no. What *The Blair Witch Project* revealed was an American moviegoing population of blue states and red states, who in this case happened to be seated right next to each other. The film also laid bare what can often be the gaping chasm between the experience inside a film festival and outside of one. Having been on both sides, I will testify that there *is* such a thing as festival fever, a delicious affliction that can result in a certain loss of... perspective. (I've most definitely succumbed, like when I saw, on almost no sleep, the scrappy, threadbare club-kid docudrama *Party Monster* and wound up making it sound like the second coming of *In Cold Blood*.) Yet if you can manage to hold on to your critical bearings, festival fever can also be one of the most enlightening deliriums a film buff will ever catch. It's the essence of movie love, a passion distilled and held up to the light and blissfully ingested.

There are trade secrets to navigating a film festival, and here are five I've discovered and have come to live by over the years. Some may sound a bit counterintuitive, but in the end, that's exactly why they're so valuable:

1. See only three movies a day. A lot of folks who cover festivals would consider this advice to be blasphemy, because at any festival, there's always a kind of cult of *how many movies did you see?* The higher the number ("Whew! This is my sixth screening of the day!"), the tougher and more devoted the movie buff in question. But if it sounds like I'm advocating a slacker approach to what is already the ultimate slacker gig— and make no mistake, that's exactly what I'm doing—there's a method to my laidback madness. The first time I ever saw four movies in a day was when I was 12, and the Campus Theater in Ann Arbor was showing all four Beatles films in chronological order. I took my brother Erik, and we gorged on Beatlemania, but *Yellow Submarine* had never felt quite so *long*, and by the time we were halfway through *Let It Be*, I felt my interest dissolving faster than the Beatles' love for one another. (Thank Jesus they didn't throw in *Magical Mystery Tour*.) A lesson took hold: *Four movies in a day is too much of a good thing.* Yes, you can do it, it's not bricklaying, but that doesn't mean it's going to feel good. At a festival, a lot of the films you see are negligible or downright lousy. Much of what you're doing is separating the wheat from the chaff, and I admit that I have less patience for chaff than most other people do. At a truly dull film, I wind up chewing my cuticles off. Three movies a day, however, creates a nice sustainable flow. It's not too many or too few; it's just right. Most vitally: It guarantees that you won't fail to respond to the nuances in that final movie of the day—and therefore wind up punishing it—all because your system is literally *fed up* with images.

2. Seek out any documentary about rock & roll or porn. This rule certainly won't work for everyone, but it does for me, because, like the three-movies-a-day principle, it's a way of revitalizing the primacy of your responses. When your senses have been dulled, a good rock or porn doc works like a sniff of adrenaline powder. At Sundance, did you just see that overbuzzed dysfunctional-family comedy that's got every phony thing but a laugh track? Swat away the synthetic afterglow with that deep-dish documentary about the Doors or Joe Strummer. At Toronto, did you make the boneheaded mistake of catching yet another of Wim Wenders' slovenly paced smiley-faced road movies? Cleanse your palette with that astoundingly researched history of the MC5. At Cannes, did you suffer through the dead-weight "progressive" drama about a Tel Aviv housewife who is drawn into an ambiguous bond with her Palestinian gardener? Time to go see the extraordinary footage assembled in that primitively fascinating look at the making of the Rolling Stones' *Exile on Main Street*. (And Mick Jagger is there to introduce it!) Rock docs on insanely specific subjects—like, say, the 2005 film devoted to Arthur "Killer" Kane of the New York Dolls—have become a kind of splinter industry. In the future, I fully expect to see entire films devoted to the life and times of Clarence Clemons, the poetic genius of Bernie Taupin, and the sonic miracle of the Moog synthesizer. And believe me, I will prioritize each of those films at whichever festival they play.

If rock docs get respect, docs about the porn world seldom do. That's because it's been proven, time and again, that outside of a former collegiate porn fan like myself, almost no one wants to see them. Even the Brian Grazer–produced *Inside Deep Throat* was shunned by audiences. Yet it took a telling look at a seismic shift in America, and that's true of other porn docs too, which at their best tease out the human vitality of sleaze. At festivals, I've encountered startling portraits of life inside the sex industry, and the most amazing one I ever saw was at Toronto in 1998, when I was one of exactly two people to sit through the only festival showing of *Wadd: The Life & Times of John C. Holmes*, a three-hour documentary about the '70s porn legend. It's one of the darkest films I've ever seen—one that connected all the ugly dots in a tale of how the pursuit of pleasure could lead to murder. My write-up of it for *EW* was quoted on the VHS box, which wound up being shelved in the porn (rather than doc) section of my local West Village video store. I didn't know if I should be proud or hang my head in shame, but I guess that made *Wadd* a true underground discovery, since almost no one but me ever discovered it.

3. Take the meals as seriously as you do the movies. More blasphemy, since at a festival, if you aren't at an official dinner, you're not supposed to treat food as anything more than the joyless Army rations that get sandwiched in between the boot-camp schedule of screenings. Everyone runs around fueled by stuff like free-giveaway "energy bars," feeling antic and physically hollow. Bad strategy! Watching movies is all about pleasure, and so is evaluating them, so I say that you need to remain in a constant dialogue with your pleasure centers. At festivals, I find places

I like to go, and I make them my touchstones, where I can take a break for half an hour and think as I revel in something that tastes *très* good. At Sundance, that used to mean Burgie's, the low-down grease-pit burger diner on Main Street (it closed in 2005), and it still means the Vietnamese place up the block whose incredible soup restores hangover-impaired functions, or Davanza's, where the ground-beef-and-mushroom pizza is an orgy of crusty tasty delight, or—a secret weapon—the rockin' festival chili dished out at the Temple Theatre. As for the Southwestern fusion restaurants on Main Street, where even the most innocent piece of fish must come encrusted in almond aioli with a side of papaya mash, do I even need to say it? Avoid these unhappy-meal boutiques at all cost.

Speaking of pizza, at Cannes, there's a restaurant that has basically become the commissary for American festivalgoers, and that's because it's a stony three-story Gallic suburban paradise, rooted in a distant era (it opened in 1960), where you can have the greatest pizza you ever tasted. Even the name of the place is perfect: It's called...La Pizza. And it is the ultimate succulent classy-lowbrow bistro parlor, where the rosé wine flows, the salads are just light green lettuce and tomato with an invisible dressing (and it's the most sublime salad you ever had), and the pizza is this insanely luscious yet classical thing that some like to have—it's a house specialty—with a sunnyside-up egg on top, so that the yolk melts right into the cheese. There may be more magical life-enhancing properties, more *artistry* in that pizza than there is in 7 out of the last 15 Palme d'Or winners.

4. Always hang out with Elvis Mitchell. Elvis is a friend, albeit a mostly long-distance one, who is one of the most compelling and mysterious figures in the universe of movie criticism. He hosts a weekly public-radio talk show out of Los Angeles, but over the decades he has held, and then left (voluntarily), more jobs than most of us have ever applied for, the most prominent one being that of film critic for *The New York Times*. Elvis is an insightful bebop maestro of a critic, a bon vivant, an iconic figure in his long graying dreadlocks, and an enigmatic hustler-survivor who seems to spin his entire life out of a whirlwind of frequent-flyer miles and friendships with prestigious maitre d's—that last item being a tad ironic, since I have never shared a meal with Elvis in which I saw him do anything other than order an entrée and eat maybe two bites of it. Elvis also possesses the rare ability to ingratiate himself into any situation on earth. If I told him, "Get a job at the White House," he'd have one in six months (and would probably quit it six months later). At a festival, Elvis is always the star, with women he has never met approaching him like groupies. When you're with him, you will always wind up at a better party and be privvy to more gossip—and film insight—than you would with anyone else.

5. The whole system wants you to be afraid, very afraid, of a Sundance crowd-pleaser. Don't be. "Crowd-pleaser" is a demagogic term. Technically, it means a movie that pleases a lot of people, but what it *really* means is: This film is guaranteed to "please" because it's the sort of calculated formulaic button-pusher that makes people feel good by reminding them of mediocre cookie-cutter television, where even the chintziest characters can become your weekly "family." In 1996, a glorified Lifetime movie called *Care of the Spitfire Grill* became the first high-profile bogus Sundance crowd-pleaser. Then came the egregious buddy sitcom *Happy, Texas*, then the wacked-family shenanigans of *Tadpole* and *Pieces of April*, and then, finally, the movie that became the ne plus ultra of Sundance crowd-pleasers: *Little Miss Sunshine*, with each of its characters—loser dad! surly teen son who refuses to speak! shticky naughty grandpa played by Alan Arkin!—a walking, talking screenwriter's index card. The insidious thing about experiencing any of these films at Sundance is that *the very fucking reason people love them so much* is that they incarnate everything that Sundance is suppose to stand against. They're watchable polished-turd entertainments *posing* as organic movies. As soon as you say to someone, "I thought *The Way, Way Back* was third-rate" or "*Little Miss Sunshine* is synthetic to the core," you're branding yourself as the kind of curmudgeonly pariah who doesn't know how to run with the crowd. Don't let it bother you, though. Because you're right and they're wrong.

There's always a chance to meet celebrities at festivals, but the question is: Can you have a genuine encounter? As opposed to one of those hey-I'm-a-big-fan/what-are-you-working-on? conversations that can thrill you when you're 25, but that you begin to realize isn't all that different from a photo op with a star at a Golden Globes dinner. It certainly helps if the celebrity in question isn't quite a celebrity yet. At a Miramax cocktail party at Sundance in 1997, I was besieged by the genial smart-aleck grin of an actor I'd seen in one or two middling movies but had barely even registered. His name was Ben Affleck. I couldn't help but be drawn into the conversation, because the first thing he told me is that he and his buddy, Matt Damon (who I'd met once briefly years before, also pre-fame), were big fans of mine. I'd grown used to being flattered, especially at Miramax parties, where Harvey Weinstein always found a way to amble up to me and growl out something like, "How's the best critic in America?" I liked Harvey, I enjoyed his huckster shamelessness, and I even appreciated his ass-kissing, but I always knew, of course, that I was being played, mostly because when you looked at Harvey, the two eyes that stared back at you were jarringly different from each other. One was wide open and looked right at you, and the other just about squinted shut and seemed to look right *through* you. That, I decided, was Harvey's gangster eye.

Affleck, on the other hand, was all easygoing sincerity, so I indulged myself in a conversation that rather amusingly treated *me* as if I were the bigger star. Ben told me that he and Matt were fixated on one line I'd written. Reviewing *Disclosure*, the 1994 Michael Douglas/Demi Moore sexual harassment thriller, I'd said: "We know the face, by now, almost too well. The glittery charmer's eyes, the long hair swept back with rakish panache, the mouth whose corners bend down into a pout of cold rage—it's Michael Douglas under siege again, battling to save his job, his marriage, his sexual honor. Fight on, beleaguered white man!" Ben and Matt relished that "Fight on, beleaguered white man!" Affleck told me that they said it to each other all the time. I adopted it as well: From that point on, Ben and I became friendly, talking at length whenever we ran into each other at a premiere party, and our version of a high-five was "Fight on, beleaguered white man!" Ben was always brimming with highly articulate and informed opinions, just as he is on *Real Time with Bill Maher*, but after I got to know him, I had to review a *lot* of bad Ben Affleck movies, like *Forces of Nature* and *Reindeer Games*, and in writing about them, I admit that I probably did take that ten percent off my fastball. I would pan the movie, but maybe go a *little* easy on Ben. I couldn't help it; I felt for him. The truth is that I always wondered how this guy who was so quick, sharp, and engaging in person could come off as such a cloying doof on screen. I decided that he was too analytical to be a truly good actor (which was probably why he liked to gamble so much—to liberate his left brain), but then, when he became a director, it all finally made sense. *That's* what he was meant to do. Behind the camera, he even figured out a way to liberate his extra-rational quick-brain energy *on* camera.

If Affleck, the tall kid next door, was someone I never had to feel a trace of intimidated awe around, it was quite the opposite the night I went out drinking with Russell Crowe. He showed up at Sundance in 2002 with *Texas*, a tiny sliver of a documentary about the rock band he was in, called 30 Odd Foot of Grunts. After 20 years as a critic, I'd grown used to thinking that no movie star was ever going to have the kind of pure idol-worship effect on me that the fabled actors from my youth did—De Niro and Pacino, Travolta in *Saturday Night Fever*, or Mickey Rourke. But then I saw *Gladiator*. I thought—and still think—that it's the single greatest *movie star* performance of the last 30 years.

Ever since the dawn of Eastwood, Bronson, and Bruce Lee (followed by their steroidal cartoon heirs, Stallone and Schwarzenegger), a great deal of movie culture has been ruled by the righteous heroics of mad-dog vengeance. The telegraphed aggression, the snarl of resolve, the perfect line of dialogue ("Well, *do* ya, punk?" "You're luggage!") that dispatches an enemy as if the very words were a lethal weapon. Russell Crowe, in *Gladiator*, was in many ways the apotheosis of these men. The difference is that he portrayed the brusque brutishness in three dimensions. He gave it heft, tragedy, soul. He was the ultimate thinking man's badass, channeling lightning bolts of clenched fury into how Maximus would stare at Joaquin Phoenix's Commodus and say, without so much as raising his voice, "The time for honoring yourself will soon be at an end." (Translation: *I would like to scrape your eyeballs out with my thumbs.*) Now, here I *was* with Russell Crowe. Was I man enough? Sorry, but this is the sort of thing that runs through your head. Or at least mine.

I figured that things would be okay as soon as he ordered a bottle of white wine instead of beer. Crowe, who had his girlfriend with him, the petite blonde Danielle Spencer (whom he married the next year, and who never said a word the whole night), took me to a music bar on Main Street, and we were ushered into the back, where we guzzled several bottles for a few hours. He was a true Aussie, with an aggressive but corny sense of humor (it was like hearing British rim-shot jokes made with a bigger drumstick), as well as a touchy-feely buddy camaraderie that I wasn't at all used to. At one point I had a piece of lint on my sweater, and when he noticed it, he reached across the table to flick it off, something that no guy in the United States would ever do. There was something cool about the gesture; it said, "We're dudes, we've got to look out for each other." He called people "Mate" and was quite cordial, answering all my pesky questions about *Gladiator*, and talking, with more than a hint of ruefulness, about how challenging it was even for him to find roles he really liked.

At one point, I did get a glimpse of the feral, short-fused Crowe who was not quite yet the stuff of telephone-tossing legend. The bar that night was featuring a special musical entertainer: Russell Hitchcock, who was one-half of the soft-rock duo Air Supply, who were also from Australia. So the choice of venue hadn't been an accident. Hitchcock decided that it would be fun to have Crowe join him onstage to sing "I'm All Out of Love," and he dispatched the manager of the bar to ask him. Crowe waved off the request, but then the manager came back, now making the mistake, in his clueless Park City rube way, of trying to *pressure* Russell Crowe into getting up on stage. Crowe's brow lowered, his look hardened into an ice-pick glare, and when he said, "I'm *not*...going to *do* that," it was with an unsettling "Back the fuck off" vibe (*I would like to scrape your eyeballs out with my thumbs*), the steam starting to come out of his ears. It wasn't acting, but it was no mere reckless display of temper either. It was why Russell Crowe was a movie star.

People tend to reveal themselves when they get angry. I learned a lot about Roger Ebert during one overheated run-in I had with him standing on line for a movie at the Toronto Film Festival in 2000, the year of *Almost Famous*. It had been close to a decade since I met Roger, and I often ran into him at festivals, where our chats were friendly, but there was a competitive gleam to them. Roger was used to dominating conversation, and was more than happy to be thought of as the most bombastic person in the room—but he didn't seem to realize, when he was shooting opinions my way, that my big-dick critical ego and ability to talk anyone in earshot under the table (and maybe even drive them nuts in the process) was as huge as his. We started to talk about *Almost Famous*, which Roger thought was unquestionably the movie of the year. Since I loved it as well, I thought we'd find nothing but common ground. But I happened to mention that a lot of people at *Entertainment Weekly* didn't like the movie nearly as much as we did, because they thought it viewed the early '70s, especially the drug scene, through rose-colored glasses. I told Roger that I thought they were too young to know how accurate the film really was: Back then, cocaine hadn't really exploded yet, and the movie's mellow booze-and-dope vibe caught the mood of the time exactly.

That's when Roger fixed me with one of his testy glares and said, "So *what* if it isn't authentic? Who cares? It's still a great movie."

I thought: *Really?* I said to him, "I don't agree with that at all, Roger. I *do* think it's a great movie, but if it didn't capture the period so authentically, I wouldn't like it half as much. That's actually the key to what's great about it."

To my surprise, Roger dialed up the outrage. "That's nonsense!" he declared, his voice rising to high dudgeon. "You're treating it like it's a documentary. It's the emotions that carry it."

I could tell this was going nowhere. *Almost Famous* was an entrancingly emotional film, but to me the emotions were rooted in reality, and that was its glory. In a fluky way, though, this movie-line debate explained Roger Ebert to me. He seemed to possess a world-class bullshit detector, but when he was in a movie theater, authenticity really *didn't* matter to him as much as...well, as much as it mattered to me. To the point that he could champion *Almost Famous* yet verge on loving it for the wrong reasons.

Another encounter that left me a bit flummoxed was when I got introduced to Michael Stipe at Sundance. The two of us were standing in a parking lot, and Stipe, who was wearing one of those big floppy Dr. Seuss hippie hats, grasped my hand in a friendly fashion, but all he said was a terse, "I've read your name." I noted the insulting subtext, but it still made me glow a bit to know that Michael Stipe considered me worthy of his condescension.

Groundhog Day, of course, isn't *really* about a day that repeats itself over and over again. It's about a day that keeps changing, in subtle transformative ways that culminate in that day finally being redeemed. At a film festival, I revel in the ritual of repetition (until I've OD'd), but what I'm really searching for is the movie that will bust me out of it—the one that *pings*, the one that will change my world by changing me. That's the ultimate payoff of festival fever, and the first time it happened to me was at Cannes in 1997. I went to see the new film by Atom Egoyan, a director of quizzically outré Canadian puzzle films who in seven years had never made much of an impression on me. But now, out of the blue, he'd lifted his game to a nearly miraculous dimension. In *The Sweet Hereafter*, he made a lyrical sin-drenched disaster movie about how one forbidden relationship can mystically ripple through a community, sparking vibrations that gather into a cataclysm. At the end, I walked down the stairs of the Palais balcony quite literally dizzy; the film had hit my senses like opium.

I had a comparable bliss-out at Toronto in 2000 when I saw *Together*, a movie that confirmed the extraordinary new voice of Sweden's Lukas Moodysson. It was an exquisitely deadpan comedy set in a quarrelsome commune in Stockholm in the 1970s, and it brought me back to the dreams of my youth, because it was really the film that no one had made—until now—about the '60s, about why the counterculture was doomed to fail because it was rooted in such an astoundingly pious premise: that we could all "care about others" as much as we care about ourselves. I'd once believed that (when I was 11), and Moodysson, who was 10 years younger than me, probably believed it when *he* was 11. He surveyed the narcissism of his characters with supremely saddened amusement, yet he cherished them anyway. He was my kind of cynical compassionate humanist.

And then there was the mother of all festival epiphanies, the movie that made me feel born again, the one that let me know there was order in the disorder of the universe. That movie was *Boogie Nights*. In 1997, I went to the world premiere showing of it at the Toronto Film Festival and came out feeling like I would never be the same. I admit I was the perfect audience. I was someone whose sexual consciousness, whose very *being*, had been formed to a degree by pornography, yet I'd never been proud of the fact, because there was no context in which to be proud of it. Porn was a cheap scandal, a joke, a bad habit that got no respect. Taken as *culture* (which is kind of what I thought of it as), it was looked down upon by the puritan right *and* the liberal left. But now, here was an epic movie, made with a virtuosity that swirled *GoodFellas* and Altman and *Pulp Fiction* and Demme together with a swizzle stick of bravura all its own, that dared to present the L.A. porn subculture of the late '70s as a skin-game utopia, a truly naked Garden of Eden from which we were destined to fall.

The movie fixated on the moment when porn on 16mm film was replaced by porn on videotape. It fixated on how erotic joy began to morph into hate-fucking, on how the lust to acquire started to flow into greed. And it said that all those things—the rise of technology, the rise of hate, the rise of a ruthless money culture—were spokes jutting out of the same wheel. *Boogie Nights* didn't just show you the skeeved-out porn subculture. It *used* porn to catch a grander reflection of the moment when the pleasure principle of the '70s gave way to an invisibly colder, controlling spirit. Mark Wahlberg's Dirk Diggler got high on sex, drugs, cash, and ego, to the point that he could barely fuck anymore, and when he and his buddies went over to the home of Alfred Molina's deranged drug dealer, who was lighting firecrackers in his living room, I was literally struck with terror. Then the soundtrack flooded with "Sister Christian," and it was like the first time I ever heard "Let It Be." The movie, I felt, was desperate to forgive Dirk, to forgive all of us who had sinned. *Boogie Nights* was a jubilant vision of a world that once was. But it was really the great vision of a scarier world that was coming.

CHAPTER 18

THE OWEN AND LISA SHOW

The crackling was back, and I now realized with depressing certainty that it wasn't going away. At first I thought it was a fluke, a random hint of scraped sandpaper coming through my stereo speakers. I replaced the fuses in back, which I figured would take care of the problem (and did for a few days), but now the sound was constantly cluttered with distortion, and I could no longer deny what was happening: My beloved Polk Audio speakers were dying. For me, this was no casual demise. I'd purchased them in 1974, when I was a sophomore in high school, and that was 26 years ago, but my attachment to these big brown boxy rectangles of sound was more than nostalgia. I was no audiophile, but I did know sound, and more than a few audiophiles I'd spoken to over the years agreed with me that there was *something* about the speakers made in the '70s—an aural depth, a roomy kick of three-dimensionality—that was baked into the ethereal physics of how they were built. When I played music, it didn't matter whether it was Eminem or Elton John, Green Day or Paula Cole, Fatboy Slim or Hanson—the bass and drums *kicked*, as if they were right there in the room, and I often cranked up the volume to enhance that. I had always fought complaints from neighbors, including one Japanese exchange student who spoke little English but found the words to literally threaten to kill me if I didn't turn my music down. To me, though, that *kick* from my music was essential; it was a life force. And now it was fading.

That this was happening in what I finally had to admit was my horrible new apartment only added to my slow-gathering spectre of loss. Stupidly, when my building went full co-op, I declined the opportunity to purchase my beloved Barrow St. apartment at an insider's price. I would have had to borrow money from my parents, and though I'd resumed speaking to them, I was too proud to enter into that kind of financial arrangement; I felt I had to do everything on my own. And since I was still carrying on an unreasonable love affair with my West Village neighborhood of Sheridan Square, I wound up renting a scuzzy place right above the Lion's Head, the once-fabled journalists' tavern that was now an anonymous collegiate hangout. My third-story walk-up, while it did have a nice soothing treetop view, was one of those glorified garrets with a brick-walled "bedroom" literally the size of my bed. I'd somehow convinced myself that hanging a gorgeous 4-by-6-foot European poster of *Run Lola Run* over the headboard would redeem the place—but no, my new apartment was a hole I was disappearing into. There was only one solution: I must get new and even more magnificent speakers!

So I took out the Yellow Pages and found a high-end audio place in Times Square, right along a legendary row of musical-instrument shops. This, surely, would be my salvation. I went to the store on a Saturday afternoon, and the only person there was a solitary salesman. I told him about the kind of speakers I was searching for, and he took me to the listening room in the back. He had the look of a lean, bushy-haired ex-roadie, but I saw that he walked with a rather severe limp, and that had a downbeat effect on me; as cruel as it may sound, I felt like I was in a store for damaged people. I sunk into a cushy chair, and there, about eight feet away, were the speakers I was going to be listening to. They were large—like thin blocks of mahogany that were four feet tall. I stared at one of them; it stared back like the monolith in *2001: A Space Odyssey*. The salesman gave me a little booklet of CDs, and I chose *Play* by Moby, which had been out for about a year. It was an album I adored, and I knew that it would be excellent speaker-testing material. He turned it right to "Why Does My Heart Feel So Bad?" The piano played, the vocals started, then the drums kicked in, then the synthesizers, and then, at last, the song's majestic hook, that soaring period soul trill from the Shining Light Gospel Choir (*"Heeee'll...* open doors!"), and as I sat there bathing in the power of it, I realized that the sound was better than great. It was perfect. And in the very clarity of that perfection, I saw what my life was becoming, maybe what it already was: It was going to be me and this music and this... *speaker*, this monolith of sound, all of us sitting there together in my shitty apartment. That speaker was going to be my life partner. If I wanted transcendent sound, I could have transcendent sound, but what I now realized is that I was the one who was limping. It made me just about run out of the store. (I did not buy the speakers.)

This is the sort of thing that can happen to you when you're living inside the fever of movie-freak fanaticism, not to mention the Peter Pan comfort zone of serial-monogamy-with-quick-burnout-flings-in-between, and one day you look up and realize that you're 40. Otherwise known as: *TOTALLY GODDAMN FUCKING OLD.* There may not be a biological clock for men, but some kind of clock was running out. What was the best response to this condition? In movies, I craved the bold and the daring and the new, but in life I did not seek change in any concrete way; in truth, I abhorred it. Almost pathologically, I wanted everything to stay the same, from my speakers on down. One of my best friends at *Entertainment Weekly* was Jeff Gordinier, the magazine's boldest and most talented feature writer, who had the office right next to mine. Jeff and I were quite different—he was a severely debonair California WASP, I was an aggressively antsy Midwestern Jewish mutt—but our pop passions overlapped (as did our towering conversational egos), and we spent many, many hours talking. Jeff developed a theory, which he wrote about for *EW*, that 1999 was "The year that changed movies." He catalogued the convention-shredding DNA of films from *Being John Malkovich* to *The Matrix* to *The Blair Witch Project* to *Run Lola Run*. In each case, he was talking about the eminently malleable, splice-and-dice consciousness of the new digital era, when the world—or at least a virtual version of it—could spin on a dime. I agreed with Jeff and relished most, if not all, of the films he was spotlighting (yes, *The Matrix* was a blast, but the fact that it set up the profound issue of mind control only to "resolve" it with great smeary gobs of slow-mo kung fu was rather lame). If the cutting edge of cinema was now avidly evolving into the 21st century, I thought: Bring it on! But the other changes happening around me added up to a single unsettling thought: *Now that I'm old, what am I going to lose next?*

Even *The Sopranos* made me feel like I was losing something. When the show made its debut on HBO, I was over the moon about it. It was obvious that the series was intoxicating, revolutionary—a great *movie*, at long last, created for television. I saw that David Chase didn't just devise his own intricate *Son of GoodFellas*, an extension of Martin Scorsese's vision of the day-to-day grisly Middle American banality of the Mob (the suburban Mob, the *real* Mob). I saw that he'd beaten Scorsese at his own game by giving us a protagonist who was infinitely richer and more reso-nant than Ray Liotta's glib sharpie Henry Hill. As Tony Soprano, James Gandolfini did for the small screen what Brando did for Hollywood in the '50s: blasted it into the orbit of a new psychodramatic dimension. I often saw Gandolfini around my neighborhood (we went to the same video store), and in person he looked even scarier than Tony. He was an awesomely large man who wore a blue kerchief on his head that made his don't-come-up-to-me stare look like that of an oversize crazy pirate.

Given my ecstasy over *The Sopranos*, you'd think I'd have to be a world-class Debbie Downer to even *consider* finding a negative side to the series' game-changing triumph. Well, maybe that's what I was; or maybe I was just good at reading writing on the wall. I got invited to do some pieces for WNYC, New York's National Public Radio station, and one of the first ones I did ran after the first season of *The Sopranos*. I said that the show was the greatest thing ever to happen to television. But I also said that it might prove to be one of the worst things ever to happen to movies. If TV, I wrote, now becomes the place where people flock for human drama, for complex script-driven tales of words and characters and ideas, then where does that leave movies? "It leaves movies," I said, "as the place for spectacle—for visual dazzle and larger-than-life fantasy. It leaves movies, as we have known them, in the dust." I guess I take a bit of pride in having foreseen, back in 2000, the full implications—for movies—of the rise of the renaissance era of television. But I've never been more depressed by an insight I was proud of.

Another shift that felt threatening, even though it was actually good news, is that my term of service as the office creep was finally coming to an end. It was time to wave the white flag; ten years of failure and humiliation was enough. Tellingly, the last nail in the coffin of my ludi-crous non-career as an office pickup artist were my feeble attempts to hit on Gillian Flynn, who was then a talented assistant just starting to work her way up the *EW* power chain. A lot of guys in the office had crushes on Gillian, because she was smart and sly and beautiful, and so amiable on the surface, with flashing warm eyes and a homespun smile, and after she told me that her father was a film professor, I thought—with ultimate geek myopia—that gee, maybe she'd be interested in a film critic like me! Gillian indulged my attempts at conversation, but after a while I saw that I was getting nowhere, and I began to notice that she was always silently *amused*. I began to divine her borderline invisible rolls of the eyes, though it was only many years later, after I'd read *Gone Girl*, that I realized: My God, the whole time that I was talking to Gillian, she was probably fantasizing about garroting me. I finally got a clue as to what really went on in her head when, during a Sundance group dinner, she did an impromptu performance of her Jeremy Piven monologue, giving her infamous take on what a doltish narcissist she found him to be when she was doing a story on him (this was several years before *Entourage*). The sheer ruthlessness of Gillian's account, especially when she imitated a hip-hop number that Piven had improvised about himself, told me that I never, ever wanted to hear that Gillian had done a monologue about *me*. I decided right then and there that the office could no longer be my (failed) lounge-lizard singles' bar.

One change that haunted me, because it was drenched in beauty yet saturated in tender torment, was a musical revelation/discovery/epiphany that shifted something around in my soul. It began, innocently enough, with a movie, and an unlikely one at that: *The Thomas Crown Affair*, the 1999 Pierce Brosnan remake of the late-'60s romantic heist caper. The remake, like its hero (and unlike the clunky original), was clever and light-fingered and suave, and during the climax, the fantastic trickery of Crown's robbery of an art museum was accompanied by a piano that burbled like a furious river atop a rapid walking bass and what sounded like a man from the West Indies singing something about how "I run to the rock." It was one of the most thrilling pieces of music I had ever heard. After the movie, I hunted it down: It was a song called "Sinner-man," by Nina Simone. I had heard of Nina Simone, but I knew next to nothing about her; I thought of her as some now barely relevant singer from the ancient days of Sinatra and JFK. I bought an album with "Sin-nerman" on it, and what I heard was a performer who merged the soul majesty of Aretha Franklin with the scarred power of Janis Joplin with the elegance of a hypnotic chanteuse—and, more than that, who made every song into a *journey*. No contemporary music outside the pop-rock sphere had ever affected me so profoundly.

I haunted the Nina Simone section of Tower Records (which was vast: She seemed to have about 100 albums), and her songs hovered like a blessing and a warning. The two that had the greatest effect on me were "Lilac Wine," a sublime ode to the lush life that I always imagined accompanying the death-by-quasi-willful-overdose of Lily Bart, the heroine of Edith Wharton's *The House of Mirth* (my favorite novel after *Harriet the Spy*), and "Sinnerman," which as I dove deeper into its bounding, percolating mysteries I began to experience as a message delivered directly to me from Nina Simone, singing as God's messenger. "Oh sinnerman," she sang, "where you gonna run to?" Where, indeed? The rock won't hide him, the river won't hide him, the sea won't hide him, and he can only pray. And I realized that the sinnerman was me, my sin being the single-minded pursuit of pleasure, which seemed harmless (except, of course, when it harmed someone), but even then it was starting to hurt me, because the problem is that it was only *about* me. I couldn't hide from that forever. For now, though, there was nothing to do but listen to Nina Simone and drink glass after glass of lilac wine and wonder why my life was starting to look like a glass half empty.

At *Entertainment Weekly*, I got a real wake-up call, one that I'd been quietly dreading, and that's when the emotional slippage started to gather into an avalanche. Jim Seymore summoned me into his office, and this time it was not to tell me that one of my reviews had gotten the name of that bomber in a World War II thriller wrong. Jim explained that he'd finally come to the decision that he wanted me to divide the movie section down the middle with Lisa Schwarzbaum. We would be co-critics: equal on the masthead, the food chain, and out in the world. My days as *the* film critic of *Entertainment Weekly* were over. I knew that Lisa had been lobbying for this, and the way that Jim put it to me was: "She's earned it." Lisa had been doing lead reviews (one out of every four, then three) for several years, yet my identity as lead critic of *EW* had grown to be fundamental to me. I was crushed by what I saw as a major demotion. My question to Jim was: What have *my* years of work earned? It was an unanswerable question, because the truth is that I had nowhere to go but down, and the things that I wanted at *EW* that I didn't have—more space to write, a more adventurous sense of what movie I could choose as a lead review—were, by now, clearly not built into the structure or spirit of the magazine. After a decade, *EW* was what it was. I still had a great deal of freedom, but I wasn't about to get any more of it.

Because I viewed Lisa's ascendance as a devastating career setback, I allowed certain aspects of it to bug me, and I got on my (private) high horse about them. In hindsight, the two of us were creating a new prototype for criticism in the 21st century, and the gender divide was an essential part of that. The vast majority of film critics were still men; what Lisa represented was the rise of women in an aggressively insular and opinionated testosteronic universe. In theory, I had no problem with that, given that the most important writer of my life—the whole reason I'd ever dreamed of becoming a film critic in the first place—was Pauline Kael. Yet in the summer of 2000, when Lisa began to split the movie section with me, her rise at *EW* was buoyed in the office by a fair amount of attitudinal rhetoric about how there were "boy movies" and "girl movies"—a whole *Men Are from Mars, Women Are from Venus* notion that the sexes responded profoundly differently to movies. I was torn: I knew there was truth to this notion, yet a part of me bitterly resented and rejected it, because my whole critical ideology, via Pauline, had been steeped in the belief that empathy trumped all. It didn't matter (or shouldn't) if you were a man or a woman, black or white, Jewish or WASP, Hispanic or Hindu: The essential miracle of movies—and of understanding them— was that they transcended all those pesky boundaries. I knew that I had the luxury of contemplating all this from within the most "privileged" category (I confess! I'm a white male!). But the whole boy movie/girl movie thing sounded suspiciously to me like some nightmare consumerist version of identity politics, a way of dividing movies into demographic slivers, with the appropriate critic appointed to endorse each one.

None of this was fair to Lisa. She truly *had* earned it, review by review, but there was a lot of "You go, girl!" spirit around the office that played into my ideological concerns, and so for a while I looked at her askance. The two of us had always circled each other with polite wariness, anticipating on some unspoken level that we both knew this day was coming, and my sense of defeat didn't exactly increase my friendliness. Ironically, though, a powerful corrective to my trepidation was built right into what movies were becoming. The vast majority of them *weren't* girl movies—they were boy movies. And that meant that Lisa, if she wanted to survive, was now going to be compelled to write about them with a powerful dose of the insider spirit—and the lack of prejudice— that I exalted. She had taken a lot of grief from readers for her negative review of *The Matrix*—an honest piece, excoriated in part because she *was* a woman. (The attitude was: Where does this *chick* get off mocking our ultimate cool trench-coat head-trip sci-fi movie?) I think the tidal wave of flack she caught for that review taught her a lesson: You can say anything you want about a "boy movie," but you had better *know your shit*. She did, taking on the most hard-hitting action films as her rightful terrain. And that set the tone for something: Almost from the start, the key to the Owen and Lisa show was that our writing and opinions *didn't* necessarily fall into those neat, false, gender-centric, demographically correct categories.

For years, a film-critic question I was asked constantly—right behind the proverbial "How many movies do you see a week?"—is "How do you and Lisa divide the movies?" People had a way of asking it with a voyeuristic pushiness, as if they were poking into some top-secret zone, where the answer just *had* to be something dicey. What they really seemed to be saying was: *Come on, fess up! You two must fight like cats and dogs!* I would always answer in a playfully casual way, saying, "Well, it's pretty simple: We switch off on lead reviews," because it was true: Whatever the major movie was that week, that's the one that Lisa or I would end up doing. It was all random, luck-of-the-draw stuff. But inside the section, we would horse trade, leading with our enthusiasms, which meant, for instance, that I reviewed a lot more documentaries, and that Lisa tended to grab the ambitious foreign film of the moment.

In my view, there was an extreme downside to the arrangement, and it always plagued me. It did make a certain sense for each of us to write about the films that we loved. What that meant, though, is that if you *didn't* like something, the probability that you might get to write a naysaying review of it was drastically diminished. I felt that robbed me of a crucial arrow in my critical quiver. There were times when even the most acclaimed movies needed to be questioned, taken down. The whole go-with-your-passion format of the Owen and Lisa show turned us into boosters more than either of us would have been on our own. I chafed at that, and couldn't do much about it. Yet there was a companionable rhythm to our arrangement. Each week, our planning meetings, led by the movie-section editor, were filled with comments like "I did the last two bad Bruce Willis movies. Could you please take this one?" or "I *really* think it's my turn to do the Coen brothers." We competed, teasing each other with a "This dud's got your name on it" one-upmanship that wouldn't have been out of place in a screwball comedy about two rival film critics.

If that movie had ever been made, it would surely have been directed by Nora Ephron—which means, of course, that Lisa would have liked it, and I would have trashed it. A running joke between us, led mostly by Lisa, was that our sensibilities had a brand-like predictability to them. I kind of hated that joke (but indulged it to get along), because I rejected any implication that I was predictable. But there was undeniably a brand dimension to our temperaments. Lisa, tall and angular and zero-body-fat thin, with a mop of curls and an ageless face that could look a bit harsh when it wasn't bursting into a smile, had a chatty, other-directed snark-driven gossip-queen knowingness; she was always highly attuned to What People Were Talking About. I was chatty too, but also moodier, more earnest and private, less interested in what others were saying than in my own theories, which became a pet peeve of Lisa's. She would say: "Here comes another Owen theory!" (*Yes*, I would think to myself. *And isn't it a good one?*)

The true secret of our partnership, reflected in the way that our last names made us sound like the marquee of some law firm from the Lower East Side (Gleiberman, Schwarzbaum & Plotznik!), is that, like a long-lost sister and brother, we shared a high-strung verbal neurotic understanding of the universe, and of the movies that reflected that universe. It's no trivial coincidence that both Lisa and I were former classical musicians. I'd played the violin, Lisa had played the viola, and I think that background informed a lot of our shared rigor about a movie's flow and rhythm and structure. (Although we never said it out loud, I think both of us also knew how the hyper-competitive aspect of classical music could mess you up.) Lisa liked to push the whole *you say tomato/I say tomahto* aspect of our tastes, because I think she believed that it helped her politically in the office, making her sensibility into a valuable piece of turf. And yes, there could be no doubt that I *did* love Oliver Stone movies (except when I didn't) and strange dark kinky indie movies (except when they were bad), and Lisa *did* revel in lacy Jane Austen–meets–Hugh Grant period adaptations (except when she didn't) or any movie made in Iran or by Wes Anderson (well, okay, she really fucking did, every time). Yet a close reading of the Venn Diagram of our likes and dislikes revealed an extraordinary underlying commonality, one that only grew over time. What we shared, as critics and as human beings, was a tough-nut fusion of enlightenment and common sense. I came to think of the two of us as powerfully twisting and idiosyncratic plants growing out of the same thick viny stem. Yet I admit that it took me a while—more than a year, probably—to get over my deep territorial heartache at having to divide the *EW* movie section with Lisa. And it would be several years into our partnership before I looked up and realized that she'd become my greatest ally. What I once saw as my mission and mine alone—carving out a place for true film criticism within the popcorn paradise of *EW*—became hers as well.

When you're a critic, certain films wind up defining you, for better or worse. They become part of your image, your folklore, your narrative. In 2000, one of those movies was my most hated film of the year, and the other was the one I loved most. A lot of people would probably have reversed them. I wrote a relatively short but scathing review that, virtually overnight, turned me into a pariah. The movie was *O Brother, Where Art Thou?*, a gum-toothed redneck period farce by the Coen brothers that I found raucously intolerable to sit through. (It was "based" on *The Odyssey*, though that was a bit like saying that *Rambo* was *The Iliad* with grease-paint camouflage and bazookas.) I had no special hate-on for the Coen brothers. I did, however, think that when they got away from the mesmerizing schlub noir of *Blood Simple* or *Fargo*, there was often a dehumanized quality to the way they used over-the-top hyperbole to poke you in the ribs, the face, the eyeballs. At times, their sense of humor was downright Teutonic, and that was *O Brother* all over. "The latest misanthropic flimflam from the Coen brothers," I wrote, "is like an extended *Three Stooges* episode featuring an even stupider version of the cast of *Hee Haw*. The Coens may be the only filmmakers in history perverse enough to make a movie that's essentially one long, goony, obvious dumb-cracker routine and to give that movie the sunstruck luminosity of an Andrew Wyeth painting." I gave *O Brother* the scarlet letter of shame—an F—and chose it as my worst movie of the year. But the film turned out to be the Coens' biggest hit to date, and its fans came at me with brickbats, as if my opinion had crossed a line of indecency. I've since tried to watch the film again, and I can't even get through it, but there's no question that *O Brother* marked a line in the sand for a lot of my readers. In the eyes of its fans, the film made shit-kicking ridicule into something nearly sacred. If you ridiculed the Coens, though, then *you* were the unforgivable misanthrope.

But then there was the skewed miracle of *Chuck & Buck*. I'd seen it at Sundance, and had done a cartwheel over it, and with good reason: It was a work of tantalizing artistry, a movie so original and fearless it was almost dangerous, yet so remarkably crafted that it made even a bent-side-of-love fantasia like Todd Solondz's *Happiness* (which I revered) look scrappy. It was shot on no-budget digital video, which was then still a bit unusual, and it had the cold utilitarian objectivity of video, but the director, Miguel Arteta, framed each shot with classical cunning. *Chuck & Buck* should be shown in every film school in America as an example of how, if you truly know how to stage and shoot a scene, the lowest budget in the universe can produce a mise-en-scène worthy of Howard Hawks.

The movie was written by its star, Mike White, and it was clearly a confessional psychodrama—by which I mean that it reflected White's life not in any actual way (though for all I know it did), but rather as a lyrical projection of the kind of agonizing arrested development that so many of us grapple with. White, letting the camera drink in the vulnerability beneath his carrot-topped, pasty-faced leer, plays Buck, who has clung to the moment he was 11 years old, when he was best friends—and more than that—with a kid named Chuck. Years later, Buck shows up in L.A. to visit Chuck, and he keeps hanging around, turning himself into the kind of "innocent" pest who doesn't even realize he's a stalker. His actions are creepy and indefensible, yet there's a purity to them: They express the kind of formative erotic-romantic longing that can drive an adult's behavior for years. Let's just say that I related. White, I wrote, "gives a phenomenal performance, and that's partly because the movie, with its digital elementalism, allows us to register every tic and quaver of Buck's shyly stuttering yet emotionally naked psycho–Howdy Doody persona. . . . I felt as if I was watching the past literally come to life."

I received a very nice thank-you note from Mike White about that review, which helped to offset a nasty letter I got from Denis Leary, who decided that my constant panning of his screen work must somehow be related to the time that we were casual acquaintances in Boston. "I would love to know why you have such a giant hair across your ass about my performances in everything from 'The Ref' to 'Suicide Kings,'" he wrote. "Either way, please do the professional thing and inform your boss that you are no longer capable of imparting a non-bias opinion of any film featuring me. . . . Otherwise, I will take this bias of yours public within the context of my own arenas (comedy, satire, HBO). Threat? Better believe it." In a P.S., he added, "And if perchance we meet again, I shall personally redefine the word 'flyweight' for you." Gulp!

I chose *Chuck & Buck* as my movie of the year, and no film I've ever selected for that honor has inspired half as much reaction. All of it was good: For years, countless people have come up to me and said, "I *love* that you made that movie number one." I always found the compliment gratifying, yet at the risk of sounding churlish, I also found it annoying. There was nothing about how I chose *Chuck & Buck* as my movie of the year that made it any different from how I chose *The Silence of the Lambs* or *Nixon* or *Boogie Nights* or *Saving Private Ryan*. People were trying to say: *Dude, what a bold, quirky, balls-out choice!* But it wasn't at all; the movie chose me. In lionizing my alleged "daring," what people were really doing was acknowledging that they *expected* a mainstream critic to be playing by the rules of corporately approved taste. They were acting like (no pun intended) I'd bucked the system. And that wasn't a compliment at all. It was a sad testament to what the system was becoming.

The real testament to what the system was becoming were the orgy of accolades that swirled around a certain darkly meandering, nomenclature-crazed storybook fantasy that should rightfully have been greeted with deeply respectful yawns. I speak of a journey without end; of dwarves and wizards and hairy-footed homunculi; of destinies forged in the molten furnace of clan warfare. I speak—yes—of *The Lord of the Rings: The Fellowship of the Ring*. When I came out of the screening

room after sitting through the first installment of Peter Jackson's trilogy, I knew that he'd visualized Tolkien's epic with a misty foreboding
grandeur that did full justice to the over-the-hills-and-far-away sprawl
of Tolkien's vision. I also knew that Jackson's obsessional pizzazz had
not succeeded in making Tolkien's characters (sorry, but there's just no
other way to put this) *very interesting to watch.* They weren't the dull-
est characters you had ever seen; they were just... *kind* of dull. Orlando
Bloom as Awesome Blonde Elf Rinse Job, Viggo Mortensen as Valiant
Blue Steel Warrior—they had presence, but they didn't have personality.
They didn't need to; they were part of a *fellowship.* The movie wasn't
about characters, about layers of suspense and dramatic intrigue—it was
about the clash of forces, the sinister mad lure of the ring, the whole
beautiful annihilating *world* of the film. Tolkien, it turned out, wasn't
a creature-feature classicist so much as the patron saint of videogames.

A day or two later, I was in the office when someone told me that
Peter Travers' 10 Best of the year list had come out in the new issue of
Rolling Stone, and that his movie of the year was *The Lord of the Rings:
The Fellowship of the Ring.* I actually wondered if I had misheard. I said,
"You're fucking kidding me." A quick word about Peter Travers, who
has, of course, been a walking punchline for years: The shameless blurb
whore! The bi-weekly ejaculator of middlebrow gush! Yet the true nature
of his corruption is not widely understood. Because here's the thing
about Peter, apart from the fact that he's actually a very personable guy,
always dispensing a quip or a nugget of gossip. The reason that he's featured in every movie ad isn't *just* because he makes a point of decorating
each review—even a lot of the pans—with yellow-highlighter lines of
floridly "literate" praise. No, the reason that he's in those ads, week after
week, and often weeks ahead of time, is that it's essentially the result of
an ongoing arrangement with the studios. That said, Peter shores up his
cred by plugging himself into the zeitgeist of hip/cool acclaim. When
he clangs the bell of praise, he's generally ahead of the curve. So when I
heard that he'd chosen *The Fellowship of the Ring* as the best movie of the
year, I thought, "Oh, *fuck.* Here we go." I knew, right then, that the critics were going to shower this thing with praise, that they were going to be
joining in a fellowship of hype.

You might ask: Okay, Owen, does *every* movie have to be a subtle and earthly real-world experience? Isn't there room for art that's rooted in the primeval power of spectacle? I would say: Of course there is. Yet what made *The Fellowship of the Ring* the gateway to a new era can be seen by contrasting it with the first *Star Wars* film, which was so clearly influenced by Tolkien. Back in 1977, *Star Wars* was a zappy space opera with a dash of the mystical in its awestruck view of the Force, and in Alec Guinness' ultra-Gandalfian Obi-Wan Kenobi. Yet there was snap and tension to every encounter, and you didn't have to be a geek of galactica to relate to it. It was a playful and bristling movie, one that kept popping. Mark Hamill was no one's idea of a good actor, but the way Luke's conflicts were sculpted, he didn't have to be. That's the way great pulp works.

The Fellowship of the Ring, on the other hand, was sodden and glum, without a motor to the interactions. It had way too many scenes like the one in which Hugo Weaving's Elrond, eyebrows knifing into his forehead, says, "This evil cannot be concealed by the power of the elves! [Shakespearean pause; voice now rising with urgent gloom:] *We do not have the strength to fight both Mordor and Isengard!*" I'm clawing for air by the end of those two sentences, because the two lines don't really have a lot to do with each other. Elijah Wood may be a better actor than Mark Hamill, but as Frodo, he's trapped in his Hobbit-caught-in-headlights imp-with-a-perm saintliness, with no language to define him. And why does the image of the Eye of Sauron look for the all the world like a vagina on fire? It looks like a vagina on fire because the ethereally evil Sauron, as well as the ring he forged, is really a Very Stuffy English Metaphor for the sinister lust for power embedded in the curse of sexuality. It's all so numbingly severe and effete, so *precious* (as Gollum, that rock star of decay, would put it).

But then, the soggy grand cosmic vagueness points to what was truly visionary about Tolkien, and so paradigm-shifting about the film version of *The Lord of the Rings*. Sitting there in his Oxford study in the '30s and '40s, smoking his pipe as he dreamed up his catalogue of Middle-earth cataclysm, Tolkien reached all the way back to a medieval mode of storytelling and turned it into something post-Freudian—a tale too starkly mythic to contain psychology. As a novel, *The Lord of the Rings* should have been subtitled: "How I Learned to Stop Worrying and Love the Fairy-Tale Trivia Geek-Out." The book might almost have been a conspiracy to turn the entire human population into YA fundamental-ists. And that's the mission that the movie finished off: By the time it had been seen by everyone, and given the collective endorsement of a critical establishment that should have known better, the evolution of movies that people had been griping about since *Jaws* and *Star Wars* was finally, truly complete. It's not just that fantasy and spectacle had taken over. It's that movies would now aim for an ideal of all surface, all mythology, all cosmology, all terminology, with what used to be their vital insides scooped out.

CHAPTER 19
COME WHAT MAY

It's part of Pauline Kael's legend that she almost never saw a movie twice. Her explanation for that was usually something along the lines of, "I got it the first time." She probably did, but I always thought that Pauline's aversion to second viewings was driven by an undertone of anxiety. Once you've written and published a review, it becomes your statement about a movie. If you go back and change your mind (about the whole film, or about this scene or that actor), then even if you're the only one who knows you've changed your mind, you're essentially saying: *I no longer agree with myself.* And that's a threatening thing to feel when your whole job consists of having opinions and standing by them. I've always gone back to see movies again and again, usually for the sheer compulsive pleasure of it (would you play an album you loved exactly once?), but sometimes, yes, to check out if I was "right." And if you're willing to do that, then you'll inevitably confront a moment when you were *wrong*. It's not fun; it can be agonizing. Yet the pain of having written something that you no longer agree with can be offset by the increase in your total earthly quotient of aesthetic delight. For me, a second viewing often goes something like this: I'll see a movie I liked well enough the first time, and now I know that I like it much more. The "flaws" melt away; they don't even seem like flaws anymore. Or, just maybe, I've transitioned from liking a film to falling in love with it. (So in hindsight, that original "like" now falls crucially short of the mark.)

In all my years as a critic, no movie ever put me through that experience as head-spinningly as *Moulin Rouge!* I totally get why. When I first saw Baz Luhrmann's visionary musical, I responded to some of it. Ewan McGregor, I wrote, "lapses into a woozy warm rendition of Elton John's

'Your Song,' and damned if the movie doesn't caress our eardrums with romance. Moments later, the black sky has gone twirly psychedelic. The rock opera, of course, is nothing new, but in *Moulin Rouge!*, the spectacle of rock employed in a period setting, funny and absurd as it often appears, speaks to us in a new and galvanizing way. It slashes through the distance that so many of us feel toward musicals, not just because the songs here really are our songs, but because the very incongruity evokes that casual, private dream world in which rock has become the daily libretto of our lives."

The "Your Song" sequence of *Moulin Rouge!*, driven by the high-beam sincerity of McGregor's charisma, was a special delight, its magic only heightened by the weird semi-glitch of the change in lyrics from "while" to "now," so that the song's key line became: "How wonderful life is, *now* you're in the world." (The pesky grammarian in me was crying out for it to be: "now *that* you're in the world.") At the same time, I complained that *Moulin Rouge!* is "an extravaganza of shrill camp," and that "the film seems to have been directed by a madman with a palm buzzer." I was mixed, and gave the movie a B-minus. What I didn't realize is that I was grading it entirely on the basis of a promising but problematic first date.

Before I compile my 10 best of the year list, I make a point of seeing a number of key films a second time, and the main reason I ever locked that ritual into place is *Moulin Rouge!* Because at the end of 2001, I *didn't* see it a second time, and being the "mixed-bag" B-minus movie it was, it was of course left off my list. I didn't think twice about it. But then, a few months later (it was February 2002), I was having a drink with Patricia Clarkson, the brilliant, fast-on-her-way-to-becoming-fabled actress who I'd become friendly with. I spotted her one evening in Balducci's, the West Village yuppie Italian grocery store, and since I'd been a major supporter of *High Art*, the movie that kind of put Clarkson on the map with her performance as a haughty German junkie actress vamp, I introduced myself, and we started talking, and it turned out that Patty was one of the most sweetly incisive people I'd ever met, and that she was also that rare thing (in fact, she may be the only one): an actress who believed in critics!

She and I started to get together, quite casually, maybe three times a year, but this particular night turned out to be the only time we ever went to a movie together. We decided to see *Moulin Rouge!* at the Village East, where it was playing in one of those cruddy airless Manhattan-multiplex shoeboxes. And watching it a second time, I fell madly in love with the parts I'd liked the first time, but what I really saw was how the whole gorgeous Brechtian pop-kitsch-opera mosaic fit together. Yes, the opening 45 minutes was brittle and in-your-face, and the movie bounced back and forth between delirious passion and cold camp, but that was all part of its voluptuous design. I now saw that *Moulin Rouge!* was the most epic of swoons, a kind of *ultra* romance in which love keeps getting crushed by the world (which only makes it more desperately enticing), and I saw that Luhrmann expressed the specialness of love by turning it into a cracked aria of rapture tucked inside an assaultive fusion of Ken Russell and MTV and *Cabaret* and Bollywood. The outside of the movie *had* to be harsh to make the inside so luscious.

After Patty and I came out of the movie, I walked her home, and as I made my way to my own apartment, I realized that I had just seen, without doubt, the greatest movie of the year. I was exhilarated, but I also thought...*fuck*! Why hadn't I realized that the first time? In *EW,* I had chosen *Memento* as the best film of 2001, and though I did love Christopher Nolan's backward head-game puzzle-movie noir, it loomed up in hindsight like a virtuoso exercise that somehow didn't matter. The movie that now mattered, that now consumed me, was *Moulin Rouge!* If I could have done it all over again, I would have made it my movie of the year, and I still think my not doing so is the single biggest misjudgment of my career.

A misjudgment I was actively accused of—though I stood by it— was the drive-by attack I made on Robert McKee, the legendary screenwriting guru. His sprawling three-day-long "Story Seminars," in which he took to the stage to lecture on the art of screenwriting, were viewed with awe from inside the movie industry, yet it was my feeling that they'd become cult events: They celebrated *him,* but the art of screenwriting was increasingly in tatters, and my opinion was that McKee's teachings (don't overvalue dialogue, etc.) ultimately reinforced where Hollywood was heading; they would have squashed the life out of, say, Quentin Tarantino. To me, McKee's mystique was part of the problem, not the solution. In my review of *High Crimes*, an egregiously scripted Ashley

Judd–Morgan Freeman potboiler, I decided, on impulse, to call McKee on the carpet. I wrote: "There's a case to be made that Robert McKee, the guru of contemporary screenwriting, has done as much to coarsen and degrade the art of Hollywood cinema over the last two decades as Jerry Bruckheimer and Joe Eszterhas combined. For 15 years, McKee entitled his famous and influential roving class 'Story Structure,' and you can feel its elusive imprint whenever you see a movie that is nothing *but* story structure—a thriller, say, that has all the bones and ligaments of drama but none of the supple human flesh." McKee phoned me in a fit of outrage, and he told me, "You had no right to say that."

"I certainly did," I said. "It's what I think."

"I want you to retract what you wrote," he said. I refused, but suggested that the two of us meet, which we did about a month later.

He chose an empty Italian place in Midtown, and after we'd been seated and exchanged pleasantries, he blurted out that his son was in the midst of intense troubles, battling drugs, which I thought was a strange thing for him to tell me. Then I realized that he was, perhaps, looking for my pity, and that suggested that we were about to have a sympathetic encounter. A few minutes later, though, McKee ripped into me, calling me an irresponsible hack. He told me that his good friend Brian Cox, who wound up portraying McKee in Spike Jonze's *Adaptation.*, had volunteered to wring my neck. Since Cox had played Dr. Lecter in *Manhunter* (ironically, one of my favorite films), that was an image I could all too easily—or uneasily—envision. I defended my position, saying that just because McKee was a celebrated teacher didn't mean that he was above criticism. But McKee was so invested in the myth of himself that he wanted nothing less than unconditional surrender, and I wouldn't give it to him. We went back and forth, his end of the conversation getting quite heated, and it was all kind of fruitless and depressing—until the very end, when the two of us walked out together, and standing on 8th Ave., I said, "I'm a writer who took a shot at you. I have a right to do that. Why are you so angry about it?" And he looked at me, his sunken handsome Irish eyes suddenly sad, and he said, "Because you hurt me." I felt that was the first totally honest thing he'd said. And it wounded me, so I said, "I'm sorry that happened. If I could do it all over again, I'd still write that piece, but I would do it differently. I was too harsh. And I apologize." I felt that without expecting to, we had both confessed something and that it gave us closure.

The weekend after I saw McKee, I went up to the Woodstock Film Festival, one of those ardently curated but stubbornly local events that I attended only rarely, mostly so that I could hang out and decompress. At a festival party, I ran into someone I hadn't seen in several years, a gifted former NYU film student named Laurie who'd been married to the drummer in They Might Be Giants. She was a brainy upstate eccentric with a touch of the siren about her, and she was buddies with the twisty-headed animator Bill Plympton, who I had championed in *EW*. The three of us chatted and had a nice time.

A few weeks later, Laurie called me out of the blue on a Saturday afternoon. She was in New York for just a day; did I want to have a drink with her? Normally, the chances were overwhelming that I'd have *something* lined up for a Saturday night. But I had no plans at all, which made me feel like this last-minute invitation was meant to be. Laurie asked me to meet her at Dorrian's, the Upper East Side bar that was the infamous hangout of Robert Chambers, the so-called "preppie killer." She asked if she could bring a friend along, and I said sure.

There's a certain age at which a guy, if he has any sense at all, will confront the undeniable fact that we now live in a culture where *only* middle-aged men wear leather jackets anymore. The night I met Laurie for a drink, I was 43 years old, but I hadn't yet made that leap of perception, and I was wearing—still youthfully, I thought—my black leather jacket with the built-in belt, the one that an acerbic assistant at *Entertainment Weekly* occasionally let me know what she thought of by singing the riff to "Staying Alive" when I happened to walk by in it. A great many women, especially at a place like Dorrian's, would have taken one look at that jacket and wanted to run screaming from the room. But one woman who didn't feel that way was Laurie's friend Sharon, who also lived upstate. The two walked into Dorrian's about 45 minutes late, and Sharon later told me that that jacket was the first thing she noticed about me, and the first thing she liked.

Given that she was 23 years old, that should not have been part of the script. But it was, and so was the part where I talked to Sharon, just to be polite (the person I really wanted to talk to was Laurie), and we weren't discussing anything I can remember, but what I noticed is that though she had a radiant smile and laughed easily at my jokes, there was a soft gravity to her, a weighted solemnity that seemed almost pre-verbal. She lacked even a recessive version of the irony gene, and that gave her conversation the quality of an embrace. Just talking to her about nothing, I felt like I was curling up in her arms.

I always like talking to women about movies, not just because it allows me to show off, but because it's a fast way to learn about who they are. Sharon had seen a lot of movies, and at one point we spoke of *Moulin Rouge!*, and it turned out that she'd had the same idiosyncratic experience that I did: She'd seen it twice, having mixed feelings the first time and completely falling for it the second. That overlapping collusion spoke to me. I thought, "Wow, *Moulin Rouge!* really *is* a tricky movie to warm up to. But maybe that's because when you surrender to it, you go all the way." Another thing Sharon and I had in common that struck me was that neither one of us had ever been on an Internet date. At the time, I was steadfastly against them (it seemed like people acting as their own yentas), and so, it turned out, was she. By the end of the night, I got Sharon's number and felt the promise of something.

I'd been looking for an apartment, finally deciding to bite the bullet of guilt and borrow money from my parents, and literally the day after I met Sharon, I bid on a one-bedroom in my former Barrow St. building, in the same line as my original beloved apartment. The bid was accepted. As far as real estate went, I was going back to the future.

But at *EW*, the future was rushing toward us in a far less toasty way. Jim Seymore had been told that his reign as managing editor was coming to an end, and instead of knighting a successor, he dithered. That's because he didn't want to go. (I genuinely felt his pain.) There were four senior editors at *EW* who could have stepped in to replace him and done an inspiring job: the Jedi triumvirate of Mark Harris, Maggie Murphy, and Mary Kaye Schilling, and also Pete Bonventre, an avuncular pal of Jim's whose career reached all the way back to the days when he covered Muhammad Ali for *Newsweek* in the early '70s, and who I had become friends with, because I responded—as so many did—to Pete's rock-solid loyalty and hard-nosed curiosity about everything under the sun. Pete looked a little like Wally Shawn, but he was no nerd. He was a bon vivant, very plugged in, who claimed that a relative of his had given Francis Ford Coppola the line "Keep your friends close, and your enemies closer." Pete was a longtime regular at Elaine's, and when I had dinner with him there, I felt like I could meet...anybody. And did. People like William Kennedy and Gay Talese and Elaine herself, who was a trip— I loved the way that she made her croaky, imperious starfucking into something iconic. Like a lot of people at *EW*, I would have been happy with any of those four as managing editor. But instead, John Huey, the eloquent but bellicose deputy editorial director of Time Inc. (he was the kind of Dixie hardhead who had a chip on his shoulder about people he thought had chips on their shoulders), decided to install his protégé from *Fortune* magazine: Rick Tetzeli, who had never held a job in the field of entertainment journalism.

Personally, I didn't hold that against Rick. He was smart and responded to pop culture, and I figured that he would learn, which he did. The trouble with Rick was his temperament: He was a tall, handsome, but morosely soft-spoken sort who yearned to be "cool" (he prided himself on keeping up on "cool music"), and as soon as he fell into the job, the atmosphere around the office began to change. It became less freewheeling, more contained, more of a reflection of Rick's low-key control-freak personality. And that was true of the magazine as well. The weirdest thing about Rick Tetzeli's version of *Entertainment Weekly* is that it had a bit of the pod person about it: It was still an accomplished magazine, one that looked like *EW*, felt like *EW*, and mostly read like *EW* (though Rick, in a misguided attempt to win awards, favored the occasional faux-*Esquire* "bonus" feature, like an endless story on Vaughn Meader, an early-'60s political impressionist whose career was cut short by the assassination of JFK). At the same time, something intangible was missing. It was the same thing that seemed to be missing from Rick's personality. The word for it is "joy."

I should add that Rick treated me quite well and, if anything, had fewer problems with my art/snob/highbrow side than Seymore did. I knew things were going to be okay, a month or so into his tenure, when Rick sent me an e-mail telling me how much he loved my review of *Far From Heaven*, Todd Haynes' sublime dream mirror of a Douglas Sirk soap opera ("The entire movie is a picture-perfect, nearly fetishistic re-creation of the four-hankie, Technicolor melodramatic style that Sirk made famous…Haynes gets at something more elusive: the mood, and mystery, of the past. Nudging his story into areas of sexuality and race that would have been taboo at the time, he at once preserves and pokes through the repressed spirit of the '50s, fashioning the era into an eerie echo of our own"). I got along with Rick, but like everyone else in the office, I always thought I was going to be fired when I passed him in the hallway, because even though he looked, from a distance, like he could have been a tawny-haired surfer dude, he had a way of skulking past you as if he was mad about something. (I'd heard that his family nickname was "Lurch.") And it was Rick who, during his first year, oversaw a re-design of the *EW* review sections that cut down our space—not enough to be calamitous, but enough to put those sections on a slippery slope. I'd always sought feedback from civilians about *EW*, and right up until the end of Jim's era, the feedback was always ecstatic. But after that redesign, I started to hear people lodging the same complaint, over and over, often by using the same cliché: "*EW* wasn't broke," they would say. "So why did they fix it?"

There was no good answer to that. None at all. The only answer was: Why ask why?

A week after I met Sharon, I invited her to have a drink at Bar Six, an elegant Village hangout that was the place I usually went for drinks with Patty Clarkson. Sharon, who drove down from New Paltz, where she'd gone to college and was still living, came into the bar and sat down opposite me at one of the small round copper tables, and the first thing she did was to pull out two jokey plastic dolls, one male and one female, that she'd brought along as a lark, saying, "I got these for us." The dolls were a throwaway, but the moment she said "us," a volt went through me. It was two minutes into our first date, and I felt as if we already *were* an "us." Laurie, who'd facilitated our getting together (without at all trying to), warned Sharon that whatever she did, she should *not* to go back to "the lion's den" (i.e., my apartment). But after taking Sharon to dinner, I did bring her back to the lion's den. I put on No Doubt's *Rock Steady*, and it was when the sugared Quaalude reggae groove of "Underneath It All" came on that we kissed for the first time.

That Sharon was 20 years younger than me sounds like the ultimate insecure-older-guy cliché. Except that dating younger women was something I almost always made a point of avoiding, and for a simple reason: They tended to bore the shit out of me. I was an ardent enough conversationalist that few things struck me as more tedious—or dispiriting—than feeling like the old-lech protagonist of Steely Dan's "Hey Nineteen," trying to connect with a "babe" I had no connection to. Sharon and I talked all night the evening we met, and after that we never stopped talking. I trumped her in worldly experience, but it was clear that she was one of the most psychologically astute people I'd ever met. She saw her way right into others. It was supreme fun to go to a party or an event with her and then do the postmortem, hearing what her take was on everybody, because it was always witty and laser-like in its perception. And our erotic connection was immediate and intense.

But what about the hunger? The serial monogamy? The four-month mark?

I went to visit Sharon for a weekend in New Paltz, and on Saturday night we wound up sitting in her car in a shopping mall parking lot, listening to music. I noticed that she had a Nina Simone CD called *Let It Be Me*, which I owned as well, from Simone's post-'70s comeback period, when her voice, due to age but also to the psychotropic drugs she was on, had grown a bit pitchy and had lost layers of its shimmering vibrato. Yet even diminished by time, her majesty rang out. Sharon told me that she adored Nina Simone, which I took as a deep omen, and she and I sat there listening, over and over, to "Balm in Gilead," which I at one point jokingly improvised stupid hip-hop lyrics to (my attempt to outdo Jeremy Piven?). But as I listened to the real lyrics ("There is a balm in Gilead, to make the wounded whole,/There is a balm in Gilead, to heal the sin-sick soul"), I felt as if Sharon and I were being baptized by the high priestess of soul.

And then, finally, it was time to stop listening to music. I looked at Sharon, and took her in my arms and drew her close, and I said something, slowly and deliberately, that I'd never said to any other woman before. I said, "I love you." And she said, "I love you, too."

And I thought: How wonderful life is, now you're in the world.

CHAPTER 20

HOW I BECAME A NUTTER

In September 2003, a website called efilmcritic.com compiled a list of quotes in movie ads culled from the preceding year, all to find out which film critics were quoted the most. The results were not surprising. Roger Ebert came in first (with 67 quotes), followed by his partner, Richard Roeper (39 quotes), and then Kenneth Turan of *The Los Angeles Times* (33 quotes). I was somewhere in the middle (with 20 quotes). The only surprise is that every critic on the list was represented simply by name and affiliation—except for me. Under my name were two prominently displayed quotes *about* me. The first said: "Owen Gleiberman, hands down, is the biggest nutter. He strikes me as someone who feels he needs to be contrarian to have any street cred; I don't trust that he reacts authentically to a film. —New York magazine editor." The second one said: "Owen Gleiberman's taste worried me. I often use it as a reverse litmus test. —Manhattan-based writer/filmmaker." By 2003, I'd certainly learned to take hostile comments on the Internet with an oversize pinch of salt. Yet these two anonymous takedowns did not appear in a vacuum; I was starting to read comments like that all the time. In the minds of a great many people, I was becoming a "contrarian," a crackpot, a cranky iconoclast, the only critic in the universe who hated (or liked) *X* or *Y*, and on and on and on. I of course had to ask myself: *What the fuck is going on?*

I knew that if my tastes really were all that screwy, I would probably never have survived at *Entertainment Weekly*. It was, after all, about as mainstream as a magazine could get. I'd developed a sixth sense for knowing when a review of mine ruffled the feathers of an *EW* editor (as often as not, you didn't need the sixth sense—they would just tell you). It happened periodically, but the days when I was known as the pariah of

Pretty Woman were behind me. And to the extent that I did ruffle feathers, or put forth a view that was "out of step" with the general current of opinion, I didn't just defend the right to do so. I thought it hardly *needed* a defense. My opinions emerged from the unique individual I was. If what I thought about movies was truly nutty, then I suppose that would be worthy of comment, yet every bone in my body told me that I was being singled out not because my opinions were so provocative or bizarre but because they were so resolutely—and, yes, uniquely—mine. As it happens, I'd walked straight into the buzzsaw of the New Groupthink.

The right to have your own idiosyncratic opinion, even when it cuts against the grain of conventional or popular taste, has always been, for me, one of the primal joys of moviegoing. Not because I'm a "contrarian," but because I revel in discovery, and in the sensation that underlies it: the freedom to think and react however you want. The reason I know I'm not a contrarian or an iconoclast—literally, one who tears down icons—is that I hold both states of mind in complete contempt. I actually think they're close to being the same thing as jumping on the bandwagon (or maybe they're just the flip side of it). The person who loves a film because everyone else does, and the person who hates a film because everyone else loves it, has, in each case, based his or her opinion on *what everyone else is doing.* That's two different shades of lame. The most infamous contrarian critic of our time, the perceptive but hectoringly perverse Armond White, is someone I believe *does* periodically construct his opinion around what others are thinking (I say that only because he's constantly talking about the opinions of others in his reviews—he seems more obsessed with others than he does with himself). Around the time of that "nutter" comment, a lot of Internet chatter began to pair me with Armond, as if we were criticism's reigning twin devil assassins. I thought that *was* nuts.

Here's why you hardly need to be that tacky third-rate thing, a *contrarian*, to be naturally, organically, *honestly* contrary. Every time you walk into a movie, you have the pleasure of two discoveries at once: You get to see the film, and you get to experience whatever you thought and felt about it. There's what's up on screen, and what's in your head and heart. When I catch up with a movie that's thought of as a classic, I'm never more thrilled than if it lives up to its reputation. It's one more movie to love! Yet from the moment I saw *Jules and Jim* as a college student and hated it, I took note of the fact that you could be down on a "classic" and that was okay. Civilization would stand; no small animals would be harmed. I had no bias against Truffaut: *Day for Night* was the movie that christened my love affair with movies. (Later on in college, I cherished *The 400 Blows* and *The Story of Adele H.*) But the point is that even with a classic, you never know what *you're* going to think. That's the tingly adventure of it.

There is, of course, a "canon" of great films—the attempt over the decades by critics and academics and the rarefied DVD programmers of The Criterion Collection to lend shape and value and meaning to the history of cinema, so that it can enjoy a sibling relationship with the canon of great literature. I don't have a major bone to pick with the canon, yet I'm not really a big one for canonical thinking. There's a fine line between accepting the canon and respectfully kowtowing to a creeping fascism of aesthetic authority. The true movie freak finds his or her own canon. As I gorged on film history, I discovered the many ways that my taste flowed in and out of accepted cinematic and critical dogma. I loved Kurosawa's *Seven Samurai* but found the majority of his films to be overrun with garrulous and badly plotted scenery-chewing. (*Cue the screams of outrage!*) I vastly preferred the delicately brutal portraiture of Yasujiro Ozu. I reveled in the '70s glory days of Jack Nicholson but loathed the much-loved *Five Easy Pieces*, which I thought was a crock right down to its famous yet badly written chicken-salad scene (what waitress in a diner on this earth wouldn't let you order a side of toast?). I thought *Full Metal Jacket* was Stanley Kubrick's greatest film, and that *The Shining* was his worst. I truly did think *Citizen Kane* was the greatest movie ever made, but apart from *Touch of Evil* and *Lady from Shanghai* I could scarcely watch anything else by Orson Welles, who I thought was a stiff-jointed, hollow virtuoso. (*Cue the screams of outrage!*) I thought Nicolas Roeg's greatest head game wasn't *Don't Look Now* but the now all-but-forgotten *Bad Timing: A Sensual Obsession*. I found Luis Buñuel's deliriously acclaimed mock-the-swells landmark *The Discreet Charm of the Bourgeoisie* to be a hellacious bore without end. And on and on.

You may be picking up on a theme here: I'm often down on foreign films that other people love. I've been seared for this by what I think of as the Highbrow Structuralist Cinema Collective—the kinds of critics who make a fetish of quality out of films that are "challenging," like Hou Hsiao-Hsien's *Flowers of Shanghai*, a period drama set in a brothel that has an atmosphere so saturated in repression that it takes half the film before you realize its story has slid off the rails and into a ditch. Yet to critics in certain circles, if you reject a movie like *Flowers of Shanghai* for being—God forbid—obtuse, then you're only revealing your own obtuseness. The problem isn't that the film is barely watchable (though take my word for it, it is). It's that *you* weren't smart enough to get it. There's now a crypto-academic snob-contest side to film criticism: Who can be the most rigorous and daring critic who "gets" the movies that no one else does? One recurrent world champion is Amy Taubin, a veteran New York critic of true talent I used to have very nice chats with, but as the years went by I saw her friendliness congeal into a scowl of Maoist disdain, her disapproval only deepening each time I let drop that I didn't care for the latest masterpiece by one of her critical darlings, like David Cronenberg (the scowl really dug in when I griped about the implausibility of *A History of Violence*) or Claire Denis (creator of ascetic leftist-feminist French wallpaper).

Let's be clear: I am not a cinematic xenophobe. I've loved and championed countless non-English-speaking films, from the despairing ecstasy of early Robert Bresson to the puckish humanity of late Agnès Varda, from De Sica and Murnau and Renoir to Ray and Visconti and Cocteau, from the tormented dreamscapes of Carl Dreyer to the twisted passion plays of Ingmar Bergman, from the haunting true-life parables of Werner Herzog to the lyrical outcast portraits of Lukas Moodysoon, from the X-ray of oppression that is *The Lives of Others* to the primal shock theater of *Irreversible*, from Wong Kar-wai's rapturous *In the Mood for Love* to Asghar Farhadi's scalding *A Separation*, from *Run Lola Run* to *4 Months, 3 Weeks and 2 Days.*

Some observers might say: Fine, but in this entire book, there has scarcely been one film you've talked about being obsessed with that has subtitles on it. It's true! Guilty as charged. As a viewer, I feel much, much closer to American filmmakers—to their subjects and styles, moods and visions. Maybe that's because I'm an American, and maybe it's because— let's be honest—we kind of created this shit. But there's no denying that I will never win the United Nations humanitarian award for enlightened global film criticism. Especially when it comes to three legendary directors who are almost universally considered geniuses, and whose work, with rare exceptions, has left me in a state of high indifference. They're the filmmakers I think of as the cinema's holy trinity of postmodern detachment: Jean-Luc Godard, Rainer Werner Fassbinder, and Pedro Almodóvar. I apologize to the gods, their fans, and to Amy Taubin, but the simple truth is that I do not like them. I think their films (mostly) suck.

Godard, of course, is the most important of these filmmakers, because he revolutionized (and, to a degree, invented) the language of modern cinema, and in that sense he's as seismic a figure as Brando or D.W. Griffith. I've been grappling with his work for 45 years, ever since I saw my first Godard film—*One Plus One*—in junior high and thought, even aside from the scenes with the Rolling Stones, that it was "interesting." (The friends I went with wanted to tar and feather the projectionist.) I love *Breathless* and Godard's one other "conventional" film, *Contempt*, a blistering snapshot of marital breakdown, plus bits and pieces of his others—the first 45 minutes of *Masculin Féminin*, the traffic jam in *Weekend*, the performance of Yves Montand in *Tout Va Bien*. Yet even the films from Godard's vintage '60s period are so fractured and self-referential and self-conscious with meaning yet obscure that I find most of them nearly impossible to sit through. (I caught up with one I'd never seen, *La Chinoise*, only recently; by the end, I wanted to shoot myself.) As an artist, Godard seems fixated on modes of communication—advertising, language, videotape—that somehow have the effect of trapping and submerging his own desire to communicate. He's basically an avant blowhard of semiotic deconstruction in the sheep's clothing of a filmmaker.

Fassbinder, because he's so much less interesting cinematically, I find even more intolerable: an arid absurdist whose desperate, driven characters should theoretically tug at our sympathies, yet they rarely come off as engaged—or fully realized—human beings. I do respond to one Fassbinder film, the touching and shocking May-December romance *Ali: Fear Eats the Soul*, and I love his revelatory work as an actor in *Fox and His Friends*, which seems to communicate, quite directly, all the angst and trouble his other films chew on like badly written cud. Mostly, he seems like an auteur from another planet.

Then, of course, there's planet Pedro, a place I've always longed to enjoy because it looks like everyone there is caught up in such a delirium of spiked passion. Yet it's all so poker-faced preposterous! So wrapped in spicy cheesy layers of artifice. So dutifully outrageous and, therefore, not outrageous at all. Almodóvar's films strike me as over-the-top Telemundo soap operas on very cheap harsh drugs, and watching one of them, I can never connect to what's happening. I feel like I'm staring at a slow-moving aquarium of bad behavior.

Of course, my views on Godard, Fassbinder, and Almodóvar may not have meant all that much in the *Entertainment Weekly* era. Far more significant, in terms of building up my image as a contrarian, were my perpetual disagreements with Media Mike—that imaginary (but all too real) dictatorial dude who had the effect of anointing critical darlings that reviewers felt they were virtually forbidden to go against. I first noticed how big Media Mike's influence was becoming around the time of *The Insider*, the 1999 Michael Mann drama about a tobacco-industry whistleblower that the entire media world seemed locked into declaring a neo-'70s landmark. The trouble was, the film was much ado about nothing. Leaving aside that the "news" on smoking, addiction, and lung cancer was 40 years old (we got endless science-class lectures about it in junior high in 1971), *The Insider* was a movie that presented the issue of whether a story would or would not be aired by *60 Minutes* as a metaphor for the freedom of information. The film didn't seem to understand that *60 Minutes* is not *The New York Times*; it's an advertising-driven entertainment-feature show posing as hard journalistic news. (The pose is part of what it's selling.) The tobacco story in *The Insider* that got "crushed" by "Big Media"? It ran a short while later in *The Wall Street Journal*. I said all of this in my review, but no one could hear the argument, because *The Insider* had achieved the status of a fearless piece of muckraking.

The power wielded by Media Mike only grew, culminating in 2007. I was a major Pixar fan, but I had mixed feelings about *Ratatouille*, the Brad Bird culinary fairy tale that looked *mah*-velous (and had a great critic character) but was, I felt, built around way too bland a hero. I hardly thought that was a subversive judgment, yet Media Mike had ruled: *Ratatouille* was the greatest Pixar film…maybe ever! *New York* magazine's Vulture site branded me an "outlier" (for giving a Pixar movie a B!), and people kept wanting to know why I didn't like it more. There were other overblown Media Mike faves, including some I didn't write about, like *Oldboy*, *The Diving Bell and the Butterfly*, and that flatly drawn animated version of a fantasy rummage sale, *Spirited Away*. (*Cue the screams of outrage!*) It was supremely ironic that Paul Thomas Anderson, a director I had championed, turned into a Media Mike superstar just at the moment his films were becoming top-heavy art statements without the exuberant flow that had made *Boogie Nights* (and, to a degree, *Magnolia*) indelible. *There Will Be Blood* was a Media Mike orgasm, a movie the whole world declared to be etched in greatness, even though the film's "flaw" was epic: It established, within half an hour, that Daniel Day-Lewis' John Huston–voiced oil tycoon was a squinty greedhead sociopath, and it then did increasingly flamboyant variations on the same didactic lesson—*greed is bad!*—in scene after scene. *There Will Be Blood* should have been called *Watching an Asshole Grow Bigger and Bigger*.

My personal Media Mike Waterloo was probably *Let the Right One In*. I had only a 90-word capsule in which to summarize why I didn't care for this Swedish vampire drama about two 12-year-olds, one a boy, the other a bloodsucking girl who *looks* like a boy (something the boy doesn't blink an eye at—it's a bit like *The Crying Game*, but also a bit like the film is selling pint-size enlightened transgender politics). And I screwed things up by making a mistake in my review: I got confused about the relationship between the girl and her guardian. (When I saw the film a second time, I realized why I was confused: The film is hopelessly vague about it. Because it's backing off from the pervy implications of the original novel.) It's always agonizing to get a plot detail wrong, but people jumped on my glitch, using it to invalidate my dislike of the movie. *Let the Right One In* became a cult film, and people grow unreasonably attached to those, but the level of intolerance for my dissenting view was off the charts, and it became another black brick in the wall of my anti-cachet—the ultimate variation on "Who cares what Owen Gleiberman thinks? He's the guy who hated *O Brother, Where Art Thou!*" or "He's the guy who didn't like *The Insider!*" or "He's the only guy who gave a good review to *Epic Movie!*" Now it was "He's the guy who trashed *Let the Right One In!*" I don't mean to go all victim card on you, but my ultimate thought was: After 100 years of cinema, why should one glum, rather slackly edited, erotically pious Swedish vampire film suddenly be *the* movie that you're not allowed to dislike?

There were two essential answers to that, and I had sympathy for one, and contempt for the other, but both were depressing. Though it was only a trickle so far, like the first droplets of water leaking through the crack in a faulty dam, a disquieting pattern had emerged: Film critics were starting to lose their jobs. The trend began at daily newspapers, essentially for economic reasons. The decline of print had begun, a product of the rise of the Internet. There were fewer advertising dollars (and a lot less *classified* advertising dollars—that's where newspapers really got murdered), so budgets needed to be cut and writers had to be laid off. Critics—of every art form—made for an easy target, and the reason seemed unassailable on the surface: If it came down to a newspaper having to choose between, say, losing a school-board reporter or a second-string film critic, then there appeared to be no contest. Especially because the hole a critic left could be plugged by wire copy from a nationally syndicated reviewer. (That may not have been a *great* option, but at least it would work.)

The slowly gathering drumbeat of critics losing their jobs, even when the attrition was still in its infancy, cast a quiet chill over the world of film criticism. But not just for the obvious reasons. The chill was accompanied by an ideological shift—a new reactionary attitude toward criticism in the culture at large, also brought about by the rise of the Internet. With commentary about film now saturating the Web, a new reality—or mythology—emerged: *Anyone can do it! Anyone can be a film critic!* And this mythology produced a corollary: If anyone can do it, then the people who get paid to be film critics are just…the lucky ones. The lottery winners. They've got the most enviable jobs in the world, but they really could be anyone, including you or me.

This mythology was rooted in the degradation of criticism. It was anchored in the belief that "anyone can do it" because what "it" actually is isn't really all that much. (It's recommending a good blockbuster over a bad one. Fighting with your fellow fanboy like Siskel and Ebert tossing spitballs at each other. Being the smart version of a chucklehead geek.) And this degraded notion of what criticism is got piled on top of the *old* anti-critic ideology, the one that went underground in the Kael/Sarris '70s but never really went away: the belief that critics were annoying snoots like Addison DeWitt. That they weren't part of *the people*.

All of this resulted in a change in criticism. In the new millennium, the slow but steady loss of critic jobs, coupled with an increasingly vocal belief that those jobs were being lost because no one deserved to have them in the first place, created a situation in which critics were suddenly a lot more anxious about the reviews they were writing and how those reviews might affect their futures. The kinds of comments I'd dealt with for a decade and a half at *Entertainment Weekly* ("Watch out, it's another one of those movies Owen likes!" Rick Tetzeli passing me in the hallway: "How could you not like *Little Miss Sunshine*? It's *fun*!") added up, for a lot of critics, to a not-so-veiled threat. If a newspaper critic, or even one at a glossy magazine, panned the latest $200 million-grossing space opera and then went to bat for a "tiny" art film that emerged from the remains of Romania, that critic's editor, stoked by the new "populist" atmosphere of anyone-can-be-a-critic reductionism, was liable to start wondering, "Why is it, exactly, that we're paying this person...?"

But that's where the New Groupthink came in, and where it came to the rescue. If critics, living under a trigger of insecurity, could now bond together, agreeing on which movies were "worthy" and standing behind them for the noble cause of art, then *that* became the answer they could offer their editors as a way to protect their jobs. To wit:

"So what's this Romanian film you love so much? The one about abortion?"

"It's really extraordinary! And it's the most acclaimed film of the year! I think it could be big at awards time!"

Translation: *"Please understand, Mr. Editor Sir! I know this is a tough movie, but I'm not the only one who likes it! Everyone does!"*

The trend toward collectivist enthusiasm began to take hold in a way that even the critics who were driving it barely realized. And that probably had a more chilling effect on what criticism *is* than the loss of jobs. It was critics trying to carve out a place for art by "speaking in one voice," which seems selfless and admirable. But it was really critics colluding in the loss of their own individuality, and thereby contributing to the very degradation of criticism that they were ostensibly fighting. By turning themselves into enlightened ditto-heads, they really *did* make criticism into something almost anyone could do.

The trend only got whipped along by the Internet itself. The Web has always been hailed as a place of democratization and diversity, of a thousand flowers blooming, and it certainly can be all those things. But one of the products of that round-the-clock digital orgy of fragmentary voices is that people are now more fixated than ever on finding an antidote to all the fragmentation. They're hungry for agreement, clubbiness, solidarity. They're looking for a mirror in the void. When the website rottentomatoes.com launched in 1998, it was immediately successful, because it served an obvious consumer function, aggregating reviews so that people could get an instant scan of what "the critics" thought. But rottentomatoes was also insidious, because in the case of almost any film, the site's big money shot—the percentage of critics who gave that film a "fresh" rating—became, in effect, a weapon to beat down critics who didn't agree with the majority. Here was clear statistical data showing that they weren't with the program. It was a reboot of the *Star Wars* paradigm: How big is your movie club? How universal? You say that Michael Mann's *The Insider* got a 96% fresh rating? Okay, let's look up the naysayers. The nasty, negative, out-of-step 4%! Who are they? *Are you now or have you ever been a critic who didn't like* The Insider?

There had been tallies of critics before, most obviously Critical Mass in *EW*. The difference, however, is that something about the metaphysic of the Internet—the sheer vastness of the technology—encourages people to rotate their entire focus outside of themselves, and to devalue what's inside. Each night, Jimmy Fallon kicks off his monologue by saying, "Here's what everyone's talking about!" Here's what's lighting up Facebook, here's what's trending on Twitter, here's what *everyone else* is saying and thinking. Everyone! And, of course, the numbers game of rottentomatoes also fed into the contemporary fetish for *systematizing* things. What was being systematized was a way to read what everyone else thinks as a conduit to figuring out what *you* think.

I saw all of this embodied in the experience I had with a smart New York writer who is still a fixture in film criticism. We were friendly, and after screenings, we would sometimes walk down the street together, hashing over the movie we'd just seen for five or ten minutes, enough time to give a fairly detailed sense of what we thought. One day, not too long after we'd done this, I looked up his review of the movie we were discussing, and I noticed that the opinion in print didn't match the one he'd given after the screening. It's as if his feelings had evolved, as if he'd changed his mind. I figured that could happen, but then I noticed that it happened again, and again, and *again*, and I realized that the opinion he was putting forth in print was, quite consistently, a subtle amalgam of what he thought and what he thought he was *supposed* to think. He's a good critic, but an even better politician. Film criticism, I hated to say it, was becoming a racket—a high-minded racket, but a racket nonetheless.

And here was the absolute insanity of it. The tendency of human beings to check out what other humans are thinking—and to be greatly influenced by it—is, of course, only human. But if there's anyone in society who's *supposed* to put his own opinion first, to be impervious to the influence of others precisely so that others might be swayed by the higher insight of his judgment, it's the critic. That is his mission. *That is his job.* If he fails to do that, then he's violating the oath of his job—the basic trust of it—as surely as a postman does if he opens your mail. I became a critic because in some adolescent art-loving egomaniacal but earnest way, I yearned to tell the world *what I thought.* I always felt that there was something deeply American about my love of criticism: It was a total exaltation of the individual. Yet it startled me when I realized how much the New Groupthink overlapped with the old groupthink—the one I'd experienced with Pauline, and had seen first-hand with her acolytes. That was the brainiac version: Could you live up to the brilliance of what she was thinking by matching it? This was the low-minded version: Could you fit in with the feelings of the film-critic collective? But in each case, you were being told: Find a way to be something other than you. In science fiction, that's called being an automaton. I call it misplacing your soul.

CHAPTER 21

THE BOOK OF ELI

My father's favorite movie was *Children of Paradise*. It's a film that's also widely known by its French title, *Les Enfants du Paradis*, and that's how my dad insisted on referring to it, letting those nasally deep-throat French syllables ring out—*Lays awn-fawwwn du para-deeee!*—in a way that allowed him to take tangible pride in his casual mastery of the language. For my father, the reverence for art was all bound up with middle-class 20th-century notions of taste, refinement, and intellectual self-improvement. That was one of the driving forces behind his worship of Shakespeare and classical music—the belief that loving those things made him a higher, even superior creature. And yet you can be an obnoxious middlebrow art snob (which he was) and still have a genuine love for art (which he did). The music of the baroque era spoke to him deeply—I think he wished he had lived back then—and though he held to the benighted notion that theater was superior to film, there were certain movies that spoke deeply to him too.

The first time I ever saw *Children of Paradise*, it was with my father. I was in my late twenties, and on one of my holiday visits home it was playing at Cinema Guild, the U of M film society devoted to classic old movies. My dad and I sat in the same hard seats we did when he took me to see my first Hitchcock film, *Sabotage* (the one he dismissed as "parrot shit"), and when he brought me along at age 12 to see *Chronicle of Anna Magdalena Bach*, an impossibly static black-and-white German film of the late '60s that basically consists of Bach's music being played in breathtakingly accurate historical settings. It was a woefully inappropriate movie to take a kid to, and it literally put me to sleep (though it's a film I now adore—in honor of my dad, I watch it by myself after midnight every Christmas Eve). But I certainly woke up later in the parking lot, when I had the horrifying experience of watching my father talk his way into a fistfight—and get the shit kicked out of him. As he was backing the car out of its parking space, he came close to another parked car, with two people leaning up against it: a guy and a girl, probably in college, who were making out with writhing abandon. My dad honked the horn (he claimed accidentally), which led to angry words, which led to my dad (who was 40 at the time) haphazardly punching the guy, which led to the guy punching *him* and smashing his glasses, which essentially left my dad blind, at which point he put up his hand from a crouched position and said, "Okay, okay..." An embarrassing moment of defeat for the former Jewish Catskills bodybuilder, and also for his mortified son. But what struck me even more than the humiliating fisticuffs was that, with my pre-adolescent Freudian feelers, I had an instinct about what had happened: Even if the horn honk was an "accident," it was my feeling that my father started this fight because he was jealous. To me, he wanted to be the one making out with that girl.

By the time I went with my dad to see *Children of Paradise*, I knew all about his hidden side—his addictive adulterous liaisons, as well as his relationship with Laura White, the woman he told me he was in love with. In that light, watching the film was a shocking experience. *Children of Paradise* is a one-of-a-kind theatrical pageant of a movie that's famous for a few reasons. The entire film was shot in secret, over a period of nearly two years (starting in 1943), during the Nazi occupation of Paris (the story is told on such a vast scale, with mad swirling crowd scenes, that it's nearly impossible to imagine how this was done), and it's surely the grandest achievement of the director Marcel Carné. Set in Paris in the 1820s and '30s, it's a tale of the theater, of actors and mimes and bohemians and criminals, and most of all it's about the diverse colors—the spectrum—of love. In almost every frame, I could see what Eli cherished about it: The notion of theater-as-a-metaphor-for-life, the literate elegance of the film's structure and design, the quaint but glorious antiquity of it.

Yet the reason *Children of Paradise* shocked me is that it may be the most agonizingly romantic movie ever made. It's a stately French period piece, but it has a swoon factor comparable to that of *Gone with the Wind* or *Casablanca*, and it's more tragically bittersweet than either. It's a film that says that true love is deep and real and standing right in front of you... and, just maybe, impossible to attain. There has never been a big-screen beauty quite like the central figure, a courtesan named Garance. As played by Arletty, who was in her mid-forties when the film was shot, she's the rare eroticized screen goddess who's a figment of radiant maturity, with a smile so complexly insinuating she makes Garbo look like Anna Faris. Every man in the film falls for her, and we can see why, but there's only one who loves her purely—the angelic mime Baptiste, played by Jean-Louis Barrault as an ingenuous harlequin of a man who is doomed to have his dreams fulfilled and his heart broken.

Children of Paradise is haunted, like almost no other movie, by the spectre of love as something tantalizing and eternal yet out of reach. When I saw the film again years later, I was struck by how much it resembled *Moulin Rouge!*, the most joyful and despairing romantic movie of *its* time. The ragtag Paris artistes, the sense that you're watching the action through a proscenium arch, the smiling purity of the hero's love and the way that Garance winds up in the clutches of an effete autocratic count: It was *Moulin Rouge!* minus "Your Song" and "Lady Marmalade." In *Children of Paradise*, I saw my father's life flash by: his hunger for love, his flirtation with finding it, his letting it go. I had asked him on several occasions why he didn't just leave my family and set up a new life with Laura, given that he claimed to have loved her, and he always said something head-shakingly downbeat yet vague like, "It just wouldn't have worked out." But whatever the particulars, I now grasped the poetic outlines of his life. Certainly, he was old-fashioned, and didn't want to risk his stability. But he had also touched love and lost it because on some level, perhaps, he didn't think he deserved it.

He may not have thought he deserved to live. In January 2008, my parents called me: My father had been diagnosed with stage-four lung cancer, and he was dying. He had, at best, six to nine months. Except that he'd been ignoring his symptoms for several years. On the day that Sharon and I got married, in September 2006, everyone in the wedding party wandered through Central Park as we had our photos taken, and Eli, who had just turned 76, could barely keep walking in the mild late-summer heat; we wondered if something was wrong. In the summer of 2007 (eight months before he was diagnosed), he told me that he was having mild chest pains, and he proceeded to do absolutely nothing about it. He was never a smoker, but by passively ignoring those symptoms, he may have helped to bring about his own death more than someone who smokes four packs a day for 40 years does. The man, after all, was an oncologist; he spent his entire career treating cancer patients. He knew the symptoms—literally—inside out. There was no excuse for him, of all people, to fail to get himself checked out.

My father's decision to ignore the warnings of illness was of a piece with the way that my brothers and I were rarely taken to doctors when we were growing up. My dad figured that he could keep tabs on our condition for free. (The result? When Erik disjointed his finger playing basketball, he wasn't given any treatment, and the finger healed crooked.) By the time I was in my twenties, I'd come to realize that my dad's blasé attitude toward our family's health was a form of passive aggression (if not abuse). But in his own case, considering the symptoms, I think it was even worse. I believe it was a passive/repressed form of suicide. Of course, if he were here now, I know just what he'd say, in his tone of calm, dour exasperation: "Owen, you don't understand. There's nothing they could have done…"

Sharon and I flew out to Ann Arbor, and it was clear as soon as we got there that Eli wanted to die. He agreed to get radiation treatments, but he had no desire to undergo chemotherapy to extend his life by a few months. He'd spent decades observing the ravages of chemo, and for him it wasn't worth it. He wanted to go quickly; he wanted to snuff the pain. Eli was still handsome, with the squarish contours of his wavy hair intact, but he'd stopped shaving in recent years, and his grayish-white beard, combined with eyes that narrowed in anger even more than they once had, gave him the look of an aging cobra. I decided, with the arrogance of someone making an executive decision who had no business making it, that he should indeed get the chemo: Why not try to give himself more time, so that it could give *all* of us the chance to talk and heal and grow together? I got very "Kumbaya" about my insensitive-jerk dad. I had an ongoing argument with him about the treatment, but I was really just giving him a taste of his own medicine, interacting with him in the way that he'd taught me, turning every encounter into a conflict fraught with negativity. I fought so vehemently to extend his life that I burned up most of the time he had left doing so.

The other thing I did, which may have been even stupider, was to buy him a great big cache of DVDs, maybe 30 or 40 of them, so that he could alleviate his suffering by watching them. Hey, it had worked for me! I tried to give him films I thought he'd respond to, a mix of old classics (like *Stalag 17, The Adventures of Robin Hood,* and *The Court Jester,* starring his favorite actor, Danny Kaye) with more contemporary titles I thought might prove appealing (Bergman's *The Magic Flute, Gladiator, Much Ado About Nothing, Rain Man*). If I'd just casually given him a few movies, that would have been fine, but dumping this load of cinema into his lap was a self-centered act of regression on my part. In a way, I was dealing with my father's death by *channeling* him; it's as if that's how I was now going to keep him alive. He was a solipsistic crank who had never really been able to see me through the fogged lens of his obsessions, and now, I was doing the same thing. *Watch these movies while you die, Dad! Take it from your son, the film critic! They'll be good for you!*

I should have just tried to talk to him. But, of course, I did that too, and as always I ran into the brick wall of his indifference—his tired-ass stories about what a tough upbringing he had, and so forth. With death on the horizon, my father did not proceed to get all self-reflective and philosophical. (In that way, I truly *wasn't* a chip off the old block; I could get self-reflective and philosophical about a trip to McDonald's.) He remained himself: blunt, hardheaded, merciless. An atheist resigned to doom. (Resigned to the impossibility of love.) When I was younger, I occasionally asked him where he stood on things like the afterlife, and his opinion on such matters was beyond cynicism. "Dead is dead," he'd say, as if it was a profound insight. Somehow, a statement like that spoke more to his feelings about life than death.

Now, though, there was a moment that bridged the stiff-jointed dad I knew with something a trace more unexpected and soft. He and I were sitting together in the living room, and he said to me quietly, wistfully, as if imparting some great secret: "You know, every time I look at Sharon, there's someone I can see she looks exactly like. Do you know who I'm talking about?"

He asked it as if there *was* a right answer, one that I, of course, should know. "No," I said, suddenly quite curious. "Who?"

With a look of forlorn reverence, he said, "The Mona Lisa."

The thought had never even crossed my mind, but now that it did, I could see what he was talking about. It was something in the placid melancholy of Sharon's thousand-yard stare, the roundedness of her face, the sincerity of her ironic smile. Now that I thought about it, she *did* kind of look like the Mona Lisa. In that comment, I also heard my father's need to elevate his daughter-in-law to a plateau of "classicism" he could approve of. Yet he made the comparison so tenderly that it took me back to an incident from my boyhood—just about the only one—when I felt a whisper of the same tenderness. Maybe it's no surprise that it hinged on a major malfunction.

In the middle of a sleepy Ann Arbor summer, after I'd finished the fifth grade, I signed up to play a violin solo in a recreation-department talent show. I'd been playing the instrument in school for two years, and this lifted me up in my father's eyes; it was me taking baby steps into his pantheon of culture. My father took me to the talent show himself, which he never would have bothered to do had I been part of, say, some junior pop-music trio. No, this wasn't about me. It was about me and the *violin*. Which is to say, it was all about *him*.

I'd been in a few grade-school orchestra concerts, and I knew the piece I was going to play by heart—it was not a challenging piece. But I'd never performed a solo before, and when I got onstage, I was startled by how it looked from up there. You couldn't see the audience at all. It was just *black*, with a glaring spotlight, and halfway through the piece, I went blank. I couldn't remember the notes, and I stood there, frozen, as the pianist accompanying me vamped away. It was one of those moments of horror that attain an out-of-body quality, where I felt like I was standing there watching myself. Try as I might, I could not remember my way back into the piece. So I just... stood. I felt like an actor in a play on live national television who'd forgotten his lines.

It seemed to me that the world had ended. After I got offstage, my father met me, and I don't remember what he said—I was locked in a bubble of devastation—but the look on my face must have been different from anything he had ever seen. Because what he did that night was different from anything he had ever done. He took me to a place in Ann Arbor that I'd never been to but had always wanted to go to, because it was known as a noisy palace of fun: a restaurant called Bimbo's, which was a 1920s-styled ragtime-kitsch parlor (the waiters wore straw boaters and looked like soda jerks), and the specialty of the house was pizza. Famously succulent wonderful pizza. Just getting to finally go inside Bimbo's and see what it looked like felt magical, and my spirits lifted a bit. My dad and I sat there, soaking up the atmosphere, saying almost nothing; we didn't speak much the whole night. But that was all right, because I knew that he'd brought me there as a gift, and since it was *so* out of character for him, I could tell that he was giving this gift because he could feel the pain I was in. And when the pizza arrived, it was the greatest thing I'd ever tasted, and with every bite, the pain melted away, because I was tasting something I had never tasted so completely before: my father's love.

He never did anything like that again. And it's probably very fucked up that *I* had to fuck up so badly to inspire him to do something like that. Then again, maybe forgetting that piece in mid-performance was my way of reaching out to him. Maybe I was asking him to fill in the music I couldn't remember. Now that he was dying, I wanted to do the same thing for him. But I didn't know how.

It wasn't the only death I was facing. It had been fifteen years since rumors last swirled around the possibility of *Entertainment Weekly* being shut down. But now, all of a sudden, the rumors of *EW*'s demise were back. In the space of just two years, the magazine had undergone one of the most jaw-dropping downhill slides in the history of high-gloss journalism. I thought: How could this be happening? How could *EW* go from having its most financially successful year, which was 2006, to knocking on death's door?

It was a perfect storm of events. But it began, ironically, with a major victory on the business side. It had taken *EW* all the way to 1997 to turn even a small profit. Then a deal got struck with Musicland to sell *EW* subscriptions at the checkout counter. And that's when fate smiled: A year or so later, Musicland was gobbled up by Best Buy, a fluky bonanza that transformed the magazine's fortunes. The same subscription deal was offered, only now at Best Buy, on a much more vast scale, and to an even more tailor-made audience. Spurred by that revenue, and by the accompanying rise in circulation and ad rates, the magazine, beginning in 2003, turned into a mini-blockbuster, with profits leaping from $15 million to $35 million. By 2006, they had reached $53 million. That figure was dwarfed by the hundreds of millions of dollars in profit generated by *People* magazine, but for *EW*, it still looked like champagne time.

None of this made my job any better, or increased my clout as a critic; if anything, it just added weight to my wings. For there was a major catch built into the victory: The eruption of revenue generated by the Best Buy deal was destined to run its course once that market had been saturated with new *EW* subscribers. But Ann Moore, the head of the publishing side of Time Inc., didn't want to see it that way. Like any relentless 21st-century CEO, she wanted the profits to rise, and rise, and rise...

After 2006, the Best Buy revenue dried up, and the ad sales nosedived—the early, ominous rumblings of what would turn into the economic earthquake of 2008. But at *EW*, there was also an X factor. The first four years of Rick Tetzeli's reign had been the most successful in the magazine's history. Yet that happened mostly for external business reasons. It happened *despite* what I felt was the creeping lack of *joi de vivre*, the hard-to-put-your-finger-on robo quality that had wormed its way into the pages of *EW*. So when the downturn hit, a lot of people looked at this weirdly chilly and suddenly emaciated magazine and thought: Whoa, this thing really *is* looking like a shadow of its former self. At the end of 2007, *EW* held an all-day-long "off-site" (i.e., the entire staff was marched over to a conference room in the Time & Life building) in which a member of the business side made a big speech imploring us to "get your swagger back." It was embarrassing, and I thought: How are we going to get our "swagger" back with a managing editor who doesn't know how to swagger? I figured, or hoped, that the ad situation would take care of itself, but by 2008 *EW* had grown thin enough that media websites were starting to make cracks about its impending death. So were the suits at Time Inc., who figured, in their wisdom, that it must be time to resurrect...the *EW* culture war! To them, the magazine was once again facing oblivion because it *still*—according to the myth—wasn't mainstream enough. (John Huey, the editorial director of Time Inc., decided the problem was that the print was too small. He made it much larger, and the result was that *Entertainment Weekly* began to look like *My Weekly Reader*.)

The death of my father. The—possible—death of *EW*. This was death in the elemental way that I had long understood it: as the end of something. Yet death wasn't always so obvious. It was something that could lurk in the shadows, something that could eat at you in invisible ways. And I didn't discover that until the day Sharon threatened to leave me.

It was Thanksgiving Day, two years after we'd met. Sharon had moved to New York and was teaching at a fractious public grade school in Washington Heights, but the two of us weren't living together; I was still slouching toward intimacy. The year before, I'd gone to Albany on Thanksgiving to meet her family, and late that night we went over to the home of her oldest friend, Liz, and had a second round of Thanksgiving dinner, thanks to the hospitality of Liz's father, Elmo, who was an extraordinary cook. He served us the mouth-wateringly moist flavor-bomb turkey of your dreams, with stuffing that was classic (no annoying berries or anything) but *so* tasty that you couldn't stop eating it, the mashed potatoes a buttery blanket of velvet bliss... *how did he do it?* I had to know. Elmo gladly shared his recipes and secrets: the way he cooked the turkey in a bag, the way he made the stuffing with sausage and Bell's Seasoning, and on and on. He wrote it all down on a three-by-five card that I took with me.

A year later in New York, Sharon and I were now going to try to cook that same dinner. I was doing last-minute shopping and was supposed to meet her in the apartment (she had a key). But when I got back, instead of Sharon I found a short note propped up on the couch. It said:

Dear Owen,
  I love you, but I can no longer be with you unless you make up your mind about having children.

                                          Love,
                                          Sharon

The issue of children had become a sticking point between us. Sharon had always said that she wanted kids, and I, not a hundred percent sure but leaning the other way, told her that I was "ambivalent," that I hadn't made up my mind yet. It was the truth; the door wasn't shut. But what I had shoved under the rug was the reality that a woman who wants to have kids also wants to be with a man who says, and with enthusiasm, "Let's have kids!" The timing of her note seemed less than great (my first thought was, "What about Thanksgiving?"), but here it was: A choice that had been on the back burner was now threatening to burn down the room. I felt the potential to be destroyed. I felt like Sharon might just be...gone.

Sharon wasn't answering either of her phones, and I knew, from the brusqueness of her note, that she didn't want to meet to "talk it out." That was the point; we had done enough talking. After 15 minutes of tormented fretting, I decided that I would get through the day by doing Thanksgiving all by myself. I would make Elmo's turkey! And the stuffing. And everything else. I would drink a lot of wine. And that sparked another idea.

There was an album I had planned, with drooling anticipation, to go out and buy that weekend: Brian Wilson's *Smile*, the legendary long-lost Beach Boys album that had, after four decades, been resurrected and revamped, completed by Wilson and an ambitious young collaborator, Darian Sahanaja; it was being released for the very first time. The Tower Records on lower Broadway was a ten-minute walk from my apartment, and I decided to stroll over there on the off-chance that Tower might actually be open on Thanksgiving. I didn't expect it to be...but it was. I took that as a sign.

On the way home, carrying *Smile* in an orange Tower Records bag, I stopped by the wine store and bought two bottles of Santa Margherita Pinot Grigio. I almost never drank until evening, but this day was different; the only way I was going to be able to cruise through it was on a wine buzz. I returned to the apartment at noon and got down to work making the food: seasoning the turkey and sliding it into its bag, cooking that layered stuffing—melting a mountain of onion and green pepper down to surprisingly manageable size in the sauté pan, dousing the crumbs in chicken stock, browning the sausage. Finally, it was all put together and in the oven. With wine in hand, I turned to *Smile*.

I didn't know what to expect, but the splendor of the opening chorale hit me in the solar plexus: It sounded like the Beach Boys reunited in Heaven. Then came "Heroes and Villains," a classic song any fan knew well, and it dazzled me as always, but then I was struck, as I never had been (for I knew a version of this song, too, from *Smiley Smile*), by the melodically topsy-turvy chromatic gorgeousness of "Wonderful." Transposed to the harpsichord, it suddenly sounded like a song that Bach had written on OxyContin.

And then I heard something extraordinary.

"Wonderful" got slower and slower, and just as it was on the verge of stopping, it transformed into a punchy, urgent beat topped with shimmering chords of nearly unbearable sweetness that sounded like they'd been plucked out of an aural rainbow. The track, though I didn't know it at the time, was called "Song for Children," and as it swirled around me, I heard those incandescent chords, and what sounded like a marching band playing a fragment of "Good Vibrations," and lyrics that seemed to be floating through the chords until they sounded like a nursery-rhyme dream chant (*"Child child child, father of the son... Where is the father, father of the sun... Where is the wonderful me, wonderful you?"*). I was spellbound. I thought it was the most beautiful two minutes of music I had ever heard in my life. And I still do.

Hearing that song, I began to weep. Readers of this book will by now have registered that I am something of a crybaby, but I've never had a catharsis of tears like this one. The whole thing about crying—maybe this is just the way a critic sees it—is that it can be happy or sad, or maybe both at once, but what it *really* is is a moment of emotional eye-opening. And at that moment I asked myself: *"Why don't you want to have children?"*

I didn't know the answer. But I started to think about something— about the fact that I was a film critic. I don't mean that I did it for a living; I mean that that's who and what I *was*. And it dawned on me that so many giants in the world of film criticism, at least in the era I hailed from, did not have children. Andrew Sarris and Molly Haskell. Vincent Canby. Stanley Kauffmann. John Simon. Roger Ebert. Pauline Kael, of course, had a daughter, but it always seemed as if that fact was somehow extraneous to her identity.

What was it about film critics and children that did not mix?

The obvious answer is that movies can grow into an obsession that fills that space. I'd always sort of known that; it didn't hit me with any force of revelation. But then I began thinking, through my tears, about what movies *were*. A person could become obsessed with any art form (books, painting, music) or with other things that were just like art (cooking, gardening, customizing cars). But movies had seduced me because they were the art form that seemed to be the most vivid reflection of life. The most perfect *imitation* of it. The seduction—the insane glory—of movies is that you could watch them and actually believe that they *were* life.

But, of course, they were not. So what were they? A miraculous mirage? Movies looked like people, they looked just like life—especially the movies *I* loved, like *Nashville* and *Sid and Nancy* and *Breaking the Waves*. I'd always thought of movies as a life force that infused me, and I hadn't changed my mind. But now I saw that they were also something else. At the movies, you drank in an alternative existence that did not, in fact, exist. Movies were the shadows on the wall of Plato's Cave. And suddenly it hit me: I wasn't just a man who loved movies. I was a man who worshipped undead images as if they were alive. I lived under their spell. And maybe that made *me* undead as well. Movies had saved my life, but now my life needed to be saved from movies.

Quite spontaneously, I fell into my version of Philip Seymour Hoffman's "I'm a fuckin' idiot" scene from *Boogie Nights*, though as I sat on my couch, drunk, listening to *Smile*, what I said over and over again is, "I'm an asshole... I'm a fucking asshole." Because I was. I loved Sharon, I loved movies, I loved being a critic, I loved my friends, I loved *Entertainment Weekly*... but I did not love *life*. Not in the raw. Not in a way that transcended my love—and hatred—for myself. And what I realized, right then, is that the only way I *could* love life, in the way I always thought I wanted to, was to have a child. It's not something I would do to hold on to Sharon (though frankly, I couldn't imagine life without her). It's something I would do to touch the life in myself. To find the real higher love. To stop, for once, looking at the shadows and to know the mystery of the things they reflected.

• • • • • •

After three or four days of hanging out with my father, during which we watched the Academy Awards and, on the last night, a DVD I thought might put him in a good mood (a collection of Wallace and Gromit shorts; it did not), Sharon and I returned to New York. I assumed I would get to spend some more time with my dad, but I didn't just underestimate the cruelty of lung cancer. I didn't count on the craziness of my response.

In recent years, I'd begun to develop a set of anxieties about flying; they never kept me off a plane, but they did leave me superstitious. When I decided that I should probably go back to Ann Arbor on my own, the superstition hardened into something unyielding: I developed what might be called a karmic phobia—the overwhelming feeling that if I now took a plane trip to visit my dying father, the plane would crash, because that would be the final fulfillment of his unconscious desire. (Maybe I really should have smoked less dope in college.)

That fear kept me away, until the week my mother called and said that Eli had taken a turn for the worse. He was in a bed that the hospice workers had set up in the living room. I decided to travel to Ann Arbor on Amtrak, because that would be slow but safe. I got a ticket for Tuesday. Early Sunday morning, my mother called and said: "He died." I had blown the chance to be with my father in his final days, his final moments, because I was all tangled up in my fears and obsessions. How much like my dad was that? It was *so* Eli it was practically a tribute. Like asshole, like son.

Sharon and I took a plane to Ann Arbor that night, my phobic ban on flying having instantly dissipated now that my father was no longer around to put a hex on me. That whole week, as we planned the funeral and memorial service, I took time every afternoon to go to Sweetwaters, an Ann Arbor coffee bar that was a soothing place to write. I didn't yet own a laptop, but I took my notebook to jot down the words I would say about my father at his service. I needed to write it out, and to take the time to do so, because I was a writer, and I felt there were things about him that I wanted to get right. Each day, as I sat there scribbling, the same music played on the Sweetwaters sound-system loop, and one song hit me like a balm of saddened rapture, because it was a haunting Bruce Springsteen song that, to my surprise, I didn't know: "Girls in Their Summer Clothes."

My days of Bruce obsession were miles behind me. I'd worn out copies of *Darkness on the Edge of Town* and *Born in the U.S.A.*, but he lost me around *Human Touch*, and I'd never really come back. But "Girls in Their Summer Clothes" was like the long-awaited sequel to "Glory Days," a song I was old enough to have heard in two different ways. When I was 25, the line "Glory days, well they'll pass you by,/Glory days, in the wink of a young girl's eye" made me think: Wow, I bet I'll feel that way some day. When I was 35, you'd better fucking believe that day had come. In "Girls in Their Summer Clothes," Bruce seemed to be singing about an even later day, and hearing him each afternoon at Sweetwaters, where he seemed to be singing right to me, I felt that he was singing the love song of Eli, the one that could have been mine: *"And the girls in their summer clothes, in the cool of the evening light,/The girls in their summer clothes, pass me by."*

My father worked hard and got married, had three sons and paid them little mind, idolized art and chased women. But really, he'd arranged his whole life so that the girls in their summer clothes passed him by. I'd come close to doing the same thing, but I was lucky enough to have one of them turn my way. My mother told me that when she found my father's body, early Sunday morning, he wasn't in his bed. He was facing the side of it, on his knees, his hands laced in front of him. She was sure he was praying.

CHAPTER 22

BRANDED

On April 1, 2008, just 12 days before my father died, all the fretful murmurs that had been echoing through the world of film criticism came to a head. The *schadenfreudish* chatter of the blogosphere, the anxious talk amongst critics themselves—all the gloom and doom was placed, for the first time, in the glare of mainstream media when David Carr, the esteemed media reporter/analyst for *The New York Times*, devoted an entire column to the subject. The headline kind of said it all: "Now on the Endangered Species List: Movie Critics in Print." Carr namechecked the latest reviewers to lose their jobs (Gene Seymour and Jan Stuart of *Newsday*, the gifted and outrageous Nathan Lee of *The Village Voice*, the veteran short-form master David Ansen of *Newsweek*, who at 63 was taking a voluntary buyout). The peg that Carr hung his piece on was the notion that with less criticism around, good, worthy, smaller movies—the kind that needed critical support—would now suffer. It was a telling take on the subject, and Carr did his usual impeccable job of reporting, but I couldn't help but feel that he'd missed the forest for the trees.

The issue of how much "influence" critics have is something that's discussed a lot more than it's understood. In our era, it's become a cynical cliché to say that film critics have lost their relevance because they no longer hold sway over the box office. The mass audience now just ignores them and heads off to the megaplex to catch the latest "critic-proof" comic-book/action/franchise wad of diversion. The truth of this seems undeniable, yet there has long been a lie embedded in that truth. The lie is the implication that it was ever much different—that there was some high renaissance moment of critic/audience symbiosis in which moviegoers, on any kind of populist scale, actually *listened* to film critics and heeded the wisdom of their recommendations. Hello? I'd like to know when that moment was.

When I first got hired to write reviews in the '80s, it was decades before anyone was talking about the waning of film criticism, but all the lofty critical breast-beating in the world did nothing to stop people from reflexively licking up the grade-Z catnip of *Porky's* and slasher movies and *Conan the Barbarian* and *Rambo* and godawful Richard Pryor comedies and *Cocktail* and *Return of the Jedi* and *Police Academy* sequels and what have you. A decade before that, in the sunlit days of the New Hollywood, critics championed the bold new American cinema—but with the rare exception of something like *The Godfather* or *Taxi Driver*, those were not necessarily the films that people were consuming on a weekly basis. They were going out to see *The Towering Inferno* and *Smokey and the Bandit* and *Walking Tall* and *Logan's Run*. (To take one random week: On May 30, 1973, here, in order, were the top 20 films at the weekend box office: *Last Tango in Paris*, *The Poseidon Adventure*, *Billy Jack*, *Slither*, *Theatre of Blood*, *Mary Poppins*, *Soylent Green*, *The Day of the Jackal*, *Brother Sun, Sister Moon*, *Deep Throat*, *Coffy*, *Class of '44*, *Fists of Fury*, *Hitler: The Last 10 Days*, *The Devil in Miss Jones*, *The Mack*, *The New Centurions*, *Dirty Little Billy*, *The Godfather*, *Camelot*.) Pauline Kael, the most avidly read critic of her time, never stopped anyone from going to see the schlock she excoriated. The kinds of movies that David Carr said critics could have an influence on were the *only* kind, really, that they'd ever had much of an influence on.

And yes, it was now true: With fewer critics around, good small films might conceivably suffer. That was something I did not take lightly. Yet to reduce the value of film criticism to How Critics Help Small Films was, in its way, to say something accurate but also to view criticism as essentially a consumerist endeavor, a well-meaning tool in the capitalist equation. It played right into the arguments made by editors who viewed critics as a quasi-useful quasi-diverting quasi-annoyance.

I was friendly with David Carr, and God knows I wrote for a magazine that flaunted the consumerist side of criticism, yet in all my years at *EW* I tried not so much to fight against that side as to go beyond it. What I wished that Carr had found at least one sentence in his article to say is that film criticism mattered *for its own sweet sake.* Because it meant something to people. Because it was exciting opinionated writing that expressed things readers might care about beyond the question of which films they did or did not choose to see. But the fact that a writer as trenchant, and as sympathetic to pop culture, as David Carr didn't even try to make that argument was proof that that argument was going the way of the dodo bird.

In the context of an increasingly harried and financially desperate journalistic culture, the reason that critics were losing their jobs—not just the economic reason, but the ideological reason it fused with—came down to one very simple thought: *The world as we know it does not need film criticism.* After all, it's not White House reporting, it's not brain surgery, it's not knee surgery, it's not farming or bricklaying or teaching math or policing the streets, it's not even some guy coming over to fix your dishwasher. The thought was: It's a kind of frippery, an indulgence, nice to have around, and if people want to do it on the Web for not very much money (or, better yet, for free), that's dandy, but criticism isn't something that's *necessary.* And anyone who thought it was is living in cloud cuckoo land. Once that line of argument takes hold, it's awfully hard to reverse. Because you can't claim—not really—that film criticism *is* as important as any of those other things. The case for why it matters cannot be made in practical terms.

So why *does* it matter? In the franchise era, the consumer-guide aspect of criticism may, in fact, be less crucial than ever. And that leaves the real heart of the matter: What criticism offers, when it's great, is an alchemy of enlightenment and delight—a heady space where each of those things can become the other. Film criticism, when it's great, has a light *inside* it, one that emerges from the nature of movies themselves. It lights up your mind and lights up your senses; it merges them until truth becomes beauty and beauty becomes truth. The question of whether film criticism is something that our journalistic culture can "afford" seems to have everything to do with economics, but really, it has to do with what our journalistic culture *values.* There will always be room for it—and money—if enough people want it to be there. That's economics, too.

I already knew that Carr's piece was running, because he had interviewed me for it. But I still read that headline and gulped. I should have gulped harder. My mother saw the article and called me, saying that she was worried about my situation. "Don't worry," I said. "I'm fine. A lot of places are losing critics, but *Entertainment Weekly* has a slightly vested interest in covering...you know, *entertainment*. They need their critics." I meant it. I was certainly sure that they needed me. All my concerns about *EW* remained focused on the magazine itself. I felt that if it survived, so would my position as a critic. But I decided that I was going to make absolutely sure that the people running the magazine felt that way too.

My first wake-up call about the meltdown of criticism came in 2007, when I was invited to Boston for a seminar in film criticism hosted by the Coolidge Corner Theatre, which had always been my favorite revival house. (It's where I would smuggle in a six-pack to watch *Mad Max* for the fourth time.) A whole "seminar," consisting of three panels over two days, sounded like a navel-gazing event, but I figured it would be fun to take a tour of my old stomping grounds (I hadn't been back to Boston for more than a decade). Besides, I loved being on panels, having long ago figured out the dirty secret of all panels: None of them—not one!—mean a thing, so you can say any damn thing you want. I knew all the critics invited, including my old rival Ty Burr, now of *The Boston Globe*; the ardent and irascible Glenn Kenny of *Premiere*; and the eloquent Stephanie Zacharek of Salon. When I got to Boston, I wandered around for a few hours and finally stumbled upon a copy of the *Phoenix*. It was a scary shadow of its former self, and I could see that its days were numbered. And then...the first panel! We gathered in the Coolidge Corner Theatre, where seats and microphones had been set up. We sat and waited. And when it was time for the panel to begin, I'm not actually sure whether there were more people in the audience or on the panel. Basically, *no one* had come. No one wanted to hear film critics talking about film critics. I thought, "Uh-oh."

A year later, just in time for the catastrophic global economic meltdown, Time Inc. unleashed a massive round of layoffs, and *Entertainment Weekly* was hit particularly hard, losing 25 people in one day (about one-fifth of the staff). I was not alone in feeling that the bloodbath at *EW* had a glimmer of punishment to it. To the Time Inc. suits, the magazine was failing...despite all those damn geek eggheads who work there! What the hell do they do anyway? Time to slice the baloney of this magazine down to size! When the triage was over, it felt like the *EW* staff had been liposuctioned. At least now the remains of us could be squeezed into our new offices, which occupied one floor of an adjunct to the Time & Life building. In 1990, Jeff Jarvis had made a point of keeping the magazine away from corporate central, but now corporate central was "welcoming" us back. And with a new mantra. The problem, as it was explained to us, is that *EW* had lost its mojo because it had forgotten what it was supposed to be covering... and not covering. The buzzwords of the moment were "on-brand" and "off-brand." Popular sitcoms starring people like Tina Fey? *On-brand!* Reality TV? *Off-brand!* (I thought: Really?) Franchise movies? *On-brand!* Indie rock? *Off-brand!* I didn't ask, but I was pretty sure that k.d. lang was still off-brand.

In addition to having a new mantra, we had a new editor. Rick Tetzeli had been protected by his mentor, John Huey (who'd made the highly questionable decision to hand him the plum *EW* gig in the first place), but now that former *People* magazine editor and *InStyle* creator Martha Nelson had ascended to the position of Time Inc. editor-in-chief, it was time for Tetzeli to go. Nelson disliked Tetzeli—she thought he was arrogant and entitled—and in his place she installed her own protégé, Jess Cagle, whose roots were deep in *EW*. He had been there for the first 10 years (before going on to *Time* and *People*), and he was someone I'd always liked a great deal. I had respect for Jess' editing chops and enjoyed his airy corporate version of shade-throwing wit, and I felt that he might be the perfect person to recharge *EW*'s pleasure centers. I told a lot of my colleagues, "He's exactly what we need."

Be careful what you think you're glad for.

Entertainment Weekly was entering a new era, and so was film criticism. I knew the time had arrived to shake up what I did. But how? I didn't have to think about it for very long. The choice seemed obvious: I would blog! The decision was nothing more or less than an act of survivalist politics on my part fused with an undertone of honest curiosity. I wanted to prove that I was industrious (to this day, I've produced more words for *EW* than any other writer), but I also knew that the digital platform was where the whole world was headed. I wanted to show that I was at home there. What I never guessed is that writing for the Web would prove my creative salvation.

I'd already written a handful of pieces for ew.com, and one of them, at least, pointed toward what I found thrilling about it; that was my analysis of the last episode of *The Sopranos*. I had an interpretation of the famous final moments that I think still stands: In that audacious cut to black, we felt just what it would be like for Tony Soprano to be killed (and therefore, I said, he *was* killed); we also felt what it would be like for him *not* to be killed (and therefore, I said, he survived). It wasn't one or the other, it was both—or, rather, letting the audience have the sensation of both. This was, if I say so myself, a rather complicated idea (and yes, for the last time, I probably did smoke too much dope in college). But right or wrong, it required the kind of extended meditation that the Web invited. There would have been no context for my piece in the pages of *Entertainment Weekly*. But as a post on ew.com, it fit perfectly.

That said, I didn't taste the full flavor of writing for the Internet until the 2008 Sundance Film Festival, the first festival I covered on-line every day. I still hadn't gotten a laptop (as I've said: *very* late adapter), so each day at Sundance, I would head to my favorite haunts, or just crouch in a stairwell, and scribble down posts in my notebook, then type them into one of the computers at the *EW* photo studio. The retyping was laborious, but every day, after my post went up, Sharon left a message on my voicemail saying something like, "That's the best piece you've written in a year." She was onto something, and she wanted me to be onto it too. I thought the posts were ragged and inconsistent, but I could tell what she meant: They had a spark to them. They were more free than my magazine reviews, because they'd been written without me looking over my shoulder, in every paragraph, at the space restrictions that were starting to crunch down on me.

There's a parlor game you can play called "Who was the first blogger?" (I don't mean in the Internet era; I mean in the historical literary sense that *Jack Kerouac was the first blogger* or *James Joyce was the first blogger*...you get the idea.) For me, the question can plausibly be answered by naming either of my two writing gods. (Actually, I have a third writing god: Edith Wharton. But she was *not* a blogger.) There's a fine case to be made that Norman Mailer, in the columns he wrote for the January through April 1956 issues of *The Village Voice*, where he first began to experiment with his rolling analytical confessional nonfiction style, crystallized a prehistoric tryout of the blogging spirit. But you could also answer the question by saying that Pauline Kael was the first blogger. I think that's one reason her writing pulsates with such an exhilaratingly haphazard joy: The happiness of it is encoded in the spontaneity with which she wrote. She really was *riffing*. In taking to the Web, I quickly figured out that I wasn't doing anything new. I was going right back home.

At first, I fooled around and amused myself. It was fun to take a movie like Greg Mottola's '80s coming-of-age drama *Adventureland* and devote an entire post to the question of why, if you lined up what was now the trilogy of great youth-nostalgia movies (*American Graffiti*, *Dazed and Confused*, and *Adventureland*), the time period between the year each film was set and the year it was released was getting so much longer. For a while, I was drawn to think pieces dunked in nostalgia, rarely missing a chance to look back on the 40th anniversary of, say, Woodstock or the Manson murders (I justified the latter by saying that they became a part of popular culture: "Every time Charles Manson gets let out of his cage, he's smart enough to put on a good show.").

From the start, I found the whole click-bait, how-many-hits-can-you-get? aspect of blogging to be a fascinating and compulsively addictive game, even though it's the thing that journalists are supposed to hate. Philosophically, I hated it too—I saw all the ways it could be used against me—but since my prime motivation for blogging was to try and enhance my job security, I framed the challenge of it like this: Could I figure out a way to write vivid and sincerely good pieces that became click bait on their own merits? I saw how big a post could blow up when I seized on Roman Polanski's 2009 arrest in Zurich to revisit the eye-opening documentary *Roman Polanski: Wanted and Desired*. In that case, it was obvious the post caught fire because of the tabloid subject (and the fact that the readers of ew.com had long wanted to see Roman Polanski drawn and quartered). But the post that truly opened my eyes on that score was unexpected: a blog on *Inglourious Basterds* that I headlined "Does Quentin Tarantino have the right to rewrite World War II?" It was a question—specifically, about the film's *hey, let's blow up Hitler!* ending— that was inspiring pockets of debate on the Web, and though I loved *Inglourious Basterds*, defending the ending was even more interesting than reviewing the movie. I wrote, "The great, sick joke of the film's grindhouse logic is that even though what it shows us didn't happen, in a larger, almost abstract sense it did happen...If you think back on all the World War II movies that were made in the period after World War II—like, say, *Sands of Iwo Jima* (1949) or *The Longest Day* (1962)—the real, and insidious, illusion may be that *they* offer a 'true' vision of what actually went on during the fighting of that war." The post was huge, and the message was: Taking pop seriously works.

And then there was *Twilight*. I think I speak for every living film critic when I say that no one ever looked forward to reviewing a *Twilight* movie. Not because they were really *so* bad (at moments, I got caught up in their chalky-skinned update of '50s-youth-movie romanticism), but because they had lumpy, disorganized plots that made them a total pain in the ass to try to write about with any coherent flair. At *EW*, being on the *Twilight* beat always felt like getting the short straw (Lisa and I alternated on them: I reviewed the first, third, and final installments; she did the second and fourth). But blogging about *Twilight* was another story, because you could bypass the whole stupid when-moody-girl-met-vampire teen soap opera and plunge into the retro resonance the books and films had built up in the culture. "Why the frothing torrents of resentment?" I wrote after the release of *New Moon*. "Frankly, I think it's this: The ascendance of the *Twilight* saga represents a paradigm shift in youth-gender control of the pop marketplace. For the better part of two decades, teenage boys, and *overgrown* teenage boys, have essentially held sway over Hollywood....No more...And that gives teenage girls a new power and prevalence. Inevitably, such evolutions in clout are accompanied by a resentful counter-reaction. For if power is gained, then somewhere else (hello, young men!) it must be lost."

I keyed into something when I wrote a post called " 'Shutter Island': Did you see the twist ending coming?" I didn't give the ending away, but having to wrestle with the issue—to reveal or not to reveal?—made me realize how annoying, and corrupting, the whole business of "spoilers" had become. Everyone—my readers, my editors—was suddenly obsessed with it, which made no sense to me. It had always been obvious that certain plot twists should not be given away in a movie review. Beyond that, though, my readers were starting to balk at too much description of *anything*, which made me think: If you don't want a movie to be "spoiled," then don't read an entire fucking review of it before you see it! The very word *spoiler* hearkened back to that demagogic view of criticism as an elite endeavor practiced by gloomy cynics who were out to *spoil* your fun. The trouble was that newspaper and magazine editors had picked up on spoiler mania. I was now being told, as I never had before, "You can't give this point away in your review—it's a *spoiler.*" The editorial machine was using the spoiler issue as one more way to cut criticism off at the knees.

When I blogged, nothing had to go through anything or anyone, and the freedom was intoxicating. There was no editing; not a comma got changed. And given how many casual comments I ever got from any of my editors about what I was writing on-line (in five years, maybe a total of about three comments), it seemed that they weren't even reading the stuff. Their attitude was: If your piece didn't need *them*, how important could it be?

Blogging about whatever I wanted was sheer joy. I talked about the rebirth of Matthew McConaughey in *Magic Mike* ("In an overly youth-fixated Hollywood, time hasn't simply caught up with him. It may, at last, have set him free...You realize that the ingratiating soft voice, the dimpled smiles, the friendly surface—the whole Matthew McConaughey-ness of it all—is now a mask. And what's beneath it is a little sinister"). I talked about the *Dark Knight* massacre in Aurora, Colorado ("Looking at a real person and seeing, in essence, the flesh-and-blood version of a digitized 'target' may be one of the key mental/metaphorical leaps of our age. And that's why I believe that writing off a tragedy like the *Dark Knight* massacre as an instance of simple 'insanity,' while technically correct, may miss one dimension of what's really going on. For what has gradually decayed, in our society of screens, *isn't* sanity. It's empathy... It makes perfect sense that James Holmes, in his grotesque obsessed-fan Joker costume, chose the very first midnight show of *The Dark Knight Rises* to uncork his arsenal of madness. He opened fire on a roomful of Batman fans, and he wanted to kill every last one of them. Maybe his real fantasy was to be the only fan left"). I used the death of Tony Scott to talk about whether or not he was actually a good director ("The very qualities that excited audiences about his work—the propulsive, at times borderline preposterous popcorn-thriller storylines; the slice-and-dice editing and the images that somehow managed to glow with grit; the fireball violence, often glimpsed in smeary-techno telephoto shots; the way he had of making actors seem volatile and dynamic and, at the same time, lacking almost any subtext—were the same qualities that kept him locked outside the gates of critical respectability... *Top Gun*, in its James Dean–meets–joystick way, is an indelible movie. And that's why I would say that it's also a good movie. It hooks you on what it is. It gets you pumped about being pumped"). And I talked about whether *The Wolf of Wall Street* was reveling in the bad behavior it showed you, and why, perhaps, that was justified ("None of us would be watching this movie if we didn't want to *feel* the heady selfishness that fueled the Wall Street players of the go-go '90s, and that still fuels them today. We want to vibrate in synch with the raw power of their desire. And that means, at least for a while, dramatizing without apologizing").

I've always had the stubborn critical virtue of curiosity. I can honestly say that there has never been a film, no matter how mediocre it sounded, that I wasn't on some level curious to see, experience, think about, meditate on, deconstruct, place somewhere along the scale of reverence to ridicule, and contextualize within the larger culture. (Actually, there is one exception: anything with the word "Pokémon" in the title. I saw the first *Pokémon* film, and it was like having dental surgery without anesthetic.) I always feel a special surge of contempt when I hear a critic refer to a movie as "critic-proof." Because it's one thing for Hollywood executives and marketers to think that way (critics have zero impact on the popularity of *Transformers 9*, and so forth). It's quite another for a critic to say that we're "irrelevant" to a film simply because we don't influence its box-office grosses. We are *commentators*. That means that we're never more relevant than when a movie is popular.

At *EW*, my dream was to comment on everything. Yet if all the *Saw* sequels and paint-by-numbers chick flicks could never dull the kick of writing reviews, I admit that the kick did start to get tamped down a bit with the gradual accretion of restrictions I was dealing with. Each year, our space got a little shorter, "small" movies (i.e., a lot of the best films of the year) got a little more marginalized, and even what you could say in a review now had to pass through the Spoiler Police. To most people, these gripes probably sound beyond preposterous. It's as if I got to go to Candy Land every day and was complaining that the package of Gumdrops I was given now had three Gumdrops in it instead of four. And every so often, the stars did line up, as when I got what I'd taken to calling a "Proustian" 730 words to write about a great movie like *The Social Network* ("With his close-cropped curls and pursed lips that make him look like a Jewish-preppy John Lydon, [Jesse] Eisenberg plays [Mark] Zuckerberg as an egomaniacal whiz-kid creep who's the smartest dude in any situation because he's inside it and outside it at the same time... The power of *The Social Network* is that Zuckerberg is a weasel with a mission that can never be dismissed. The movie suggests that he may have built his ambivalence about human connection into Facebook's very DNA. That's what makes him a jerk-hero for our time"). But more and more, if I blogged on a movie that I also reviewed, the blog post would be the piece I took pride in; to me, it was the real review. And that's because all the rules and niggles and space cut-backs were the result of a newly reined-in environment at *EW*.

Here are two rather startling facts. Lady Gaga's first album, *The Fame*, was released in August 2008 and took its time to build, making 2009 the year that she rose to become the most ecstatic and revolutionary pop figure since the '80s heyday of Michael Jackson and Madonna. But did *EW* do a major cover story on Lady Gaga in 2009? No. She was considered too strange and threatening for the *EW* audience. In other words: *Off-brand*. In June 2009, Conan O'Brien took over *The Tonight Show*, and we all remember the three-ring circus of multiple talk-show-host mayhem that resulted: the flameout of Conan, the weaseling back in of Jay Leno, with Jimmy Fallon, who debuted *his* show in March 2009, already escalating the potential options. It was the most explosive entertainment story of the year, but did *Entertainment Weekly* do a major cover story on the late-night wars? No. Why not? *Off-brand*.

Where was all of this genius strategizing going on? Much of it took place in the office of Martha Nelson, since Jess Cagle, from the moment he came in, was required to run pretty much everything he did past his meddling mentor. It wasn't his decision; Nelson had appointed herself Micro-Manager-in-Chief of *EW*. She and Jess became a two-headed beast, and the result is that it was hard to tell where Nelson's decision-making left off and Jess' began. Either way, I felt that the two-headed beast, which seemed to have one gargantuan paw still stuck in *People* magazine, had conceived the *on-brand* version of *Entertainment Weekly* as a bizarrely polite and vanilla place, where a star of utter obscure irrelevance like Lady Gaga wasn't allowed to mess things up.

Let's be clear about something: In his first two years at the helm, Jess Cagle saved *Entertainment Weekly*. He whisked it back from the dead and made it crackle again. He's a deft and creative editor who transformed *EW* back into a living, breathing, and successfully amusing magazine. At the same time, while anyone in the powerful position of running a magazine like *EW* needs to cultivate relationships, and maybe a few friendships, with publicists, it soon seemed clear to me that Cagle, in the years since he had left, had embedded himself in the publicist-industrial complex—a matrix of flacks he seemed intent on stroking. He didn't like "negative" stories (maybe that was why *EW* never jumped on the battle over late night?). And there was a trio of movie stars he appeared to have placed on a special perch where little seen as hurtful to their careers could be published in *EW* or on ew.com. The stars were Tom Cruise, Julia Roberts, and Will Ferrell. Ferrell may have seemed like he didn't belong on that scared scroll, but that only suggested to me that the reason for the dictate—though no one quite knew where it came from—was connected to some deal Jess had made with the publicity devil.

I was never told that I couldn't give Tom or Julia a negative review. But I was told not to write a blog post about Cruise's career woes, and there was one moment that I experienced as a real clampdown. I actively despised *Duplicity*, the spy-vs.-spy romantic thriller starring Julia Roberts and Clive Owen. It was the second film directed by Tony Gilroy, whose first film, *Michael Clayton*, I revered. But *Duplicity* was a vintage sophomore slump, an unwatchable shell game of headache-inducing convolutions, and so, at the end of 2009, I included it on my worst of the year list. Jeff Giles, the editor in charge of movie coverage, came into my office and told me that I should strongly consider taking it off the list. Jeff, who was like a Gen-X version of Roger Sterling (terminally ironic in a passive-aggressive likable/bullying way), was someone I had a good relationship with, and I listened as he tried to make the case that the movie didn't belong on my list (it was "ambitious," etc.). But *Duplicity* was just the kind of overreaching dud I often tweaked at the end of the year, because it's the kind of movie that drove me nuts. I'm convinced it wasn't an aesthetic judgment that KO'd my choice—it was the presence of Julia Roberts. The return of the curse of *Pretty Woman*!

I was past my days of purist self-righteousness. I knew that even if I did take *Duplicity* off my worst of the year list, the world—and criticism—would stand. My real fear, though, was that Jess, in his new mode of pathologically "friendly" let's-boost-the-product advocacy, had altered his view of critics. The Jess Cagle I knew back in the '90s believed in what we did. He had once complimented me on a review I wrote for the stage section of *EW* about the Broadway revival of *Wait Until Dark* that featured Quentin Tarantino. I'd used it as a chance to tweak QT's acting, and I remember Jess saying about my piece, "That was good *EW*!" It made me feel a deep solidarity with the magazine. I felt like Jess was saying: This is what *we* do. We tell it like it is.

But that Jess was gone. The Jess who had taken his place didn't seem to want criticism that challenged or provoked or dissed what was popular; what he wanted was a weekly celebration of product. If a lead review was negative, he wouldn't say "Why don't we like this movie?" but he might say, "Why are giving so much space to something we don't like?" (It's good he wasn't a post-9/11 Middle East bureau chief.) And even more disturbing to me, he wasn't operating in a vacuum. The critical "values" (or lack thereof) he was now playing up seemed to represent a channeling of the zeitgeist.

Time Inc. kept having layoffs, and early in 2013, there was a major round that included a stunning loss: Ken Tucker, our stalwart and eternal TV critic, was given the boot. It was not a good moment. And then, to escalate the stun into shock, Lisa Schwarzbaum, maybe because she was good at reading writing on the wall, chose that moment to take a voluntary buyout. I could see the atmosphere at *EW* had begun to get to her.

With Lisa and Ken suddenly gone, a lot of people began to come up to me, everywhere I went, armed with the same phrase. They would say, "You're the last man standing." They didn't just mean at *EW*. They meant that *so* many critics had left their jobs, for one reason or another, that the ones still working on a high-profile scale for major media outlets could be counted on practically one hand. A part of me liked being the "last man standing," but since I wasn't stupid, another part of me asked: How long will I be standing? I projected all of my anxieties onto the issue of *EW*'s survival. But then came the warning signs. Like chest pains.

I was the one big-dog critic left at *EW*, and that gave me an illusion of security. I not only wrote more than any other critic there. I was known for my obsession with writing on-line, which was now officially The Future. Chris Nashawaty, the longtime *EW* feature writer and video and DVD critic who replaced Lisa in the movie section, was an elegant stylist and a good friend of mine, but he was only just finding his way as a film critic (a new role for him). I felt that the magazine needed me as much as it ever had.

That fall, I was nominated for an award for best on-line column in the min Editorial & Design awards. It wasn't as prestigious as the National Magazine Awards, but it meant something (the nominees in all the categories sprawled across the major magazines, from *Time* to *Rolling Stone* to *The New Yorker* to *Vogue*). In an irony that no one but me could possibly have taken notice of, I owed the nomination in part to my attempt to avoid writing any negative stories about Tom Cruise, Julia Roberts, or Will Ferrell: When the Cruise sci-fi movie *Oblivion* came out, I didn't feel I could do the "Is Tom Cruise still a movie star?" post that I desperately wanted to, so instead, I used the film as a springboard for a column called "Do post-apocalyptic movies still speak to us?" ("The future as wasteland isn't a revelation anymore, it's a rerun"). At the awards ceremony, the moment arrived for my category, the nominees were read... and I won. My very first journalism award.

Three hours later, I was back in the office, walking down the hallway, and who should be coming the other way but Jess. He gave me a terse "Hello, Owen," and that was all. No congratulations, no acknowledgment that I had just won an award for *EW*... nothing. I wasn't hurt or insulted, because I felt that it wasn't a snub. It was something far more grave: a sign. That my days were numbered.

Two months later, Jess was appointed managing editor of *People* magazine, with the provision that he would continue to oversee *EW*. A new editor came in: Matt Bean, who struck everyone as a frat-house bro, though I also noticed that he had energy and ideas. He didn't seem too worried about propping up the "mainstream" priorities of *EW*, and I was looking forward to working with him. But I never got the chance. On April 2, 2014, a day of entirely unexpected layoffs, Matt called me into his office, and I already knew what for.

"We're letting you go," he said.

A shudder went through me, but I held it together enough to say, "Can I ask why?"

I knew that Matt would be reading from a script, and I wanted to keep him talking long enough to force him to go off-script. He was new at this kind of thing, and still awkward in the role of executioner. "There's going to be a lot of changes at this company," he said. "Moving forward, we may not even *have* a full-time film critic." That wasn't a bad line (it played off the waning of film criticism), but I knew that it was one. When I asked if he had a problem with my work, he began to sputter and flounder.

"We might want someone with a show on YouTube," he said.

"Okay," I replied, "I'd be happy to do a show on YouTube."

"But you don't have one now!" he said. That struck me as a bit of a reach (was *this* why I was being tossed out of *EW*?), even as I took it to be a coded dig at the idea that I was too old...without his coming out and saying it. The "too old" rationale was something the company *couldn't* say out loud (without risking an age-discrimination suit), but unspoken, it could pass for you-don't-fit-into-our-plans-for-the-future thinking. I tormented Matt by making him tap dance a bit more. But then I stopped, because I decided that what his non-answers revealed was that he had little to do with this. A critic like myself was no longer viewed as an asset to the magazine. It was not personal, but to me the stark reality was that under Jess Cagle, *EW* no longer believed in what I did. And frankly, I was starting to wonder who did.

I'd sensed in my reptile brain what was coming, yet getting kicked out of *Entertainment Weekly* left me shell-shocked. I thought about the fact that people all over the country were losing their jobs, and that so many of them were in a far worse position than I was. There are benefits to having worked for a major American corporation for 25 years. I went home, absorbing it all, trying to keep my head from spinning, and that evening, a moment came when there was no one in the apartment but me and Daphne, our beloved Cavalier King Charles Spaniel. As she curled up with me, I realized, to my intense surprise, that I felt calmer—in my body—than I had in a very long time. I'd been carrying a truckload of tension, and now it had all leaked out, as if I'd been given a cosmic massage. Inside, I felt devastated. But I also felt reborn.

In 33 years, I'd been blessed to hold two full-time jobs as a film critic, and in the end I got axed from both of them. I don't know what that says about me, but it certainly says *something*. It seemed as if Big Media was finally done with me, and maybe, for the first time, I was done with Big Media. But maybe the thing that Big Media was done with wasn't *me* so much as a critic—any critic—like me. A full-blown, hellbent, do-or-die movie freak. For a moment, I drifted back to Joker's words at the end of *Full Metal Jacket*, when he's still stuck in the middle of war yet his spirit has come out the other side of it: *I am so happy that I am alive, in one piece... I am in a world of shit, yes. But I am alive. And I am not afraid.*

CHAPTER 23

CRITICAL MORASS

If you open up *The New York Times* on a typical Friday to get the lay of the movie landscape (I realize that simply by referencing the print edition of the *NYT,* I just made myself sound 150 years old), you'll see that there are 20 or more new movies opening on any given week—more movies than anyone with a life, or even the most hardcore junkie cinemaniac, could ever hope to see, or maybe even want to see. When I was in college, honing my identity as a movie fanatic, my addictive fantasy was to be a devout "completist" who saw every movie ever made. That goal, though, has now come to sound as exhausting as it is impossible; it would be like saying that you wanted to consume every meal ever served. It's a dream of binging that makes one fantasize about purging.

The movies now open on a tier system, a descending hierarchy that ranges from the 4,000-screen wide-release juggernaut to the infinitesimal art speck, from the prestigious and high-profile and acclaimed to the scuzzpit anonymous. Any given weekend will, of course, mark the arrival of several major new studio releases. One is called something like *Captain America: Attack of the Drones* (a craftsmanly piece of product that critics under 30 find to be a bold leftist statement), and it might be opening alongside the latest bad-boy urban-suburban comedy starring Kevin Hart (title: *Straight Outta Akron*), followed by the few independent releases that are actually relatively visible (that swoony and ironic Greta Gerwig comedy; that George Eliot adaptation starring Kristen Stewart, Glenn Close, and Jude Law; that Alex Gibney documentary chronicling the secret history of the Arab oil cartel). And that's just tier one and tier two. There is also the Jason Statham heist movie, *One Percent of Nothing* (it's directed by Guy Ritchie, so is it dumb trash or hip trash? And do you care?), along with a shitty romcom, *BFF*, pairing Anna Kendrick and Adam Scott that no one pretends is going to do the kind of business that shitty romcoms once did, but there it is anyway, opening at a theater near you.

Thanks to a fusion of budget, advertising, and what remains of movie-star marquee power, each of these films, good, mediocre, or abysmal, will imprint itself on your brainpan as a do-able slice of artistry or diversion. But then there's the *next* 10 films. They're mostly the collected muck of indiedom, maybe worthy, maybe not, but definitely on the barely visible spectrum of the radar: a collection of movies that could, theoretically, turn out to be masterpieces but that will, in all likelihood— not to sound like I'm prejudging!—prove to be incredibly trivial. There's the five-hour drama about Lithuanian monks that was the toast of the New York Film Festival (it's paced like a Sunday in an Amish waiting room), the transgender documentary that dares to throw shade to power (though it's not nearly as fun, or enlightening, as any episode of *RuPaul's Drag Race*). There's the scrappy low-budget indie neo-noir starring a solemnly revamped Jeremy Piven, the lesbian Latina homage to *She's Gotta Have It* that took an acting award at Sundance, and the documentary called *Eat to the Beat* devoted entirely to '70s New Wave drummers...

All of this choice, all of this cinema, all of these *movies* should rightfully be considered a weekly haven for film buffs. And maybe they are. Yet what they feel like is an endless cinematic shopping mall in which everything is possible and nothing is totally at stake. The prospect of a 20-new-films-a-week smorgasbord may be a New York and L.A. phenomenon, but the rest of the country is catching up fast; it now has more immediate access to that same roster of films than ever before. Many of the movies can now be watched, via video on demand or Netflix, in tandem with—or even ahead of—their micro theatrical runs; yesterday's rarefied platform release is today's cable-and-Internet fodder. I'll never forget the moment when I learned just how transformative the VOD revolution was going to be. It was 2011, and we were in a movie section meeting at *Entertainment Weekly*, trying to decide in which issue to run a review of *Melancholia*, Lars von Trier's talky postmodern gloss on *Deep Impact*. Should we do it the week of its limited 19-screen New York and L.A. opening? Or perhaps wait a week? Then someone piped up with a news flash: The film was *already playing* on video on demand. It hadn't even officially opened yet—not anywhere—but you could see it, that very night, on your big-screen TV in Boulder, Colorado, or Bangor, Maine. My jaw dropped through the floor: This was not your father's art-house release, or mine. It was a paradigm shift—arguably the biggest one in movies since the introduction of the videocassette. It marked a whole new instant-entertainment ballgame.

If movies, and the possibilities for watching them, are multiplying like something out of a physics equation, then what's happening to criticism? It's multiplying, too, though in this case the physics get really twisty: The more writers there are who get to have their say, the less variation there seems to be in what they have to say. One opinion is worth a thousand echoes. Even as one critic after another has lost his perch in the mainstream media, there now appears to be a critic nearly everywhere you look, though it must be said that a lot of them don't get paid much more than if they were fetching lattes at Starbucks. The notion that this is a justifiable, let alone viable "profession" is fast melting away...but that doesn't mean there isn't a galaxy of volunteers lining up to do it!

You can find critical voices on the printed and digital pages of newspapers and magazines, and on the on-line film sites, from the earnest and urgent indiewire to the brash and mouthy Hollywood-elsewhere. You'll see critical takes on movies in gossip magazines (where every film seems to get at least three stars), on throw-everything-at-the-wall-and-see-what-sticks buzz-machine aggregator websites, and on countless personal blogs. You can also tune in to a heady babble of impromptu criticism when you scan the comments section of almost any on-line review, for the old adage that "everyone's a critic" has never been more actualized than it is today. Of course, that other old adage also holds true ("Opinions are like assholes: Everybody has one"), but in our era, it's not rare to encounter unconstrained commentary on a movie review that is more perceptive, and better written, than the piece it's commenting on. The different sites, the competing echelons, the whole shifting-sands landscape of media cacophony—when it comes to criticism, the different levels (print and digital, professional and amateur) now flow into each other, like tributaries all feeding into one giant rushing river. And yet, maybe as a result, there's a sameness, a don't-rock-the-boat orthodoxy that tames and organizes the babbling brook of opinion.

Media Mike, who I now think of as an old friend (though really, he's the eager-beaver office boy who gets Big Brother his coffee), is rampant, issuing orders on his microphone, sketching in the parameters of what to think and what to say. If people now look skeptically at critics, that could be because they register, on a nearly unconscious level, that the once fearless and mighty declaration of opinion is too often, these days, ground hamburger: a safely seasoned, familiar, pre-chewed assertion. You can see it, and feel it, in the reaction to movies both highbrow and low. A new *Planet of the Apes* sequel is coming out? Media Mike has decided that the revamped series is a work of pop brilliance, and that Andy Serkis' Caesar is the Daniel Day-Lewis of chimps. If you say, as I did, that the series is plodding, or—God forbid!—that it's not as much fun as the original schlocky dystopian *Apes* films, then you're going to wind up sounding like a clueless primate who didn't get the memo. Certain independent features now come with critical bows wrapped around them. I thought *Beasts of the Southern Wild* was a perilously awkward, Scotch-tape "visionary" student film, yet it wasn't just praised—it was anointed. After taking a swipe at it at Sundance ("It's uncontaminated by the vulgarity of trying to entertain you"), I wasn't allowed to review it for *EW*; the machine wanted a review that reflected what the machine had agreed to think. The landscape of film criticism is now driven by a kind of oxymoron: enlightened conventional wisdom. It's not that the official opinion is dumb, or even *wrong*. It's that it's so damned cautious. It's pointing the way with a finger held up to the wind. It's an act of following that pretends to look like leading.

If I now voice a question that burns through my intestines, through all these media developments and technological innovations, these *evolutions* that we're all supposed to bow down before, then surely I risk sounding like a man trapped in an ancient time. Yet I will ask the question anyway, just to hear what it sounds like. The question is this:

Why does it seem like all this shit once mattered more than it does now?

My answer is *not* that movies aren't as good as they used to be. The blockbusters, there's no denying it, are too often packages of cynical, airless bombast, and it's been painful to see the movie universe split itself, like a dividing cell, into two adjoined spheres—the popcorn/mass and the arty/indie, and rarely the twain shall meet. That division, which everyone now accepts without thinking, is an assault on the basic dream of movies as a populist form.

Yet if you consider the sheer abundance of good movies that come out in any given year, there's a powerful case to be made that we're still in the middle of a golden age. Movie art is thriving, sometimes even as popular art (*Sideways, Brokeback Mountain, Casino Royale, Precious, Inglourious Basterds, The Social Network, The Kids Are All Right, Lincoln, Bridesmaids, World War Z, American Hustle, Boyhood, The Grand Budapest Hotel, Guardians of the Galaxy*). It's become a waste of time to cry over the fact that so many inspired films are now officially designated as "small." So what? At least they're *there*. Which leads me to ask yet again: *Why does it seem like all this shit once mattered more than it does now?*

I think there are three reasons, three explanations for why the *perception* that movies—and critics—don't matter all that much anymore has mutated into a reality.

1. The Internet, touted as a liberator, now squashes art with overkill. In a perfect world, the experience of a movie could (and maybe should) exist on its own, with nothing to come between the viewer and the screen. The only true value of a critic—ever—should be to enhance the experience. Yet we have now reached a state in which the profusion of criticism, much of it overly reactive and second-rate, creates a vastly different dynamic: In the digital age, the movies and everything that gets written about them all merge into the same twitchy information/hype stream. Criticism, instead of being an added value, is often a case of more being less. Why less? Because the reflexive echo chamber of opinion *demystifies* one's responses, corralling thoughts and feelings into increasingly rigid categories of social-media positioning. Twitter, which every writer and editor has been browbeaten into thinking is the greatest gift to communication since the telephone, has been a disaster for criticism: a psychological version of the ankle monitor one wears during house arrest. With its constant noodging and checking in, Twitter chains a person to what everyone else is thinking, and critics use it to plug themselves, hour by hour, into the matrix of opinion. It enslaves them to the world outside themselves.

2. The new renaissance era of television, while all too genuine, is also about the re-embrace of our status as couch potatoes. With *The*

Sopranos, TV at last caught up with the aesthetics of movies, and a handful of other series have built on that achievement. Yet unless you're talking about a highly select number of elite shows (we all know what they are: *Mad Men*, *The Wire*, *Breaking Bad*, a couple of others), the notion that serial drama on television regularly attains more "complexity" than movies, simply because of its long-form, multiple-episode nature, is a canard, one that trashes the essential truth of movie history. (If you applied it to the New Hollywood, then *Bonnie and Clyde*, *M*A*S*H*, and *The Last Detail* would all look less "complex" than *Days of Our Lives* or *Dallas*.) It's true that the sprawl of a television show can feel novelistic, but the miracle of a great movie is that it doesn't *need* more than two hours to be a great novel (and 99 percent of the world's great movies don't need to be a minute longer than they are). While I stand behind no one in my reverence for *The Sopranos* or *Mad Men*, the people who are sitting around watching *House of Cards* or *Homeland* or *Louie* or *Orange Is the New Black* and saying "TV is better than movies!" are simply rationalizing what the old, pre-renaissance era of TV addiction was always about: making "friends" with a show, or with the characters on it, so that revisiting them each week returns you to a place of holistic comfort. Appointment television *is* comforting, even when it's lousy. That's why TV recaps are almost always positive: If last night's episode was *on*, then that was enough; that's all it needed to be—at least, according to recap culture—to be an acceptable slice of TV. What the new age of television has allowed people to do is to elevate that couch-potato feeling into something that replaces entering the darkness of a movie theater as *the* sacred pop-culture experience. It may be an aesthetic revolution, but it's also a habit, a choice, a canonization of caution.

3. Reality has now conquered art. In the '70s, movies channeled the gritty realities that surrounded them (Vietnam, Watergate, the violent decay of our cities), and that's what infused the era's cinema with its daring, cathartic flavor. Today, on the increasingly rare occasions when Hollywood tries to turn topical reality into vital moviemaking, the attempts often seem tone-deaf. A lot of the reason, though, is that the audience no longer cares. After 9/11, we were deluged with "important" movies that took stock of the new world in which America found itself, and while most of those films were so-so, there was an underlying sense

that the problems themselves—the rise of radical Islam, the secret corruption of America's attempts to fight it—were too vast to be solved, or
explained, or even channeled by a mere *movie*. The cataclysms of Vietnam and Watergate were rooted in the mythological order of the Cold
War, but the post-9/11 world speaks to a profound, turbulent disorder
that touches too many raw nerves to be salved by the elixir of populist
storytelling. The savagery of global terror, the slow-motion collapse of
the American middle class: These are issues that movies have almost no
tools to illustrate, because the issues weigh on the audience with a severity that transcends diversion. I would argue that America now faces its
most unnerving set of problems since the end of World War II. Next to
those realities, how can movies, in all honesty, really mean that much?
In a sense, the fanboys have got it right: How can movies today represent
anything but escape?

· · · · · ·

One reason that movies today might mean a little less to *me* than they
once did is that I now have two daughters, Lily (age 5) and Sadie (age
3), and both of them, to me, are movie stars. While fatherhood hasn't
stopped me from being a movie freak, it *has* made it much harder for me
to find a movie—any movie—that can give rise to the feeling, "Holy
shit, that film just changed my life!" That's the sensation I was on a cru-
sade for in my teens and twenties and thirties. It's why I got hooked on
certain films like they were toots of crystal meth. They helped to create
me by altering who I was; each one of them felt like a genesis of faith.
The last time I got addicted to a movie the way I got addicted to *Carrie*
or *Nashville* or *Boogie Nights* was in 2005, when I saw Steven Spielberg's
Munich five or six times because I couldn't stop going back. I still think
it's the one transcendent big-screen expression of the post-9/11 world—
the one that unravels the enigma of *why* vengeance doesn't work, why it
sets off a destructive karma that is destined to eat itself. *Munich* infused
the docudrama form with a dread-soaked poetry. As had happened to me
so often before, I yearned never to leave its spell.

Did it change my life? I'd like to think a movie could still do that,
but my primal dynamic has shifted: When I look at Lily and Sadie, I feel
it's my role to be the sun they revolve around, and much of my ADD

addiction to the flow of images, to *change*, is soaked up by the astonishment of watching them change. I don't need movies as voodoo anymore.

After Lily was born, a lot of people asked me, with an almost jejune eagerness, *"What movies are you going to show her?"* (It was like hearing the new version of *"How many movies do you see a week?"*) I think a lot of them honestly imagined me sitting down with Lily once she was about six and opening up a sacred DVD box as I explained, "Okay, sweetheart, now we're going to watch a movie by someone named Martin Scorsese. It's all about a man who drives a taxi cab. He is sometimes very lonely. But he just wants to find a friend! And by the way, pumpkin, keep an eye out for those hypnotic rack-focus shots." I've noticed that people I know who are films buffs tend to take excessive pride in the budding cinephile tastes of their children (they're hooked on Chaplin! their favorite movie is *Bringing Up Baby*!). To avoid becoming one of those people, I decided that when it came time to introduce my children to movies, I would intentionally place myself a little behind the curve. I had no desire for their tastes to be a pale carbon copy of mine. Before I even had the chance, though, I began to notice something about Lily that shocked me: Whether or not she turns out to be a movie freak, she is every inch the daughter of a critic.

I saw it, without fully realizing it, the moment she was born. Less than 10 seconds after she popped out, she turned toward a window, and she was really looking, *staring* outside it. Already, she was studying the world. At the time, I dismissed the thought, but that, as it turns out, is Lily all over: scrutinizing and dissecting everything she sees, hungry to know how it all works—on screens, big and small, and in life. I truly think it's genetic, and I would never have guessed that before; she's made me realize that my own relentlessly analytical, deconstructive temperament was built into my cells more than I ever imagined. In my case, however, it's also spiced with adaptive behavior, because as different as I am from my father, I can hear the reverberation of his voice—blunt and slicing, with a merciless shrug of *my way or the highway*—in the compulsive need I have to spray the world with my opinions. It's a way of being that strikes many as impolite or even eccentric but that, for me, will always feel right.

I do, of course, have a squishy-sentimental side (you can't think *It's a*

Wonderful Life is one of the 10 greatest movies ever made without one), but now that my dad is gone, I confess I rarely miss him, though I believe there's a telling reason for that. At the funeral of a family member, you'll tend to feel the absence, almost physically, of that person. But at my father's funeral, what I felt was the presence of his absence. Yes, he was no longer there; but that made me realize that he had never quite been there. His testy, cutthroat bluster appeared to be who he was, but I believe it was also his way of shrouding his identity. His life—his real life—will always feel like a movie that I never got to see.

It would be easy to say that I'm a better dad than he was, but the truth is that I inherited a huge streak of his selfish impatience. I am too often restless in the presence of my children (I'll pray that they finally go to sleep so that I can watch that DVD at midnight!), and when it comes to the upbeat, rah-rah playground camaraderie of parenthood, I am often a monosyllabic curmudgeon; I have way too little of that New Dad eagerness. I find the endless prattle about which school your kid is going to attend to be soul-killing in its barely disguised competitive monotony. Yet when I look at my daughters, I feel compelled, at every moment, not to let them down. My father had passion, but he kept it mostly to himself, whereas I became a critic to let my passion flow, and to encourage it to flow in others. And I know that pop culture matters because it's a form of love.

I felt that powerfully the first time I finally sat down with Lily to show her a movie outside the *Frozen*/Pixar/Hannah Montana orbit—a movie that *I* wanted to show her. It was *Yellow Submarine*. A Beatles cartoon! Just like the ones my father guilt-tripped me about watching 50 years ago. I hadn't seen *Yellow Submarine* since the early '70s, but I needed to revisit it for a piece I was writing, and I thought: "It's a cartoon. Maybe Lily will go for it." At first, she balked; it looked like one of "daddy's boring movies." But then she sat down, and kept watching, and I could see that she was lured by the mod trap-door psychedelia, and by the mystique of the Beatles, who she kept asking about ("Do they all live in that house?"). She asked to see the film again the next morning, and the day after that, and she began to talk about what she was seeing ("They have lots of pointy shoes in this movie!"). She was fascinated by the towering, apple-dropping henchmen of the Blue Meanies ("I'm scared of their tallness"). She was fascinated by the undersea creature with a vacuum-cleaner snout who, at one point, ingests the entire picture ("Did he vacuum the world? And then did he vacuum himself?" He did!). When "Hey Bulldog" came on, she did a happy bouncing canine dance, holding her hands in the air like paws.

I relished watching *Yellow Submarine* with Lily, and what possessed me as much as it did her was the "Lucy in the Sky with Diamonds" sequence. I hadn't truly appreciated it when I was younger. But now I felt like it might be the single most bedazzling sequence I had ever seen in a movie, with kaleidoscopic colors that strobe and pulse until they spill out of the drawings, dissolving into sheer scrumptious beauty. What I hadn't appreciated before is that as the images grow more messy and ragged, less pinpoint gorgeous, they become even more incandescent. I saw the "Lucy in the Sky" sequence as an idyllic acid trip, though for Lily, already immersed in princess culture, it was a vision of girl-on-a-horse divinity.

Through it all, I could see that she *knew* the Beatles were special. She kept wanting to look at pictures of them, so I showed her the covers of my albums, and she began to carry around the four cellophane portraits of the cartoon Beatles that came inside the *Yellow Submarine* DVD box. After a few days of this, I wanted to see if Lily knew her Beatles, so I pointed to the drawing of John, in his purple bellbottoms and *Sgt. Pepper* moustache, and I asked, "Do you know who that is?"

Without missing a beat, she looked up at me and said, "Henry?"

I think I chuckled out loud. Who could be less of a *Henry* than John Lennon? But then a strange thought came into my head: Maybe she sees a quality in John that I don't. *Maybe she's onto something.* I thought: Why do I always have to impose my own point of view? Why not try to see it her way?

I looked at Lily and smiled. "Yes," I replied. "That's Henry."

ACKNOWLEDGMENTS

A great deal of what I know about movies I learned from talking about them, and I want to thank three people, especially, for carrying on a conversation with me that has never ended: Hugh Cohen, my beloved mentor and comrade; Christopher Potter, my undergraduate leader of the pack; and Godfrey Cheshire, my blood brother of cinema.

I also want to tip my hat to the wit and wisdom of David Browne, who has had the grace and patience to interface with every last one of my theories, even when he knew better. I'm grateful to Lise Suino for always helping to bring the past into the present. And I thank everyone I ever worked with, over 24 years, at *Entertainment Weekly*, for being part of the most awesome and fun of all magazine staffs.

I'm not sure I could have finished this book without Carrie and all the fine folks at Veselka, who always gave me one of those tables in the back when I needed a place to write. Finally, I want to salute the dedicated team at Hachette Books, notably Michelle Aielli, Betsy Hulsebosch, Ashley Yancey, Christopher Lin, and Mari C. Okuda. I'd also like to express a boundless debt of gratitude to my agent, Erin Hosier of Dunow, Carlson & Lerner, who has been there at every stage with her impeccable insight and support, and to my inspiring editor, Mauro DiPreta, who believed in this book and made it so much better.

INDEX